The working class in welfare capitalism

International Library of Sociology

Founded by Karl Mannheim

Editor: John Rex, University of Warwick

Arbor Scientiæ
Arbor Vitæ

A catalogue of the books available in the **International Library of Sociology** and other series of Social Science books published by Routledge & Kegan Paul will be found at the end of this volume.

The working class in welfare capitalism

Work, unions and politics in Sweden

Walter Korpi
Swedish Institute for Social Research

Routledge & Kegan Paul
London, Henley and Boston

First published in 1978
by Routledge & Kegan Paul Ltd
39 Store Street,
London WC1E 7DD,
Broadway House,
Newtown Road,
Henley-on-Thames,
Oxon RG9 1EN and
9 Park Street,
Boston, Mass. 02108, USA
Printed in Great Britain by
Redwood Burn Ltd
Trowbridge and Esher

British Library Cataloguing in Publication Data

Korpi, Walter
The working class in welfare capitalism.-
(International library of sociology).
1. Labor and laboring classes – Sweden
2. Labor and laboring classes – Case studies
I. Title   II. Series
301.44'42'09485   HD8576.5   78-40093
ISBN 0 7100 8848 5

For
Martin, Anja, Tomas and Jane

Contents

CONTENTS

Figures

Tables

Preface

This book has its origin in a study on unofficial strikes
in the metal working industry which the Swedish Metal Workers' Union commissioned me to do in 1965.   As a part of
this project, I carried out a survey study among the
metal workers in 1966-7.   In the spring of 1968 I gave my
report on the strikes to the union.   In this report, however, I had not been able to fully analyse the available
data.   The Bank of Sweden Tercentennial Foundation therefore gave me a grant to continue the study.

For several reasons, the main report from this study
has taken time to complete.   Some of the reasons have
been research-related.   The mainstream theories in sociology and industrial relations indicated that the explanations to actions like unofficial strikes were to be sought
in conditions within the firm, primarily in the technological context of work and in the workplace bargaining systems.   Such an approach, however, soon appeared too
narrow.   More and more I came to see industrial conflict
as an important symptom of societal change.   The relatively dramatic changes on the Swedish labour market since
the late 1960s underscored the necessity of a broader approach.   My research therefore became focused on the analysis of the role of the working class in the capitalist
industrial societies.   The result was this book, which
takes Sweden as a 'test case' for the development and
position of the working class in the western societies.

Contemporary social science offers more or less well-
defined and competing approaches to the understanding of
the western societies and their changes.   Since the
1960s, the Marxian view has again come to the fore as an
important alternative approach.   It is my opinion that
the social sciences have much to gain from a dialogue between scholars with marxian and more mainstream approaches, where efforts are made to clarify and pinpoint dif-

ferences between the competing approaches and to evaluate
them with the aid of empirical data.   The work with this
book has also brought home to me the importance of the
historical dimension for the understanding of contemporary
society.   This book deals with issues which are central
in the political debate.   Although striving for objecti-
vity in the analysis, all social scientists have value
premises and biases from which the analysis starts.   I
hope that my particular biases have been made sufficiently
clear to alert the reader about their existence.   The
book is written with a view towards use in undergraduate
courses.

My work with this book has been aided and facilitated
by many persons.   First and foremost I wish to thank the
metal workers who have responded to my questions.   I also
wish to thank those at the headquarters of the Swedish
Metal Workers' Union who in different ways have supported
this study, among them Sven Forslund, Henry Karlsson,
Ingvar Liljeros, Bert Lundin, Åke Nilsson and Holger
Olsson.   My thanks are also due to the Swedish Metal
Trades Employers' Association, represented by Mr Åke Gustafsson, and to the Iron and Steel Works' Association as
well as to the member firms of these associations, which
generously have facilitated the carrying out of the empirical part of the study.

During different phases of this project I have had the
privilege to work together with the following research
assistants: Göte Bernhardsson, Horst Hart, Jan-Ivar Ivar-
sson, Ove Källtorp, Elisabeth Lindgren, Gunnar Olofsson,
Sven E. Olsson, Casten v Otter, Lena Sahlin, Claes-Göran
Stefansson, Sune Sunesson, Karin Tengvald, Nils Wickberg
and Denny Vågerö.   In the beginning of the project I had
the opportunity to co-operate with Bengt Abrahamsson.
The following persons outside the Swedish Institute for
Social Research have read longer or shorter portions of
the manuscript: Phyllis Arora, Satish Arora, Edmund Dahlström, Olof Frändén, John H. Goldthorpe, Lennart Gärdvall,
Bernt Kennerström, Casten v Otter, Lars G. Pettersson,
Veljko Rus, Richard Scase, Rudi Supek, Göran Therborn,
Hannu Uusitalo, Wlodimierz Wesolowski and Rune Åberg.   I
wish to thank them for valuable criticisms.   It goes
without saying that none of them should be identified
with the views expressed herein.

My colleagues at the Swedish Institute for Social Research have served as a decidedly pluralistic and excit-
ingly critical audience for the draft chapters of this
book.   They have provided a stimulating work environment
and have in numerous ways helped to improve the book.
Anne-Maj Folmér-Hansen has done a lot of typing for me.
To them all my collective gratitude.

As mentioned above, this research has been supported by the Swedish Metal Workers' Union and the Bank of Sweden Tercentennial Foundation.

Koutojärvi, Sweden   Walter Korpi
1977

1 Grave-diggers or angels in marble?

In its beginning capitalist industrial society created a
class of wage workers. Soon developing into its numeri-
cally largest category, the working class came naturally
into the focus in the thinking on the future development
of this type of society. In a more or less literal
sense, the working class was the foundation upon which the
economic and social structure of the society rested. It
was seen as having the potential to shake and shape its
social order. This potential was regarded with hope as
well as fear.

Those who felt that the burden and distress of the
workers under early industrialism was unjust, and rooted
in the economic system of society, foresaw that the working class would become its own liberator. 'Wage labour
rests exclusively on competition between the labourers,'
said Marx and Engels in 'The Communist Manifesto' in 1848.
But with the development of capitalism the organizational
potential of the workers increases. The weakness of the
workers, based on internal competition, will give way to
collective strength, founded on class-based organizations.
'The development of Modern Industry ...cuts from under
its feet the very foundation on which the bourgeoisie produces and appropriates products,' wrote Marx and Engels in
the Manifesto, and claimed that 'what the bourgeoisie,
therefore, produces, above all, is its own grave-diggers.'

Those who feared the growing number and power of the
workers came to hope for a gradual domestication of the
working class. They saw no basic conflict between the
higher and the lower layers of the population and assumed
that, with time, the workers would consent to their role
in society. The Conservative statesman Disraeli, who had
supported the extension of the franchise to the workers,
expressed such ideas. In 1883, on the second anniversary
of his death, 'The Times' wrote that 'in the inarticulate

1

mass of the English populace, [Disraeli] discerned the
Conservative workingman as the sculptor perceives the
angel prisoned in a block of marble.' (1)   When their
true features were revealed, the working men would prove
willing to accept their station in society.   Later
thinkers assumed that the processes inherent in industrialism would not unify the working class, but would decom-
pose it and integrate the workers with the rest of society.   Industrialization would thus gradually render the
working class innocuous to capitalism.

The debate on the working class in capitalist industrial society has continued up to the present along these
two divergent lines.   In this debate two issues have been
central.   The first concerns the nature of this society,
focused on the question of possible conflicts of interest
between workers and employers.   The second is how actual
and potential changes in the position of workers in the
class structure of capitalist industrial society will
affect its future development.   The standpoints on the
first issues are often reflected already in the choice of
terms for describing society.   Those who use the concept
'industrial' society tend to regard the technological organization of production as the distinguishing characteristic of society;   they stress the possibilities for har-
monious relationships between workers and employers (e.g.
Dahrendorf, 1959;   Kerr et al., 1960).   On the other
hand, those who use the term 'capitalist' society tend to
see the economic system of society as basic;   they tend to
hold that the relationship between workers and employers
is marked by inherent conflicts of interests (e.g. Westergaard and Resler, 1975;   Miliband, 1969).   The question of the relative importance of private ownership of
capital in these societies appears to have been the lynch-
pin in the debate on the working class.

This book is about the working class in advanced capitalist societies and about the probability for a socialistic development in these societies.   Its focus is on
one such society, Sweden.   This country is often seen as
the prototype of the welfare state, if not of modern society (Tomasson, 1970).   The Swedish trinity of rapid
economic growth, industrial peace and an apparently successful welfare state has intrigued foreign observers. (2)
It is often overlooked abroad, however, that Sweden remains basically a capitalist country.   Compared with
Britain, France, West Germany and Italy, for instance, the
nationalized sector of Swedish industry is smaller.   On
the other hand, compared with most capitalist countries,
public interventions to attempt to assure the welfare of
the wage-earners have been more common in Sweden.   The

extensive use of political measures to attempt to affect
the distribution of welfare in Swedish society reflects
the strong influence of its working-class-based political
parties and labour organizations.

Swedish society is not however a welfare state in the
sense that it has an even approximately equal distribution
of welfare. Its social and economic structure further
tends to make the welfare of large segments of the population hazardous. It would appear that the Swedish combination of a capitalist economic system with extensive
political measures attempting to counteract the outcome of
the capitalist market principles and to redistribute welfare in society according to principles of social justice
can, instead, be described as *welfare capitalism*. (3)
Welfare capitalist states are marked by the tensions between, on the one hand, power based on ownership of property exercised through the capitalist economic system and,
on the other hand, power based on the mobilization of the
mass of the population in political parties and unions.
The capitalist economic system can be seen as producing an
inequality of welfare, while political interventions reflecting the power of working-class-based organizations
attempt to counteract these inequalities with varying but
never full success.

Because of its long period of Social Democratic government Sweden offers an illuminating case, if not a test
case, for the divergent theories on the development of the
working class and on the probability of a socialist development in capitalist industrial societies. Different
interpretations of the Swedish case would, however, appear
possible. The Swedish working class could thus be seen
as integrated into and innocuous to the capitalist economic system. This argument has been proposed from two
different perspectives.

As an advanced industrial nation combining an economy
based on private ownership with a democratic, interven-
tionist state, Sweden has been seen as revealing the
future for the successful incorporation of the working
class into welfare capitalism. The downfall in 1976 of
its Social Democratic government, which had been in power
almost without interruptions since 1932, could be seen as
confirming this interpretation. From a different perspective the same development has been interpreted as a
deviation along the road of reformist social democracy,
which disarms the working class through class collaboration while retaining the state primarily as an agency for
the economic power holders in society.

The balance of the theoretical and empirical analyses
to be presented in this book, however, points to a

different interpretation. Unions in Sweden have gradually come to organize the overwhelming proportion of the
labour force, workers as well as white-collar groups,
underlining their common position as sellers of labour
power and opposition to employers. Political parties
questioning the legitimacy of capitalism continue to be a
major force in its political life. The argument of this
book is that in Sweden the basic prerequisite of capitalism, the internal competition among the wage-earners, is
now on the verge of being abolished. The grave-diggers
of capitalism are thus still at work and the future of
capitalism remains open.

The Swedish case however not only provides the possibility to study social democracy in action. In the
latter half of the 1970s, the mass Communist Parties of
Western Europe appear to have abandoned the strategy of
the dictatorship of the proletariat associated with the
Third International and are on the threshold of assuming
governmental office within the framework of capitalist-
democratic states. In some significant ways, the new
strategy of 'Eurocommunism' resembles a reformist socialist strategy with which the Swedish Social Democrats have
traditionally been associated. The Swedish experience is
therefore of interest also in attempts to assess the
problems and prospects of the new political developments
in Continental Europe.

The book contains analyses of theories attempting to
explain the role and position of workers in Western industrial societies and brings empirical data on Sweden to
bear on these theories. It discusses the historical
changes in the position of workers in Swedish society and
the development of their organizations. Basic issues
dealt with concern the extent to which work experiences
continue to make workers dissatisfied with their position
in society; the role of the work-related social relationships as bases for solidarity and organization; the
functioning of the main class-based organization, the
labour union; the political views and choices of the
workers; and industrial conflict.

The focus of the book is on a core sector of the Swedish working class, the metal-workers. The empirical
data comes from historical sources, union archives and
sample surveys, the main one being a comprehensive survey
among the metal-workers. These data are analysed against
the background of wider developments in Swedish society.
In the theoretical frame of reference, a central role is
assigned to changes in the distribution of power resources
in society.

The debate on the position and role of the working

class in capitalist society has been and continues to be
both scientific and political. To paraphrase Myrdal
(1953), one can say that the political element has been
transparent in the development of theories in this area.
Underneath the debate on the working class, however, differing conceptions and theories of class and class conflict can be discerned. It is therefore helpful to begin
with an exposition and analysis of the major theories in
this area, as a background against which the development
of the working class can be understood. If differences
in basic assumptions between these theories can be delineated, we can hope to specify divergent hypotheses concerning the development of conflict groups and interest
organizations in capitalist industrial societies. These
hypotheses can then be evaluated in relation to empirical
data on developments in Sweden.

1 SOME THEORIES ON CLASS AND CLASS CONFLICT

The progenitors of much of the ensuing theories on class
and class conflict have been Karl Marx and Max Weber, and
our discussion starts with them. It must be recognized,
however, that the writings of Marx and Weber reflect the
ideological climate of their times, as well as their personal social positions and political commitments. Therefore these 'classical' writers have to, and deserve to, be
treated as living thinkers rather than as dead saints.

Marx

Although the concept of class is central to his social
and economic theories, the writings of Marx do not contain
any concise treatment of the class concept. His works
reflect, instead, a continuous discussion and analysis of
problems related to class. As is well known this situation has led to some disagreements among his interpreters.
The writings of Marx reveal, however, the following central themes of relevance in this context. (For secondary
sources see e.g. Avineri, 1968; Aspelin, 1969 and 1972;
Mills, 1962; Robinson, 1966; Therborn, 1971; Giddens,
1973.)
    A key to the theories of Marx is that he consistently
takes work and the sphere of production as the point of
departure in his analyses of society. Through goal-
directed work, man changes himself and his environment.
Work presumes and generates co-operation and interaction
among men. In the sphere of work the basic economic and

social relations between men are thus created. The way
in which production is organized is assumed to be decisive
for the structure of society and of societal institutions.

The pattern in which men co-operate with and relate themselves to each other in the sphere of production depends
on the conditions of production in society. These conditions reflect the level of development of the 'forces of
production', a concept which refers to the material and
technical conditions of production as well as to knowledge
relevant for production. The level of development of the
forces of production in a society determines the amount of
products that can be produced in a period of time i.e. the
'productive force of work'. With the development of
technology and knowledge, the productive force of work
will increase.

In a society production can be organized in different
ways. The concept 'relations of production' is used to
describe the economic relationship of people to the means
of production and to the products, i.e. to indicate who
owns and controls the material resources in the society.
The ways in which men relate to each other in the sphere
of production also generates the classes in society. The
relations of production further form the material base for
the legal and political superstructure of society. (4)
In the more developed societies, the relations of production have been antagonistic in the sense that they have
generated conflicts of interests and differences in power
resources between different classes. In these societies
a relatively small class of people has been able to appropriate the surplus of production, the surplus which is
retained when the necessary resources for continued production have been set aside.

With changes in the conditions of production, the prevailing relations of production can come into conflict
with the development of the forces of production. This
means that the forms of ownership and control which previously facilitated the development of the forces of production, now limit and restrict further progress. When
the forces of production have developed as much as the
prevailing relations of production allow, a period of
social change begins.

The relations of production then change so that the
forces of production are again allowed to develop. With
changes in the relations of production also the way in
which the dominant class appropriates the surplus of production changes. In this way different modes of production have appeared and disappeared. The ancient socie-

ties based on slavery were followed by the feudal system
and the latter, in turn, by the capitalist mode of production.

Upon these fundamental assumptions Marx created a
theory on capitalist society. This theoretical structure
should not be seen as a philosophy or as a set of laws
determining the future development of society. It is
more fruitful - and in accordance with Marx's own posture
as a scientist - to view his theories as a set of interrelated assumptions and hypotheses concerning tendencies
in the development of capitalist society. These hypotheses must be continuously tested and amended in the
light of empirical observations concerning the way in
which capitalist society functions and changes.

In the course of the historical appearance and growth
of the capitalist mode of production, a societal structure develops where the basic cleavage is between those
who have to make their living by selling their labour
force on the labour market, i.e. the wage workers, and
those who own the means of production and buy labour
force, i.e. the bourgeoisie. The structure of this society is thus characterized primarily by the fact that a
dominant class exploits the subordinate class and appropriates the surplus of production. These classes are
interdependent but the relationship between them is marked
by strife and is inherently unstable. Marx was aware,
however, that these classes are not internally homogeneous. In capitalist society, social relations are characterized by competition. Repeatedly Marx pointed to
this internal competition and division of labour which
generates 'an infinite fragmentation of interest and rank'
and splits labourers as well as capitalists (Marx, 1967,
III, p. 886). A central theme in his work is the attempt
to analyse the conditions under which this internal fragmentation becomes limited and makes possible the formation
of major coalitions, which can appear as the principal
conflict groups or contenders in specific historical
situations.

The relations in the sphere of production also form the
basis for the political domination by the bourgeoisie over
the wage earners, as well as for a legal and ideological
superstructure, which supports the underlying class relationship. The state expresses the basic pattern of domination founded in the sphere of production; it functions
also as a co-ordinator of capitalist production.

The exploitative relationship between sellers and
buyers of labour power leads to an unequal distribution of
the results of production. The formation of unions, however, counteracts internal competition between workers,

and makes possible collective action whereby workers are
able to protect themselves against some of the consequences of their subordinate position. Although the
writings of Marx are somewhat ambiguous at this point,
the 'emiseration' (Verelendung) of the working class must
thus not be understood as a universal process, plunging
workers into ever deeper misery. It would appear, instead, to affect primarily the 'industrial reserve army',
i.e. the unemployed and those with precarious positions on
the labour market.

The motor of change in the Marxian theory of capitalist
society is provided by the fact that production is geared
to the creation of profit, not to the satisfaction of
human needs. In order to maintain and increase profit,
the bourgeoisie has to initiate continuous changes in the
processes of production. These changes lead to an increasing division of labour and make possible the great
contribution of capitalism, the remarkable increase in the
productivity of human labour. Production for profit,
however, also implies waste and generates recurrent economic crises.

Changes initiated by the capitalists have also had
other effects. Enhanced by recurring economic crises,
the concentration of capital in fewer and fewer hands continues. Parallel to this development, work becomes increasingly social in character (Vergesellschaftung).
This is manifested in the increasingly co-operative and
collective nature of the work processes, which necessitates the co-ordinated action of increasing numbers of
people and makes different sectors of society more interdependent. At some point, the centralization of capital,
and the increasingly social nature of work, leads to a
situation where the capitalist mode of production hinders
the development and realization of the potentials of production.

At the same time social change accompanying this 'maturation' of capitalism facilitates the building up of the
organizational power resources of the working class. In
'The Communist Manifesto', Marx and Engels stated this
hypothesis in the following way (quoted in Bottomore and
Rubel, 1961, p. 192):

In the early phases of capitalism the labourers still
form an incoherent mass scattered over the whole country, and broken up by their mutual competition....
But with the development of industry the proletariat
not only increases in number; it becomes concentrated
in greater masses, its strength grows and it feels that
strength more. The various interests and conditions
of life within the ranks of the proletariat are more

and more equalized, in proportion as machinery obliterates all distinctions of labour, and nearly everywhere reduces wages to the same low level.

By generating processes that overcome the fragmentation introduced through the division of labour and that change the social consciousness of workers, in the long run the capitalist mode of production leads to the formation of coalitions or conflict groups on the basis of economically defined classes. This is expressed in the development of organizations, beginning with unions and extending to working-class-based political parties. The nominal 'class in itself' (*Klasse an sich*) is thus converted to a conflict group, a 'class for itself' (*Klasse für sich*).

With the 'maturation' of capitalism the strength of the working class thus increases. At the same time the contradiction between the private ownership of the means of production and the increasingly social nature of work becomes more acute, leading to economic insecurity, irrational organization of production and inefficient use of resources. At some point the increasing consciousness among the workers of the nature of these problems and of their increasing power makes it possible for them to resolve this contradiction on their terms, by abolishing the capitalist mode of production. *The demise of capitalism results, then, from social change accompanying the development of capitalism which creates both serious societal problems as well as the conditions for their solution on the terms of the originally weaker class.*

Marx did not assume that the abolishment of the capitalist mode of production would necessarily involve the use of violence. He was also keenly aware that the two-class division central to his analytic model was not found in existing societies at the time of his writing: 'Middle and intermediate strata ... obliterate lines of demarcation everywhere ...' (Marx, 1967, III, p. 885). To a greater extent than often has been acknowledged, Marx recognized that the development of capitalism would generate counter-tendencies towards class polarization. While he assumed that some sectors of the middle classes, e.g. the small entrepreneurs, would tend to sink into the working class, he also expected that there would be a 'constantly growing number of the middle classes, those who stand between the workman on the one hand and the capitalist and landlord on the other. The middle classes ... are a burden weighing heavily on the working base and increase the social security and power of the upper ten thousand' (Marx, 1969, II, p. 573). These new middle classes would grow with the expansion of capitalist production, which is exploitative and antagonistic, and which

therefore necessitates a control structure over and above
that required merely for the co-ordination of work.   As
Marx noted 'the exploitation of labour costs labour'
(Marx, 1969, III, p. 355).

Weber

Most of later sociological theorizing on class can be seen
as explicit or implicit criticisms of the Marxian stand-
point.   Foremost among these critics is, of course, Max
Weber.   The extent of his disagreement with Marx and the
nature of his views, however, often appear to have been
misrepresented to a point where one is tempted to talk
about 'vulgar Weberianism' (Giddens, 1973, pp. 41-52;
Cohen et al., 1975; Pope et al., 1975; Therborn, 1976;
see also Bendix, 1974).   The following themes in the
thought of Weber seem to be of primary relevance in the
present context.

The basic difference between the class conceptions of
Marx and Weber would appear to be that, while Marx sees
classes as arising from the ways in which people are
related to each other in the sphere of production, for
Weber classes are primarily expressions of differentia-
tions based on what people have to offer on the market,
i.e. on their market capacities.   According to Weber
classes are characterized by the fact that a majority of
their members 'have in common a specific causal component
of their life chances', this component consisting of
their control over goods (Besitzes) and services or performance capabilities (Leistungen) (Weber, 1968, p. 927).
The control over goods and performance capabilities on the
commodity and labour markets thus determines their poten-
tialities on these markets;   and 'the kind of chance on
the market is the decisive moment which presents a common
condition for the individual's fate.   Class situation is
in this sense, ultimately market situation' (Weber, 1968,
p. 928).

Weber further assumes that class situations are differentiated on the basis of the type of goods and property
its members control, as well as in terms of the type of
services and performance capabilities they are able to
offer on the market.   Class situations thus become highly
diversified and form the bases for a plurality of classes.
Control over various types of property leads to the formation of different 'property classes' (Besitzklassen).
Among the propertyless differences in terms of marketable
skills, based e.g. on education or occupational training,
introduce differences in market capacities and form the

bases for 'acquisition classes' (*Erwerbsklassen*).
'Social classes' (*Soziale Klassen*) are defined in terms of
social relations between people and are characterized by a
low degree of individual and inter-generational social
mobility (Weber, 1968, p. 302).
The Weberian class concept is related to the Marxian
one, since ownership of property is a major determinant of
market capacities. '"Property" and "lack of property"
are ... the basic categories of all class situations'
(Weber, 1968, p. 927). Weber would, however, appear to
have used the class concept primarily as a tool for explaining differences in life chances of individuals, while
Marx also stressed the crucial importance of class relation, founded in the sphere of production, for the long-
term development of society.

A major difference between these two classical writers
in their views on the future development of society arises
from the fact that, in contrast to Marx, Weber assumes
that the sphere of consumption is also an important basis
for the long-run development of conflict groups. Similarities in style of life, rooted in family experience
and reflected in the sphere of consumption, thus underlie
the formation of status groups (*Stände*). Status situations are determined by 'a specific, positive or negative,
social estimation of *honor*' (Weber, 1968, p. 932). Class
and status can, however, not be seen narrowly as two different aspects of social stratification. Instead, market
capacity, based on class, and 'honor', reflecting belong-
ingness to a status group, stand in partial opposition to
each other as bases for the distribution of life chances
(Weber, 1968, pp. 930, 936).

Status groups and classes are on a par as potential
bases for conflict groups, and they acquire importance in
an alternating pattern. 'Where the bases of the acquisition and distribution of goods are relatively stable,
stratification by status is favored. Every technological
repercussion and economic transformation threatens stratification by status and pushes the class situation into
the foreground' (Weber, 1968, p. 938). Since the relative importance of the status order and of the economic
order tends to fluctuate in an alternating manner, and
since every group is a part of both orders, the long-run
development the structure of society and of the class
system becomes indeterminate (Bendix, 1974). This in-
determinateness contrasts with the Marxian assumption of
the long-run dominance of the sphere of production, which
leads to hypotheses about basic changes in the class
system and the structure of society.

Dahrendorf

Among the later generation of sociological critics of the
Marxian class theory following more or less closely in the
footsteps of Weber, the theories of Dahrendorf have enjoyed relatively wide currency.   Dahrendorf (1959, ch. 2)
holds that central parts of the Marxian theory of class
have been factually refuted.   The polarization and 'emiseration' of the working class predicted by Marx has not
taken place.   The state has not been subordinated to
capital but has played a quite independent role in equalizing living conditions in society.   The Marxian emphasis
on the importance of property was also exaggerated.
Status differences based on income and occupation have reduced the saliency of class divisions.   Dahrendorf sets
forth his own theory as a positive critique of the Marxian
position, although he acknowledges that the two approaches
depart from each other.   This departure is basic, indeed, and hinges on two different sets of assumptions.

The first set of assumptions is that property relations
are only a special type of basis for authority;   it is
authority, i.e. the legitimate exercise of power, that
should be seen as the central variable for class formation. (5)   In every social organization authority is
differentially distributed, and the incumbents of some
positions have the right to exercise authority over the
incumbents of other positions.   This differential 'distribution of authority in associations is the ultimate
"cause" of the formation of conflict groups' or social
classes (Dahrendorf, 1959, pp. 172-3).   Within each association it gives rise to two conflict groups, those with
and those without authority.   Ownership of the means of
production is thus only one of a multitude of possible
bases for authority;   it gives rise to classes or conflict groups in only one of an almost infinite number of
different associations or social organizations.

In early capitalist society, conflicts arising in
industry were superimposed on a number of other lines of
cleavage, especially in the political sphere, which
tended to give society a two-class character.   The second
and most important set of Dahrendorf's assumptions is that
in modern, 'post-capitalist', society this superimposition
has been dissolved.   While post-capitalist society still
is a class society in the sense that authority remains
differentially distributed in all of its multitude of organizations, the lines of cleavage no longer tend to
overlap.   Most importantly, conflicts in industry have
been 'institutionally isolated' from conflicts in politics.   This is because the determinants and mechanisms

that now allocate positions in industry tend to become independent of those that allocate positions in the political sphere. Thus 'membership in an industrial class leaves open to which political class an individual belongs', and 'the participants of industry, upon leaving the factory gate, leave behind them with their occupational role their industrial class interests also. The manifest contents of industrial class interests are no longer identical with those of political class interests' (Dahrendorf, 1959, pp. 271-4).

Dahrendorf's central thesis of the dissociation of industry and society in post-capitalist society thus goes contrary to the Marxian view of the fundamental importance of the economy and the material base for the structure of the whole society, including, of course, the political arena. By postulating a great number of independent lines of cleavages, he redefines the Marxian class society into a non-vertical mosaic of the post-capitalist society, with an almost infinite number of criss-crossing cleavages.

Industrialization and embourgeoisement

In retrospect, it appears evident that the theory developed by Dahrendorf reflected the dominant climate among bourgeois, liberal intellectuals in the West during the 1950s. This intellectual climate, shaped in the Cold War atmosphere against a background of an unprecedented rate of economic growth and serious electoral difficulties for the reformist socialist parties in postwar Europe, is also reflected in other influential schools of thought on class and politics that emerged in this period. These ideas came partly to serve as legitimations of the status quo, but they also offered influential alternatives to the Marxian interpretation of the development of capitalist society. As rivals of Marxian ideas, they were largely based upon the earlier Weberian critique of Marx. Central to these theories has been the assumption that the process of industrialization, while not changing the class position of citizens in the Marxian sense, is accompanied by changes in technology and economic organization which affect, in Weberian terms, their market and status position.

A fundamental assumption in several of these theories is that the exigencies of a common basic technology impose a set of imperatives on the social structure of societies undergoing industrialization. This 'logic of industrialization' tends to generate convergence in the develop-

ment of social institutions and social life in these societies (Kerr et al., 1960, 1973; Kerr, 1968; see also
Galbraith, 1967; Aron, 1967; Lipset, 1964; and Parson,
1966). The forces of industrialization are assumed to
change the pattern of social stratification by increasing
the requirements of education and technical skill in the
labour force. The middle strata will therefore tend to
expand and the stratification hierarchy will tend to
become diamond-shaped. Cleavages based on occupation
will be increasingly important in the working class.
Social, geographical and occupational mobility is expected
to increase. The working class will therefore tend to
disintegrate and gradually to merge with the middle
strata.

While conflict remains, 'the industrial society ...
develops a distinctive consensus which relates individuals
and groups to each other and provides an integrated body
of ideas, beliefs, and value judgements' (Kerr et al.,
1973, p. 53). The peak and critical period of worker
protest comes relatively early in the process of industrialization. It reflects the breakdown of social bonds
and societal institutions in its early stages. After
this critical stage protests decline in intensity. This
is largely a result of the appearance of new institutions
- political democracy, the growth of unions and the emergence of a 'web of rules' in the sphere of industry -
which again make it possible to regulate and resolve societal conflicts. The institutionalization of conflict
and the separation of political from economic conflict -
the former taking place in the sphere of democratic elections and the latter through collective bargaining limited
to 'economism' - is thus seen as rendering conflict innocuous to the fabric of capitalist industrial society. (6)   Technological advances from the mass production phase to continuous or automated production contribute to this development by increasing the prospects for
moral integration of the workers in the firm (Blauner,
1964, pp. 154, 162-5, 181). Based on experiences in the
most advanced industrial nation, the United States, a
decline of the unions is expected. 'The union belongs
to a particular stage in the development of the industrial
system. When that stage passes so does the union in anything like its original position' (Galbraith, 1967, p. 27
p. 274).

With the development of industrialism, unions are seen
as gradually losing their class character and becoming
sectional and special interest organizations (Lester,
1958; Galbraith, 1967, chs 23 and 24). 'Labour organizations will not be component parts of class movements

urging programs of total reform, for the consensus of a
pluralistic society will have settled over the scene, nor
may they be heavily identified by industry.... Rather,
they may tend to take more the craft, or perhaps better,
the occupational form.... (P)rofessional-type interests
should mean more to workers than industry or class ties'
(Kerr et al., 1973, p. 274).

As the choice of terms indicates, these theorists see
the technological aspects of production, not the type of
ownership of means of production, as the crucial characteristic of advanced societies. Patterns of ownership
are accorded only minor importance, and all industrial
societies, the capitalist ones in the West as well as the
communist ones in the East, are assumed to follow largely
converging paths of development.

Recent theories on the 'post-industrial' society also
have been based on the assumption that changes in production technology crucially affect the class structure of
society (Bell, 1972; Touraine, 1974). As the production
processes become more advanced, a decreasing proportion of
the labour force will be involved directly in manufacturing, while service occupations will increase in importance. The technological changes also imply that theoretical knowledge of specialized kinds will confer power
to individuals in much the same way as did ownership of
property in the earlier phases of industrialization.

These rivals to the Marxian theory of the development
of industrial societies share some characteristics with
the theory they attack, mainly in their 'historicistic'
flavour, i.e. the claim that they can discern the ultimate
goal towards which human societies are developing (Goldthorpe, 1971). Unlike the Marxists, however, for whom
the future still was ahead, especially for the American
exponents of the rival theories, the future had already
begun. Political democracy of the western type was seen
as 'the crowning institution' of modern society (Lerner,
1958, p. 64). The combination of political democracy and
capitalism was as 'the good society itself in operation'
where 'the fundamental political problems of the industrial revolution have been solved' (Lipset, 1960, pp. 403,
406).

In Europe, the ideas central to the 'logic of industrialism' school of thought appear more fragmented; but
they focus on the prediction of the increasing 'embourgeoisement' of the working class (for a summary and criticism of these views see Goldthorpe et al., 1971). These
ideas reflect attempts to explain the electoral difficulties faced by socialist parties in postwar Europe, especially in Britain. Again, technological changes are

assumed to blur the distinction between manual and non-
manual occupations; the working class is seen as declining and disintegrating, marked less by class consciousness
than by a striving for middle-class status.   Contributing
to these tendencies are changes in patterns of housing, in
particular the splitting up of old, homogeneous working
class communities and the growth of new, more anonymous
and mixed housing areas.

Critical responses

Among some writers of a Marxist bend, the response to the
ideas of the decline and decomposition of the working
class has partly been to question them on empirical
grounds (e.g. Westergaard, 1970; Westergaard and Resler,
1975).   Many 'neo-Marxists', however, appear to have been
willing to accept the description of the actual changes
in the position of the working class implied by the 'embourgeoisement' thesis, but have advanced alternative
interpretations of the causes of these changes.   Alienation, retarded subjective consciousness owing to the
social authority or 'hegemony' of the bourgeoisie, and
the creation of a labour aristocracy made possible through
exploitation of underdeveloped countries have thus been
suggested as causes for the presumed 'embourgeoisement'
(Marcuse, 1964; Nicolaus, 1968; Mann, 1973).   Some of
them, however, do not see the changes in the stratification system as necessarily disarming the working class as
a revolutionary force (Gorz, 1964).
It has also been hypothesized, especially in France,
that the 'new working class' - consisting of highly
skilled workers and technicians who experience the 'contradictions' between the need for autonomy in their work
and the limitations for such autonomy in their present
work organizations - will be a revolutionary section of
the labour force (Mallet, 1963; Touraine, 1974). (7)
Based on ideas of Lenin, French theorists have also viewed
the 'uneven development' of different levels of capitalist
society as a cause of revolution.   They have also seen
revolutions as being 'over-determined', i.e. caused by a
multiplicity of factors, of which important ones are
found on the level of the 'superstructure' while the
material base comes in only 'in the last instance' (Althusser, 1969; Poulantzas, 1971).   The similarity of
such theories to academic functional sociology has been
pointed out (Parkin, 1975).
The theses on the 'logic of industrialization' and the
'embourgeoisement' of the working class have also been

criticized on empirical grounds.   Hamilton (1967 and
1972) has questioned assumptions about decreasing class
differences in consumption standards, as well as about
the dependence of workers' political views on their
standard of living.   Goldthorpe (1966) found that the
assertions of decreasing differentials in income and
wealth, and of increasing mobility rates, were unsupported
by empirical data.
     In an influential study, Goldthorpe et al.
(1968a, b,
1969) examined empirical data on affluent British workers
in Luton, selected so as to maximize the degree of 'embourgeoisement', but by and large they failed to verify
hypotheses derived from the 'embourgeoisement' thesis.
On the theoretical level, the Luton research group
stresses the fact that the class situation of the workers
does not change with increasing wages, enlightened management or changes in patterns of housing.   'Despite such
changes the workers must gain their livelihood by placing
their labour power at the disposal of an employer in
return for wages' (Goldthorpe et al., 1969, p. 157).   The
conditions under which the workers earn their living, not
the size of income or the ways in which income is con-
sumed, are the hard facts that set the frames and conditions for their actions.   For the great majority of the
workers collective action remains the primary way in which
they can further their interests.
     The Luton research group points, however, to a trend
towards a convergence of some sections of the middle class
and of the working class around the values of 'instrumental collectivism' to further a privatized and family-
centred way of life.   In the white-collar group, increasingly large administrative units, reduced opportunity for
'career' mobility and rapid inflation have led to a
greater reliance on collective action through trade
unions of an instrumental and apolitical kind (Goldthorpe
et al., 1969, pp. 157-9).   Among workers, nearly full
employment, the gradual erosion of the traditional work-
based community and the institutionalization of industrial
conflict have reduced the solidaristic involvement of
workers in their work, workmates and the union.   Instead,
instrumental orientations become more common and work is
seen primarily as a means to achieve high wages to support
a privatized way of life.   Although the exclusive reliance on the 'cash nexus' between workers and their employers make strikes on wages likely, the dominance of
instrumental orientations to work limits the aspirations
of workers to high wages, and the probability for a basic
challenge to the capitalistic system thus declines.

Giddens

Among the recent generation of academic critics of Marixan
class theory, Giddens (1973, p. 101) considers the most
important inadequacy of the class theory of Marx to be
that it is based on a two-class model, which makes it conceptually difficult to recognize the existence of 'middle'
classes, in the Marxian case most clearly the existence of
the 'new middle classes' in capitalism. According to
Giddens, this flaw in the Marxian position is based on the
assumption of an almost dichotomous distribution of power
between the owners and the non-owners of the means of production; thus, 'Marx failed to recognise the potential
significance of differentiation of market capacity which
do not derive directly from the factor of property ownership' (Giddens, 1973, p. 103).

Giddens follows and extends the Weberian critique that
ownership of the means of production should be seen as
only one of several possible bases for bargaining power
in the capitalist market. Other bases of similar importance are occupational skills and formal education, which
differentiate the propertyless sectors of the population.
Giddens thus identifies market capacity - defined to include all forms of relevant attributes that individuals
bring to the bargaining encounter - as the central variable in class formation. This leads to the acknowledg-
ment of multiplex bases for the formation of classes.

The main problem for Giddens then becomes to analyse
what he calls the 'structuration' of class relationships,
i.e. the processes whereby the multitude of economic
classes, defined in terms of differences in market capacities, become translated into relatively few social
classes, i.e. socially identifiable aggregates of individuals. One important factor in this context is the
degree of social mobility in society, which determines the
extent to which common life experiences are reproduced
over generations. The division of labour introduces
other factors, primarily by involving a physical separation of manual and non-manual labour, and by allowing a
proportion of the non-manual employees to participate in
the framing and enforcement of authority to which the
manual workers are subjected. In the sphere of consumption, tendencies towards housing segregation reinforce the
separation created by market capacities. The degree of
overlap between these factors generally tends to create a
threefold class structure generic to capitalist society:
i.e., a differentiation between an upper, a middle and a
lower or working class (Giddens, 1973, pp. 107-10). In
his class analysis, Giddens thus departs from Marx and
arrives at a position close to that of Weber.

Giddens also departs from Marx in that he does not see
the working class as a threat to the capitalist economic
systems of advanced societies.   He maintains, on the
contrary, that social democracy is the normal form taken
by the systematic inclusion of the working class within
the capitalist system.   While this incorporation is
potentially unstable, the instability is not related to
the increasing 'maturity' of capitalism, as Marx assumed.
Giddens (1973, p. 287) argues instead that 'revolutionary
consciousness tends above all to characterise the point
of impact to post-feudalism and capitalism-industrialism,
and is not endemic to capitalist society itself.'   Following the French neo-Marxists, Giddens (1973, p. 117)
argues that 'the sources of revolutionary consciousness
will tend to be linked either to those groupings on the
fringes of "incorporation" into a society based upon industrial technique (e.g. peasants whose traditional mode
of production has been undermined), or conversely to those
involved in the most progressive technical sectors of
production.'

2   THE ROLE OF PROPERTY

The heuristic value of the concept of class and of class
theories is in facilitating the understanding of the distribution of privilege and life chances in society;   the
'structuration' of class relationships;   the formation of
economic and political conflict groups;   and the pattern
of social change.   Some of the confusion and controversy
surrounding class theories derives from the failure to
distinguish clearly between causal and descriptive uses
of concepts and variables.   In this context a distinction
must thus be made between, on the one hand, the latent
(or causal) variables introduced into the class theories
and, on the other hand, the manifest (or dependent) variables, which are derived from the latent variables and
the assumptions of their interrelationships.
One example of the unfortunate mixing of latent and
manifest characteristics in the context of class theories
is the debate on the number of classes to be recognized. (8)   Neo-Weberians like Giddens thus criticize the
'two-class model' of Marx on the grounds that it cannot
deal with middle classes and, related to this, that it
fails to recognize the important effects of market capacities other than property.   But this criticism appears
to be misdirected;   the two-class model of Marx was not
intended as a description of the societies of his time
but rather as a causal model of the long-run development
of capitalist societies.

In the Marxian model the pattern of ownership of the means of production, which in capitalist societies divides the population into two classes, is taken as the pivotal causal variable.   This causal variable, however, is not immediately and completely manifested in society.   Instead the central hypothesis is that, as capitalism develops *in the long run*, ownership of the means of production will dominate over other factors which fragment and rank the propertyless sectors of the population.   The ensuing homogenization of the conditions of life among the wage-earners will thereby facilitate the formation of a unified conflict group among them.   The observations of Marx that internal competition and the division of labour introduce an infinite fragmentation of interest and rank among the labourers, and his extended analyses of the conditions under which this fragmentation can be overcome, indicates a keen awareness of the relevance of factors other than property for the formation of conflict groups.   In his causal scheme, however, these other factors (e.g. occupational skills, formal education and status) must be seen primarily as intervening variables dependent upon the basic causal variable, the pattern of ownership of the means of production.

A unifying theme of non-Marxian theories of class formation is, as we have seen, the stress upon the limited and decreasing role of the ownership of the means of production, with several other factors given equal or even greater weight.   Weber, for instance, thus considered the command over skills and education to be as important as property, and regarded status as being on a par with class as an axis along which conflict groups are formed. Dahrendorf and Giddens explicitly state that ownership over the means of production is only one among many factors determining the formation of conflict groups.   In the theories on the embourgeoisement of the working class it is obviously assumed that private ownership of the means of production is of little significance in modern societies.   The 'logic of industrialism' school also relegates ownership of the means of production to a marginal role, focusing instead on technology and industrial organization as the basic aspects of modern societies.

The fundamental disagreement between Marxian and non-Marxian approaches to class theory does not therefore concern the number of classes to be recognized, or whether power in society is dichotomously distributed, or whether market capacities like education or occupational skill are significant.   It concerns, instead, *the relative importance of the defining characteristic of capitalist societies - the private ownership of the means of production - for the distribution of life chances, class structuration, the formation of conflict groups and the pattern of social change in capitalist industrial societies.* While the Marxian approach to class theory makes the mode of production the pivotal causal variable in this context, and sees occupational skills, education and status primarily as intervening variables in this process, the non-Marxian approaches generally relegate the pattern of ownership of the means of production to a position of, at the most, one among many independent variables. This aspect of the differences between Marxian and non-Marxian approaches to class theory can be crudely summarized as in Figure 1.1.

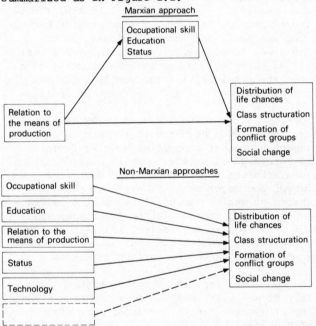

FIGURE 1.1 Schematic representation of differences between Marxian and non-Marxian approaches to class theory

When evaluating the fruitfulness of Marxian and non-Marxian approaches to class theory for the explanation of social change, class structuration and the formation of conflict groups, it can be noted that the sphere of production in many ways is a more basic category than the market and the area of consumption. Although mutual influence can be expected between them, it would thus appear that changes in the productive system of society will have decisive effects on its social structure, market

relations and consumption patterns, while changes in
market relations and consumption patterns generally can
be expected to reflect, rather than to initiate, structural change.   It can be argued, then, that to base
class theory in the sphere of production, as is done in
Marxian class theory, is for important purposes potentially more fruitful than the stress on the market and
on consumption, which is found in most of the non-Marxian
approaches.

The Marxian as well as the non-Marxian class theories
recognize ownership over the means of production, formal
education, occupational skills and labour power as power
resources in bargaining encounters and in social conflict.
It is thus also possible to evaluate the potential fruitfulness of these theories in terms of a comparison between
capital, on the one hand, and 'human capital', on the
other hand, as power resources.   Of particular interest
is the actual and potential degree of concentration of a
power resource, the possibilities for mobilization and
transformation of the resource and its range of applicability.

One can note, then, that the actual as well as potential concentration is much higher with respect to capital
than with respect to market capacities such as formal
education and occupational skills.   While mass education
has come to characterize modern capitalist societies,
those who control the major means of production and the
dominating shares of wealth can still be counted in fractions of a percentage of the population (Atkinson, 1975;
Diamond, 1975; Westergaard and Resler, 1975; SOU, 1968;
LO, 1976).   Capital and wealth can thus be and are concentrated in much fewer hands than are other market
capacities.

Such a high concentration level implies that changes
in the property of an individual assume major significance
only when they affect ownership or control over significant parts of the means of production.   Ownership of
durable consumer goods, a home or small savings, signifies
primarily some degree of independence for the owner but
does not generally function as a crucial power resource.
Changes in the level of education or occupational skills
of an individual, however, are of significance also at the
lower level of the distribution.   Formal education, in
fact, tends to yield diminishing returns after a certain
level is reached.

These differences in the pattern of distribution of
market capacities imply that, in individual bargaining
relationships, he who controls the means of production
generally has an upper hand also over the educated or

skilled person and, of course, over him who only controls his own labour power.   The value of these other market capacities as power resources in bargaining can be enhanced through collective actions, which limit internal competition and concentrate, so to speak, the value of the small individual power resources on the market to one point, where bargaining on behalf of all can take place. Such concentration, however, requires collective action, something that often is difficult to achieve in large collectivities.   The mobilization of power resources based on capital is thus generally much easier than the mobilization of power resources based on labour power, skill and education.

As power resources, capital and wealth also differ from occupational skill and formal education with respect to the range of applicability and the ease of transformation. Capital and wealth are versatile power resources, which can be used and deployed for a great variety of purposes and quickly transformed.   'Human capital' such as education, skill and labour power has a much more limited range of use and is difficult to transform into other capacities.   As every wage-earner knows, the transformation of labour power to money takes time and requires suitable opportunities for such transformations, i.e. jobs, which can be difficult to find.   On the basis of ownership of the means of production, large-scale changes can be initiated on different levels of the economy, but labour power and other similar market capacities are primarily limited to use for defensive purposes or as checks on the initiative of capital.

It is thus obvious that, through their *potential and actual concentration, ease of mobilization, ease of transformation and range of applicability, capital and control over the means of production are unique resources, which confer great power to a small fraction of the population.* The primacy accorded to this type of power resource in Marxian theory would thus appear to be well founded and potentially fruitful.

If control over the means of production is the major power resource of the buyers of labour power, organizations that co-ordinate collective action become the major alternative power resource for the sellers.   Marx and Engels identified the potential for collective action of workers, channelled through the unions, as a power resource that could counterbalance power based on property. Unions, wrote Engels in 1845 (Engels, 1969, p. 245),

> imply the recognition of the fact that the supremacy of the bourgeoisie is based wholly upon the competition of the workers among themselves, i.e. upon their want

of cohesion.... If the competition of workers among
themselves is destroyed, if all determine not to be
further exploited by the bourgeoisie, the rule of
property is at an end.

Marx and Engels predicted, however, that the workers
would find union action too limited and therefore would
also organize themselves politically into a party in class
conflict.   Economic conflict would thus be fused with
political conflict and turn into conflict between classes,
which would eventually lead to the overthrow of the bourgeoisie.   Marxian theory thus implies an assumption that,
under certain circumstances, organizations for collective
action among the wage-earners can become more important
power resources than control over capital.

3   MARXIAN AND WEBERIAN APPROACHES TO CLASS CONFLICT: SOME HYPOTHESES

A central question raised by the foregoing discussions
concerns along what lines of cleavage conflict groups will
tend to form in industrial capitalist societies.   The
formation of conflict groups can be seen as a process of
coalition formation.   Assuming rational actors, we would
expect that the main factors affecting coalition formation
are similarity of interests and the relative distribution
of power resources which determines the chances for success (Caplow, 1968; Gamson, 1961; see also e.g. Riker,
1962).   Similarity of position within the division of
labour can be expected to generate similarity of interests.   In advanced societies the occupational structure
can thus be assumed to be the main axis along which conflict groups are formed.   Through the occupational structure, the division of labour is closely related to the
distribution of market capacities such as property, education and skill, and thereby to the distribution of power
resources in society.

Status and prestige can be seen primarily as being
derived from other power resources (Lenski, 1966).   Factors such as these can therefore be expected to be of
secondary importance as bases of cleavage in the formation
of coalitions or conflicts groups. (9)   Experience indicates however that, especially if correlated with market
capacities, religion and ethnicity can serve as important
lines of cleavage among the propertyless (Bonachich,
1972, 1975).   The degree of social mobility, and of
physical and social separation of occupational groups both
on and off work, can also be of relevance for class structuration and for the formation of conflict groups.

An important potential line of division can be expected between the higher echelons of the occupational structure, to which belong those who own and control the means of production, and the lower levels of this structure.   The main reason is that this 'upper class' generally fills major positions as controllers of the means of production, while the great majority of the labour force offers its labour power on the market.   Other lines of potential cleavage are related primarily to occupational skill and formal education.   One must remember however that, contrary to what is assumed in the functionalistic theory of stratification, (10) skill and education do not lead to differentiation of rewards merely because of their instrumental value for society.   More subtle processes emanating both from the buyers and the sellers of labour power are at work here, and complicated interactions can be expected between coalition formation and the shape of the occupational hierarchy.

One set of factors affecting the differentiation of rewards in the occupational hierarchy is related to the increasing size of enterprises and the need for co-ordination and planning of work within them.   Although most types of production organizations require control structures and a differentiation in positions, the antagonistic nature of capitalist production puts additional requirements on the control structure for maintaining the pattern of dominance within the firm.   This control structure will be differentiated with respect to power delegated to its positions.   Differential rewards to incumbents in the position of power serves partly as a control device and reflects efforts of the employers to win sectors of the 'new' middle class into their fold (cf. Dreyfuss, 1952).

Another source of differentiation emanates from the sellers of labour power.   The value of labour can be enhanced by collective actions aimed at controlling its availability.   Now the scarcity value of labour power can be increased according to two different principles, *inclusion* or *exclusion*.   Where power resources are widely distributed and depend on numbers, the most rational strategy would appear to be inclusion of all possible sellers in the coalition.   Industrial unionism is an expression of this strategy.   If, however, power resources are based on acquired skills, an alternative strategy would be to control and restrict the possibilities to acquire these skills, i.e. to monopolize a sector of the labour market.   As Weber noted, when competition increases it is common that 'one group of competitors take some externally identifiable characteristic of another group of (actual or potential) competitors - race, language, religion, local or social origin, descent, residence, etc. - as a pretext for attempting their exclusion' (Weber, 1968, p. 342). (11)   Craft unions and professional organizations are expressions of such a strategy.

As is well known, the main types of interest organizations or conflict groups on the labour market have been employers' organizations, white-collar unions, professional societies, craft unions and industrial unions. Because of their divergent assumptions about the relative importance of capital and other market capacities for the formation of conflict groups, the Marxian and the Weberian approaches to class theory would appear to lead to divergent hypotheses concerning the development and patterning of these interest organizations.   We will now specify some hypotheses on the development of these organizations on the labour market.   Although not derived from the above approaches to class theory in any strict sense, these hypotheses nevertheless appear to capture the basic thrust of these approaches and thus to make them partially amenable to empirical elucidation.

One area of divergence concerns the *bases for the organization of unions*.   The Weberian approach, with its stress on status and a multitude of 'acquisition' classes, leads to an expectation of a relatively large number of union organizations which primarily reflect differences in market capacities and status.   Weber reminds us that 'the direction in which the individual worker, for instance, is likely to pursue his interests may vary widely, according to whether he is constitutionally qualified for the task at hand to a high, to an average, or to low degree' (Weber, 1968, p. 929).   Unions based on occupation or craft could thus be expected to play the central role.   The Marxian stress on the predominance of the split between sellers and buyers of labour would, instead, lead us to expect that the bases for the organizations will be wider and involve e.g. a whole branch of industry.   Thus industrial unionism would be expected to be increasingly important, leading eventually to class-based organizations and decrease of internal competition.

Another difference between the two approaches concerns the *level of organization*.   The Marxian emphasis on the split between sellers and buyers of labour power predicts an ever-increasing level of unionization among the sellers as well as of organization among the buyers.   In contrast, the Weberian approach, with emphasis on the multitude of relatively small organizations with unclear lines of demarcation, the status similarities cross-cutting the cleavage between sellers and buyers of labour power and

the alternating importance of class and status as bases
for the formation of conflict groups, appears to predict
a lower level of unionization.   Although classes represent possible, and frequent, bases for social action,
Weber (1968, p. 929) thus stresses that 'the emergence
of an association or even of mere social action from a
common class situation is by no means a universal phenomenon.'

The Marxian and Weberian approaches to class conflict
would also appear to lead to differing hypotheses concerning the *relationship between economic and political conflict*.   The Marxian emphasis on the importance of the
economic base for the political, legal and ideological
institutions of society leads to the prediction of a close
relationship between political and economic conflict.
If, however, status groups based on styles of life and
patterns of consumption are equally important, the relationship between economic and political conflict can be
expected to be highly attenuated.   Later in this book
(chapters 3 and 4) the above set of hypotheses will be
evaluated against the background of developments in
Sweden.

4   THE PLAN OF THE BOOK

In this chapter we have attempted to specify the theoretical assumptions on class and class conflict that underlie
the diverging positions in the debate on the working class
in capitalist industrial society.   Our conclusion was
that the crucial difference between these two approaches
is related to the role and weight accorded the defining
characteristic of capitalist society, the private ownership of the means of production, for the structuration of
classes and conflict groups in these societies.   In
chapter 2 we will continue the analysis of the theoretical
underpinnings of the debate on the working class, and consider especially the themes of argument that concern the
potentiality of basic structural changes in the capitalist
system, i.e. the 'transformation' of capitalism into socialism.   A model of social conflict will be developed,
that integrates two diverging approaches to conflict
theory in modern sociology and political science, one
stressing the subjective aspects or desires of the participants in conflict, the other viewing conflicts as power
struggles.   This model specifies the role of structural
and subjective factors in social conflict and will be used
as a background for the discussion of theories on the
probability of the transformation of capitalism.

Chapter 3 intends to increase the reader's familiarity with the most important changes during the last hundred years in the social structure of Sweden, the country upon which our case study of the working class in advanced industrial societies will be based, and to discuss these developments against the background of the divergent theoretical standpoints.   The growth of the interest groups on the Swedish labour market is thus analysed in relation to the hypotheses derived above from the different approaches to class theory.   The development of political conflict and of the political strategies of the Swedish labour movement are taken up, and an interpretation of the long-term changes in the level of industrial conflict in Sweden is suggested.

The two subsequent chapters move into an analysis of the role of work among manual workers, where the empirical data primarily refer to metal workers.   The purpose is to provide a multiplex and nuanced basis for the discussion of the present situation and future development of the Swedish working class.   Central issues here are, to what extent work experiences affect the subjective readiness and desire of workers for structural change, and to what extent social relations created around work promote or hinder the organization and mobilization of the workers as a collectivity.   Chapter 4 starts with an analysis of the factors in industrial work that create work dissatisfaction.   The theory predicting that work dissatisfaction no longer constitutes a motivation for structural change in capitalist society, but is accepted as part of an instrumental orientation to work that makes high wages the central goal of work is central for the discussion of the future role of the working class. This theory is subjected to an empirical test.   In chapter 5 we will look at the role of modern industrial technology in shaping social relations around work in ways that may affect the cohesiveness and solidarity of the working class, and thus its power resources.

Departing from the analysis of shopfloor social relations among the metal workers, the subsequent three chapters are focused on the development and internal functioning of the union organization, a main vehicle for the mobilization of the power resources of the working class.   Chapter 6 looks at the workplace union and on the meaning that workers give to union membership.   The probability of the continued commitment of workers to unionism of a solidaristic type, especially in the younger generation of workers, is discussed.   Factors affecting the degree of participation in union government, as well as the internal functioning of the workplace union, are also analysed.

In chapter 7 we take up the 'classical' problem of
union democracy and membership influence, which is of
relevance for the direction that union action takes in
situations of class conflict.   The historical development
towards an increasing centralization of decision-making
within the union is documented, and alternative explanations for this trend are discussed.   Chapter 8 is an
analysis of the debate within the working class on strategies and tactics in class conflict, which is reflected
in the internal opposition to union leadership.   This
opposition has at times been vigorous among the metal-
workers with ties to left-wing political groups.   The
nature and basis of strength for the internal opposition
is discussed and its role in the history of the union is
analysed, partly on the basis of quantitative data derived
from union documents.

The political views and standpoints of the wage-earners
are, of course, of crucial importance for the future development of society.   In chapter 10 we look at the trend
of class voting in Sweden during recent decades, to see to
what extent class continues to structure and shape party
preferences in the electorate.   We also examine the
social roots of party preferences among workers, especially the 'deviant' preferences for the communist and the
bourgeois parties.   The function of the workplace political climate and of the workplace union for the political
preferences and activity of the workers are analysed.
The relationship between the Social Democratic Party and
the union, a key issue for working-class action, is discussed.

In the final chapter 11, an attempt is made to bring
together the various lines of argument and evidence and
to discuss the significance of developments in the 1970s
for the future of welfare capitalism in Sweden.

5   EMPIRICAL DATA

In this study different sources of empirical data are
utilized as bases for the discussion of the development
of the working class and its organizations in Sweden.
Secondary analyses of nationwide surveys carried out in
the period 1973-5 are used, e.g. to analyse work experiences and party preferences.   In the analysis of the
historical development of membership influence and of
the left-wing union opposition within the Swedish Metal
Workers' Union, internal union documents are relied upon.

The main source of data, however, comes from a survey
study among metal-workers carried out in the winter of

1966-7.   This survey was originally undertaken as part of
a study commissioned by the Swedish Metal Workers' Union
to probe into the background of unofficial strikes in the
metal-working industry.   It involved a two-stage sampling
procedure.   A purposive sample of forty-eight firms representing different sizes, technologies and community
types were included.   The workers in these firms thus
constitute the population of this survey.   The firms included range in size from 50 to 4,300 workers.   Shipyards, the electro-technical industry, steelworks and
auto assemblies, as well assdifferent types of engineering
firms, are represented.   The firms are located in varying
types of communities: small and middle-sized service and
commercial towns, heavily industrialized communities some
of them dominated by a single firm, and the three largest
cities in the country (cf. Appendix 2).   In comparison
with the whole metal-working industry, large firms are
over-represented in this sample.   An attempt was also
made to include firms with varying levels of unofficial
strikes, but this turned out to be rather unsuccessful.
Within each firm a random sample of workers was selected
with stratification according to level of participation in
union affairs.   Altogether about four thousand workers
were included and were asked to complete a questionnaire
during working time.   The response rate was 97.2 per cent
(for details see Appendix 1).

Society undergoes continuous change.   The purpose of
this book is not primarily to describe the present situation in Sweden but, instead, to attempt to understand some
of the processes of change that take place in its working
life, in its union organizations and on its political
scene.   Such an analysis must involve a historical perspective and consider a longer period of time.   In
attempting to understand the changes that presently take
place in society, we need to know what the situation was
like before the changes as well as to have information
about the factors that are of importance in the processes
of change.   From this point of view, it is an advantage
that an important part of the data here refer to the situation in the late 1960s, to the period immediately preceding the years of change on the Swedish labour market
beginning in 1969.   Although this limits the possibilities to describe the present situation, it broadens our
possibilities to understand the background to the changes
in the 1970s.   The present book is thus a partial and
time-bound analysis of processes of change in capitalist
society.   It gives points of departure and bases for
comparison for future studies of the working class and its
organizations in Sweden and perhaps also in other
countries.

2 Social conflict and structural change

Already Marx and Engels had foreseen difficulties in the
process of change in the capitalist system because of
counter-tendencies to class polarization related to the
growth of the middle classes; because of conflicts between different sectors of the working class, e.g. through
the existence in Britain of a 'labour aristocracy' made
possible by Britain's position as an imperialist power;
and because of corruptability among some union leaders. (1)   The obvious failure of the expectations of an
early socialist breakthrough in the industrial countries
forced some rethinking in the Marxian camp.

On the one hand, the revisionists with Eduard Bernstein
as a leading figure, pointed to the rising standards of
living of the workers and to the growing size of the
middle classes and questioned the philosophical foundations of Marxist thought.   They argued that the overthrow
of capitalism was going to be a long, gradual process
where the trade unions would play a crucial role.   Lenin,
on the other hand, maintained that as long as unions are
limited to bargaining for wages, workers will remain integrated in the capitalist system, since wage demands can
be satisfied within this system.   Only if 'trade union
consciousness' is transcended through the infusion of
revolutionary ideology by a revolutionary political party
can such an integration be avoided. (2)   As we have seen
the dominant critics of the Marxian position in modern
sociology have asserted that the working class in advanced
industrial societies constitutes no basic threat to
capitalism.

In the continuing debate on the working class, several
related themes of argument have thus appeared.   One theme
has concerned the objective possibilities for the working
class to effect basic changes in the capitalist economic
system because of its weak power resources as reflected in

31

difficulties of union and political organization. Another often stressed theme has centred around the subjective conditions and readiness for action in the working class, related to its level of aspiration, class consciousness and awareness of possibilities of an alternative society. A third theme has maintained that the growth of unions and mass political parties has led to the creation of effective institutions for conflict regulation and the separation of political and economic conflict, which has undermined the revolutionary potential of the working class and incorporated it into capitalist society.   Thus, somewhat paradoxically, the increasing strength of the working class is assumed to decrease the possibilities for basic structural change in advanced capitalist societies.

In the present chapter we will discuss some of the major themes of argument along which the debate on the working class has continued.   Central to this debate are problems concerning objective and subjective factors in structural change and social conflict.   We will therefore begin here by analysing the two diverging approaches to social conflict in modern sociology and political science;   one stressing the subjective aspects of social conflict, with relative deprivation as the central concept, the other viewing conflicts primarily as power struggles. A model of social conflict incorporating the central concepts in both these divergent theories will be developed. We will then analyse the relationship between industrial and political conflict, consider the role of the state in social change, and discuss the relationship between conflict and structural change.

1   OBJECTIVE AND SUBJECTIVE FACTORS IN SOCIAL CONFLICT (3)

Social conflict and structural change in a society can fruitfully be viewed as being generated by the attempts of citizens to solve important problems confronting them. One basic problem area confronts them when they go about the business of making their daily living.   The extent to which problems in this area generate social conflict and change depends partly on the extent to which given outcomes are defined as unsatisfying, i.e. on the levels of aspiration and awareness among the citizens.   It also depends on the actual possibilities of the citizens to affect changes in the circumstances under which they live.

Modern students of conflicts such as revolutions, race riots and other forms of collective violence have attempted to explain conflict largely in terms of the subjective states and desires of the participants concerned.   In

this *expectation-achievement approach* to conflict theory,
conflicts are thus seen primarily as responses to an in-
tolerable gap between the normative expectations and
actual achievements of the actors created by accumulated
experiences of hardships, i.e. as a result of increasing
relative deprivation (e.g. Davies, 1962; Feierabend et
al., 1969; Gurr, 1970). (4) The dominance of this
approach in the postwar period has led to the neglect of
structural factors that determine the actual possibilities
for achieving change, i.e. primarily the distribution of
power resources between the participants concerned. (5)
In a review of postwar conflict research, Converse (1968,
p. 489) thus observes that 'power frequently is handled as
a factor to be dropped out by assuming that two conflicting parties are roughly equal in "power".'

The expectation-achievement approach to conflict has
recently been attacked on theoretical as well as on empirical grounds. Its critics have proposed power resources, the mobilization of power resources and the
struggle for power as the central features in an alternative approach to conflict theory (Snyder and Tilly, 1972;
Tilly, 1973; Oberschall, 1973; Shorter and Tilly, 1974).
In this alternative, the *political process approach,* manifest conflicts like collective violence or revolutions are
seen as closely related to, and produced by, the central
political process; a collectivity within a population
makes a claim to certain privileges and this claim is
resisted by another collectivity. The process of acquiring control over power resources is seen as a necessary
condition for possessing the capacity to contend for
privileges. Conflicts are assumed to be most frequent in
periods when parties acquire or lose control over power
resources. The proponents of this approach to conflict
theory tend summarily to reject motivational concepts like
relative deprivation as being theoretically unfruitful or
empirically unsupported (Oberschall, 1973, pp. 37-8 and
Snyder and Tilly, 1972).

The expectation-achievement approach to conflict theory
is obviously inadequate to the extent that it puts exclusive emphasis on the motivation, or wish, for improvement
among the potential participants, and overlooks the actual
possibilities for achieving the desired change, the latter
being determined primarily by the differences in power resources between the parties concerned. In many situations, where the desire for change grows in a collectivity
with increasing relative deprivation or hardship, the
actual possibilities for alleviating the situation may
simultaneously decrease as a result of the changing
balance of power among the parties. This approach thus

shares the weakness of class theories that put great
stress on status and status groups.

The political process approach to conflict is fruitful
through its stress on the primacy of power resources and
the mobilization of power in social conflict.   Yet it
seems necessary to include also the subjective aspects and
consciousness of the actors in attempts to explain social
conflict.   This is because any theory of conflict that
focuses on the mobilization of power resources will, at
least implicitly, have to come to grips with motivational
concepts like relative deprivation, since motivational
factors are generally accorded a central place in theories
of mobilization (Atkinson, 1964; Blalock, 1967, ch. 4).
The Marxian theory of class conflict, with its focus on
structural factors involving the power relations is society and its simultaneous stress on the importance of
subjective aspects and motivation embodied in the concept
of class consciousness, would appear to be a potentially
fruitful approach in this context.   Such an approach,
however, must be confronted with later theories in sociology and political science, and can be further developed
via an attempt to reconcile the divergent approaches in
modern conflict theory.

We will therefore here develop a model of conflict
that incorporates the central concepts from both the
expectation-achievement approach and the political process
approach.   In this model, which might be called a *power
difference model of conflict,* relative deprivation as well
as differences in power resources between the parties are
included.   The difference in power resources between
parties is used as the central independent variable.
Utility of reaching the goal, expectancy of success and
relative deprivation are introduced as intervening variables to relate the effects of changes in the balance of
power among the parties upon the probability of manifest
conflict between them.

Concepts and assumptions

The conflict situations that are of central concern here
are those that in one way or another relate to class conflict and to the struggle over how the surplus in society
is to be distributed among different collectivities or
parties (Lenski, 1966, ch. 3).   These conflicts can be
regarded as bargaining situations (Schelling, 1960, pp.
4-5; Rex, 1961, p. 123; Patchen, 1970, pp. 389-408).
In such bargaining situations the strategy of conflict
adopted by the parties generally involves the use of

rewards as well as punishments over a period of time. This implies that conflict should be analysed as an inter- action over time.   Both short-term and long-term effects of changes in the difference in power resources between the parties need to be considered.

The term 'conflict' here refers to manifest conflict, i.e. to interaction between parties with incompatible interests (Axelrod, 1970; Bergström, 1970; Fink, 1968). For conflict to occur, *both* parties have to resort to the use of punishments.   If one party turns the other cheek or returns good for bad, no conflict becomes manifest in the present sense of the word.   Conflict, however, need not involve violence.   The parties entering into conflict can be individuals, groups or collectivities such as classes.   Parties are assumed to be rational and to be satisficing rather than maximizing (Simon, 1957, pp. 196-206).

For simplicity, the analysis here is limited to con- flict situations with only two parties.   This is of course an over-simplification, since conflicts between two parties often are affected by third parties and other en- vironmental factors.   The issue of third parties, how- ever, brings up the question of the formation of conflict groups, where we find two unreconciled theoretical trad- itions in modern conflict theory.   According to the 'criss-cross' or 'cross-cutting cleavage' theories, intro- duction of third parties may decrease the probability of conflict (Coser, 1956; Galtung, 1966).   Such assumptions are implicit in ideas that assume that the decomposition and internal differentiation of the working class will decrease the probability of class conflict.   The second contemporary theoretical tradition, 'coalition theory', deals with the process by which three or more actors com- bine into two opposing camps in the conflict situation (Caplow, 1968; Gamson, 1961; Riker, 1962).   In the present discussion therefore we have to exclude third parties from the discussion. (6)

Viewing conflicts as a part of bargaining situations suggests the possibility of carrying out the analysis within the framework of an exchange approach, utilizing some of the concepts from exchange theory.   But parties entering into exchange or conflict must not be assumed to have equal access to power resources, an assumption that is often made in exchange analysis. (7)   On the contrary, the difference in power resources is used as the central independent variable in the present analysis.   Power re- sources are the properties of an actor that provide the ability to reward or punish another actor and must be dis- tinguished from exerted power, or power in use (Blalock, 1967, pp. 118-19).

Exchange between two parties can be characterized by a going rate of exchange according to which the transactions of the parties are executed (Blau, 1964, pp. 155ff.). Each party is also assumed to evaluate the outcomes (the going rate of exchange) in the relationship according to its normative expectations (level of aspiration), which indicates what outcomes in the relationship it evaluates positively and considers to be fair and just.   The aspiration level of a party in a particular exchange relationship is assumed to be determined by knowledge of outcomes gained by its own or by vicarious experiences in similar relationships (Thibaut and Kelley, 1959, pp. 81-3).   The difference between the level of aspiration and the going rate of exchange defines the degree of relative deprivation experienced by a party in the relationship. (8)

We will assume further that in the long run the going rate of exchange is determined primarily by the difference in power resources between the parties.   This implies also that the availability of power resources, other than those directly concerned in the exchange, i.e. not only the supply and demand for the goods exchanged, can affect exchange rates. (9)   The going rate of exchange is usually arrived at through some kind of explicit or implicit bargaining between the parties.   If bargaining fails to bring the going rates above the aspiration level of a party, exchange may still take place if the party lacks better alternatives; however, the result may also be a termination of the relationship, or a conflict. (10)   In the latter case, use of punishments can be viewed as an attempt by one of the parties to change the going rate of exchange: conflict is thus the continuation of bargaining by other means.

In the long run the weaker party, through internal psychological processes, will tend to adjust its aspiration level towards the going rates of exchange in the relationship (Thibaut and Kelley, 1959, ch. 6).   Since the outcomes in exchange relationships known to parties through personal or vicarious experiences result from the prevailing balance of power in these relationships, it can be assumed that through a process of learning these parties also will have their aspiration levels directly and strongly influenced by the perceived difference in power resources between them.   We can also assume that the stronger party will use its power to 'engineer consent' and to influence the weaker party to accept as legitimate the rules for, as well as the going rate of, exchange in the relationship (Rex, 1961, pp. 181-2; Westergaard and Resler, 1975, pp. 141-7).   In the short run, however, aspiration levels may often deviate from the going rates of exchange.

The term 'mobilization of power resources' has two distinct meanings, which often are not separated. It can refer to the process whereby a party acquires control over power resources that it did not previously have (Gamson, 1968, p. 98; Snyder and Tilly, 1972; Tilly, 1973, p. 437); to the process whereby a party invests or uses the power resources already under its control (Blalock, 1967, p. 110); or to both these processes (Oberschall, 1973, p. 28). In the present context it is important to keep these aspects separate. For the propertyless groups, the development of organizations to co-ordinate action is the central power resource. We will refer to the acquiring of control over this type of power resource as the process of organization, and it involves the formation of conflict groups of coalitions. The process of organization thus affects the difference in power resources between the parties concerned, i.e. the basic independent variable in the present model. The term 'mobilization' is used here to refer only to the process of investing or using power resources already under one's control. (11)

A power difference model of conflict

In order to facilitate the presentation and understanding of the power difference model, the variables assumed to affect the probability of mobilization of power resources by a party are outlined in Figure 2.1, with causal relationships between the variables indicated by arrows. In the following presentation and discussion of these hypothetical causal relationships, each hypothesis is numbered serially in the order of presentation; this number also identifies the corresponding arrow in the figure. Plus

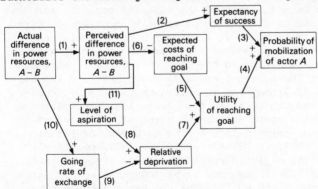

FIGURE 2.1 Causal relationships between main variables assumed to affect the probability of mobilization of actor A in a situation of potential conflict with actor B

signs (+) on the arrows indicate positive relationships
between the variables, whereas minus signs (-) indicate
negative relationships.

As stated above, the basic independent variable here
is the actual difference in power resources between the
parties.   We assume that, before taking action, rational
actors will attempt to assess the difference in power resources between themselves and their opponents.   Let us
further introduce a probabilistic element into the perception of the difference in power resources, but make
the assumption that on the whole the actual difference in
power resources tends to be correctly perceived by the
parties. (12)   Thus, when the difference in power between
two parties, A and B, changes to the benefit of party A,
the probability that A will perceive itself as the stronger party will increase monotonically (*hypothesis 1*).

Following Atkinson (1964, p. 242) and Blalock (1967,
p. 127) we will assume here that the degree to which a
party will mobilize power resources is a multiplicative
function of perceived probability of achieving the goal
(expectancy of success), and of the utility to the party
of achieving the goal.   Now if party A perceives its
power resources as larger than those of the opponent,
party B, its expectancy of success will naturally be
higher than if it perceives itself to be the weaker party.
We can thus assume a positive relationship between the
perceived difference in power resources and expectancy of
success (*hypothesis 2*).   Ceteris paribus, the higher the
expectancy of success of a party, the higher is the probability of mobilization (*hypothesis 3*); further, the
higher its utility of reaching the goal, the higher is the
probability of mobilization (*hypothesis 4*).

The utility to a party of reaching the goal is here
assumed to be a function of the expected costs in reaching
the goal, and of the degree of relative deprivation with
respect to the goal.   In a situation of potential conflict, the anticipated costs of reaching the goal will to
a large extent depend on how the other party is expected
to react.   The relevant costs of power here are the costs
to party A of attempting to influence party B by pressure
resources and the costs to B of resisting A's influence
attempts, both costs defined in terms of the value of
opportunities forgone in choosing to attack or resist
(Harsanyi, 1962, pp. 67-80; Baldwin, 1972, pp. 145-55).
The higher the expected costs to a party are, the lower
its utility (13) is assumed to be (*hypothesis 5*).   Expected costs for reaching the goal are assumed to be negatively related to the perceived difference in power
resources.   Thus, the larger the difference to its

advantage that a party perceives, the smaller are the
expected costs (*hypothesis 6*).

The relative deprivation of a party was defined above
as the difference between the going rate of exchange and
the level of aspiration of the party.   The higher the
relative deprivation of a party with respect to the goal,
the higher is its utility of reaching the goal assumed to
be (*hypothesis 7*).   Ceteris paribus, the higher the level
of aspiration of a party, the higher is its relative
deprivation (*hypothesis 8*); but the higher or better its
going rate of exchange, the lower is its relative deprivation (*hypothesis 9*).   The latter two hypotheses are
implied by our definition of relative deprivation.

As indicated above, the more advantageous the difference in power resources is to a party, the better, in the
long run, is its going rate of exchange in the relationship (*hypothesis 10*).   The level of aspiration was assumed to be affected primarily by previous experiences of
outcomes in similar exchange relationships.

Thus, the more a party perceives that the balance of
power is in its favour, the higher is its level of aspiration in the relationship (*hypothesis 11*): by personal and
vicarious experiences it has learned to expect that in
similar situations the stronger party will strike the
better bargain and will tend to get 'the lion's share' of
the goods to be distributed. (14)   This *dependence of the
level of aspiration and thus of social consciousness on
the actual and perceived difference in power resources* is
of crucial significance.   It has, however, often been
overlooked in discussions of the determinants of levels of
aspiration and social consciousness.   Usually other factors are seen as the important ones in this context (e.g.
Gurr, 1970, ch. 4).

The above discussion leads to the conclusion that, the
more advantageous a party perceives the balance of power
in the relationship to be, the higher is its utility of
reaching the goal.   Since parties are here assumed to be
satisficing rather than maximizing, the effects on utility
of further improvements in the balance of power of an already stronger party will however gradually decrease.
Now a change in the actual difference in power resources
between two parties, which is to the favour of A but to
the disadvantage of B, will increase the expectancy of
success as well as the utility of party A.   From this
follows that, ceteris paribus, such a change will increase
the probability that party A mobilizes power resources
(but will decrease the corresponding probability of party
B).

We have assumed that the probability of manifest con-

flict between the two parties depends on the probability
that they both mobilize power resources at the same time.
For manifest conflict to occur, one of the parties has to
initiate conflict through a punishing move against the
other party, who then has to retaliate.   Where the difference in power resources between the actors is large,
the stronger party is highly probable to make punishing
moves against the weaker party, and also to defend himself against possible attacks from the weaker party.
Since, however, the probability that the weaker party
will retaliate to the attack from the stronger party is
low, as is the probability that the weaker party himself
will attack, the probability for manifest conflict remains
low in this situation.   When the difference in power resources between the actors begins to decrease, the probability of mobilization of the stronger party decreases,
while the probability of mobilization of the weaker party
increases.   This increases the probability for manifest
conflict.

The above discussion therefore indicates that we can
expect a curvilinear relationship between, on the one
hand, the difference in power resources between the parties and, on the other hand, the probability of manifest
conflict between them.   In contrast .to other models of
conflict, which usually assume maximum probability of
conflict at the point of parity in power resources between
the parties (Gurr, 1970, pp. 234, 277; Timasheff, 1965,
pp. 156-8), a *bimodal distribution* of the probability of
manifest conflict on the difference in power resources
between the two actors is predicted here.   The probability of manifest conflict is thus assumed to be low when
the power resources of the parties are greatly unequal,
to increase up to a point with decreasing differences in
power resources, but to drop around the point of parity
in power resources, where something like a 'balance of
terror' between the parties is approached. (15)   An increase in the difference in power resources between actors
with unequal power resources will, correspondingly, generally decrease the probability of conflict.

Once the parties have mobilized their power resources
and entered into conflict, the outcome of the conflict may
affect not only their perception of the difference in
power resources between the parties, but also the actual
balance of power.   In this way *feedback mechanisms* are
introduced into the model.   Certain structural features
promote action, which in turn may affect structure.

Time and relative deprivation

Conflicts often unfold during relatively long time
periods.   The effects of the time dimension are incorporated into the power difference model through an assumption
that a change in the difference in power between parties
affects the going rate of exchange and the aspiration
levels of the parties with different degrees of delay.
We assume that the aspiration level of a party is slow as
it moves downward but that it moves upward more easily.
When the difference in power resources between two parties
changes, the most immediate effect of this change is
assumed to be an increase in the aspiration level of the
party that benefits from the change.   If the new balance
of power remains stable, the going rate of exchange in the
relationship will tend to change accordingly as a result
of bargaining or conflict or both.   With time the aspiration level of the losing party will then also approach
the new going rate of exchange in the relationship.
     Thus changes in the difference in power resources be-
tween two parties will affect the aspiration level of the
gaining party before the going rate of exchange becomes
modified.   Not only the actual size of the difference in
power resources, but also the rate of change in power resources may therefore have effects on relative deprivation.   If the originally weaker party experiences a rapid
improvement in its power position, it will feel greater
relative deprivation than after a slower increase, which
gives time for a gradual readjustment of the going rate
of exchange.
     The above assumptions imply that increases as well as
decreases in the difference in power resources between
the parties will increase the relative deprivation of the
parties in the period immediately following the change.
If the new balance of power becomes stable, however, relative deprivation will decrease with time.   This makes for
an intricate relationship between relative deprivation and
the probability of conflict, which we shall now consider.

Relative deprivation and conflict

Relative deprivation has been assumed to increase according to three basic patterns.   Decremental deprivation
occurs in a situation where one's expectations remain
stable but where one receive less and less.   If one's
expectations rise while achievements remain stable, aspirational deprivation is created.   The third type is
progressive deprivation, which occurs when a relatively

steady improvement in one's social and economic conditions generates increasing expectations but is followed by a sharp reversal in the trend of improvement (Gurr, 1970, pp. 46-58).

An increasing difference in power resources will change the going rate of exchange to the disadvantage of the weaker party. Since aspiration levels are assumed to be slow in moving downward, this decrease in achievements will lead to decremental deprivation. This type of relative deprivation is thus usually the result of an increase in the difference in power resources between the parties. The probability for conflict can be expected to decrease in such a situation, since the deteriorating balance of power will decrease the expectancy of success of the weaker party and increase the expected costs of reaching the goal.

A common cause of hardships experienced by many groups in society is probably that their command over power resources relative to that of other groups in society is slipping. In spite of their high motivation to achieve improvements and a high degree of relative deprivation, collectivities losing power are less likely to enter into conflict. In other words, assuming that mobilization is a multiplicative function of utility and expectancy of success, if expectancy of success is low, a high utility or desire for change will normally not lead to a high probability of mobilization. (16)

The power difference model of conflict allows for increases in relative deprivation of a party even when the difference in power resources and the going rate of exchange remains stable, i.e. for aspirational deprivation. Aspirational deprivation will increase the utility of mobilization of a party. But since the balance of power between the parties can be assumed to be stable, expectancy of success will not increase, nor will expected costs for reaching the goal be affected. Because of the multiplicative relationships assumed between expectancy of success and utility - since expectancy of success remains low - aspirational deprivation thus will have relatively small effects on the probability of mobilization of a party and on the probability of conflict.

Progressive deprivation has been assumed to occur in connection with a rapid improvement in the social and economic conditions of the lower social strata (Davies, 1962). To the extent that this improvement is the result of a more equal distribution of the surplus in society, we can assume that the power differences between higher and lower strata have decreased. A decrease in a large difference in power resources between two parties is expected

to increase the probability of conflict.   This follows
primarily from the assumptions made in the present model,
that the probability of conflict between two parties is
higher if the difference in power resources between them
is small than if the difference is large.

But the rate of change in power resources may also have
some independent effect on the probability of conflict.
A rapid improvement in the power position of the weaker
party will increase its level of relative deprivation more
than a gradual improvement will;   it will thus bring about
some additional increase in its utility of reaching the
goal and to some extent also in the probability of mobilization.   When a formerly large difference in power resources between two parties begins to decrease, the probability of conflict is therefore expected to be especially
high.   In contrast to the other forms of relative deprivation, progressive deprivation is thus assumed to be
associated with, albeit not the major cause of, an increase in the probability of conflict.

If the new balance of power between parties with formerly large differences in power resources becomes stable,
the probability of conflict can be assumed to decrease
with time, since through bargaining or conflict the going
rate of exchange will change in favour of the party gaining in power, and since the aspiration level of the losing
party will gradually move towards the new going rate of
exchange.   The probability of conflict, however, will
remain higher than it was when the more unequal balance of
power prevailed between the pargies, unless the point of
parity in power resources is being approached.

Differences between approaches

In contrast to the expectation-achievement approach to
conflict, the power difference model of conflict outlined
here does not predict a positive correlation between relative deprivation and conflict.   Only increases in progressive deprivation will be associated with a strong increase in the probability of conflict, this being an
effect primarily of the underlying decrease in power differences between the parties.   Increasing aspirational
deprivation will generally add little to the probability
of conflict, while increasing decremental deprivation
tends to be associated with a decreasing probability of
conflict.   These diverse trends, when taken together,
would make us expect that the overall correlation between
relative deprivation and probability of conflict will be
insignificant.

In the political process model of conflict, the acquisition or loss of power resources are seen as the central
variables in the development of conflict; they affect the
capacity of the parties to make claims for privileges and
advantages which, if resisted, lead to conflict.   Acquisition and loss of power resources thus are assumed similarly to affect the probability of manifest conflict.
According to the power difference model of conflict, however, we would not generally expect parties losing power
resources to contend for privileges as often as parties
gaining in power.   Only where a balance of power resources between parties has been prevailing can we expect a
growing imbalance to increase the probability of conflict.
In situations where there are already considerable differences in power resources between the parties, a further
widening of the power gap is here predicted to decrease
the probability of conflict, while a narrowing of this gap
is predicted to increase it.

2   INSTITUTIONALIZATION OF INDUSTRIAL AND POLITICAL CONFLICT?

The analysis above indicates that the distribution of
power resources between social collectivities is a crucial
aspect of social structure.   Changes in the difference in
power resources can be assumed to have wide-ranging repercussions on the distribution of privileges and life
chances in society, on the social consciousness of the
citizens, on the level of manifest conflict and on the
nature of societal institutions.   Important aspects of
the development of Western industrial societies during the
last hundred years can be interpreted broadly in terms of
the effects of decreasing differences in power resources
between social classes, resulting from the growth of
unions and working-class-based political parties.   The
improving power position of the workers thus has led to
increasing aspirations and demands, which in turn resulted
in an increase in the level of industrial and political
conflict since the end of the nineteenth century. (17)
It also has resulted in some improvements in the relative
life chances of the workers. (18)   The most significant
institutional changes reflecting the increasing organizational power of the working class has been the introduction of political democracy and the institutionalization
of collective bargaining.
   The above analysis also indicates than an unequal distribution of power resources between major social collectivities or classes can and will have crucial effects

on the distributive processes in society even if the power
resources of the dominant group are not mobilized or acti-
vated.   Power resources can instead affect the processes
of exchange indirectly, through the institutional structure of society and through the social consciousness of
the citizens.   The distribution of power resources in
society thus largely determines the nature and type of
societal institutions, e.g. the legal and political
arrangements and such institutions as the commodity market
and the labour market.   The rules and patterns for the
operations of these institutions reflect the distribution
of power resources.   The dominant groups can thus benefit
from the routine operations of these institutions without
having continuously to exert power.   Institutionalization
thus implies an economical use of power resources.

Power resources can further be used to 'engineer consent' and to implant acceptance of the rules of operation
of the societal institutions.   If such efforts are successful, the exchange processes taking place within the
framework of these institutions can become regarded as
more or less legitimate and may not be widely questioned,
even if they maintain and generate inequality.   Where the
rules are questioned, the perceived differences in power
resources may make the weaker party feel that opposition
is futile.   Also, where conflicts of interest between
collectivities or classes are latent, conflict will thus
only sometimes become manifest.

As we have seen in chapter 1, a dominant line of
thinking among modern social scientists has been that,
while the early stages of industrialization contained possibilities for the overthrow of capitalism, this probability has decreased close to insignificance as a result
of the separation of industrial and political conflict and
of the institutionalization of conflict.   Giddens (1973,
pp. 202, 287) assumes that the separation of the manifestations of conflict in the political and in the economic
spheres is inherent in capitalism and derives from the
fundamental separation of the economy from the polity in
capitalist society.   Therefore capitalism will not in
itself generate a class consciousness among workers to
the point of questioning the continued existence of the
capitalist system.

The assertion of the separation between the 'economic'
and the 'political' in capitalist society is based on an
important observation.   In contrast to feudalism, production in capitalist society is carried out within the
framework of a market system, where the citizens enter,
in principal, as free individuals, each possessing at
least some resources for exchange (the main ones being

money and labour power).   Transactions on the market are
in principal carried out without the authoritative allocation of work or rewards from the polity.

The weakness of the arguments for the separation of
the 'economic' and the 'political' spheres in capitalist
societies derives partly from the tendency to overlook the
central role of power differences and the extent to which
institutional arrangements reflect and mediate the influe-
ences from the power structure.   On the market the parties are formally free and equal, but in practice the
market as well as the polity are structures of power.
The labour market can serve as an illustration.   The
actual power differences between the formally free and
equal partners on the labour market in the early days of
industrialization were captured by the dark irony of
Marx (1967, I, p. 176).   On this market,

the money-owner ... strides in front as capitalist:
the possessor of labour-power follows as his labourer.
The one with an air of importance, smirking, intent on
business; the other, timid and holding back, like one
who is bringing his own hide to market and has nothing
to expect but - a hiding.

The growth of unions and collective bargaining has decreased the imbalance in power resources between the parties on the labour market but it has not abolished it.

A related weakness of the assertions of the separation
between economy and polity is that the basic assumption
of the near-separation of the collectivities that confront
each other in economic and in political conflict (e.g.
Dahrendorf, 1959, pp. 271, 277) does not square well with
the facts.   In most Western countries the coalitions
formed in these two spheres of conflict show a considerable overlap, as indicated by the structure of political
parties, labour unions and employers' organizations.

These assertions of the institutionalization of conflict also overstate the importance of institutions.
Institutional arrangements of conflict resolution must be
seen more as intervening than as independent variables
affecting the level of conflict.   The power difference
model of conflict indicates that, if differences in power
resources between classes remain relatively stable for a
longer period or if the classes are close to the point of
parity in power resources, institutions for conflict regulation can be expected to develop.   These institutions,
however, must not be taken as the primary causes of the
decrease in manifest conflict.   Instead, both the decrease in the level of conflict and the growth of regula-
tory institutions reflect changes in the underlying difference in power resources between the parties.

The assertions of the gradual separation between industrial and political conflict in capitalist society are unsatisfactory since they are not based on evidence of basic changes in the positions of the workers on the labour market since the days of early capitalism.   Because labour power cannot be separated from the worker, the sale of labour power involves also the person of the worker. The 'delivery' of labour power therefore leads to the subordination of the worker to the employer.   The labour contract continues to make explicit the subordination of the worker to management.

The transactions on the labour market therefore still involve power over human beings, something that in a basic sense is a political issue.   The subordination of the workers can be expected to generate inequality in work-related rewards.   The extent of dissatisfaction with these rewards will depend on the aspiration level of the workers, which in turn can be expected to reflect their power position in relation to the employers. (19)   If the power position of the workers continues to improve, this can be expected to affect their social consciousness and to generate a desire for improvements, potentially to the extent of abolishing the institution of wage labour. (20)

The assertion of the separation between political and economic conflict also hides important aspects of how the relationship between conflict in the industrial and in the political arenas has changed over time.   The organization of the working class started naturally with unions which in the first years often were limited to 'economism'.   With the growing strength of the labour movement, however, industrial action extended its focus towards political goals, e.g. the achievement of the general suffrage.   Thus in this early period of growing strength but relative weakness of working-class organizations, the flow of issues was generally *from the political to the industrial arena*.   Where the unions and working-class-based political parties have remained relatively weak and without a dominant role in the government, industrial conflict has continued to be directed towards political goals.

But where the increasing strength of the labour movement has enabled the working-class-based political parties to dominate the government, this has opened the possibility of solving problems emanating in the industrial arena, through political action.   The flow of issues between the two arenas can then change direction.   In countries where reformist social democratic parties dominate government legislation on various social,

economic and labour market issues thus reflects the flow
of issues of conflict *from the industrial into the political arena*.

In many countries the growing political strength of
working-class-based parties has limited the scope of the
operation of market principles, e.g. by placing health
and education in the public sector.   Since the 1960s the
debate on 'incomes policy' and the increasing responsibility of the state for investments in industry also
point to the basic interdependence of the political and
economic sectors and to the fragility of the border between them.   If the market is seen as a structure of
power (e.g. Giddens, 1973, pp. 101-2), we can expect it
to be closely related to the political power structure.

3   THE ROLE OF THE STATE

The divergent views on the future of the working class in
industrial capitalist societies are to a considerable
extent related to differing conceptions of the state.
The state can be defined to include the central and local
decision-making organs of a nation, i.e. the parliament,
the government, the central bureaucracies, the judiciary,
the police, the military organs and local government. (21)
Basic to the non-Marxian, 'pluralist' interpretation of
the state is the idea that the state is, by and large,
'neutral' in relation to the various social groups or
strata in society;   it merely carries out their collective
decisions.   The state does thus not play any important
role in these theories.   In the most simple versions of
Marxian theory the state is, instead, seen primarly as an
agent of the dominant class in society, the bourgeoisie,
although it is granted a certain independence in relation
to various fractions within this class as the carrier of
their common long-term interests.   Basic to the Marxian
view is the idea that the state emerges out of the internal conflicts of society and serves to regulate these
conflicts in terms of the relative power positions of
different classes. (22)   In reformist, social democratic
ideology, the state assumes an important function as an
agency through which society can be reformed.

In purportedly Marxian discussions, the state sometimes
receives an 'organismic' character, and is given an independent existence over and above the competing group or
classes in society.   Power resources are seen as resting
with the institutions of the state, not in the collectivities or classes in society.   In my view, the activities
of the state can be seen, instead, as reflecting the

distribution of power resources between the major collectivities or classes in society. (23)   We have assumed
above that the major sources of power are, on the one
hand, control over capital and the means of production
and, on the other hand, political and economic organizations which make possible collective actions by the wage
earners.   While the officials in the state apparatus to
some extent have independent power resources, their
'degrees of freedom' must be seen as being severely limited by the power resources resting with the major societal
collectivities or classes.   The direction of bias in
state activity is therefore likely to reflect the distribution of the major power resources in society and its
changes (cf. Wesołowski, 1972).

Actually, both the Marxian and the 'pluralist' views of
the state appear congruent with the above assumption.
The differences between these theories arise instead from
differing views on the extent to which power resources are
diffused in society.   In the days of Marx, the working-
class-based organizations were very weak and state actions
then clearly reflected the overwhelming dominance of the
bourgeoisie.   If, however, the relative power position of
the working class improves owing to improved organization,
this can be expected to be reflected in the degree and
direction of bias in state action.   The state can therefore be a potential agency for social change.   Obviously,
however, the mere extent of state intervention in the
economy can not be taken as the indication of the role of
state actions.   The increasingly social nature of production has necessitated an increasing reliance on long-range
planning and state intervention in all modern capitalist
nations, and much of the enlarged state activity can be
congruent with the interests of capital (Westergaard and
Resler, 1975, ch. 4).

4   CONFLICT, POWER AND STRUCTURAL CHANGE

It is often assumed that conflict is a necessary or sufficient cause for social change (see Cohen, 1968, pp.
83-6).   Similar ideas are also reflected in discussions
on the probability of basic structural changes in the
economic organization of capitalist societies and in the
debate on the future of socialism.   Neo-marxists as well
as neo-Weberians thus often assume that the probability of
basic changes in capitalist institutions is presently
greatest in countries like France and Italy, because of
their relatively high levels of industrial conflict, often
directed towards political goals (e.g. Mann, 1973, pp.

9-10, 72; Giddens, 1973, p. 293).   This probability,
however, is generally discounted for countries like
Sweden, where industrial conflict in the postwar period
has been infrequent and not directed to political goals.
These interpretations must be questioned.

The above discussion indicates that the background to
and the relationship between manifestations of conflict
and structural change in society are considerably more
complicated.   In our analysis we have singled out the
difference in power resources between societal collectivities and the changes in this difference as a major
factor affecting the functioning of society.   We have
thus assumed that changes in the difference in power resources between societal collectivities affect the distribution of life chances between different sectors of
the population as well as the levels of aspiration and the
social consciousness of the citizens.   Further we have
assumed that the changes in power resources affect the
level of manifest conflict as well as the location of the
manifestations of conflict between the industrial and the
political arenas.   We have also seen the functioning and
change of societal institutions as reflecting the power
structure in society.   These basic assumptions are summarized in Figure 2.2.   The nature and type of manifest
conflicts in society as well as the probability for social
change thus all depend on the changes in difference in
power resources between societal collectivities but need
not be affected in identical ways by changes in the power
structure.

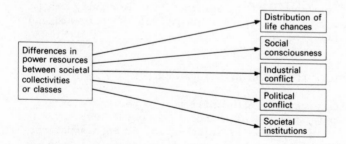

FIGURE 2.2   The dependence of the distribution of life
chances, social consciousness, industrial conflict, political conflict and societal institutions on the differences in power resources between societal collectivities or
classes

To the extent that our analysis is correct, countries

like France and Italy would appear to reflect a situation
of gradual strengthening of relatively weak working-class-
based organizations, which is accompanied by an increase
in the level of industrial conflict.   Since the unions
lack efficient political channels to press their claims,
industrial conflict is also directed towards political
goals.   This situation in some ways resembles that of
Sweden up to the early 1930s.   Political strikes are thus
generally a sign of the relative weakness of a labour
movement.

Our analysis indicates that the difference in power
resources between major social collectivities is the
critical variable affecting the probability of changes in
the economic organization of society.   From this point
of view the level and nature of industrial conflict is a
more superficial phenomenon.   In a country where the
working-class-based parties dominate the government, the
wage-earners' disadvantage in power resources vis-à-vis
the employers can be smaller, and the probability of
basic institutional changes thus greater, than in countries where the level of industrial conflict is high and
fused with political elements.   According to this analysis, in the mid-1970s the probability for basic changes
in the economic organization of society are thus greater
in Sweden than in France or Italy.

The predictions of the integrations of unions and reformist labour parties into advanced industrial societies
have been based on observations after the Second World
War in the western European countries and in United
States.   Before projecting these observations into the
future, it must also be remembered that the postwar period
has been characterized by an unusually rapid economic
growth.   This has provided opportunities to convert the
conflict of interests between workers and employers from a
'zero-sum' type of conflict to a 'positive-sum' conflict
situation, where improvements for both parties have been
possible without changes in their relative positions.   If
the possibilities for rapid economic growth decrease as
they did in the mid-1970s, the projection of these policies into the future need not be warranted.

The proponents of the thesis of the integration of the
working class into capitalist society have not shown why
the workers would continue to accept the negative consequences of their subordination on the labour market if
their power resources continue to increase.   According to
the present analysis, we would instead expect this subordination to become increasingly vulnerable to questioning as the relative power resources of wage-earners
improve through economic and political organization.   A

*social order marked by inequality in rewards can be main-
tained only if it is supported by inequality in the distribution of power resources.*   A central issue in the
discussion on the future development of capitalist industrial societies is thus, under what conditions can the
power resources of the wage-earners based on political and
economic organization continue to increase in relation to
the power resources of the employers based on control over
the means of production?

5   COLLAPSE, LIBERATION AND MATURATION

Marx and his early followers assumed that the downfall of
capitalism would come about through internal processes of
change inherent in capitalism.   These processes of maturation would gradually increase the unity and strength of
the workers to a point when the power resources of the
working class would surpass those of the representatives
of capital, making it possible for the workers to resolve
societal problems generated with the maturation of capitalism on their terms.   So far, this has remained only a
theoretical possibility.   In this century, the anti-
capitalist changes in economic systems have instead
occurred through processes distinctly different from the
one envisaged by the early socialists.

One type of anti-capitalist transformation process has
taken place in connection with the collapse of a regime,
generally as the aftermath of war.   In the near power
vaccum thus created, minority groups of revolutionaries
have been able to seize power and to establish anti-
capitalist regimes.   The main illustrative case here is
the collapse of tsarist rule in Russia as a result of its
military defeat in the First World War.   In a situation
where the total power resources in the nation were scattered and difficult to mobilize as a result of the war,
an elitist communist party supported by parts of a relatively undeveloped working class and groups of peasants,
were able to mobilize enough power resources to topple
the weak tsarist regime and its successor.   Similar but
abortive attempts were made in Finland and Hungary in 1918
as well as in Germany at the end of the First World War.
The communist takeovers in eastern Europe after the Second
World War also came after breakdowns of the old regime,
but - with Yugoslavia and Albania as clear exceptions -
in these countries the presence of the Soviet Army played
a crucial role.

A different type of anti-capitalist transformation
process has taken place in the former colonies in the

Third World in connection with wars of liberation against
the colonial powers.   Aided in a decisive way by forces
of nationalism and ethnicity, socialist and communist
groups have been able to rally major sectors of the population, dominated by peasants, against the foreign
oppressors and their agents.   Typical cases here are
China, Cuba, Vietnam and some African nations.

In countries where the capitalist system was abolished
after the collapse of the old regime - again with Yugoslavia as an exception - elitist and bureaucratic power
structures based on state ownership of the dominant part
of the means of production have been established.   Since
these regimes have only had the support of a minority of
the population, their maintenance has necessitated more
or less widespread political oppression.   In the Third
World countries, where capitalism was replaced after wars
of liberation, the new systems have usually had relatively
wide support and have developed different types of mass-
based, one-party regimes.

The abolishment of capitalism through the process of
the 'maturation' of capitalist societies has thus not yet
become true.   We have here assumed that basic structural
change is generated through efforts of citizens to solve
important societal problems with which they are confronted.   The persistance of capitalism draws attention to
two circumstances: on the one hand the role of societal
problems and crises, on the other hand the relative distribution of power resources in society.   Although structural change is a reaction to societal problems, these
problems need not reach the dimension of a big crisis,
like for example the Great Depression.   Economic crisis
situations appear, instead, to indicate that the power
resources in society have changed to the disadvantage of
the working class, and that the probability of change
thus is low.   Experiences of problems and crises, however, may also have long-term consequences through effects
on the social consciousness of citizens.

If the capitalist system is to be transformed through a
process of maturation, societal problems that are difficult to solve within the framework of a capitalist system
must thus increase in significance.   The distribution of
power resources in society must further change to the advantage of the originally weaker collectivities.   The
changing distribution of power also affects which conditions in society are regarded as problems and how important these problems are considered to be.   There is thus
a two-way relationship between power distribution and
problem definition in society.   Since structural changes
resulting from processes of maturation involve shifts in

the distribution of power resources in society, the solutions to the problems generating this type of structural change are likely to have support from the majority of the population.

3 The Swedish labour movement and class conflict

Our discussion on the position of the working class in capitalist industrial society is based and focused on the working class in one country, Sweden. Since Sweden is the country where a social democratic party has had the longest tenure as the dominating government party - from 1932 to 1976 - it offers a unique case for the study of the possibilities and limitations of reformist socialism. In this chapter we will describe and analyse key aspects of the Swedish experience against the background of the diverging positions in the debate on the working class, beginning with an outline of changes in the social and political structure of Sweden during the last hundred years.

1 CHANGING ECONOMIC AND POLITICAL STRUCTURE

The process of industrialization started relatively late in Sweden. (1) In 1870 almost three-fourths of its economically active population was still engaged in the primary sector, mostly agriculture, with only 9 per cent in manufacturing and crafts (Carlsson, 1966, p. 281). By comparison, Britain, the first country to industrialize, at this time had only 15 per cent of its population in agriculture but 43 per cent in industry and crafts (Scase, 1977, p. 18). The agricultural population in Britain was outnumbered by that in industry and crafts already in the first years of the nineteenth century, while this did not occur in Sweden until more than a century later (see Figure 3.1).

The development of Swedish industry was based on the utilization of natural resources, primarily iron and wood. The export of iron had old traditions in Sweden. Export of sawmill products started around 1850 and accelerated up

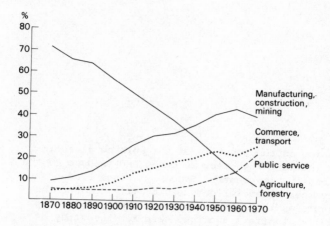

FIGURE 3.1 Distribution of economically active population
in Sweden by sectors of the economy, 1870-1970

to the 1880s.   Based on iron and wood, early industrialization in Sweden took place in the countryside rather
than in the big cities, which were primarily centres for
administration and commerce.   This pattern of decentralized industrial location was to remain important during
the industrial expansion of the 1870s.   During this
decade the engineering industry expanded rapidly.   The
building of railroads, mostly by the state, accelerated
and facilitated the expanding export of grain, primarily
to England.   The electrification of industry was rapid in
the years around the turn of the century.
    The number of workers engaged in manufacturing and con-
struction increased by 30 per cent in the 1870s and again
as much in the 1880s, and by a further 37 per cent in the
1890s (Jörberg, 1961).   In the following decades the increase was somewhat lower.   The agricultural population,
however, remained important even between the world wars.
    Owing to the increasing importance of exports, the
Swedish economy became sensitive to international business
fluctuations.   After a boom in the 1870s came a period of
depression towards the latter part of the 1880s.   In the
1890s a new boom period started, lasting up to 1907 with
only minor interruptions.   This expansion was felt especially in engineering and in the new paper industry.
After a slump around 1908 came a period of economic up-

swing which continued to the First World War.   An up-
swing around 1919 was followed by a brief but deep depression in 1921-2, whereafter came a boom period.   The
international depression hit Sweden severely first in
1931, with maximum unemployment in early 1933.

The process of industrialization changed the composition of the economically active population in terms of
the type of occupation and type of relationship to the
means of production (see Therborn, 1976, and Olofsson,
1976, for more detailed analyses).   Among men the proportion of independent farmers and their co-working family
members decreased from 36 per cent in 1870 to 11 per cent
in 1960, the decrease being especially rapid after the
Second World War (figure 3.2).

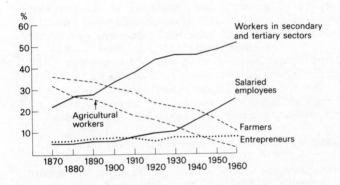

FIGURE 3.2 Distribution of economically active men by
occupational standing in Sweden, 1870-1960

Also, the number of workers in the primary sector, i.e.
farming and forestry, decreased markedly.   At the same
time the number of workers in the secondary and tertiary
sectors continued to increase up to the mid 1960s.   This
increase was especially marked in the years from 1890 to
1920.   The relative size of the working class thus has
been fairly stable, around 55 per cent among the economically active men, during this period of one hundred years.
Since the 1960s the number of workers in manufacturing has
decreased slightly while it probably has increased somewhat in the tertiary sector.

The salaried employees have expanded considerably, especially in the decades after 1930, and comprised about
half the number of the workers in 1960.   The proportion
of entrepreneurs outside agriculture, i.e. largely the

petty bourgeoisie category, has remained relatively
stable, 5-8 per cent, throughout the century.   The number
of entrepreneurs, however, has decreased somewhat in manufacturing and commerce since 1950.

Industrial expansion around the turn of the century
gave rise to a class of large entrepreneurs, among which
the wholesale dealers played an important part.   Foreign
capital was of some importance in early industrialization.
Enterprises came increasingly to be organized as corporations.   In 1872 corporations employed 45 per cent of all
workers, a figure that rose to nearly 80 per cent in 1912
(Jörberg, 1966).   The distribution of workers in manufacturing by size of workplace, however, has been surprisingly stable throughout this century. (2)

Since the Second World War Sweden has undergone rather
drastic social changes.   Urbanization has increased: by
1970 less than 20 per cent of the population lived in
sparsely populated areas.   The expansion of the tertiary
sector, especially the public services, has been marked.
An increasing proportion of married women have been entering the labour force (Silenstam, 1970, p. 105).   The
proportion of economically active married women was thus
14 per cent in 1950, 23 per cent in 1960 and 58 per cent
in 1975.   The increase in female employment in recent
years has come primarily in the public sector.   The large
category of women in domestic service has all but disappeared.

From being a nation with large-scale emigration, culminating in the 1880s, Sweden in the postwar period has
become a recipient of immigrants.   Those from the Nordic
countries, especially Finland, have dominated, but the
influx of southern Europeans also has been substantial.
The immigrants have found work primarily in manual occupations.   In the early 1970s the proportion of foreigners
among manual workers is estimated at somewhat over 10 per
cent.

The process of industrialization has had one crucial
consequence for the class structure of Sweden: an increasing proportion of the economically active citizens
are wage-earners (Figure 3.3).   The increase in the proportion of wage-earners has been especially rapid in the
decades after the Second World War and reached 90 per cent
in the 1970s.   Of particular importance is that the married women increasingly often enter the labour market as
wage-earners.   The differentiation within the working
class in terms of market capacities may have decreased as
a result of the advent of mass production technology. (3)
The expansion of the tertiary sector as well as the increasing number of salaried employees, however, has tended

to increase differentiation among wage-earners.   The
increasing influx of women and immigrants has added to
this differentiation.

FIGURE 3.3   Estimated percentage of wage-earners among
economically active men and women in Sweden, 1870-1970

The changes in the economy have, of course, affected the
political and legal institutions of society.   The old
system of political representation based on the four
estates was abolished in 1866.   In its place came a bi-
cameral Riksdag, where the first chamber was to reflect
an older electoral opinion as compared with the second
chamber.   The restriction of franchise based on property
and income, however, gave the right to vote only to about
5 per cent of the population. (4)   The indirectly elected first chamber was dominated by the upper class, while
big farmers came to dominate the lower chamber.
    In the following decades political struggles centred
around the extension of the franchise.   Here the petty
bourgeoisie and the growing number of industrial workers
joined ranks against the upper class, the state church
and the king.   The franchise was extended in 1907 and in
1909; the principle of general franchise for men in elections to the second chamber of the Riksdag was accepted,
although rules relating to property and income still restricted franchise in the indirect elections to the first
chamber.   In practice, however, the rules for eligibility
continued to restrict franchise even to the second

chamber: in the 1911 elections, for instance, only 71 per
cent of the workers but 88 per cent of those in other
groups had the right to vote.

In spite of opposition from the King and the conservative groups, the breakthrough for the principle of parlia-
mentarism came in a government crises in 1917. Against
the background of revolutions abroad and manifestations of
increasing dissatisfaction among workers within the
country, universal suffrage for women as well as men was
legislated in 1918 by a coalition between Liberals and
Social Democrats and became effective in the 1921 elections (Söderpalm, 1969). Proportional elections favouring a multi-party system were introduced in 1919. In
1970 the bi-cameral system was replaced by one chamber,
subject to re-election every third year, and voting age
was lowered to eighteen years.

2   THE LABOUR MARKET ORGANIZATIONS

On the basis of an assumption of conflict of interest
between sellers and buyers on the labour market we would
expect interest organizations, or conflict groups, to
develop, especially among the wage-earners. In chapter 1
we outlined some diverging hypotheses concerning the
levels and bases for unionization derived from the different importance accorded control over the means of production, formal education, occupational skills and status
in Marxian and Weberian approaches to class theory.
Within this framework, we shall now examine the development of organizations on the Swedish labour market.

Manual unions and employers' organizations

The organizational history of wage-earners in Sweden
clearly illustrates the importance of differences in
market capacities for the development of unions. This
is reflected in the lines of cleavage between organizations for manual workers and salaried employees, as well
as between skilled and unskilled workers. Other factors,
however, have modified the effects of the cleavages based
on market capacities.

The main organizational attempts began in the 1870s,
primarily among skilled workers; they included efforts
to monopolize sectors of the labour market from the competition of unskilled labour migrating into urban
areas. (5)   Of about 260 local unions existing in 1890,
two-thirds were craft unions. Only towards the end of

the century did membership in unions for unskilled workers exceed that of the craft unions (Lindbom, 1938).

The unions began to combine into local co-ordinating committees at an early stage and later, especially in the 1890s, into national unions.   By the end of the century thirty-two national unions had been formed, among which was the Swedish Metal Workers' Union, founded already in 1888.   A central task of these national organizations was to increase the level of unionization among workers in their field.   Unions thus grew out from the centre, a significant factor for the relatively centralistic pattern of decision-making that developed within them.

It is also crucial in this context that from the very beginning the development of unions was intertwined with politics.   Among the about seventy organizations sponsoring the foundation of the Social Democratic Party in 1889, no less than fifty were local unions (Lindbom, 1938, p. 123).   The party became active in organizing unions. During the 1890s the non-political and liberal groups, which had been especially strong in some of the craft unions, lost out against the Social Democrats.   A liberal 'yellow' union organization existed from 1899 to 1910 but was of relatively small importance (Myrman, 1973).

In 1898 the confederation of the national unions, Landsorganisationen (the LO), was formed.   This organization was primarily intended as a mutual insurance agency in lockouts but was also to have co-ordinating functions. A Social Democratic party man was elected its first chairman, and the union branches were required to become collective members of the Social Democratic Party.   This very close connection between the unions and the party was resisted by some of the larger unions, which stayed outside the LO until the connection was weakened a few years later.   Also in the years to follow, however, the issue of 'separationism' between unions and the Social Democratic Party was to be one of significance. (6)

In the long boom period around the turn of the century the number of union members increased rapidly, especially among the semi- and unskilled workers, and tripled from 1900 to 1907.   In 1907, at the peak of the boom, about one-third of male workers in the secondary and tertiary sectors of the economy were unionized.   In the core sectors of industry, e.g. in the metal-working industry, the level of unionization was even higher - above 40 per cent (Figure 3.4). (7)   Among men in the primary sector, however, as well as among the women, the level of unionization at this time was low.

Although collective bargaining on the local level was common already in the 1890s, employers often tried to

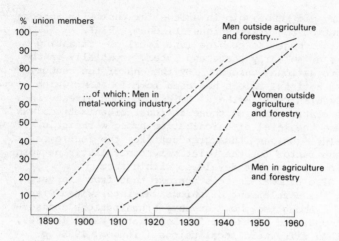

FIGURE 3.4 Estimated level of union membership among male and female workers by sectors of the economy, 1890-1960

crush the unions (Karlbom, 1969, p. 145; 1955, p. 109). In addition, legislation was used to hinder their growth: a law in 1899 thus made even attempts to stop strike-breakers a crime subject to public prosecution (Eklund, 1974). (8)   The nationwide strike in 1902 for general suffrage brought home to the employers the need to organize themselves.   The formation of the Swedish Confederation of Employers' Organizations (Svenska Arbetsgivareföreingen, the SAF) later the same year was thus an indirect recognition of the necessity to fight the unions on their own terms. (9)   Subsequently, collective bargaining on the national level gained ground. - In 1905, after a large lockout, the first major industry-wide contract (10) was signed in the engineering industry; it included partial recognition of the right of unionization and minimum wages.   A local conflict in 1906 involving the right of organization led to negotiations between the LO and the SAF; this ended with the 'December Compromise' of the same year, where employers recognized the right of unionization and the LO accepted the prerogatives of management to hire and fire and to lead and direct work. (11)   This compromise thus excluded the 'closed shop' and made union membership voluntary.   Attempts to use strike-breakers continued to the early 1930s. (12)

The newly organized employers started to use large-scale lockouts and threats of lockouts against the unions. Although the big engineering lockout in 1905 failed, several others were effective.   In the recession of 1909 the proclamation of a large lockout led to the declaration of a general strike by the LO.   The strike lasted for one month and was lost by the workers.   This disaster almost halved the membership of the LO, and it took a decade to recover the losses.

In contrast to the situation in several other countries, e.g. the United States and France (Shorter and Tilly, 1974, ch. 6), where union membership among manual workers has been stagnating, unionization among manual workers in Sweden has been increasing almost continuously in absolute as well as in relative numbers during the present century.   The exceptions to this trend are the period after the general strike in 1909, a minor setback during the depression around 1922 and a brief period of stagnation in the Depression a decade later.   A sizable proportion (20-30 per cent) of the workers, especially in the public sector, belonged to unions that remained outside the LO during the first decades of the century.   In the 1930s, however, the majority of these joined the LO, and by 1940 only about 2 per cent of the organized workers remained outside the LO. (13)   In the half-century from 1920 to 1970 the total number of organized workers thus has more than quadrupled while the number of members in the LO has increased six times.

Complete and industrial unionism

As Figure 3.4 indicates, the rapidly increasing absolute number of union members reflects an increasing level of unionization among the workers.   Among male workers in the secondary and tertiary sector the level of unionization shows a gradual but continuous increase up to the recent years, when a point of saturation at a very high level of organization (above 90 per cent) is being approached.   Among men in the core sector of manufacturing, i.e. the metal-working industry, the level of unionization follows the same pattern but on a higher organizational level.   Among men in the primary sector, however, the increase sets in first in the 1930s, reaching only a medium level (somewhat less than 50 per cent) in the 1960s. (14)   Among women in the secondary and tertiary sectors the increase in the level of unionization also starts in the 1930s, but there the rate of increase is higher, leading to a level of unionization almost comparable with that among the men.

The continuous rise in the level of unionization is of considerable significance.   It indicates that, contrary to what is sometimes assumed (Shorter and Tilly, 1974, pp. 151-5), the advent of mass production technology need

not have adverse effects on the possibility to organize
workers.   The lower level of unionization and the slower
breakthrough for unionism among women and among workers in
the primary sector, however,   testifies to organizational
difficulties at small places of work where relationships
to the employer are personal and in sectors where employment is seasonal and where the labour force is geographically dispersed.   The *gradual* rise in the level of
unionization through the present century also in the core
sectors of manufacturing, i.e. in metal-working, indicates
that the social processes leading to unionization take
their time.   While structural factors can facilitate or
hinder the penetration of unionism, it may thus take generations to make union members.   The marked increase in
unionism since the 1930s also indicates that political
factors are of importance for the level of unionization.

Another significant aspect of unionization among manual
workers in Sweden has been the early dominance of industrial unionism, where only one union represents the
workers at each place of work.   Although in 1908 not less
than 25 of the 38 unions in the LO were craft unions,
these comprised only about one-fourth of the LO membership
(Table 3.1).   The LO congress in 1912 made industrial

TABLE 3.1 Distribution of LO members by type of union,
1908-73

Type of union	1908	1923	Year 1933	1953	1975
	%	%	%	%	%
Industrial	46	64	67	78	85
Mixed	28	16	19	12	10
Craft	26	20	14	10	5
Total	100	100	100	100	100

unionism its main organizational principle.   Because of
strong resistance from the craft unions, their importance
decreased only gradually.   In the period following the
Second World War, however, craft unions have become insignificant;   by 1975 only 5 per cent of the LO members
belonged to craft unions.   The two remaining 'mixed'
unions, in land transport and commerce, differ little from
industrial unions.

Of significance in this context is also that unions
have generally been based on open membership.   Unions
have thus not attempted to monopolize job opportunities

for their members.   Jurisdictional fights between unions
also have been rare.

The white-collar sector

Organizations among salaried employees in Sweden developed
later than did manual unions, but early when seen in an
international perspective.   The first white-collar organizations had more the character of mutual aid organizations than of unions.   The ties binding the salaried employees to their employers have been severed only gradually.   In 1922, the foremen in the engineering industry
achieved an agreement whereby their neutrality in industrial disputes was guaranteed.   The inflationary period
at the end of the First World War gave an impetus to collective efforts for maintaining wages among the salaried
employees.   In 1936 the rights of organization and of
collective bargaining were recognized by law, a step of
importance primarily to salaried employees.   White-collar
organizations in the private sector, the main ones being
among foremen and employees in banking and manufacturing,
formed a central organization (15) in 1931;   a comparable
organization in the public sector was formed in 1937.
These amalgamated in 1944 to form the Central Organization
for Salaried Employees (Tjänstemännens Centralorganisation, the TCO).   Its member organizations are based primarily on the principle of 'vertical' or industrial
unionism.   In 1947 salaried employees with academic
training formed a new organization, the Swedish Confederation of Professional Associations (Sveriges Akademikers
Centralorganisation, the SACO), which initially wanted to
include only professionals with academic training but subsequently attempted to enlarge its organizational base.
This divergent 'horizontal' principle of organisation
based on occupation, sometimes with unclear lines of demarcation, has led to some disputes between the TCO and
the SACO.   In 1966 salaried employees in the public
sector were accorded the right to strike.
     The level of organization among salaried employees is
difficult to estimate accurately, since the distinction
between salaried employees and workers in the censuses is
not clear; neither does it correspond completely with the
recruitment bases for the LO and the white-collar organizations.   A rough estimate, however, indicates that in
1940 about one-fourth of salaried employees that were
potential members of the white-collar unions were actually
unionized (Figure 3.5).   This proportion increased to
about one-half in 1950, and remained relatively stable in

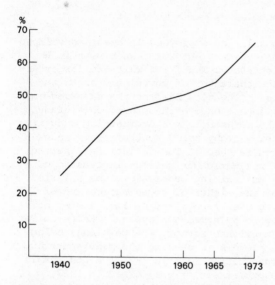

FIGURE 3.5   Estimated level of unionization among salaried
employees organizable in white-collar unions, 1940-73

the following decade.   Between 1965 and 1975, however,
the absolute number of organized salaried employees just
about doubled, bringing the proportion unionized to about
two-thirds.   The level of organization has been higher
among men than among women. (16)

Unions and occupational stratification

As the preceding review indicates, the overall pattern of
union membership among wage-earners in Sweden has tended
to reflect the system of occupational stratification.
Table 3.2 shows to which 'top level' union organization
persons in different occupational categories belong, as
well as social composition of the members in these organizations.   The data refer to men and women with full-time
employment in the spring of 1974. (17)   The table indicates that persons in the upper and upper middle classes
(social group I) are relatively evenly split between the
SACO and the TCO, but that the SACO is comprised almost
exclusively of persons from this stratum.   The majority
of persons from the lower middle class (social group II)

TABLE 3.2   Socio economic status and type of union membership among Swedish men and women with full-time employment in 1974

(a) Type of union membership by socio economic status

	Men			Women		
'Top' union organization	Social group I	Social group II	Social group III	Social group I	Social group II	Social group III
	%	%	%	%	%	%
LO	2	28	96	(0)	17	92
TCO	52	70	4	(50)	80	8
SACO/SR	46	2	0	(50)	3	0
	100	100	100	100	100	100
N	(150)	(417)	(963)	(23)	(313)	(266)

(b) Socio economic composition of different union organizations

	Men			Women		
Socio economic status	LO	TCO	SACO/SR	LO	TCO	SACO/SR
	%	%	%	%	%	%
Social group I	0	19	87	0	4	(54)
Social group II	11	72	13	18	89	(46)
Social group III	89	9	0	82	7	(0)
	100	100	100	100	100	100
N	(1045)	(405)	(79)	(297)	(284)	(21)

belongs to the TCO, but a significant minority belongs to
the LO.   While the TCO is the most heterogeneous of the
three top organizations, about three-fourths of its members come from the lower middle class.   The manual workers (social group III) almost exclusively belong to the
LO and their dominance in the LO is strong.   However, the
LO also has a small minority of members from the lower
middle class.

3 MARKET CAPACITY AND ORGANIZATION

In chapter 1 we discussed the relative importance of different types of power resources such as private property,
formal education and occupational skills for the formation
of organizations on the labour market.   The Marxian
approach to class theory and class conflict, with its
stress on the importance of the ownership of means of production, apparently predicts that the level of organization of the labour market will gradually be extended to
encompass almost all wage-earners.   A Weberian approach
to class theory, however, with its stress on the importance of skill, education, occupation and status, would
appear to predict a lower level of unionization, especially in the white-collar sector, with unionism based primarily on occupational cleavages.   To what extent does
the Swedish case give support to one or the other of
these sets of hypotheses?

As we have seen, the level of organization on the Swedish labour market has increased gradually over the years
- in recent decades especially dramatically in the white-
collar sector - and reached a level of about 80 per cent
of the labour force in the mid-1970s.   The early appearance of employers' organizations can be seen as counter-
mobilization, necessitated largely by the growing organizational strength of the workers.   Thus the Swedish case
appears clearly to support the hypothesis regarding the
level of organization derived from the Marxian approach to
class theory.

Moving then to the bases for organization, the picture
becomes somewhat less clear.   We have seen that within
the LO, and also within the TCO, the principle of industrial unionism has come strongly to dominate.   The increasing importance of the LO in relation to its member
unions in recent decades (see below) indicates that,
among workers, class is replacing occupation as the main
organizational base.   Also among the salaried employees,
however, occupation plays only a minor role as a base for
organization.

The continued importance of status and formal education
for organization among wage-earners, however, is attested
by the fact that the lines of cleavage among the three
'top' organizations have remained.   The formation of the
SACO in 1947 can be seen as a reaction against the dominating tendencies towards 'vertical' unionism within the
TCO.   As of the mid-1970s, however, approximately 80 per
cent of all union members in Sweden belonged to unions
based on the principal of industrial or 'vertical' organization.   It is also clear that since the 1960s the TCO
and the LO have been approaching each other and are now
co-operating in significant areas.   On the whole, then,
labour market organizations in Sweden are in a process of
development that would appear to support the hypothesis
concerning the bases for organization derived from the
Marxian approach to class theory.

A remarkable aspect of Swedish unionism, however, is
that it has evolved gradually over a long time.   Only in
the decades after the Second World War are Swedish manual
workers for the first time thoroughly organized in industrial unions, with important power vested in the common
class organization, the LO.   Thus the Swedish case clearly contradicts the predictions - implicit in the 'logic of
industrialism' school of thought and in neo-Weberian
approaches to class theory - of a decline in the organizational potential of the working class after their presumed
'golden age' in the revolutionary days during early industrialization.   It appears, instead, that in Sweden *the
organizational basis for the working class to act as a
'class for itself' has 'matured' only in the postwar
period.*

The rapid increase in unionism among the salaried employees in recent decades also points to the fact that
relations to the means of production continue to remain
significant in modern capitalist society.   Unionization
stresses the situation of employees as sellers of labour
power, and accentuates their collective rather than their
individual power resources.   As long as the salaried employees were relatively few, they tended to have a position objectively different from those of other wage-
earners: as representatives of the employer, they exercised power delegated to them.   Over the years, however,
the number of workers per salaried employee has decreased
drastically: in manufacturing from 13 in 1915 to 8 in
1935, to 3 in 1965 and to less than 3 in the 1970s
(Croner, 1963, p. 160).   This indicates that the position
of the average salaried employee in the structure of power
and privilege has changed considerably.   The very
increase in the number of salaried employees, which has

been assumed would lead to the formation of a new class
between workers and employers in industrial societies,
would appear instead partially to undermine the privileged
position of salaried employees, making the situation of
the majority of them, in some important respects, more
like that of the manual workers.

Organizations among salaried employees in Sweden were
formed in a period when the differences between themselves
and the manual workers in several respects were greater
than they are today.   Their organizations are still in a
process of development.   The favourable market position
of some of the professions indicate that we can expect
their organizations to continue.   In the rest of the
white-collar sector, however, various attempts at coalition formation with the LO have appeared in the 1970s.
To begin with the organizations of state employees in the
TCO and the LO formed a coalition in wage negotiations.
In the 1977 wage rounds the white-collar unions in the
private sector for the first time carried out wage negotiations in a coalition with the LO.   This co-operation
between the LO and the TCO appears to be growing in
strength.

4   POLITICAL MOBILIZATION

A striking characteristic of the party system in Sweden is
the early and persistent dominance of the working-class-
based Social Democratic Party. (18)   Already by around
the turn of the century, two decades before the advent of
universal suffrage, it had become a major political force
in the country.   During the 1920s the cleavage between
the 'bourgeois' and 'socialist' party blocks was established, with the bourgeois block based primarily on upper-
and middle-class support and the socialist block based
primarily on working-class support.

Apart from the gradual increase in the strength of the
Social Democratic Party, the most important changes in the
Swedish party system have occurred within the bourgeois
block (Back, 1967).   Since the 1930s, when the present
system of five major parties was established, the bourgeois block includes three main parties, a Conservative
Party, a Liberal Party and a Centre Party (formerly the
Agrarian Party). (19)   The bourgeois parties have varied
considerably in size as well as in their electoral base.
Since the party split in 1917, the socialist block has included small left-wing or communist parties in addition to
the dominating Social Democratic Party.   Also, the parties to the left of the Social Democrats have been rela-

tively unstable. (20)   The social bases of the bourgeois
and of the socialist blocks, however, appear to have been
relatively stable during the present century. (21)

During the first decade of extended franchise, the
mobilization of the Swedish electorate followed a rather
peculiar trend, with an early increase and a later decrease in electoral participation (Figure 3.6 and Appendix
3).   Beginning in 1928, however, voting participation has

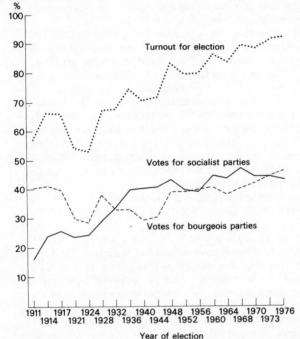

Year of election

FIGURE 3.6   Percentage of enfranchized citizens voting,
voting for socialist parties and voting for bourgeois
parties in elections to the Riksdag, 1911-76

tended to increase.   The elections in 1928, 1936, 1948,
1960 and 1968 show sharp increases in participation.
These elections can be described as *mobilizing elections,*
in which the two blocks managed to increase support, primarily from among their traditional social bases, and the
total participation rate increases drastically.   Electoral participation then tended to remain at this higher
level, reaching an internationally very high level -
around 90 per cent - in the 1970s.

Mobilizing elections have occurred after campaigns in
which alternative policies have been pitched against each
other, and the control over the government has clearly

been at stake. High and rising electoral participation
rates in Sweden indicate that the political parties have
continued to offer meaningful choices to the voters,
channelling their demands in a fairly effective way. (22)
The trend in voting participation in Sweden thus offers a
contrast to the situation in Britain (Butler and Stokes,
1969, pp. 155-6) and the United States (Burnham, 1970),
where declines in participation point to a decomposition
of the party system and to disappointment among voters
with the performance of the parties.

The pattern of change in electoral participation is
relatively similar for both sexes and for the different
'social groups', but the level of participation differs
(Appendix 3).   As everywhere, men participate more than
women, and persons with higher socioeconomic status more
than those with lower socioeconomic status. (23)   Working-class men tend to vote about as frequently as middle-
class women, but up to the mid-1950s the participation
rate increased faster within the latter group.   Working-
class women have been the slowest to mobilize.   With
time, however, differences have decreased between social
groups, and especially between the sexes.   Since the
1940s electoral participation has in fact been higher
among young women than among young men (Rudebeck, 1965,
p. 451).

The absence of religious, ethnic and regional lines of
cleavage in combination with historical factors is important in accounting for the early strength of the Social
Democratic Party.   Because of the relatively late industrialization in Sweden, the new large generations of
workers came of age in a period when the union movement
already was socialistic, and the Social Democratic Party
a major contender for political power.   Also, the extension of suffrage in the years before and immediately after
the First World War came at a time when the working class
was still in a process of formation.   Among Swedish work
ers, the non-socialist legacy, resulting from living the
politically formative years around the age of twenty deprived of a working-class-based political party, was thus
weak.   In England, where the working class had already
developed during the first part of the nineteenth century
but where the Labour Party achieved prominence only after
the First World War, this legacy has taken generations to
wane (Butler and Stokes, 1969, ch. 5).   The background to
the continued strength of the Social Democratic Party,
however, must be sought in the policies it has stood for,
something that we will return to in the next chapter.

The socialist proportion of the electorate increased
sharply during the first two decades of the century

(Figure 3.6).   After the extension of the franchise in
1909 the Social Democrats became the largest party in the
second chamber of the Riksdag in 1915.   In the 1920s,
however, the socialist vote stagnated and remained well
below a majority in the electorate.   In the 1928 mobilizing election the bourgeois parties were able to increase
their votes more than the socialists.

The socialist mobilization, however, continued in the
1930s.   In 1932 the socialist proportion of the electorate slightly exceeded that of the bourgeois parties and a
Social Democratic minority government was formed.   In the
1936 mobilizing election the socialists considerably sur-
passed the bourgeois parties.   The socialist proportion
of the two-block vote increased drastically in the wartime
elections, reaching 58 per cent in 1944, without however a
comparative increase in the proportion of the electorate.
Participation, especially by the working class, was relatively low in these elections.   The Social Democratic
victories probably largely reflected the tense international situation in these years, when Sweden was surrounded by the armies of Nazi Germany, as well as the
personal popularity of the Social Democratic leader of
the wartime coalition government.

After the war a new mobilizing election came in 1948.
The bourgeois parties mobilized better than the socialists
but did not succeed in unseating the Social Democratic
government.   In the 1950s participation rates declined
and the government was in a constant danger of being unseated, saved sometimes only by the first chamber, which
reflected an older electoral opinion.   The 1960s, however, saw a new increase in socialist vote, culminating
in the 1968 mobilizing election, when the socialist block
reached a higher proportion of the electorate than ever
before.   After the 1968 elections, however, the socialist proportion of the electorate has declined while the
bourgeois proportion has continued to increase.   A stalemate between the blocks occurred in 1973.   In 1976 the
bourgeois parties reached their record vote, unseated the
Social Democratic government and formed a three-party
coalition government.   The introduction in 1970 of a uni-
cameral system subject to re-election every third year has
made the life of any government more hazardous.

Although no supporting figures are available, we can
assume that the proportion of workers voting for the
socialist parties increased between the two world
wars. (24)   Survey data indicate that 81 per cent of
workers supported socialist parties in 1946-8 (SIFO,
1975).   During the 1960s the working-class vote for the
socialist parties decreased somewhat, while the middle-

class vote for these parties tended to increase.   These
recent changes, however, need not indicate a general
decline in the importance of class for party preferences.
Rather, it appears necessary to look for different explanations of the changes in the socialist vote among the
working and the middle classes (see chapter 1).

5   HOW UNIQUE IS SWEDEN?

Sweden, our test case for the role of the working class in
advanced capitalist countries, differs from other such
countries primarily by having a working class that is
better organized and has greater collective power resources than that found in most other capitalist countries.
This difference, in turn, reflects structural and historical circumstances, which can only be briefly hinted at in
this context.

The racial and ethnic homogeneity of the working class
in Sweden is an important structural factor facilitating
collective action.   The importance of this factor is
perhaps best seen in comparison with the United States,
which has one of the weakest labour movements among the
industrialized countries.   As Bonachich (1972, 1975) has
shown, in the United States the historical background in
the slave system created a split labour market, where
wage differentials were related to race.   This led to
three-cornered conflicts on the labour market, where the
employers often were able to play off the disadvantaged
black workers against white workers, e.g. by underbidding
of wages and strike-breaking.   The successive waves of
immigrants from various parts of Europe and Asia contributed to the ethnic heterogeneity of the workers and made
collective action on the basis of class very difficult.

Another significant circumstance facilitating the
development of the Swedish labour movement has been the
relative weakness of church and religion.   The Catholic
Church in particular has in many countries been an important counter-power to the development of a radical labour
movement.   As indicated, e.g. by experiences in Germany
and Holland, religious cleavages between Catholic and
Protestant workers have made collective action on a class
basis more difficult.

The fact that industrialization in Sweden came late and
was relatively rapid contributed to the strong socialist
dominance of its union movement and facilitated the organization of industrial rather than craft unions.   Unlike
for example its British counterpart, the Swedish labour
movement thus has not had to overcome entrenched craft

unionism, nor the historical heritage of generations of workers being socialized into a political culture where the socialist alternative was absent.

The split in the labour movement between the reformistic and revolutionary directions following the First World War came to have relatively small consequences in Sweden. While the labour movements for example in France, Italy and Finland have been divided into two directions of roughly equal size, the Swedish labour movement has been unified, something that has added to its strength.   Nor has the Swedish labour movement been disorganized by strong fascist groups or by wars.   The political actions of the Social Democratic government have also been of crucial importance in fortifying its support.   Because of the close relationship between the unions and the party, compromise solutions have been sought which to a large extent have been compatible with the interests of the wage earners.   In the following chapter we will analyse the development of Social Democratic policy and ideology.

4 The political ideas and strategies of the Swedish labour movement

Any analysis of the position of the working class and of
the political, economic and social development in Sweden
during the present century, must take into account the
goals, strategies and tactics espoused by its labour movement.   These strategies and tactics, in turn, must be
seen in the context of the choices available, as determined by the difference in power resources between social
collectivities or classes.   In this chapter we will analyse the development of the ideas and political strategies
in the Swedish labour movement up to the 1960s and look
also at the oppositional currents within the labour movement.   We will further discuss the relationship of the
Social Democratic political strategy to changes in the
level of industrial conflict as well as the effects of
Social Democratic policies on the conditions for a development in a socialistic direction in Sweden.

1 SOCIAL DEMOCRATIC IDEOLOGY AND POLICY

Reformist socialism

The Swedish Social Democrats have traditionally expressed
their central goals through the symbols of the French
Revolution: freedom, equality and brotherhood. (1)   Society should be organized in a way that permits the full
development of the potentials of each individual, while
creating solidarity among the citizens.   In contrast to
the liberals, they do not oppose freedom to equality.   On
the contrary, the demand for equality is seen also as a
demand for equality in freedom.   Because it leads to vast
differences in economic power and conditions of life, as
well as to internal antagonisms, the economic organization
of capitalist society is seen as blocking the realization

of these values.   It therefore ought to be changed, and
ownership of the means of production made communal.

According to its first programme (2) accepted in 1897,
the Social Democratic party wanted to 'completely re-mould
the economic organization of bourgeois society', and to
abolish the private ownership of the means of production.
But by stating that the means of production should be
socialized 'by degrees'; and by choosing political means
to achieve this goal, the party was reformist.   As stated
in the revised programme in 1911, 'this goal can be
achieved only through the organization and political
struggle of the working class and other groups in society,
which suffer from capitalistic exploitation.'   These
latter groups included, e.g., small farmers, artisans and
shopkeepers.   The task of the party was to unite the
masses in political struggle and to win political power in
society to 'bring about the socialistic organization of
society in the way and in the order shown by development
itself'.

The achievement of political democracy became the major
tactical goal of the party. (3)   The Swedish Social Democrats thus agreed with the contention of Karl Marx half a
century earlier that 'Universal Suffrage is the equivalent
of the political power for the working classes ... where
the proletariat forms the large majority of the population
....   Its inevitable result ... is the political supre-
macy of the working class' (quoted in McKenzie and Silver,
1968, p. 4).   In this reformist strategy, actions through
the government, under the political control of the working
class, became central.   Although socialization of the
means of production of course was regarded as essential,
pragmatism characterized the early programmes regarding
the choice of means for the realization of the socialist
society.

As a natural consequence of the very close relationship
between the Social Democratic Party and the unions, which
were involved in day-to-day struggles on bread-and-butter
issues, the party came to work for social reforms and
gradual improvements of the position of workers within the
capitalist system.   Among the proposals for social reforms, the unemployment issue was important.   Motions to
the Riksdag between 1908 and 1912 proposed the introduction of unemployment insurance and public work projects at
regular wages (Öhman, 1970; Steiger, 1972).   The early
programmes explicitly stated that the unions were important forces to counteract power based on property, and to
force employers to give a larger proportion of the product
to wage-earners.   The emiseration of the working class
thus was not seen as a necessary stage in the process of

reshaping capitalist society.   It is difficult to find
evidence for any widespread, fatalistic belief, attributed
to the party by some commentators (Tingsten, 1973; Lewin,
1967), in the more or less automatic transformation of
capitalism into socialism.   On the contrary, at an early
stage of the struggle for gradual improvements within the
capitalist system, universal suffrage, the eight-hour
working-day, better wages and social reforms were outstanding characteristics of the Social Democratic programmes and policy.

The reformist strategy and the work for social reforms
necessitated co-operation and compromises with other
groups, primarily with the Liberals.   This created a
tension between the party's long-term goals and short-term
tactics, a tension that has remained in decades to come.
In the early years, however, the distinction between reformist socialism and 'social reformism' was kept clear.
Branting, the first leader of the Social Democratic Party,
wrote in 1907 that the policy of the Liberals to combine
capitalism with social reforms was insufficient.   It is

the great illusion of all the social reformistic
forces, which in spite of their radicalism at one point
or another shrink back from a change in the foundations
of society and therefore dream of the state of balance,
where the workers acting through the state have cut the
claws of capitalism so that its ability to hurt has
been neutralized while its power of initiative has been
retained.

In the daily practical work to strengthen the resisting power of the working class, we Social Democrats
generally go hand in hand with them.   But when facing
the associations of big capital in the age of trusts,
it should be increasingly evident that the monopoly of
private ownership of the important means of production
must be abolished to radically break with the unsound
and absurd division into classes.   Only when these
means of production, in the new, gigantic size they
have reached in the era of capitalism, are converted
into public property through the large, all-encompas-
sing organization which the society constitutes, have
we blocked up the source from which now flows undeser-
ved poverty for the great majority and just as undes-
erved affluence for a privileged minority. (4)

Branting was thus fully aware of the crucial role of the
ownership of the means of production for the functioning
of society.

The party split

The rapid growth of the labour movement around the turn of
the century was accompanied by internal disagreements.
Left-wing opposition to the party leadership grew during
the first decade of the century, finding its organizational bases in the youth organizations of the party, who
questioned the reliance on parliamentary action and co-
operation with the Liberals. (5)   This opposition also
involved groups oriented towards syndicalism and anar-
chism.   In response to a lockout threat, the LO leadership declared the general strike in 1909, apparently
largely to prevent the internal oppositions from gaining
an upper hand.   After the defeat in this strike, the syndicalist union organization was formed in opposition to
the LO.
   Provoked by disagreements over co-operation with the
Liberals, internal decision-making procedures and support
for the military policy of the Conservative government
during the First World War, the internal cleavages within
the Social Democratic Party led to major split in early
1917.   The very heterogeneous left-wing groups formed the
Social Democratic Left Party - a reformist party, but more
radical and democratic than the one they had left.   The
formation of the new party was to make permanent the internal split within the labour movement, although the
opposition to the left of the Social Democrats remained
relatively small.

Lost momentum

Having regained its strength after the general strike in
1909, the labour movement was able to achieve universal
suffrage in 1918 and the eight-hour working day a year
later through a coalition with the Liberals.   Thereafter
the coalition was dissolved, partly on the initiative of
the younger Social Democrats.   A new party programme re-
affirming the socialist goals of the party, was accepted
in 1920.   Soon, however, the radical atmosphere around
the end of the First World War dissipated, giving place to
the chilly winds of the postwar depression.   In the 1920s
the Social Democratic Party came to lose its forward
momentum.
   This stagnation reflected partly the political weakness
of the working class to which the party split contributed.   The socialist parties had only weak support in the
large agricultural sector.   The extremely high unemployment in the depression years of 1921-2, which continued at

a high level throughout the decade, weakened the unions
and decreased their bargaining power.   When the depression was overcome, the Swedish economy began a period of
rapid expansion and concentration, accompanied by a resurgence of liberal, capitalist ideology.   The Social
Democrats had to choose between forming weak minority
governments or remaining politically powerless.   The
1920s became a period of shifting governments and sometimes of discrediting political compromises.

The continuing high level of unemployment became the
main political issue of the 1920s.   Not only the bourgeois parties and the employers, but also some Social
Democrats, accepted the liberal economic wisdom that
the cause of unemployment was too-high wages, which did
not allow employers to produce at acceptable prices
(Erlander, 1972, p. 171).   Support to the unemployed must
not counteract the downward pressures on wages brought
about by increased unemployment.   Relief work projects
must therefore not compete with regular production and
should offer considerably lower wages. (6)

High levels of unemployment and political weakness
forced the Social Democrats to limit their efforts to
ameliorate the condition of the unemployed.   In 1923 and
1926 Social Democratic minority governments resigned over
disputes about rules for support to the unemployed.   A
political strike was staged in 1928, to protest the proposal of the bourgeois government to make collective
agreements legally binding.   That same year the LO
accepted the bourgeois government's invitation to a so-
called 'Mond conference' for industrial peace. (7)

In the 1928 elections the socialist parties, for the
first time, were perceived as having a chance of winning
a majority.   The bourgeois parties launched a strongly
anti-socialist campaign, focused partly on a Social Democratic proposal to introduce inheritance taxation.   Electoral participation increased most strongly in the upper
middle class, however, and the Social Democrats suffered
a loss of mandates.

The historical compromise

Towards the end of the 1920s the Social Democrats developed a partly new unemployment policy.   This policy combined ideas from J.M. Keynes, the Marxian tradition of
under-consumption as the cause of economic crises and previous Social Democratic proposals of public work projects
at regular wages as cures for unemployment. (8)   According to Wigforss (1951, pp. 287-8), the chief architect of

the new-policy, 'Keynes' theories strengthened the faith
in the correctness of the teachings of common sense and
of socialism.'   Since the policies developed during the
1930s came to set the pattern for the political strategy
of the party in the decades to come, we must analyse them
in some detail. (9)

According to the familiar ideas contained in the new
unemployment policy, expanding state expenditure and provision for productive public employment at normal wages
will increase buying power, which thereby will increase
demand in the economy.   In a debate in the Riksdag in
1932 a member of the bourgeois government argued that the
prevailing crises was of such an immense scale that the
state could not possibly provide work for all the unemployed.   Wigforss taught the minister that he (Sveriges
Riksdag, 1932, p. 101):

> had overlooked a small circumstance of central impor-
> tance in the crisis.   It is so that if I want to start
> jobs for 100 persons it is not necessary that I put all
> of the 100 to work.   It is so fortunate in this world
> that if I can get a job to an unemployed tailor, then
> he can afford to get a new pair of shoes, and in this
> way an unemployed shoemaker will get work.   The crisis
> is characterized, above all, by something which usually
> is called the vicious circle and which means that first
> the income of some persons is lowered, and this makes
> that neither those persons who used to supply their
> needs, can now sell their goods and therefore become
> unemployed.   One can say that the crisis feeds itself
> once it has started.   This is a well-known fact, but
> it is also so when the recovery starts.

Public employment would thus have multiplicative effects.
Sweden appears to have been the first Western country
where this type of policy was put to work.

This new policy became the main issue in the election
campaign of 1932.   The socialist parties succeeded in
winning a narrow majority in the electorate, but the bourgeois parties retained the majority in the Riksdag.   The
Social Democrats formed a minority government and made a
deal with the Agrarian Party: the Social Democratic Party
supported a protectionist agricultural policy in exchange
for agrarian support of unemployment policies. (10)   The
growth of the movement of producers' co-operatives among
the farmers in these years contributed to the willingness
of the Agrarians to enter into this agreement (Hellström,
1976).   In the context of a general international recovery, these new policies decreased unemployment and improved the economic situation of the country.

The Social Democratic minority government had to resign

in June 1936.   The elections three months later evoked a
hard contest between the bourgeois parties, stressing the
dangers of socialism, and the Social Democratic Party,
fighting for its economic and welfare policies.   A new
increase in electoral participation, especially among the
workers, led to a clear victory for the Social Democrats.
Since the First Chamber of the Riksdag reflected an older
electoral opinion, the Social Democrats did however not
have a majority in the Riksdag.   The Social Democrats and
the Agrarians then formed a coalition government, partially motivated by the threats of war and of fascism.   In
the communal elections of 1938 the Social Democrats for
the first time received 50 per cent of the vote.

In the latter half of the 1930s there seems to have
been a widespread feeling in Sweden that the Social Democrats were to remain in government position for a long
period.   This new situation, where *political power was
separated from economic power,* made the Social Democrats
reconsider their political strategy.   The classical means
to socialism, i.e. nationalization of key sectors of the
economy, was still not a realistic policy, since it would
not receive support in the Riksdag.   The desire to give
employees opportunities to participate in the running of
firms also was seen as difficult to reconcile with large-
scale nationalization.   Minor nationalizations would not
change the functioning of the capitalist economy.
Instead, the Social Democrats developed a partially new
political strategy based on the previous pattern of gradual reforms: in the short run it aimed to improve the
conditions of the lower strata, but in the long run it was
intended to limit the power of capital and to provide increasing political support for anti-capitalist measures.

The key to the new strategy was the use of public
power, founded in organizational resources and exercised
through the government, to encroach upon the power of
capital.   Through economic policies the business cycles
would be evened out.   The level of employment, of crucial
importance for the welfare of the working class, would be
kept high through political means, and thereby partly
withdrawn from the control of capital.   State intervention would be used to induce structural changes in the
economy in order to increase its efficiency.   Public
power, above all, would be used to affect the distribution
of the results of production.   Through fiscal and social
policies a more equal distribution of income would be
achieved.   Political power, founded in control over organizations, would be pitched against economic power,
founded in control over capital;   and thus would come to
affect the distribution of an increasing proportion of the
national product.

The new political strategy developed gradually and
brought together currents of thought that had been partly
formulated earlier.   It can be viewed from three different but related angles.   From one point of view it can be
seen as an *economic growth strategy of class conflict,* intended to increase the total national product so that a
'zero-sum' type of conflict between labour and capital
could be turned into a 'positive-sum' type of conflict:
both parties could thereby profit from the increase in the
total product, even if their relative shares were not sub-
stantially changed.   Gunnar Myrdal (1945), postwar minister of commerce in the Social Democratic government, summarized the essence of this growth strategy, when he said
that

> a reformistic development presupposes a series of un-
> interrupted settlements according to constructive prin-
> ciples between the two strongest forces in the nation:
> the wealthiest entrepreneurs and the socialist labour
> movement.   A common interest in an increasing produc-
> tion should more and more become a possible basis for
> these big settlements.

Policies to keep the economy going 'at full speed' and
attempts to induce structural changes in the economy were
partly related to the growth strategy. (11)   The unions
contributed to this strategy by efforts to co-operate with
management, to avoid industrial disputes and to increase
productivity within the firms.   In the 1930s a rationalization drive, including time studies and assembly line
production, accelerated in Swedish industry.   Rather than
attempt to block rationalization and technological change,
the unions gradually came to rely on a policy of co-operation with management to increase the efficiency of production, on the condition that the consequences for labour
were taken into account.   The symbol of this 'historical
compromise' between classes and the parties on the labour
market were the negotiations between the LO and SAF starting in 1936, and leading to the Main Agreement in
1938. (12)

From another viewpoint the new political strategy could
be seen as an effort to *accelerate the 'maturation' of
capitalism.*   Many of the leading Social Democrats were
well acquainted with Marxian thought and believed that
the Swedish economy was not yet ripe for socialization.
Measures to increase its efficiency, by leading to an increasing level of economic concentration, would hasten
this maturation (Wigforss, 1967).

The new policies could also be seen as a *welfare strategy,* intended especially to improve the conditions of life
of the lower strata of the population.   Social policy and

measures to increase employment were essential from this
point of view.   A welfare strategy would also tend to
increase mass support for continuation of the new
policies.

From a new basis of strength, made evident in the increasing electoral support for their policies, the Social
Democrats towards the end of 1938 issued a formal invitation to the private business sector for co-operation.
Wigforss, the minister of finance and the leading Marxist
theoretician within the party, made it clear that the need
for co-operation arose from the fact that economic and
political power now had become dissociated, and that
within the foreseeable future neither the labour movement
nor private capital could realistically hope to resolve
the inherent conflict of interests between them through
the surrender of the other party (Wigforss, 1954, p. 111):

Expressed without euphemisms this means, on the one
hand, that those who have power over larger or smaller
sectors of the private economy must not base their
actions on the assumption ... that a political change
will take place within a future near enough that a discussion based on the possibility of concessions, ac-
commodations, compromises, becomes unnecessary.   On
the other hand it also means that the representatives
for political power admit the necessity of maintaining
favorable conditions for private enterprises in all
those areas where they are not prepared without further
ado to replace the private enterprises with some form
of public operations.

Based on a superficial reading of Marx, Tingsten (1973)
argued that the fatalistic belief in the quick and inevitable breakdown of capitalism and the more or less automatic victory of socialism was the outstanding characteristic of Marxism.   He held that, by engaging in work for
piecemeal social reforms in the 1920s and 1930s, the
Social Democrats did in practice abandon their socialistic
programme.   Others have interpreted the new political
strategy developed by the Social Democrats during the
1930s as a shift from the basic idea that private ownership of the means of production must be abolished, to a
redefinition of socialism as a combination of a planned
economy and welfare state measures (e.g. Lewin, 1967).

The second leader of the party, Per Albin Hansson, is
often perceived as a spokesman for 'social reformism'.
This interpretation must be questioned, however.   In a
well-known speech in 1928, Hansson made the 'people's
home', characterized by 'equality, concern, co-operation
and helpfulness', the goal for Social Democratic policy.
He noted: 'The Swedish society is not yet the good home

for the citizens.   To be sure formal equality in political rights previals here, but in the social area the class
society remains and economically the dictatorship of a
minority prevails' (in Fredriksson et al., 1970, p. 26).
His conclusion was that, to become the good home for the
citizens, 'democracy must be carried out and be applied
also in the social and economic areas'.   His preference
for addressing himself to 'the people' rather than to 'the
working class' was an attempt to underline that the party
wantèd to bring together all the exploited classes (Hansson, 1929, p. 338):

> An appeal to the people makes everybody listen, in a
> rallying of the people most want to join, and it gives
> everybody a clear and understandable conception of what
> we want, when we talk about a liberation of *the people*
> from the capitalistic dictatorship.

Like Wigforss, he saw the new political strategy during
the 1930s as moving society in a socialist direction,
since 'by carrying out a cautious, controlling policy we,
so to say, prepare the form for another organization of
production'(in Fredriksson et al., 1970, p. 134).

As formulated by Hansson, the Social Democratic path to
socialism had three steps.   The first step had been the
achievement of *political* democracy.   The second step, now
to be taken, was the achievement of *social* democracy.
The third and future step would be to achieve *economic*
democracy (cf. Lindström, 1949).

Since the 1920s, however, tendencies towards a redefinition of the role of private ownership of the means
of production had grown relatively strong among the younger generation of Social Democrats (Erlander, 1972, pp.
125-34). (13)   The leading idea in this reformulation was
that ownership consists of different sets of more or less
independent functions, expressed, for example, through
decisions on production, investment and employment. (14)
Through public power exercised by the state, one set of
functions of ownership could be curtailed or abolished
without making it necessary to abolish simultaneously the
other functions.   The functions of ownership could thus
gradually be limited without the necessity to abolish private ownership of the means of production. (15)

Some of the leading younger intellectuals of the
party (16) even equated socialism with extensive social
policies combined with a planned economy, directed by a
Social Democratic government.   The new strategy thus
involved clear possibilities that reformist socialism
would turn into social reformism.

The strategy of the employers

Also among the employers, the questions concerning the
strategy and tactics to be applied in the new political
situation with a Social Democratic government in power
became subject to a lively internal debate.   One group
consisting of the managing directors of the largest
Swedish export industries with multinational organizations
formed an informal pressure group, 'The Big Five', which
was active from 1933 to 1953 (Söderpalm, 1976).   This
group wanted to maintain a militant stand against the
Social Democrats and to work through the bourgeois parties
to unseat the government.   It maintained close contacts
especially with the Liberal Party.
    According to the judgment of the leaders of the SAF,
however, where the home market industries dominated, the
Social Democrats were to remain in power for a long time
to come.   In their view the possibilities offered by the
new situation to advance the interests of industry by
acting as a pressure group outside the political parties
should be explored.   The organizations on the labour
market should therefore maintain a political neutrality
and serve as counterweights to the political parties and
the state.   They should be free to arrange the rules and
institutions on the labour market without intervention
from the state.
    This latter strategy came to guide the actions of the
SAF.   In 1936 the SAF and the LO entered into negotiations that led to the signing of the Main Agreement two
years later.   During more than three decades this agreement stood as a symbol for the independence of the parties
on the Swedish labour market from the state.   This high
independence of the Swedish labour market organizations
from the state, however, resulted not from social change
of the type envisaged by the 'logic of industrialization'
but rather from a shift in the balance of power between
classes, which made their organizations reconsider the
strategies of class conflict.

Maturation of the welfare state

Experiences during the war of a 'siege economy', with
state intervention, a high level of taxation and gradually
a very low level of unemployment, were to become important for policy-making in the immediate postwar period.
The party programme, revised in 1944, retained a clearly
Marxian character.   In the same year the Social Democrats
also accepted an action programme for the postwar period,

which proposed a continuation of the policies from the
1930s but on a higher level of aspiration. Full employment, not only in the sense of avoiding depressions but
in terms of the provision of work to all those able and
willing to work, became one of the cornerstones of the
postwar policy. Economic efficiency was to increase
through structural changes and state intervention, e.g. in
the capital market and over long-term investment planning.
A more equal distribution of the results of production
would be achieved through social and fiscal policies.
Important among the social policies were improved old-age
pensions, special allowances to families with children,
public health insurance and housing allowances. A new
tax scheme was also proposed, which increased the pro-
gressivity of income taxation and increased company taxation as well as property and inheritance taxes. The
postwar programme was seen as moving society in a socialist direction. The Communist Party also chose to support
it.

After the end of the Second World War, the militant
groups among the employers gained an upper hand. An
intensive political fight arose concerning the taxation
schemes and state interventions in the economy outlined in
the postwar programme. The bourgeois parties viewed
state intervention as leading to inefficiency and as dan-
gerous for democracy. (17)   The climax came in the intensive campaign preceding the 1948 elections, when electoral
participation again rose drastically. The bourgeois parties, however, did not manage to achieve a majority in the
Riksdag.

The violent anti-socialist feelings aroused during the
campaign against the planned economy, however, did weaken
the political support for the Social Democratic Party,
placing it in a defensive position. Economic instability
was serious; the major problem became how to combine full
employment with stable prices. To attempt to curb the
high rate of inflation, the government persuaded the LO to
consent to wage freezes in 1949 and 1950. Wage freezes,
however, tended to increase the share of profits in the
total product and relegated unions to a passive role.
Leading liberal politicians and economists argued that the
goal of economic stability should be given a higher priority at the expense of full employment. (18)

Towards the end of the 1940s, a theoretical model for
the solution of the employment-inflation dilemma, compatible with full employment and with the traditional role
of the unions, was developed by economists at the LO. (19)
The main feature of this model was the key role assigned
to an active manpower policy for the stabilization of the

economy.   Full employment should not be maintained by
creating excess demand in the economy, because this would
lead to inflation.   Since the level of demand always
varies between different sectors of the economy, it was
more efficient to maintain a moderate overall level of
demand combined with selective measures designed to affect
the labour market in areas with unemployment.   These selective measures would include public work projects, shel-
tered employment, support to firms in depressed areas and
the stimulation of geographical as well as sectional
mobility of labour.   This manpower policy would shift
workers from less efficient to more efficient areas, and
would accelerate structural change and productivity increases.   Aided by the high level of employment, unions
could increase wages.   To diminish the possibility of
price increases, demand would be curbed through increases
in indirect taxation.   Profits would thus be squeezed
between high wages and limited buying power.   The government would come to control the distribution of an increasing proportion of the national product.   As discussed
below, only parts of these policies were put into effect.

The 'solidaristic wage policy' that the LO has increasingly stressed during the postwar period came to function
partly as a complement to the economic policies.   By requiring equal wages for equal work, irrespective of the
profitability of the enterprise, the least profitable
firms would be squeezed out from the market.   It also
left the most profitable firms with a large share of the
profits to be used for continued expansion.   By tying
wage increases to increases in productivity, this wage
policy came to include an element of incomes policy.   The
stress on decreasing wage differentials, however, was to
have important consequences for the unions.

The 1950s evolved as a period of political and ideological retreats for the   Social Democrats. (20)   The conservative forces were strong during the Cold War.   In the
fact of economic instability and international tensions,
the Social Democrats entered into a coalition with the
Agrarians in 1951.   The contemporary theories of the increasing embourgeoisement among wage-earners in industrial
society (see chapter 1) gave the electoral difficulties of
the Social Democrats the status of a scientific law.

During the 1930s, and also in the postwar programme,
the fundamental principle of Social Democratic strategy
had been that state planning and co-operation with the
business community should take place on terms laid down by
labour, and that public power would be used to induce
structural changes in the economy that would facilitate
the 'maturation' of capitalism.   The decreasing political

strength of the party during the 1950s, however, and the political necessity to maintain full employment, placed private enterprise in a very strong bargaining position vis-à-vis the government.   To maintain full employment it was necessary to achieve a high rate of economic growth. By and large, decision-making in the sphere of production was left to the managers, and planning became directed to providing them with resources for expansion - labour as well as capital.   Economic growth was stimulated through various devices, e.g. a decrease in effective company taxation (Meidner et al., 1975, p. 54).   The role of the state became limited more and more to affecting distribution of the results of production, by channelling an increasing proportion of the national product to public consumption.

These new practices were reflected in the revision of the party programme in 1960.   While basic criticisms of capitalism were retained, the programme received a liberal flavour.   Socialization of the means of production was treated more or less as an emergency measure to be applied in areas where private enterprise had proved itself unworkable.   This liberal flavour was also present in an economic programme prepared for the LO congress in 1961 by members of its research staff (LO, 1961).   Since the latter part of the 1960s, however, this 'social reformistic' political strategy has again been questioned.   This questioning has been stimulated by indications that an efficient capitalist system combined with welfare state measures could not ensure the welfare of the citizens.

The early signs of a departure from social reformism can be traced back to the late 1950s.   The coalition with the Agrarians broke up in 1957 on the issue of supplementary pensions.   The Social Democrats had proposed a system of supplementary pensions for all, which would build up vast pension funds under state control.   This proposal was seen primarily as a major reform to increase social justice; but through the creation of large pension funds it also had important implications for the distribution of economic power in society.   The Social Democrats again were able to leave their defensive position.   After hard election struggles they carried through this issue to a victory.   The elections in 1960 became a fight for or against a Social Democratic government, which wanted to channel an increasing proportion of the national product to public consumption.   Again participation increased and the Social Democrats strengthened their position, especially among white-collar groups.   For the first time in the postwar period, they received over 50 per cent of the vote in the communal elections in 1962.

This situation, however, was short-lived as the electorate grew more volatile in the 1960s.   In the communal
elections in 1966 the Social Democrats received their
lowest electoral support in the postwar period.   This
instigated a period of self-scrutiny within the labour
movement.   A campaign focused on 'increased equality'
and full employment gave the Social Democrats their
greatest victory ever in the 1968 elections to the
Riksdag.

The 'stagflation' since the late 1960s, combining high
unemployment with rapid inflation, increasing awareness of
health hazards at work and waves of unofficial strikes
since 1969, have brought issues of power based on private
ownership of the means of production again into political
focus.   In these years increasing concern with protection
of the environment and the energy crises also have brought
ecological issues centred around man's possibilities to
survive into the political debate.   The question of
nuclear energy came into the centre of the 1976 election
campaign and was crucial for the narrow defeat of the
Social Democrats.   We will return to these developments
in the concluding chapter.

2   THE CHALLENGE FROM THE LEFT

Although a sizable proportion of workers vote with the
bourgeois parties, since the first decade of this century
there has been no organized opposition from the right
within the labour movement.   The left-wing opposition,
however, has been of significance, and has manifested
itself both in the political arena and within the unions.
For obvious reasons the unions became a battlefield in the
fight for working-class support.

During the first decades of the century syndicalis-
tically oriented groups formed the most important ideological and organizational opposition.   Instead of relying
on parliamentary action and political reforms through
state organs, the syndicalists stressed the necessity of
a militant class struggle outside parliament, based on the
unions.   The syndicalist unions reached their maximum
relative strength around 1920, with a membership about
twelve per cent of that of the LO.   After the formation
of the Social Democratic Left Party in 1917, the internal
opposition has centred around the political parties to the
left of the Social Democrats.

In the spring of 1917, when wartime deprivation was at
a peak and a militant mood was widespread among workers,
syndicalists and left-wing Social Democrats formed the

first embryo of an oppositional organization within the
LO, the Swedish Union Opposition (Gärdvall, 1974; Bäckström, 1971, pp. 244ff.; Klockare, 1967; Kilbom, 1953,
pp. 239-41).   Influenced by syndicalist ideas, its programme demanded that the unions intensify their work towards socialism and engage in militant industrial action
of various forms.   Since the local labour market was
seen as more important than the national one, local co-
ordinating organizations were to play a key role in union
work.   In contrast to its counterpart in Norway, which
became a dominant force within the Norwegian LO, the
Swedish Union Opposition attracted only a few hundred
members, and was dissolved in 1920.   Its failure reflected the expansion of the syndicalist unions in these years
and the more militant policies introduced by the Social
Democrats towards the end of the First World War (Andrae,
1975).

With the formation of the Third International, the
Comintern, in the spring of 1919, the cleavage between the
'reformistic' and 'revolutionary' directions within the
European labour movement was formalized.   In the political sphere some of the basic differences between reformistic socialism, represented by social democrats, and revolutionary socialism, represented by parties to its left,
emerged in differing positions on political democracy and
on the nature of the political party.   While social democrats have seen political democracy as a basic requirement
for the reforming of society, communist parties often have
seen 'bourgeois democracy' as less essential.   While
social democrats have organized a mass party open to all,
communist parties have been explicitly elitist, focusing
on the more class-conscious sections of the working class
and, until recent years, imposing activity requirements
upon their members.   The actual policies of both these
directions, however, have varied over time.

Membership in an international movement based on 'the
first socialist state', the Soviet Union, was probably
experienced as an important ideological and emotional
support by the oppositional minority groups within the
labour movements in different European countries.   The
Comintern also gave economic support to its sections.
But membership in the Comintern made the communist parties
dependent on an organization that was dominated by the
Soviet Union.   Its policies largely came to reflect the
national interests and internal problems of the Soviet
Union, without due consideration for the specific problems
confronting the various communist minority parties.   The
communists thus became torn between, on the one hand, solidarity with an international movement and, on the other

hand, their assessment of the situation in their own
country, which often appeared to demand policies and
solutions different from those recommended by the Comintern.

The adoption by the Comintern in 1920 of the Leninist
party principles, requiring a highly centralized party
organization and the subordination of the unions under
the leadership of the political party, drove a wedge into
the organizations to the left and continued to shake them
in the following decades (Borkenau, 1962; McKenzie, 1964;
Gärdvall, 1975; Kennerström, 1974; Arvidsson and
Berntsson, 1975).

The Social Democratic Left Party had joined the Comintern in the summer of 1919 and formed the Union Propaganda
Association, which was to co-ordinate and strengthen
attempts to influence union policy. The programme of
this association was by and large patterned after that of
its predecessor, the Swedish Union Opposition. The introduction of the Leninist party principles into the anti-
bureaucratic and decentralized Left Party led to a split
in 1921, and the birth of the Swedish Communist Party,
which became a section of the Comintern. The Union Propaganda Association became dependent on the Communist
Party (Kilbom, 1953, pp. 250-1). Its close association
with a minority party limited membership to union branches
controlled by the opposition, and it only had about five
thousand members. But its ideological influence was
relatively strong, and its membership included two future
chairmen of the LO.

The return of the revolutionary tide following the
First World War necessitated a change in Comintern policy.
Its third congress in 1921 proclaimed the 'united front'
policy, requiring work within and according to the statutes of the reformist unions and co-operation with social
democrats on specific issues. The Union Propaganda
Association, which was tied to the Communist Party, was
therefore dissolved in 1923. A split in the Communist
Party in 1924, centring around the demands for increasing
centralism in the Comintern (Arvidsson, 1975), delayed
efforts to carry out the new Comintern policy. In 1926,
however, the Committee for Union Unity was established:
according to instructions from the Comintern it was to
function as a national co-ordination committee to rally
support for 'united front' policies within the limits of
union statutes (Kennerström, 1974, p. 17). Towards the
end of the 1920s the Communists apparently increased their
organizational and political activities within the unions
(Back, 1963, pp. 90-1). At the two national conferences
in 1926 and 1929 sponsored by the Committee for Union

Unity, unions comprising about 8 per cent of the membership of the LO were represented.

By the end of the 1920s, the Comintern again shifted policy, voicing its expectation of a coming world crisis in the capitalist system, which would pitch 'class against class', the bourgeoisie against the proletariat, and where social democrats would reveal themselves as 'class collaborators' and would act as the 'left wing of fascism' or as 'social fascists'. The new policy accepted by the congress in 1928 was directed towards providing the working class with an 'independent' leadership in the impending crisis. This new 'ultra-left' policy thus openly confronted the social democrats and relied upon 'the united front from below', exemplified by strike committees including unorganized workers but excluding union leaders. In Sweden the Committee for Union Unity came out more openly against LO leadership, thereby provoking a frontal attack from the LO (Kennerström, 1974, pp. 19-20). The LO declared that support for the Committee was not compatible with membership in the LO unions.

The threat of expulsion from the LO led to a split within the Communist Party in 1929. The groups loyal to the LO, among them the great majority of the communists active in the unions, formed a communist party outside the Comintern. This party was renamed the Socialist Party when, in 1934, it amalgamated with a splinter group from the Social Democrats. The Socialist Party had an elaborate programme for 'faction work' within the unions, but enjoyed scant success (Kennerström, 1974, pp. 47-8). It also tried to find support among the unemployed through the Central Committee for the Unemployed, which organized national conferences in 1930 and 1933, where unions with 3 and 5 per cent, respectively, of the LO membership were represented (Kennerström, 1974, p. 54). In the general elections, however, this party was relatively strong as long as 'ultra-left' policies kept the Comintern Party weak. When the 'popular front' in defence against fascism was introduced by the Comintern in 1934, the Socialist Party gradually dwindled into insignificance.

During the first years of the 1930s, the Comintern Communist Party attempted to follow the militant line against the LO, and organized the Red Union Opposition in 1930. This organization remained weak, however, and in 1933, when some of its leaders and union branches under its control had been expelled from the LO unions, it was dissolved. The 'popular front' policy of the Comintern relieved the party from further attempts in this direction. As a result of dubious standpoints on foreign policy by the Communist Party, the Social Democrats almost

managed to erase the Communists from leading positions in
the unions during the first years of the Second World War,
partly by formally barring them from elected positions in
the unions.

The dissolution of the Comintern in 1943 allowed the
Communist Party to develop a policy of 'national communism', and to channel the deprivations experienced by
workers during the war.   The Communist Party reached the
peak of its strength in the general elections in 1944 and
1946, when it managed to achieve 10-11 per cent of the
total vote.   Towards the end of the war communist and
independent candidates ran in union elections under the
label 'the Free Union People' and achieved considerable
support; in the Swedish Metal Workers' Union they almost
achieved a majority (see chapter 9).   In the 1950s and
1960s, the left-wing opposition again weakened, but it
regained some strength in the 1970s.

The policy alternatives propagated by the left-wing
opposition within the Swedish labour movement have hovered
between revolutionary and reformistic socialism.   A unifying thread in these policies has been criticism of the
economic growth strategy of class conflict adopted by the
Social Democrats, and greater reliance on industrial
action to improve the situation of the working class.
While the Social Democrats have seen the growth strategy
of class conflict as a way of increasing the welfare of
the working class and of hastening the maturation of capitalism, the Communists have viewed this strategy as
'class collaboration'.   Rationalization to increase the
efficiency of production, for example, was seen as leading
to 'the stabilization of capitalism at the expense of the
proletariat' (Linderot, 1972, p. 112).   In spite of their
organizational muddle and fluctuating levels of support,
however, the left-wing groups appear to have provided a
potential channel of opposition to the tendencies towards
a conversion of reformistic socialism to social reformism
inherent in the growth strategy of class conflict relied
upon by the Social Democrats.

3   INDUSTRIAL CONFLICT

The trend of disputes

The level of industrial conflict in a country is often
interpreted as an indication of its level of class conflict.   In Sweden the frequency of industrial disputes
shows dramatic changes over time, moving between opposite
extremes.   The increasing organizational strength of the

Swedish unions, enabling the workers to resist pressures
from the employers and to voice their demands, was reflected in an increasing frequency of industrial disputes
beginning in the late 1880s (Figure 4.1).   Already in

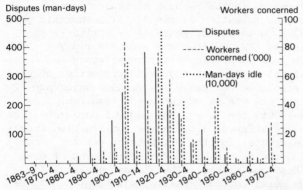

FIGURE 4.1   Mean number of industrial disputes, workers
concerned and man-days idle in Sweden, 1863-1974

the latter part of the 1880s the majority of all strikes
were led by unions (Lindbom, 1938, p. 148).   When the
employers had organized themselves and started to use the
lockout weapon, industrial disputes turned into tests of
endurance, climaxing in the general strike of 1909.

After the crushing defeat of the unions in the general
strike, a period of relative calm set in on the Swedish
labour market.   With the recovery of union strength,
however, the level of conflict again increased towards the
end of the First World War, reaching a peak in the years
following the war.   A sizable part of these disputes resulted from lockouts, often aimed at forcing wage decreases in the depression.   The level of disputes remained high through the 1920s.   When the Great Depression
hit Sweden in 1930-1, employer demands for wage decreases,
backed by lockouts, sustained industrial conflict at a
high level.

Up to the middle of the 1930s, Sweden had one of the
very *highest* relative rates of disputes among Western industrial countries (21) (Shorter and Tilly, 1974, p. 333).
As in other countries with relatively well-organized
unions, e.g. Norway, Finland, Denmark and the Netherlands,
disputes in Sweden in this period tended to be long.
They thus differed from the strike pattern in some other
European countries, especially France and Italy, where
strikes tended to be less frequent and of shorter dura-
tion, but on average with more participants (Shorter and
Tilly, 1974, ch. 12).   These differences would appear to

reflect differences in the organizational strength of the working class: weak unions, unable to endure long disputes, tend to rely on short and large-sclae protest actions aimed at influencing the government.

A decisive change in the Swedish strike pattern occurred after the formation of the Social Democratic government in 1932: a couple of years later strike rates declined markedly. (22) After the Second World War Sweden came to rank *lowest* in strike rates among the Western industrial nations. A growing proportion of strikes have also come to take place without union support, or against the wishes of the union leadership.

In the mid-1930s, the LO and the Social Democrats thus intervened to end strikes, e.g. in the construction industry, which was crucial for the attempts to get the economy going. During the Second World War some amount of unofficial strikes took place. The climax came in 1945 with the large metal-workers' strike, which union leaders were forced to declare because of rank and file pressures (see chapter 9). A wave of unofficial strikes also took place in connection with the wage rounds in 1947. Since 1969 unofficial strikes have increased again. These strikes have generally been relatively short and small. Some larger disputes in the white-collar sector in 1966 and 1971 depart from this pattern.

Up to the middle of the 1930s the well-organized Swedish employers had frequently resorted to lockouts. With a Social Democratic government, lockouts became difficult to use successfully, and have tended to disappear.

Institutionalization of conflict

The institutionalization of industrial conflict started early in Sweden, both through union-management agreements and through legislation. As noted above, collective bargaining on the local level was common even before the turn of the century. The high level of organization among employers made industry-wide bargaining possible and desirable. Gradually, industry-wide contracts covered the great majority of the LO members (Westerståhl, 1945, p. 162; Karlbom, 1969, p. 148) (Table 4.1).

Since several unions were parties to the early industry-wide agreements, and since there was a continuous threat of lockout, the LO took an active part in the bargaining process of the unions, e.g. in the negotiations leading to the engineering agreement in 1905. After the defeat of the LO-led general strike in 1909, however, the LO was forced to relinquish this active role. Towards

TABLE 4.1 Proportion of LO members working under
different types of collective agreements, 1908-74

Type of agreement	1908	1915	1936	1940	1950	1960	1970
	%	%	%	%	%	%	%
Industry-wide (or regional)	24	42	42	50	61	67	78
Local related to industry-wide		20	11	13	8	9	5
Local	76	38	46	37	31	24	17
	100	100	99	100	100	100	100

the end of the 1930s the LO again began to intervene in
the negotiations of the member unions (see chapter 8).
After the Second World War the position of the LO has
become very strong. Since the middle of the 1950s a
three-tiered bargaining system has evolved: at the top
level, centralized negotiations between the LO and the
employers' organizations take place, leading to a 'frame
agreement'; at the second level this agreement becomes
the basis for industry-wide bargaining by the member
unions; and at the third level the workplace union organization represents the workers in adapting the agreements
to local conditions.

Agreements on procedures between employers' organizations and the unions have also formed a central part of
the web of rules on the Swedish labour market. The most
important one is the Main Agreement, dating from 1938,
which established rules for grievance bargaining as well
as for protecting third parties in industrial disputes.

As indicated above, up to the 1930s state intervention
in industrial relations was relatively common in Sweden.
Around the turn of the century legislation intended to
curb the growth of the young labour movement was introduced. Some of the more important labour market institutions were established through legislation. (23)
Against the strong opposition of the LO, manifested in a
nationwide political strike, a bourgeois government enacted a law in 1928 that made collective agreements legally binding. It also established the Labour Court to ad-
judicate in breaches against agreements and in disputes
over their interpretation. According to the new law, industrial conflict was permitted with the exception that,
during the term of the contract, conflicts on issues reg-

ulated in the contracts were forbidden.   By declaring
that the managerial prerogatives concerning hiring and
firing as well as the direction of work were basic rights
accruing to the employers even if this had not been made
explicit in the contract, however, the Labour Court
drastically enlarged the peace obligation during the term
of contract.   As mentioned above, in 1936 the Social
Democratic government enacted a law on the right of organization, which came to be important for the organizational attempts in the white-collar sector.

Why decreasing conflict?

How are we to account for the decrease of industrial conflict in Sweden from an extremely high level during the
first three decades of the century to an extremely low
one after the Second World War?   An influential intellectual tradition in postwar social science, exemplified by
the 'logic of industrialization' school of thought, predicts that the level of conflict in advanced industrial
societies will decrease as a result of two developments:
the growth of institutions to regulate industrial conflict, and the separation of industrial and political conflict.   Sweden has been widely regarded as a case in
support of these ideas.   For several reasons, however,
this interpretations appears doubtful.
     To evaluate the effects of the development of institu-
tions of conflict regulation, one seeks evidence of decreases in the level of conflict subsequent to the establishment of institutions.   Such evidence, however, is
difficult to discern.   As noted above, the decisive
break in the trend and pattern of disputes can be quite
clearly located in the years around 1934-5.   Legal institutions developed gradually during the first decades of
the century and included mediation (1906), arbitration
(1920) and finally the laws on collective agreements and
the Labour Court.   The level of industrial disputes, however, remained high even after the appearance of these
institutions.   Neither did collective bargaining between
well-organized parties since the beginning of the century
decrease conflict;   the high level of organization among
both workers and employers led instead to prolonged disputes including a frequent use of the lockout weapon.
The second state in the development of the web of rules,
including the rules accepted through the Main Agreement in
1938 and the growth of the three-tiered bargaining system
in the 1950s, came *after* the decisive decrease in the
level and pattern of disputes.   The centralization of the

internal decision-making procedures within the trade
unions also occurred after the decline in disputes (see
chapter 8).   It can also be noted that well developed
institutions could not hinder the increase in strikes in
the 1970s.

The separation of industrial and political conflict in
advanced industrial societies leading to a restriction of
union interests to 'economism' is another central tenet
of the 'logic of industrialization' school of thought.
As previously discussed, this assumption is also congruent
with a Weberian approach to class theory, while on the
contrary a Marxian approach predicts a close relationship
between industrial and political conflict.

We noted above that Swedish unions, initially limited
to bread-and-butter issues, were 'economistic' in the
early stage.   Soon, however, they became socialistic,
and began to co-operate with the Social Democratic Party
in a rather closely integrated labour movement.   As exemplified by the nationwide political strikes in 1902 and
1928 at this stage, political issues generated conflict
in the industrial arena.   After the coming to power of
the Social Democratic government in 1932, however, the
pattern changes.   As discussed above, this new situation
induced changes in the conflict strategies of the labour
movement.   It was no longer necessary to attempt to
affect political decision-making through strikes.   The
unions had, instead, access to a relatively efficient
political alternative which they could use to achieve
important goals, primarily through changes in employment,
fiscal and social policies.   The decrease in industrial
disputes in Sweden after the mid-1930s must be seen in
the perspective of the new conflict strategy of the labour
movement, which moved the centre of gravity of distribu-
tional conflict from the industrial to the political
arena.   Thus also with respect to the inter-relatedness
of political and economic conflict, the Swedish case would
appear to be more congruent with the Marxian than with the
Weberian approach to class theory.

In sum, then, although the rules and institutions regu-
lating industrial disputes have been of importance for the
level and type of industrial conflict in the country, we
have thus not found evidence for the frequently made
assumption of their crucial role in decreasing the level
of conflict.   Conflict-regulating institutions can more
fruitfully be viewed as intervening rather than as major
independent variables affecting levels of conflict. (24)
The changes in the level of industrial conflict in
Sweden, leading to a low level of disputes since the
middle of the 1930s, would instead appear to be the result

of changes in the distribution of power resources in society related to the coming to power of the Social Democratic government in 1932, and of the subsequent changes
in the conflict strategies of the labour movement as well
as of the employers.

4   CREEPING TOWARDS OR AWAY FROM SOCIALISM?

When evaluating the tactics and strategies of the Social
Democratic Party, we must keep in mind that they developed
in conflict situations, where the working class was the
weaker party.   To judge from the experiences around the
end of the First World War in Finland, Hungary and Germany, where the skewness in the distribution of power resources was similar to that in Sweden, any attempt to a
revolutionary overthrow of capitalism most probably would
have been doomed to failure.   In Western capitalist
countries labour has generally lost the big battles, such
as the general strikes in Sweden in 1909 and in Britain
in 1926.   Proposals for large-scale nationalization probably also would have been very difficult to carry through
the Riksdag, and could have been used for successful
attacks against the Social Democratic Party.
    Of basic importance for the evaluation of Social Demo-
cratic policies, however, is to what extent they have laid
the basis for a strengthening of the labour movement and
of its political support.   This is essential for the possibilities of introducing future changes in the economic
system of society.   Evidence of relevance here concerns
the effects of Social Democratic policies on the citizens'
conditions of life and on social structure, as well as how
these changes have been experienced and interpreted by the
citizens.   Let us look at some indicators of interest in
this context.

Standard of living

One relevant area concerns the consequences that Social
Democratic policies have had for the standard of living of
the lower and middle social strata.   Changes in levels of
unemployment and means-tested social assistance reflect
changes in the standard of living within the working
class.
    A rough indication of major changes over time in the
level of unemployment can be obtained from two sources
(Figure 4.2).   Data on unemployment among union members
are available up to 1957;   and figures on registered unem-

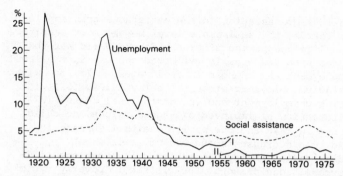

FIGURE 4.2   Percentage of unemployment among workers and
percentage receiving social assistance in the population,
1918-76 (I = unemployment among union members in the LO;
II = registered unemployment among workers in manufacturing covered by unemployment insurance)

ployment among workers in manufacturing, covered by unemployment insurance, have been published since 1956. (25)
The very high levels of unemployment between 1920 and the
mid-1940s, with the two peaks around 1921 and 1933, offer
a striking contrast to the postwar period characterized by
close to full employment.   The decrease in the unemployment rates after 1933 came when the new unemployment policies were introduced by the Social Democratic government.
The relative increase in unemployment connected with the
'stagflation' in the late 1960s, however, should be noted.
    In the postwar period the policy of the Social Demo-
crats and the LO was to give full employment priority over
economic stability, if a choice had to be made.   This
policy met political resistance but led, by international
comparisons, to a relatively low level of unemployment
(Sorrentino, 1972).   Apparently other governments, such
as those in Britain and the United States, have given economic stability a higher priority in the inflation-employ-
ment dilemma facing them in the postwar period.   In contrast to many other governments, the Swedish Social Democrats have also preferred to provide jobs through active
state intervention rather than through indirect measures
such as tax decreases, which leave solutions to the play
of market forces. (26)
    The proportion of the population receiving means-
tested social assistance each year provides a rough index
of relative poverty, indicating especially changes in economic conditions among workers (Korpi, 1975).   Assistance
rates apparently did not reflect the increasing misery
among workers resulting from the depression of 1921-2
(Figure 4.2).   Partly as a result of increasing Social

Democratic representation in the assistance granting local
welfare boards, the assistance level became more sensitive
to need.   In the period after the Second World War the
assistance rate has clearly reflected changes in the level
of unemployment and changes in real wages.   It rose with
increasing unemployment since the early 1930s, fell with
decreasing unemployment and increasing real wages. (27)
The introduction of improved old-age pensions and child
allowances in 1948 and the public health insurance in
1955 led to a decrease in the use of assistance.

Swedish social policy has achieved at least one landmark success: one phase of the classical 'poverty cycle',
poverty in old age, has been broken up.   While in countries such as Britain and the United States, a large proportion of old people live in poverty as has always been
the case (Atkinson, 1975, pp. 198-202), in Sweden old
people have become the category with the very lowest
social assistance rate.   The 'stagflation' beginning in
the 1960s is reflected in a rather dramatic increase in
assistance rates since 1965, especially among young families with children.

An illustration of how changes in conditions of life
have been experienced during the present century emerges
from replies to a retrospective question presented to a
random sample of the Swedish population in 1968 and 1974:
'Did your family have economic difficulties during your
childhood?' (28)   The responses presumably refer to experiences of respondents when they were between five and
fifteen years of age.   The percentage reporting such
economic difficulties is presented by birth cohort and
socioeconomic status of father in Figure 4.3.   In the

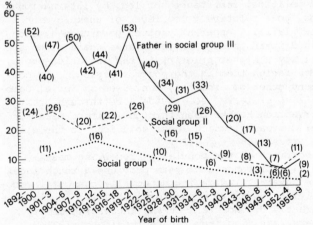

FIGURE 4.3 Percentage reporting economic difficulties
during childhood by father's socioeconomic status and
year of birth (Swedish-born only)

three-year cohorts of working-class origin (father in
social group III), the level of childhood deprivation is
high among those born in the nineteenth century, shows
peaks for the cohorts growing up during the difficult
years around 1917, the depression after the First World
War and the Great Depression of the early 1930s.   In the
following cohorts experiences of deprivation begin to decrease but show some increase among those growing up
during the Second World War. (29)   Working-class respondents who grew up in the postwar period reported dramatically less experiences of deprivation.   In the youngest
cohorts experiencing the 'stagflation' period after 1965,
however, some increase would appear to have taken place.
Our data thus indicate that, from the 1930s up to mid-
1960s, the proportion of the population subject to severe
economic hardship declined very considerably and that the
differences between socioeconomic groups in this respect
almost have vanished.

Income and wealth

The distribution of income and wealth are also of relevance in this context.   Income data in Sweden, based on
tax assessments, are weak in terms of reliability and
validity.   Available studies indicate that in the period
from 1935 to about 1950 inequality in taxable income
tended to decrease (Bentzel, 1952, ch. 6;   SOU, 1968 (7),
pp. 189-95;   Järnek, 1971;   Kuuse, 1970), probably primarily because of decreasing unemployment and a shift of
the labour force from agriculture and domestic service to
the secondary and tertiary sectors.   In the two decades
since 1950, however, the distribution of incomes among
adult men has remained relatively stable (Spånt, 1976).
The net effects of taxation and transfers has been to decrease inequality in terms of disposable income and buying
power (Bentzel, 1952, pp. 123-6 and SOU, 1971 (39), p.
61), although the effects of these factors have been relatively small in comparison with others affecting income
distributions.   Among workers, wage differentials between
men and women as well as between low-paid and high-paid
workers have decreased considerably in recent years
(Meidner et al., 1975). (30)
   Inequality of distribution of property ownership does
not appear to have decreased since the 1930s (SOU, 1968
(7), pp. 177-82;   also Spånt, 1975).   Ownership of the
means of production is highly concentrated.   The private
sector is dominated by fifteen to twenty ownership groups,
most of them families.   Among these one family, the

Wallenbergs, clearly has been the most influential.   Concentration of ownership in the largest companies appears
to be even higher in Sweden than in Britain and the United
States.   The dominance of the largest ownership groups
also has increased markedly in the postwar period (SOU,
1968 (7);   Hermansson, 1959;   Meidner et al., 1975).   In
recent decades effective company taxation has decreased,
while individual taxation, especially its non-progressive
parts, has increased (Meidner et al., 1975, pp. 51-2).
These developments presumably reflect economic policies
directed towards providing the most efficient firms with
good possibilities for expansion in order to maintain full
employment.

   Of relevance for the distribution of economic power
resources in society are also the funds for supplementary
pensions under public control.   These funds are growing
very fast and will reach their maximum strength in the
1980s.   Already in 1969 their value was equal to that of
the total stock of private companies listed at the stock
exchange (Spånt, 1975, pp. 45, 52).

The social composition of the party elite

An indicator, albeit a tenuous one, of changes in the
political centre of gravity of a party is the social composition of its elite.   The proportion of the Social
Democratic members of the Riksdag who were in manual occupations while they held their seats has never been high
(Sköld and Halvarsson, 1966;   Holmberg, 1974).   Even
during the first three decades of the century only one-
third of the Social Democrats in the second chamber of
the Riksdag were workers, a figure that has declined to
about 10 per cent in the 1960s (Figure 4.4).   An increas-

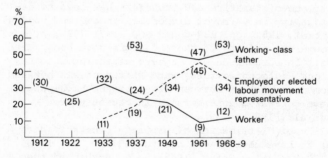

FIGURE 4.4   Social origin and present occupation of Social
Democratic members of the second chamber of the Riksdag,
1912-68

ing proportion has made a career within the labour movement.   In the earlier period, editors of Social Democratic newspapers were a relatively numerous group in the
Riksdag.   More recently full-time representatives for the
various organizations within the labour movement - primarily from the unions but increasingly often from the
party - have come to form the largest single group among
the Social Democrats in the Riksdag.   The overwhelming
majority of them have started out as workers.

The proportion of the Social Democratic members with
working-class fathers in the second chamber of the Riksdag
has been relatively stable, about 50 per cent, throughout
the century and is not much lower than that among the
rank-and-file Social Democratic voters.   The proportion
with a higher secondary education has increased only
slowly over the decades: it was 25 per cent in 1961
(Sköld and Halvarsson, 1966, pp. 420, 466).

From 1917 to 1976, eighty-one persons served as members
of Social Democratic governments.   (31)   The working-class
proportion among them is lower than among the Social Democratic members of the Riksdag (Figure 4.5).   Only about
one-third of them have had working-class backgrounds, or
started their own occupational careers in manual jobs.
Close to two-thirds of them have had a university education or its equivalent.   Somewhat surprisingly, the
social composition of the members of the government thus
has been relatively stable over the century. (32).   In
the bourgeois government formed in 1976 no members came
from working-class backgrounds or had started their occupational careers in the working class.   Those without
university education all had backgrounds in agriculture.

When comparing the social background of the Social
Democratic Party elite with that of the British Labour
Party (Butler and Stokes, 1969, p. 153; Rose, 1976,
pp. 52-4; Parkin, 1971, p. 131), two differences appear.
Before the Second World War, the working-class proportion
of the Labour Party elite was higher than that of the
Social Democratic Party.   But while the working-class
proportion of the Labour Party elite has declined drastically over the years, it has remained relatively stable
in the Social Democratic Party.   The changes in the
social composition of the Social Democratic Party elite
thus does not point at an increasing 'embourgeoisement'.

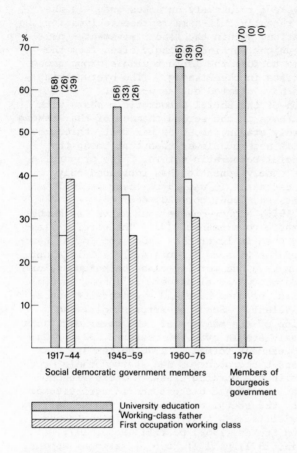

FIGURE 4.5   Social composition of Social Democratic members of government, by year of entrance into government, and of the 1976 bourgeois government

Declining status differentiation

The social changes taking place in Sweden in recent decades have created a society that in many ways is egalitarian. (33)   While Sweden formerly was perhaps a highly status-differentiated society (Lipset, 1960, p. 241), status differentiation has definitely declined in recent years.   This is of interest primarily as an indicator of underlying changes in the power structure of society.

One of the most visible signs of declining status differences is the rapid increase among the younger generation of the use of the familiar form of address, *du*, even
when speaking to unknown persons of different backgrounds
in various social situations.   As Figure 4.6 indicates,
the use of *du* has become the norm among those who came of
age in the postwar period. (34)   It is also generally
used in the mass media.   Another sign of decreasing
status differentiation is the abolishment of the system
of orders in the early 1970s practically without protests
from those concerned.   The increasingly high degree of
secularism in Swedish society should also be noted. (35)

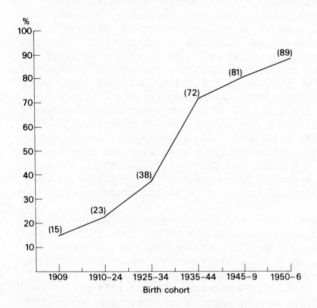

FIGURE 4.6 Percentage of the Swedish population predominantly using the familiar form of address, 'du', when
speaking to unknown persons with different social backgrounds, by birth cohort (data source: SIFO, 1974)

Persisting problems

By international comparisons, the Swedish Social Democrats have been extremely successful in developing policies that create and maintain political support.   The
full employment policy, with which the party became identified in the 1930s, and which it has continued relatively
successfully into the postwar period, has probably been

the most important part of the policy package.   The level
of employment is central for the life chances and experiences of the majority of the population; but it also has
important indirect effects, e.g. improving the bargaining
position of the workers and affecting the general climate
in the labour market and at the shopfloor level.   Social
policies directed towards decreasing want and improving
economic security have of course also been valuable but
would probably not have been sufficient.

In the common struggles against unemployment during the
1930s, the close co-operation between the LO and the
Social Democratic Party was cemented.   This co-operation,
in turn, explains why full employment was given first
priority in the postwar employment-inflation dilemma.
The mutual dependence of the unions and the party has
made party leaders seek political solutions which, by and
large, have been congenial with the interests of union
members.   The key to the political strength of the party
would thus appear to be that *it has remained a class party
which has channelled the demands and provided acceptable
solutions to the problems of the wage-earners, generated
by the conflict of interests on the labour market and by
the subordinate position of the wage-earners in the sphere
of production*.   These policies have also earned electoral
support from a sizable and increasing proportion of the
white-collar sector.   The continued unity of the labour
movement would thus appear to be the greatest asset of the
party.

The weakness of the party, reflected in the increasing
volatility of politics since the 1950s, appears to be generated by the fact that its strategy has necessitated economic growth, which to a large extent has been created on
the terms of private capital.   How growth is to be
achieved has thus been determined with private profit as
the main decision-making criterion.   This has aggravated
societal problems, e.g. rapid urbanization, regional inbalance, restructuring of the labour force and health
hazards at work.   Being focused on the maintenance of
economic growth, the party has further faced difficulties
in handling issues related to the environment, the ecological balance and the energy crises that have come into
the political focus since the 1960s.   The period of
'stagflation' beginning in the late 1960s indicates that
the economic growth strategy may not give more lasting
solutions to the problems of economic insecurity facing
citizens.   In the final chapter we will return to a discussion of the political developments in Sweden in the
1970s.   The following chapter will begin the analysis of
industrial work and its role for the labour movement.

5 Work and work orientations

Since work is the crucial junction between labour and
capital it assumes key importance in the discussion of the
working class in a capitalist industrial society. The
importance of work derives from the fact that through work
the material conditions for social life and for social
change are created. But work is important also because
it is a major context in which the social consciousness of
the wage-earners is formed. At work the wage-earner
places his labour power at the disposal of the employer,
who has acquired the right to use it through the labour
contract. Since labour power cannot be dissociated from
the wage-earner, its delivery also involves his subordination to the representatives of capital in the work situation. His motivation to accept or to initiate basic
social change can thus be affected by the way in which he
experiences the delivery of labour power. Work is therefore of relevance also for the subjective conditions for
social change.

In this chapter, work will be analysed from the perspective of its role in social change. We will explore
the ways in which the class structure of society conditions job designs, work roles and control structures in
the work organization, and how these in turn affect work
experiences. The consequences of work experiences will
also be discussed. The formation of normative expectations concerning rewards from work will further be analysed, since they are crucial when work experiences are
viewed from the perspective of their relevance for social
change.

1   GOAL OR ONLY MEANS?

The extent to which work experiences create dissatisfaction, which can motivate wage-earners to accept or to
initiate social change, depends on the difference between
their normative expectations of rewards from work and the
rewards they actually receive.   Normative expectations of
rewards, i.e. what wage-earners think that they have legitimate claims to, can vary in quality as well as in quantity.   The term 'orientations to work' has been used to
describe the pattern of rewards people expect from work
(Goldthorpe et al., 1968a).   Two main types of rewards
from work can be distinguished;   on the one hand there are
extrinsic rewards, which are primarily economical, and on
the other hand there are *intrinsic* rewards, which refer to
the satisfaction derived from work tasks and work roles.
    It is often assumed that capitalist production organi-
zations can provide for extrinsic rewards from work more
easily than they can provide for intrinsic rewards.   The
extent to which workers are 'economistic', i.e. to which
they limit their expectations of rewards from work to high
wages, is thus of potential importance for the stability
of the capitalist system.   Here, the debate on the working
class ties on to the long debate about what rewards men
seek from work.   The unifying thread is the question of
the relative weight of extrinsic versus intrinsic rewards
from work.
    Two different intellectual traditions can be discerned
in the discussions on what men seek and should seek from
work.   In one powerful tradition, work is seen primarily
as a means to other goals, and economic returns as the
main purpose of work.   This view is central to the mainstream of liberal economic theory, where work generally is
seen as a 'disutility', as 'a painful exertion of mind or
body' (e.g. Jevons, 1970, p. 188).   The theory of 'scientific management', originating in the writings of Taylor
(1913), which has shaped managerial ideologies on the organization of industrial work, is based on the premise
that economic incentives are the most important ones for
workers.   In this tradition the characteristics of work
that deprive workers of intrinsic job satisfaction are
seen as necessary consequences of efforts to increase the
efficiency of production, and thereby the economic rewards
from work.   It is also often suggested that increased
efficiency and shorter working hours can provide workers
with the possibility of 'self-actualization' outside of
work (e.g. Dubin, 1958, ch. 14;   Faunce and Dubin, 1975).
    Another intellectual tradition, dating back at least
to the Renaissance, invests work with an intrinsic mean-

ing, seeing it as a potentially enriching experience through which men can develop their aptitudes and abilities, enjoy the satisfactions of achievement and find an outlet for their creative capacity.   Marxian thinking, important within the Swedish labour movement, clearly follows in this tradition.   The 1973 action programme of the Swedish Metal Workers' Union is illustrative: 'Every individual has the right to a job which can be experienced as a creative activity.... Production must be organized ... so that every individual can experience joy in work' (Svenska Metallindustriarbetareförbundet, 1973, p. 9).

As is well known, however, Marx held that the capitalist economic system destroys the creative potentiality or work, alienating the worker by subjecting him to the will of the employer.   In an often quoted passage Marx has summarized this view (in Bottomore and Rubel, 1963, p. 177):

In what does this alienation of labour consist?
First, that the work is *external* to the worker, that it is not a part of his nature, that consequently he does not fulfil himself in work but denies himself, has a feeling of misery, not of well-being, does not develop freely a physical and metal energy, but is physically exhausted and mentally debased.   The worker feels himself at home only during his leisure, whereas at work he feels homeless.   His work is not voluntary but imposed, *forced labour*.   It is not the satisfaction of a need, but only a *means* for satisfying other needs.
This alienation, Marx assumed, would continuously stir the workers' desire to abolish the institution of wage labour.

Modern behavioural scientists continue to stress that intrinsic rewards from work are important for the satisfaction of human needs and realization of an individual's potential (e.g. Argyris, 1964; McGregor, 1960; Likert, 1961).   They tend to depart from an assumption of a hierarchy of more or less general human needs, where prior satisfaction of basic physiological needs then activates needs of a higher order, including self-actualization (Maslow, 1954).   The well-known Human Relations school underlines the importance of work for the satisfaction of social needs: it stresses the need to interact with and be accepted by members of a workgroup and one's immediate supervisors (Mayo, 1945; 1945, p. 111; Zaleznik and Moment, 1964).

While the alienating characteristics of work in industrial society are deplored by modern behavioural scientists, they focus on the considerable variation in the feeling of alienation that is found between employees. In contrast to Marx, they generally have not related alienation to the capitalist economic system; they have instead seen the feeling of alienation as caused by the large-scale organizations and impersonal bureaucracies that pervade industrial societies (e.g. Blauner, 1964, p. 3; Gardell, 1971, p. 18). Thus they generally postulate that rearrangement of the organizational structure within the enterprises can serve both the employers' need for profit and the human needs of the employees. It has further been argued that, in the advanced industrial societies, the feeling of alienation threatens to counteract economic effectiveness, which increasingly requires a relatively high degree of personal involvement and commitment from labour (McGregor, 1960; Likert, 1961, 1961; Argyris, 1964; Dahlström et al., 1966, p. 162).

2   CONTROL AND JOB DESIGN

The debate on what types of rewards men seek from work can be elucidated by an analysis of the factors that affect and condition job designs, work roles and control structures. (1) According to a dominant line of thinking in industrial sociology and psychology, these are determined largely by the factors that shape the general structure of the production organization. Three sets of factors generally are considered crucial in determining the structure of this organization: the production technology utilized by the organization (e.g. Woodward, 1965, 1970; Perrow, 1970), the size of the organization, and the environment of the organization (e.g. Stinchcombe, 1965; Burns and Stalker, 1961; Lawrence and Lorsch, 1967). These factors are generally assumed to determine organizational structure - and thus also job designs and work roles - by imposing constraints - primarily economic ones - on the organization. The members of the organization are seen primarily as adapting themselves to these constraints. This line of thinking is congruent with the Weberian emphasis on the role of bureaucratic principles in large-scale organizations, where rational pursuit of organizational goals necessitates a division of labour and control structure that makes for the subordination of the many to the few.

An alternative view of the structuring of the production organization can be suggested. The starting point for this perspective is that the production organization is created to provide profit by bringing together capital and labour. This approach thus implies that some members of the production organization have an active role in shaping its structure. The structuring of the production

organization is essentially a political process involving
the exercise of power, not one of adaption to external
constraints.   To the extent that interests of different
groups of actors within the production organization are
opposed, the power-holders within the organization can be
expected to attempt to shape the organizational structure
so as to facilitate their own continued dominance.   In
this perspective the structuring of the production organization thus is related to the class structure of society.

Some modern organizational scientists have questioned
the view that organizational structure is primarily a
product of economic constraints imposed by the environment of the organization, its technology and size (Child,
1972; Davis and Taylor, 1975).   They argue that functional imperatives and constraints do not affect organizational structure directly, but operate instead via the
strategic decisions made by those members of the organization who have the power of structural initiation within
the organization.   This power is unevenly distributed
among its members.   The strategic decisions are made by
a dominant coalition within it, and can therefore be expected to reflect the interests and goals of this coalition.

These theorists further view constraints upon structural choice as limited.   Decision-makers in large and
powerful organizations thus often have considerable opportunities to choose and to affect their immediate environment.   Although available technologies exhibit short-term
rigidities, organizational structure does not follow as a
necessary 'implication' of technology; rather, it is a
product of the decisions about work plans, resources and
equipment which organizational power-holders make out of
a consideration of their own values and the goals and environment of the organization.   They also exercise some
choice over performance standards, and are able and willing to trade off potential gains in different areas
against each other (Child, 1972).

The above discussion indicates that, while the choice
of production methods and job designs is to some extent
constrained, employers and management in the production
organizations can exercise a significant degree of discretion.   Bendix (1956) has documented the strong concern that management traditionally shows to retain and
fortify its control over the workplace.   The Swedish Employers' Association has manifested this concern through
the well-known paragraph in its statutes requiring that
the declaration that the employer has the right to hire
and fire employees as well as to lead and direct work
should be included in all collective agreements.   It is

thus clear that employers and management can be expected
to prefer organizational forms that - manifestly or
latently - support their control over the workplace, and
that they will tend to develop technologies that maintain
and enhance this control.

Through the present century, scientific management has
provided the main guidelines for managers in their thinking on the structuring of work organizations. The general principles of scientific management, which stress
efficiency, standardization of job performance and hier-
archical authority, clearly tend to augment managerial
power within the production organization. In a letter
written in 1898 to the president of the Bethlehem Iron
Company, F.W. Taylor made explicit that these principles
were intended to 'stop the loafing', to permit the running of a shop 'entirely independent of any one man or
any set of men', and to ensure 'that any policy, which may
be decided upon by the management, can be properly carried out' (quoted in Tannenbaum, 1966, pp. 12-13).

The consequences of these principles for the work organization can be summarized in the following way.
Standardization of job performance leads to the breaking
up of work into many simple and specialized tasks, each
to be performed by a different worker. The method for
performing the task is predetermined or incorporated into
machinery rather than left to the judgment of the worker.
Work tasks requiring planning, judgment and choice tend
to be separated from the actual production jobs and are
brought together into work roles higher up in the organizational hierarchy. In this way a great proportion of
all work roles at the lower levels of the production organization require the performance of what Fox (1974, p.
16) has called low-disrection work. Thus the behaviour
required is specifically defined; performance is assured
through close supervision, impersonal rules and/or incentive payments; and the co-ordination with other positions
is imposed and standardized. Those who perform low-
discretion work generally derive little intrinsic satisfaction from their work tasks. In such organizations,
involvement of workers tends to become calculative
(Etzioni, 1961, pp. 3-21).

Work tasks requiring high discretion provide an important individual power resource for workers (Crozier, 1964,
pp. 111, 160; Fox, 1974, p. 100). Low-discretion work
decreases the individual power resources of workers by
making them easily replaceable. It thus disarms a major
part of the individual power resources of the workers, and
makes numbers and collective action their main remaining
power resource. The power of management, however, is

also enhanced through the creation of a control hierarchy, where those in work roles requiring high discretion are relatively few and thus can be motivated to comply through combination of higher rewards and better possibilities for moral involvement in the work organization.

This type of work organization does not necessarily follow from the nature of the production tasks as mediated through technology; rather, it appears largely to be a solution to the control needs generated by the conflict of interests between sellers and buyers of labour power. Psychologists engaged as consultants or researchers in industry have exhorted managers to design jobs that provide better possibilities for workers to exercise discretion. Our discussion suggests that the resistance of management to such organizational changes need not be irrational from their own point of view.

It is sometimes argued that, because the same principles of work organization dominate also in communist societies, they are the necessary consequences of technological requirements (e.g. Blauner, 1964). This argument does not make sense, however, unless one is prepared to accept that communist societies have a more equal distribution of power resources and fewer conflicts of interest than is the case in democratic, capitalist societies. The proponents of this argument would probably hesitate - and with good reason - from accepting such an assumption.

It has been suggested that the negative consequences of mechanization for work satisfaction are especially pronounced on a medium level of technology, i.e. in the stage of transfer from craft to mass production. The third step of technological development, process production and automation, is expected to provide much better possibilities for work satisfaction (e.g. Blauner, 1964, pp. 182-3; Dahlström et al., 1966, p. 159). Available evidence, however, gives only partial support to such predictions (e.g. Goldthorpe et al., 1968a; Wedderburn and Crompton, 1972, pp. 135, 150; Gardell, 1971, 1976).

3   INEQUALITY IN JOB SATISFACTION

The foregoing discussion indicates that we can expect the degree of job satisfaction derived from the performance of work tasks and work roles to be unequally distributed in the labour force. Some studies (e.g. Blauner, 1960) support this hypothesis while others (e.g. Jencks et al., 1972, ch. 3) claim that intrinsic job satisfaction has little relationship to occupational status.

For the Swedish population, the relationship between

position in the occupational hierarchy and the level of
intrinsic job satisfaction can be documented by data from
a survey in 1975. (2)   One of the questions put to this
sample was, 'Is your job monotonous?'   Among men and
women employed in mining and manufacturing (N = 1157),
the percentage responding negatively to this question
clearly increases with increasing socioeconomic status as
described by the number of years of formal training required for the job (Figure 5.1).   In this sector, white-

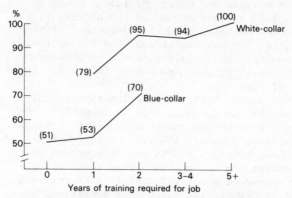

FIGURE 5.1 Percentage reporting variety in job among
persons employed in mining and manufacturing, by type of
job and years of training required for job (N = 1157)

collar jobs generally provide a considerably higher degree
of variety than do blue-collar jobs, even at the same
level of training requirements.   Among blue-collar workers in unskilled and semi-skilled jobs, about one-half
find their jobs monotonous, as against one in twenty among
white-collar employees in medium-level and higher
positions.

   Monotony at work to some extent can be alleviated
through alternation between different simple tasks.   Another work aspect presumably of greater significance for
the individuals is the extent to which their work stimu-
lates them by providing possibilities for learning.   The
above sample was also asked, 'Does your work provide you
with good possibilities to learn new things?'   Here we
find clear differences between the socioeconomic levels
(Figure 5.2).   The proportion reporting good opportunities for learning at work is more than three times higher
among white-collar employees in medium and higher positions than among the unskilled and semi-skilled manual
workers.   Differences between white-collar jobs and blue-
collar jobs on the same level of qualification, however,
are small. (3)

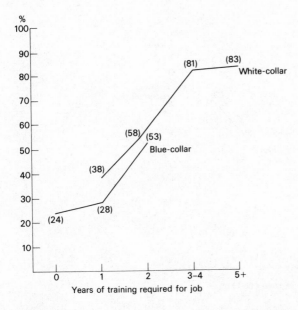

FIGURE 5.2 Percentage reporting good opportunities for
learning new things in job among persons employed in
mining and manufacturing, by type of job and years of
training required for job (N = 1157)

The above results illustrate the important differences
between, on the one hand, 'job enlargement' or job rotation in the sense of alternation between different low-
discretion task and, on the other hand, 'job enrichment',
where the level of discretion of work role is increased
(Paul and Robertson, 1970).   Job enlargement and job
rotation may decrease monotony by providing more superficial variety of the type found in the lower white-collar
jobs, but they do not necessarily provide opportunities
for personality development and 'self actualization'.
   Since position in the socioeconomic hierarchy affects
the level of earnings as well as the level of intrinsic
job satisfaction, we can expect to find a relatively high
degree of 'reward crystallization' in the labour force;
that is, those with higher earnings also tend to have more
interesting and varied work.   This is amply documented in
the above sample of men and women employed in mining and
manufacturing (Figure 5.3).   Both variety at work and
learning opportunities in the job clearly increase with
the level of monthly earnings.

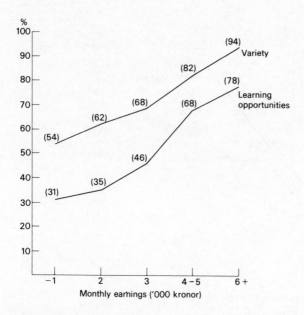

FIGURE 5.3   Percentage reporting variety in job and good
learning opportunities in job among persons employed in
mining and manufacturing, by level of monthly earnings
(N = 1157)

4   WORK CHARACTERISTICS AND JOB SATISFACTION

The characteristics of the work organization and of industrial technologies, which affect the level of intrinsic
job satisfaction among manual workers, have been exten-
sively mapped in numerous sociological and psychological
studies. (4)   Fragmentation of work into specialized and
repetitive jobs that require little skill, provide a low
level of autonomy, constrain freedom of movement and leave
few opportunities to control the pace of work has been
found to reduce the level of satisfaction derived from
work tasks and work roles.
   In our study among the Swedish metal-workers, we can
analyse what factors in the work situation affect *intrinsic job satisfaction,* which is measured by an index made
up of two questions.   One question attempts to tap
directly the type of rewards received from work: 'Some
jobs are performed only in order to get money.   Other
jobs give not only money but also a feeling of personal

satisfaction.   What kind of job is the one you have now?'
'I do it for the money only' was the response chosen by
51 per cent of the respondents, while 39 per cent stated
that their job 'also gives a feeling of personal satisfaction'.   When asked 'Do you think that your job on the
whole is varied or monotonous?' 60 per cent stated that
it is 'very' or 'rather' varied.   With dichotomous items
this index gives a classification of three levels of job
satisfaction.   Only about a third of the workers in our
population has a job that provides both variety and a
feeling of personal satisfaction.   (The details of the
construction of this and of the other indices introduced
later in this book are given in Appendix 2.)

   In this large-scale survey study, we have had to rely
on the workers' own descriptions of their work situation.
Such subjective descriptions have been found to give indications of job attributes that agree well with more
'objective' ratings of job characteristics (Turner and
Lawrence, 1965, pp. 55-8; Gardell, 1971, ch. 6).   The
indicators of work characteristics of relevance to job
satisfaction are described below.

   The *skill requirements of the job* are measured by an
index comprised of two questions: 'How long a time do you
think it takes on the average for a beginner without
training and experience in industry to learn your job?'
and 'Could just about anybody learn to do your job well?'
We find that one-third of the metal-workers have jobs requiring at least one year of learning, while two-thirds
affirm that their jobs do not require any special talent.

   The extent of *machine-paced work* is here measured by a
single question: 'Is your work-pace determined by machines or other equipment?'   In our population 38 per cent
have jobs that are machine-paced at least to a rather
large extent.   An index of *freedom of movement* is based
on two questions: 'Do you now work at an assembly line?'
and 'Are you bound to a particular station during work or
can you move around freely in the department/shop?'   In
our sample 14 per cent work in assembly line production,
while 44 per cent indicate that their freedom of movement
is restricted.   Workers in assembly line production who
indicate that they are bound to a particular station form
the category with the least freedom of movement in this
three-valued index; while workers not working at assembly
lines and indicating that they are allowed to move around
freely make up the category with the greatest degree of
freedom of movement.   An important indicator of the control structure within the firm is the type of wage used.
No less than two-thirds of the workers in our population
work on some kind of piece rate, whereas the others work
on time-rates.

The skill requirements of a job, the degree of control over the pace of work and freedom of movement, as well as the type of remuneration, constitute basic work characteristics, which can be expected to affect the level of intrinsic job satisfaction as defined above.   We can assume, however, that these effects are partly mediated through other aspects of work experiences.   One such intervening factor is the degree of *autonomy* in carrying out the job, measured by the question, 'Do you have great or small possibilities to decide how you are to carry out your work?'   Another relevant intervening variable is whether the work is considered hectic, as measured by the question, 'Do you think that your work is too hectic?' Here 51 per cent indicate relatively high work autonomy while 60 per cent indicate that their job is too hectic.

In the above discussion we use causal reasoning: factors related to production technology and control structure of the work organization are seen to affect experiences of job satisfaction, either directly or via some intervening variables.   The difficulties inherent in testing causal hypotheses in non-experimental, cross-sectional studies are well known (cf. e.g. Blalock, 1964). The empirical data we have available here are the interrelations between the different variables as ascertained in the sample of respondents from our population of metalworkers.   These correlations can be seen as results of the causal factors operating in the population prior to the study.   To increase our understanding of these causal factors we can develop a causal model that is an oversimplified model of reality in the sense that it incorporates only a small proportion of the possible operating factors. Different statistical techniques can be used to evaluate the extent to which the hypothetical causal structure is consistent with the observed correlations.   In this case we use the technique of path analysis to give a quantitative interpretation to the manifestations of an assumed causal structure.   (For readers not familiar with path analysis, a brief introduction is given in Appendix 1.)

The path diagram outlined in Figure 5.4 gives a convenient representation of the causal system assumed to operate in determining the level of intrinsic job satisfaction among the metal-workers in our population.   The four exogenous variables in this hypothetical causal system are found to the left.   As indicated by the two-headed arrows connecting these independent variables, their interrelationships are taken as given, and the correlations between them are indicated on the arrows.   The two technologically determined aspects of the work situation, machine-paced work and freedom of movement, are

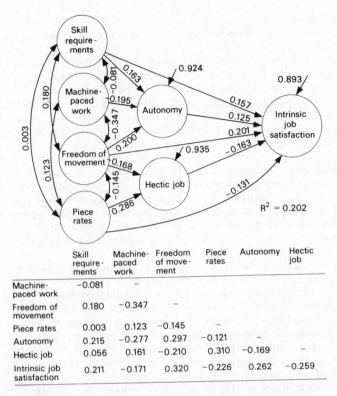

	Skill require- ments	Machine- paced work	Freedom of move- ment	Piece rates	Autonomy	Hectic job
Machine- paced work	−0.081	−				
Freedom of movement	0.180	−0.347	−			
Piece rates	0.003	0.123	−0.145	−		
Autonomy	0.215	−0.277	0.297	−0.121	−	
Hectic job	0.056	0.161	−0.210	0.310	−0.169	−
Intrinsic job satisfaction	0.211	−0.171	0.320	−0.226	0.262	−0.259

FIGURE 5.4 Path diagram and correlations between
variables assumed to affect intrinsic job satisfaction
among metal-workers

relatively strongly correlated. With decreasing freedom
of movement and increasingly machine-paced work, piece
rates become more common. Workers on jobs with higher
skill requirements tend to have greater freedom of movement and slightly less machine-paced work, while the type
of wage is not related to skill requirements.

The effects of the independent variables on the intervening and dependent variables are indicated by one-headed
arrows. The direction as well as the relative size of
these direct effects are given by the path coefficients on
each arrow. We see that freedom of movement has the
greatest direct effect on intrinsic job satisfaction, followed by hectic job, skill requirements, type of wage and
degree of autonomy. (5) Machine-paced work has little
direct effect on intrinsic job satisfaction. Rather, it
has indirect effects on job satisfaction via autonomy of
work, and through its relatively close relationship

with freedom of movement.   Autonomy at work is also affected by freedom of movement, and by skill requirements
for the job.

The extent to which work is considered too hectic is
affected primarily by the type of wage.   Thus piece
rates, by making work more hectic, also have indirect
effects on job satisfaction.   Lack of freedom of movement
also contributes to the feeling that work is too hectic.
Machine-paced work influences the feeling of hecticness
mainly indirectly via its association with freedom of
movement.

Our data thus indicate that, in the metal-working industry, technology has important effects on intrinsic job
satisfaction via constraints on freedom of movement, skill
requirements of the job and machine-paced work.   The control system implied by remuneration through piece rates
affects job satisfaction to about the same extent as the
level of skill. (6)

For good reasons, then, the workers are now voicing
more and more criticism of the extensive reliance on
piece-rates in Swedish industry.   One of our metal-
workers, a man in his forties bending tubes in a hydraulic
press, expressed the views of an increasing number of his
work-mates when he commented in his questionnaire:

'I am highly dissatisfied with the present piece-rate
system.   This baiting of people with seconds and
tenths of seconds is senseless.   Production and the
firm perhaps gain on it, but I doubt that the workers
do so in the long run.   There are many cases where
the workers, sometimes also the relatively young ones,
can no longer suffer the baiting anymore.   Then they
are moved to so called peaceful jobs, often with low
time rates.   There they lose most of what they had
gained before.   In my opinion a monthly wage is the
best one also for the worker.   Perhaps it would somewhat reduce production and thereby also wages.   But
we would certainly last longer, up to pension age, and
everything considered the loss would be small or none.
One's health is worth more than high earnings during a
brief period.'

The variables considered here can account for one-fifth
of the variance in job satisfaction ($R^2 = 0.202$).   This
relatively modest proportion of variance explained depends
partly on crudeness and unreliability in the indicators
used here.

5   CONSEQUENCES OF WORK EXPERIENCES

A large part of the waking hours of adults is spent at
work.   It is therefore of importance to analyse the consequences that different work experiences have upon employees' personality development, level of aspiration,
family relations and participation in civic affairs.   In
other words, focus should be upon what Lazarsfeld and
Thielens (1958, p. 264) have called the 'effective scope'
of an individual, i.e. 'what he perceives, what he has
contact with, and what he reaches for through his interests or his expectations'.

Different hypotheses have been proposed concerning the
consequences of work experiences for the off-the-job lives
of employees (Wilensky, 1960).   Some have hypothesized
that capacities and aspirations are relatively constant:
what cannot be used and satisfied at work is compensated
for off the job.   Others have argued that work and non-
work are now compartmentalized to the extent that work experiences will have only minor effects on activities outside work.   It is also often assumed that 'adult socialization' takes place at work; work experiences thus contribute to or hinder acquisition of skills and capacities,
expectations and aspirations, thereby 'spilling over' into
the non-work sphere of life.   The scarce data that are
available in this context appear to support this 'spill-
over' hypothesis (Meissner, 1971; Karasek, 1976; Westlander, 1976).

Among industrial workers the range of variation in the
degree of job discretion is relatively restricted.   Most
workers are thus subjected to relatively similar - and
negative - work experiences.   We would therefore not
expect work experiences to produce very great variation in
off-the-job activities among industrial workers.   To
attempt to gauge the potential role of the work situation
for off-the-job activities we have constructed an index of
job discretion, simply an additive index based on the previously described measures of skill requirements in the
job and degree of freedom of movement.   In this way, an
index with five levels is obtained: at one end are workers on assembly-line jobs with restricted freedom of
movement and low skill requirements; at the opposite end
are workers whose jobs require considerable training and
allow them to move around freely within the department or
shop.

Of special interest in this context are the effects of
the job situation on organizational and political activities of workers.   To isolate the possible effects of the
level of job discretion from 'contaminating' factors, we

have limited the following analysis to the Swedish-born
men, and have standardized each level of job discretion
with respect to age, marital status, number of children,
size of firm and type of community.   With an increasing
level of job discretion, the proportion of men with high
union activity (7) (i.e. who attend meetings of the workplace union regularly or have elected positions in the
union) tends to increase (Figure 5.5)   Similarly, the
level of political interest (as manifested in reading of
political material in the newspapers and attendance at
election meetings) also tends to increase with level of
job discretion.   Membership in sports clubs, the most
common voluntary organization besides union and political
organizations, also tends to increase with increasing job
discretion.

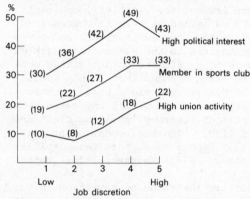

FIGURE 5.5   Percentage with high political interest, high
union activity and membership in sports clubs by level of
job discretion among metal-workers

The relationship between level of job discretion and off-
the-job activities is probably to some extent a result of
self-selection.   The above results indicate, however,
that work characteristics are of importance for the total
life situation and for the 'effective scope' of the employees. (8)

6   IMMIGRANTS AND WOMEN IN THE JOB STRUCTURE

In our population of metal-workers, about every fifth
worker was born abroad.   Migrating manual workers generally tend to filter into the lower positions on the
labour market (e.g. Castles and Kosack, 1973;   Boalt,
1968).   In Sweden immigrants are unevenly distributed

between branches of industry, and tend to be clustered
into sectors with relatively low wages, high unemployment
and an above-average frequency of occupational accidents
(Wadensjö, 1972, p. 172; Haavio-Mannila and Johansson,
1974).

When we compare the job characteristics of immigrants
and Swedish-born workers in our population of metal-workers (after standardizing for sex, age and time of employment in the firm) we find some interesting differences
emerging with respect to work characteristics (Table 5.1).
While immigrant workers do not differ much from the Swedish-born workers in terms of self-rated skill requirements, they tend to hold jobs with more negative work
characteristics.   Thus they are found more often on
assembly-line and machine-paced jobs, as well as on jobs
with a low level of autonomy, with low attention requirements and a high. frequency of piece rates.   Compared with
Swedish-born workers, however, a considerably larger proportion of the immigrants have high wages.   It would thus
appear that to some extent the immigrant workers are 'compensated' for their negative job characteristics with
higher wages;   in fact, they may have 'chosen' disutility
in work for higher wages.

Women are another minority group in the metal-working
industry.   In comparison with their male workmates, the
female metal-workers are found more often on jobs with
low skill requirements, a low level of autonomy, low
attention requirements and relatively low wages (Table
5.2).   Women also work on assembly lines more often than
men but do not have machine-paced jobs, nor have they
piece rates more often than men.

7   ORIENTATIONS TO WORK

Although the majority of manual workers have a low level
of intrinsic job satisfaction, the sociopolitical consequences of these negative work experiences depend upon
the normative expectations concerning rewards from work
that are prevailing among workers.   Without having to
resort to assumptions about universal human needs for
self-actualization, it is apparent that, since most employees are dissatisfied with the performance of low-
discretion work, such work tends to go against important
aspects of their psychological constitution.   This widespread dissatisfaction points to potential expectations
of intrinsic rewards from work tasks and work roles.
Such expectations, however, can be counteracted by circumstances that exert economic pressures on workers, con-

TABLE 5.1 Work characteristics of Swedish-born and foreign-born metal-workers with standardization for sex, age and time of employment in firm

Ethnicity	Low or medium skill requirements	Assembly line job	Machine-paced work	Low autonomy	Low attention requirements	Piece rates	Low or medium wage
Swedish	82	11	40	46	38	66	71
Foreign	85	25	48	58	46	74	59

TABLE 5.2 Work characteristics of male and female metal-workers with standardization for ethnicity, age and time of employment

Sex	Low or medium skill requirements	Assembly line job	Machine-paced work	Low autonomy	Low attention requirements	Piece rates	Low or medium wage
Men	81	13	42	47	39	67	67
Women	96	24	38	63	47	69	79

straining them to limit work to an instrumental role as a
means to high economic returns.   To the extent that workers become 'economistic' in this sense, capitalism tends
to become stabilized, since it can generally provide for
economic rewards from work more easily than intrinsic
ones.   In the debate on the working class in capitalist
society, it is therefore important to discuss the formation of normative expectations of rewards from work, or
orientations to work.

Formation of work orientations

In postwar industrial sociology it has often been assumed
that attitudes and expectations concerning work are formed
primarily through socialization on the job and that they
thus reflect immediate experiences of work tasks and work
roles.   In contrast to this 'technological implications'
approach, Goldthorpe et al. (1968a, 1969) have argued for
an 'action approach' to industrial sociology, where the
actors' own definition of the situation is taken as a
starting point for the analysis.   They thus assert
(Goldthorpe et al., 1968a, p. 138) that
   in *any* attempt at explaining and understanding attitudes and behaviour within modern industry, the probability at least must be recognized that orientations
   to work which employees hold in common will need to be
   treated as an important *independent* variable relative
   to the in-plant situation.
The work orientations that workers *bring to* work are thus
seen as being of key importance.
   The action approach to industrial sociology has been
valuable in drawing attention to the limitations of the
'positivistic' assumption that social structure more or
less directly determines human behaviour, and in underlining the importance of considering how the individual's
definition of the situation mediates between social structure and action.   But this approach must be complemented
by an analysis of the ways in which social consciousness
is socially generated, and the choice of action constrained by social structure. (9)   In any discussion of
work orientations therefore we must also consider the
long-term interaction between social structure and social
consciousness.
   Everything else equal, most employees would probably
prefer a job offering at least a modicum of learning opportunities.   Because of the differing position of employees in social structure, however, expectations concerning rewards from work tend to be socially patterned.

Sub-cultural differences in work orientations can result
from differences in the typical opportunities for intrinsic job satisfaction offered in positions on different
levels in the occupational hierarchy.   For large sectors
of the manual workers, work is, indeed, a disutility, to
be suffered only because it is a necessity.   Within the
range of available positions the option of an interesting
job is in practice often not available.   In the long run
personal experiences of uninteresting jobs can be assumed
to affect expectation of rewards (Dahlström et al., 1966,
pp. 35-53).   Among manual workers, expectations of job
satisfaction may thus gradually fall into the background.
Where such experiences are shared by many over generations, they will affect the sub-culture and thus tend to
make normative expectations of satisfying jobs less
salient in working-class culture.

Socially structured differences in work orientations
can also be created by differences in the strength of economic pressures impinging on individuals.   Where economic
pressures are strong, individuals are often forced to
relegate work to an instrumental role.   Since the intensity of economic pressures varies in the occupational
hierarchy, it may generate sub-cultural differences in
work orientations.

The degree to which extrinsic rewards are associated
with intrinsic ones in the jobs open for individuals at
different levels of the occupational hierarchy, i.e. the
degree of 'reward crystallization' in different sectors
of the labour market, can also be expected to affect work
orientations.   Compared with those higher up in the
occupational hierarchy, manual workers more often are
forced to choose between a more satisfying job or higher
income.   This is indicated, e.g., by the concentration
of incentive payments and shift work to the manual jobs.
Such forced choices may have long-term effects on work
orientations.

The job structure

The degree of 'reward crystallization' in manual jobs is
a structural factor that can be reflected in work orientations.   'Reward crystallization' can decrease as a
result of pressures from two directions.   On the one
hand, workers can successfully put pressures in support
of high wages as a compensation for dissatisfying jobs.
On the other hand, employers may have to offer higher
wages in order to attract workers to dissatisfying jobs.
The extent to which dissatisfying jobs are compensated for

by high wages depends partly on institutional factors, which may vary between countries.

In Swedish industry there has been a remarkably consistent relationship between the average wages of manual workers in different skill groups.   Throughout the present century wages of the semi-skilled workers in the engineering industry have been about 90 per cent of the wages of skilled workers (Olsson, 1970, p. 216; Torsvall, 1974).   The favoured position of skilled workers is also reflected in the job rating systems used in Swedish manufacturing.   While requirements in the areas of skill, responsibility and physical effort make up for three-fourths of the maximum possible ratings, the psychic disutility of the job, reflected for instance in monotony, accounts for only 4 per cent of the maximum possible rating (Johansson, 1967, p. 214).

The impact of institutional factors upon the degree of 'reward crystallization' in subsectors of the labour market is perhaps most clearly seen in the motor industry. In the United Kingdom as well as in the United States, auto assemblies are reputed to offer high wages for alienating work.   Swedish auto assemblies, however, do not pay markedly high wages.   While in the 1950s, wages for male workers in these firms were about 10 per cent above the average of all large engineering firms in the country, this difference had decreased to only 2 per cent by 1972. In the local labour markets where the auto assemblies are found, their wages have not departed markedly from that of other big engineering firms employing primarily semi-skilled labour, and have been clearly below those of big engineering firms with large proportions of skilled workers.

The absence of markedly high wages among manual workers in the Swedish motor industry is primarily a result of the institutional structure of collective bargaining.   Wages are established through industry-wide bargaining, where all workers within the metal-working industry are represented by the same union, which negotiates with the employers' organization covering the whole engineering industry.   This structure neither provides the same possibility for auto workers to press for sectional demands as in countries where they have their own unions, nor enables the auto firms to use high wages as an enticement.

Employers in the Swedish auto industry instead have solved the problem of personnel by decreasing skill requirements of the jobs, and by recruiting immigrant labour.   From 1950 to 1970 the proportion of skilled workers in the auto assemblies decreased from about 40 per cent to about 20 per cent.   Since the 1950s the assembly

lines have been manned almost exclusively by migrant workers, often from rural backgrounds, first from Finland and
later also from southern Europe.

Increasing instrumentalism?

In their landmark study of affluent British workers,
Goldthorpe et al. (1968a, 1971) claimed that in the postwar period increasing economic pressures were gradually
forcing manual workers to accept an instrumental orientation to work, where expectations of high economic returns
become all important.   This hypothesis was generated on
the basis of an empirical study of highly paid manual
workers at Luton, a new and growing industrial centre in
an economically expanding area, noted for its high wages
and having a high proportion of geographically mobile
workers, many of them living in new housing areas. (10)
    The salient findings of the Luton study were that,
while the semi-skilled workers generally experienced
rather intensive dissatisfaction with the low-discretion
work they performed, this dissatisfaction did *not* reflect
in any important way upon their general situation as employees.   These workers appeared to have chosen their
present jobs and retained them primarily because of the
high wages that the jobs offered.   A high degree of dissatisfaction with work tasks was thus not related to any
pronounced tendency to leave their present employment,
and it coexisted with a general satisfaction with the employer (Goldthorpe et al., 1968a, chs 2-4).
    To account for their findings the authors proposed that
the behaviour of the affluent workers in Luton be understood in terms of a markedly instrumental orientation to
work, in which the paramount expectation is for high wages
to support a way of life whose central interests lie primarily outside the sphere of work.   This interpretation
was seen as supported by several circumstances.   In a
situation of relatively full employment where choice was
possible, the reasons given for seeking and for remaining
in the present employment referred to high wages rather
than to intrinsic job satisfaction.   The workers saw employment primarily as a bargain involving money for
effort.   Relatively superficial social relations existed
between workers on the shop floor and were not continued
off work.   A low proportion of workers had joined the
union as a matter of principle or duty.   The aspirations
of the workers were directed more towards securing a continued improvement in their standard of domestic living
than towards occupational advancement (Goldthorpe et al.,
1968a, pp. 144-6).

This markedly instrumental orientation to work, the authors argued, differs significantly from the 'solidaristic' orientation to work found, e.g., among craft workers and more traditional workers, where work is also expected to give important intrinsic rewards. In this solidaristic orientation, work is defined as a group activity; ego-involvement in work is strong; work satisfies expressive needs of the workers; and social relationships at work are transferred into the out-plant life of the workers (Goldthorpe et al., 1968a, pp. 40-2).

Of particular interest in the context of the discussion on the working class in capitalist industrial societies is the hypothesis that the markedly instrumental orientations to work found among the Luton workers are 'proto-typical' of the future; and that these workers reveal a pattern of industrial life which in the fairly near future will become far more widespread. This hypothesis is based on several observations and assumptions. The traditional modes of working-class life supportive of a 'solidaristic' orientation to work are being gradually eroded by urban redevelopment, greater geographical mobility and the demonstration effects of already 'affluent' working-class families. Therefore 'models of new standards and styles of living will become both more evident and more compelling' (Goldthorpe et al., 1968a, pp. 174-5). This is assumed to intensify pressures on the mass of manual workers to increase their consumption power. Thus the unskilled and semi-skilled workers especially feel pressured to seek employment that offers high wages even at the cost of dissatisfying work.

These tendencies are also encouraged by an ongoing reorientation of working-class family life, where a more companionate, partner-like form brings the conjugal family into a more central position in the life of the manual workers. A privatized way of life focused on the conjugal family and an instrumental orientation to work are thus seen as mutually supportive.

Part of the reasoning behind the hypothesis that modern industrial workers will increasingly define work in instrumental terms lies open to question. It is thus difficult to accept the assumption that the pressure to increase consumption power is more intense for the modern industrial workers than it once was for the 'traditional' workers. (11) The high economic pressure on modern industrial workers is seen as a result of 'aspirational deprivation', where aspirations run ahead of the increasing standards of living. In traditional working-class households, economic pressures were intensified by circumstances such as low wages, large families and frequent losses of income owing to periods of unemployment and illness.   The desire to protect the family against these realities can create pressures to increase consumption power, which are at least as strong as those found among affluent modern workers trying to 'keep up with the Joneses' in the consumer society.   The high levels of unemployment in the prewar period must also have limited the possibilities of workers to choose a job according to their preferences.

Another weakness in the reasoning behind this hypothesis is that it cannot account for changes in the structure of rewards in the jobs available for manual workers. Unless the degree of 'reward crystallization' in manual jobs decreases, i.e. the reward structure changes so that higher wages are generally associated with more dissatisfying work, possible pressures towards increasingly instrumental work orientations cannot become manifest.

8   WORK ORIENTATIONS AMONG THE METAL-WORKERS

For several reasons Sweden offers an interesting test case for the hypothesis that orientations to work among industrial workers in advanced societies are becoming increasingly instrumental.   Many of the characteristics assumed to be conducive to instrumental work orientation are present in Sweden.   Continuing urbanization has led to a high degree of geographical mobility.   The majority of the workers in urban areas live in housing developments constructed in the postwar period.   The overall level of affluence in Sweden is also quite high: for instance, at the time of the Luton study the *average* wages of the Swedish metal-workers were about 50 per cent above the lower wage limit required for inclusion in the category of *affluent* workers in Luton.   To the extent that geographical mobility, new housing areas and demonstration effects of new standards and styles of living among 'affluent' working-class families contribute to instrumental orientations, they would probably be quite as pervasive in Sweden as in Britain.

On the basis of data from our study among Swedish metal-workers we can draw some inferences concerning the relative importance of expectations of intrinsic and extrinsic rewards from work for the actions of workers. We have not attempted to measure expectations of rewards from work through direct questions (e.g. Ingham, 1970, pp. 88ff.;   Wedderburn and Crompton, 1972, pp. 96-101). Instead, orientations to work are studied indirectly by measuring the extent to which intrinsic job satisfaction and satisfaction with wages are related to the tendency to quit present employment. (11)

The rationale for the approach used here is that, to the extent that legitimate expectations of rewards from work are not satisfied, the resulting relative deprivation can be expected to increase the propensity to quit present employment, if alternative job opportunities are available. If workers have markedly instrumental orientations to work, dissatisfaction with wages will be related to the propensity to quit present employment, while the level of intrinsic job satisfaction is not expected to affect this propensity. If, however, workers expect intrinsic rewards from work *in addition* to the economic ones, dissatisfaction with both wages and the job itself is expected to affect the propensity to quit present employment.

In our survey, the dependent variable, propensity to quit employment, was ascertained through the following question: 'Do you think that you will quit this firm voluntarily within the next five years?' Of the workers in our population 28 per cent indicated that they 'certainly' or 'perhaps' would do so. Satisfaction with wages was measured by the question, 'Are you on the whole satisfied or dissatisfied with your present hourly wage?' In our population 26 per cent were more or less satisfied with their wages, 37 per cent were 'neither satisfied nor dissatisfied' and 36 per cent indicated they were more or less dissatisfied. Intrinsic job satisfaction was measured through the scale presented earlier in this chapter. Among the metal-workers in our population the tendency to quit present employment falls drastically with age, and is also related to marital status and the presence of minor children in the household. Age, marital status and number of dependents are therefore added as independent variables when we look at the effects of satisfaction with wages and internal job satisfaction on the propensity to quit present employment. Many of the oldest workers would retire within the next five years. The following analysis is therefore limited to workers not older than fifty years.

Multiple-classification analysis (Andrews et al., 1973; Blau and Duncan, 1967, pp. 128-40) provides a convenient technique for describing and summarizing the relationship of a set of 'independent' variables to a 'dependent' variable. (For readers not acquainted with this technique, a brief introduction is given in Appendix 1.) In addition to the empirical or 'unadjusted' percentage expecting to quit present employment for each category of an independent variable, this technique also provides the 'adjusted' percentages on the dependent variable, which result from 'holding constant' or 'standardizing' the other independent variables included in the analysis.   The effects of an independent variable on the propensity to quit employment is measured in terms of the differences in the percentages 'unadjusted' or 'adjusted' found between the various categories on the independent variable.   The effect of an independent variable on the propensity to quit present employment can be summarized in terms of the *eta coefficient* based on the 'unadjusted differences', while the *beta coefficient* summarizes the effects of the independent variable that remain when the other independent variables are 'held constant', i.e. on the basis of the 'adjusted' percentages.

The results of multiple-classification analyses of the effects of the independent variables on the propensity to quit present employment among our metal-workers are presented in Table 5.3.   To save space, only the beta coefficients for each independent variable and the 'adjusted' percentages for the key independent variables, intrinsic job satisfaction and satisfaction with wage, are given.   With age, marital status, number of dependents and satisfaction with wage held constant, the proportion of Swedish-born men indicating that they would quit present employment within five years decreases from 43 to 25 per cent as one moves from low to high intrinsic job satisfaction.   When we move from low to high satisfaction with wages with the corresponding variables held constant, the propensity to quit decreases from 42 to 25 per cent. The beta coefficients for these two variables are of the same size.   These results do thus not support the hypothesis derived from the Luton study with regard to markedly instrumental work orientations.   They indicate, instead, that among our metal-workers expectations of intrinsic job satisfaction are about as important as expectations of high wages.

It is possible however that, owing to variations in the intensity of economic pressures, and as a result of processes of self-selection, pronounced instrumental orientations to work can be found in different subsectors of our population.   The intensity of economic pressures, for instance, can be expected to vary with family cycle, and to be especially pronounced among married men with minor children.   In fact, among married men below the age of thirty years who have dependents, satisfaction with wages has a greater effect on propensity to quit than has intrinsic job satisfaction.   This situation, however, appears to result from the more temporary economic pressures in the early phases of family formation.   Among men who have not yet reached this phase in the family cycle, i.e. single men in the ages below thirty years and without dependents, intrinsic job satisfaction has about the same effects on the propensity to quit as has satisfaction with wages.   Among married men in the ages thirty to fifty years with dependents, who have generally passed the economically most pressing phase in the family cycle, both job and wage satisfaction again have approximately similar effects on the propensity to quit present employment.

The Luton study indicated that geographical mobility of the 'pull' type can be conducive to, as well as supportive of, instrumental orientations to work.   Among the Swedish-born men below fifty years of age, only 40 per cent had spent almost all their lives in the communities in which they were presently living.   When we limit our analysis to men who had lived less than fifteen years in their present community, however, we find that internal job satisfaction has the same effect on quitting propensity as has satisfaction with wages.   French data indicate that industrial workers with rural backgrounds may have instrumental work orientations (Touraine and Ragazzi, 1961).   This is to some extent supported by our study: among those in our sample who had worked for at least one year in agriculture of forestry, satisfaction with wages has a somewhat greater effect on the quitting propensity than has intrinsic job satisfaction.

A study in the United States indicates that city culture can be conducive towards instrumental work orientations (Turner and Lawrence, 1965, ch. 2).   Among the men in our population living in the three largest cities, however, satisfaction with wages and with job have approximately the same effects on the quitting propensity.   The Luton study also indicated that instrumental work orientations were pronounced especially among those socially downward mobile men who had middle-class contacts through the conjugal family, and presumably experienced intensive economic pressures to keep up with their better situated kinsmen.   In the present sample, however, for socially downward mobile men with frequent middle-class contacts, intrinsic job satisfaction has at least the same effect on the quitting propensity as has satisfaction with wages.

Owing to processes of self-selection, we might expect to find workers with markedly instrumental orientations to work in the sectors of the labour market where especially high wages are offered for dissatisfying work.   Thus, for instance, they might tend to gravitate towards big firms, which reputedly offer higher wages but generally less satisfying work conditions than smaller firms (Ingham, 1970).   The comparison of the effects of the two satisfaction variables on the quitting propensity among men in

TABLE 5.3 Effects (beta coefficients) of intrinsic job satisfaction, satisfaction with wages, age, marital status and number of minor children on propensity to quit present employment among different categories of metal-workers and standardized percentages planning to quit present employment by level of intrinsic job satisfaction and satisfaction with wage

Variable	-50 years, all	-30 years, married with minor children	-30 years, single	31-50 years, married with minor children	Swedish-born men -50 years, geographically mobile	-50 years, rural background	-50 years, living in three largest cities	-50 years, socially downward mobile with middle class contacts
Intrinsic job satisfaction	0.159	0.113	0.242	0.226	0.160	0.106	0.167	0.186
Satisfaction with wage	0.145	0.149	0.233	0.202	0.171	0.160	0.141	0.133
Age	0.288	0.017	0.200	0.213	0.236	0.320	0.180	0.325
Marital status	0.097	-	-	-	0.063	0.043	0.200	0.055
No. of children	0.054	0.022	-	0.085	0.057	0.026	0.084	0.147
R^2	0.152	0.027	0.120	0.129	0.100	0.132	0.106	0.124
N	2201	276	401	833	762	565	519	291
Intrinsic job satisfaction	%	%	%	%	%	%	%	%
Low	43	43	60	34	47	37	41	58
Medium	36	36	61	23	40	30	40	53
High	25	50	36	12	29	26	25	37
Satisfaction with wage	%	%	%	%	%	%	%	%
Low	42	51	60	33	46	38	41	53
Medium	30	42	55	14	37	30	34	50
High	25	31	30	19	24	17	23	31

Variable	Swedish-born men			Swedish-born women -50 years	Foreign-born men	Foreign-born women
	-50 years, large plants	-50 years, individual piece rates	-50 years, married, low skill requirements, high wages			
Intrinsic job satisfaction	0.159	0.184	0.098	0.240	0.033	0.320
Satisfaction with wage	0.141	0.210	0.372	0.188	0.313	0.395
Age	0.293	0.285	0.313	0.399	0.158	0.382
Marital status	0.095	0.137	-	0.148	0.101	0.236
No. of children	0.050	0.044	0.120	0.091	0.033	0.347
R^2	0.148	0.209	0.213	0.228	0.122	0.253
N	1082	271		173	350	76
	%	%	%	%	%	%
Intrinsic job satisfaction						
Low	42	44	32	52	36	50
Medium	36	36	22	30	27	33
High	24	23	29	26	26	12
	%	%	%	%	%	%
Satisfaction with wage						
Low	41	47	16	49	54	57
Medium	30	35	15	27	22	45
High	24	21	51	34	20	15

the largest plants in the present study, however, does not
support such an expectation.   In the Swedish context,
piece-rate workers might also be expected to have chosen
higher wages for more hectic and less satisfying work.
According to our data, however, among workers on individual piece rates the two satisfaction variables have similar effects on the propensity to quit.   Only if we focus
on the small category of men where processes of self-
selection and intensive economic pressures appear to coincide - i.e. married men on jobs with low skill requirements but with above-average wages - do we find that intrinsic job satisfaction has little effect on quitting
propensity, while dissatisfaction with wages is strongly
related to this propensity.

Immigrant workers, often from rural backgrounds and
with a short time perspective on their stay in the host
country, might be expected to have markedly instrumental
work orientations.   In fact, we have already noted that
immigrant workers in the metal-working industry tend to
have negative work characteristics but relatively high
wages.   The present analysis gives additional support to
the prediction of instrumental work orientations among
immigrant men: satisfaction with wages has large effects
on the propensity to quit, while intrinsic job satisfaction is only weakly related to this propensity.   Female
workers also might be assumed to have instrumental work
orientations, since they are generally found in low-
qualified jobs with relatively weak ties to the labour
market.   But our data do not support this hypothesis.
Among both Swedish-born and foreign-born women, the two
satisfaction variables have about the same effects on the
propensity to quit the present job.

The above data thus fail to support the hypothesis that
there is any *general* tendency towards markedly instrumental work orientations among the metal-workers in our population.   Instrumental orientations to work, however, are
found in some subgroups: immigrants, migrant workers with
an agricultural background and the young married   men with
minor children, who are in a phase of the family cycle
that traditionally is known to involve strong economic
pressures.   While men under strong economic pressures may
tend to congregate at jobs offering relatively high wages
for unskilled work, these sectors of the labour market are
relatively small.

Our findings do thus not support the hypothesis that
the Luton workers are 'proto-typical' for the industrial
workers of future in their markedly instrumental orientations to work.   It is possible, indeed, that instead of
being proto-typical of the future the Luton workers may

have been rather atypical in their work orientations.
Many of the young married men were in a stage of the
family cycle when economic pressures are most intensive.
Luton was also known as a place where high wages were
offered for semi-skilled work.   Among the workers in
Luton there was an unusually high proportion of geographically mobile men as well as socially downward mobile
persons.   It is thus likely that the high proportion of
men with markedly instrumental orientations to work was a
result primarily of intensive but temporary economic
pressures in the early stages of the family cycle and of
processes of self-selection, which made workers in search
for high wages congregate at this highly visible
community.

9   THE FUTURE OF WORK ORIENTATIONS

We have assumed here that orientations to work among industrial workers are the result of an interaction between
social structure and social consciousness.   Widely shared
psychological characteristics tend to predispose most
people to experience favourably a modicum of variety,
challenge and learning opportunities on the job.   This
provides a latent basis for expectations of some degree
of intrinsic rewards from work.   The extent to which
these expectations become manifest appears primarily dependent on the way in which the 'opportunity structure' on
the labour market is differentiated in terms of the level
of intrinsic rewards offered at different levels of the
occupational hierarchy, the degree of association between
extrinsic and intrinsic rewards and by the economic pressures experienced by the individuals.

    But work orientations among industrial workers cannot
be expected to have direct effects on the structure of
rewards on the labour market.   Although for example
changes in working-class family life may make an increasing proportion of modern workers potentially willing to
forsake intrinsic job satisfaction for higher wages, these
expectations cannot be realized unless the job structure
changes so that intrinsic and extrinsic rewards in manual
jobs become increasingly dissociated.   Neither need expectations of intrinsic job satisfaction among workers be
reflected in the reward structure.   This structure can
instead be assumed to reflect primarily the strategic
choices made by the production organization's dominant
coalition consisting of owners and the upper levels of the
managerial hierarchy.   These strategic choices appear
guided by one overriding decision criterion, the necessity

to make a profit.   Changes in the way in which different
sectors of the labour market are structured in terms of
rewards.would thus appear to depend primarily on the results of considerations and choices by managements.   In
the long run, however, the results of these strategic
choices can be expected to affect the normative expectations of the workers.

The limits for the strategic decisions by managements
that affect the structure of rewards in manual jobs are
set by the distribution of power resources between the
parties on the labour market.   For example, where unemployment is high managements can expect to fill vacancies
irrespective of the degree of job satisfaction offered in
the position, and workers may thus, in the long run, come
to view work primarily in instrumental terms.   In recent
decades, however, relatively full employment and improved
social insurance systems appear to have increased the
power resources of workers in a way that may affect the
strategic choices of management of relevance for the
reward structure.

Relatively full employment, for instance, makes possible a fairly high turnover of personnel.   Improved
health insurance systems permit a higher level of absenteeism.   Turnover and absenteeism probably to some extent
are related to the level of intrinsic job satisfaction.
The increasing costs of personnel turnover and of absenteeism may affect the calculations behind the strategic
choices of management, requiring them to consider the
alternative of providing more attractive jobs in order to
have a more dependable work force.

Most firms can accept rather high calculated risks in
terms of turnover and absenteeism.   But a firm runs a
more serious risk if it cannot recruit enough personnel.
This appears to have been the position of the Swedish auto
manufacturers in the late 1960s, when changes in legislation made the recruitment of immigrant workers more difficult and when the costs of personnel turnover increased.
The auto firms responded by starting programmes for job
enlargement and worked out alternatives to the assembly
line.   Some of these experiments attracted international
attention.   This development illustrates the way in which
the direction of technological changes is shaped by the
priorities of management and by changes in the alternatives available to them.

As a result of political and economic organization, the
power resources of workers have improved during this century.   This has helped them to increase their standard of
living, as well as their protection against circumstances
such as unemployment and illness.   The fatalistic outlook

often assumed to characterize traditional workers was probably an adjustment to the fact that they had little control over the circumstances determining their fate. Such outlooks have probably become less prevalent as a result of these changes. The improving power position of the workers has probably also resulted in increasing levels of aspiration. If workers have latent expectations for intrinsic rewards from work, it is difficult however to see why the expectations generated by their improving power position will be limited to high wages.

The Swedish experience, again, indicates that with an improving standard of living the quality of working life becomes more, not less, important for workers. Beginning in the late 1960s, for instance, there has been a mounting drive among workers and union leaders to decrease the high frequency of piece rates traditionally found in Swedish industry. They argue that piece rates make work more hectic, increase exhaustion and decrease job safety. As a result of this drive, the proportion of time worked on piece rates in Swedish manufacturing decreased from 69 per cent in 1970 to 47 per cent in 1976. The increasing concern with the quality of work environment also illustrates that workers are becoming less willing to trade disutility in work for higher wages.

Alienation of labour thus continues to incite modern workers to question the conditions under which they work and, potentially, the economic structure that generates these conditions.

6 Social relations in work and community

The power of the working class rests in its potential for organization through which the small individual power resources of workers can be combined into concerted, collective action at the workplace and in society. This organizational potential, in turn, to a considerable extent reflects the network of social relations among workers, formed through encounters at work and in the local community. Ongoing changes in production organizations and in community structure may affect the contexts in which social relations among workers develop and may thus be of importance for the organizational potential of the working class.

In the present chapter we will describe and analyse different aspects of social relations among metal-workers, focusing on their potential dependence on the organization of production in the firms where the workers have their jobs and on the structure of the communities in which they live. The purpose here thus is to shed light on the underpinnings of the organizational potential of the working class, and to give a background to our subsequent discussion of the functioning of the union organization. We are interested primarily in the consequences, or objective role, of social relations among workers rather than in their expressive role as sources of satisfaction of affective needs. A distinction must also be made between the 'horizontal' relationships among workers and the 'vertical' relations between workers and managements.

1 THE ROLE OF TECHNOLOGY

Social interaction in the work situation takes place in a setting that has been more or less consciously structured to facilitate achievement of the goals of the production

organization.   Central features of this setting are production technology, and the firm's control system.   The
concept of technology is surrounded by some confusion.
For the present purposes, however, we can say that technology includes 'the plants, machines, tools and recipes
available at a given time for the execution of the production task', while the controle structure or the administrative system of the firm refers to 'the supervisory
structure and other arrangements made to carry out and
control the production of the organization' (Reeves,
Turner and Woodward, 1970, pp. 4-5).

The influential 'technological implications' approach
to industrial sociology assumes that the production technology of the firm largely determines worker behaviour by
prescribing specific actions or goals, and by constraining
and structuring opportunities of workers to engage in
particular kinds of behaviour (Woodward, 1965, 1970;
Emery and Trist, 1960; Kuhn, 1961; Sayles, 1958; Scott
et al., 1956; Perrow, 1967).   The quality of industrial
relations in the firm is also assumed to be determined
mainly by technology which further, at least in the short
run, sets limits to the control structure of the organization.   The change from a medium level of mechanization,
including e.g. assembly-line technology, to a high level
exemplified by process technology has been assumed to
provide good opportunities for the moral integration of
workers into the firm and thus for an improvement of the
vertical social relationships at work (Blauner, 1964).

This strong emphasis on the role of technology in the
shaping of social life within a plant has been criticized
by proponents of the social action approach, who stress
the importance of the worker's own definition of the situation (Goldthorpe et al., 1968a; Silverman, 1970).
Their criticism centres on the necessity to complement an
analysis of attitudes and actions of workers in the plant
by considering the expectations that workers bring to
work, and their definitions of the work situation.   These
definitions are related to their out-plant roles as members of families, communities and social classes.   According to the social action approach, the role of technology in structuring work-related social relations is
thus limited and mediated through the workers' definitions
of their work situation.

As previously indicated, the sample in the metal-workers' study was selected so that firms with different
types of technologies would be represented.   We can thus
attempt to analyse to what extent and in what respect
technological variables are related to social life within
these firms.   In attempting to classify our firms

according to the predominant type of technology, we use a
modified version of the well-known typology of Woodward
(1965), who proposed a threefold classification of production technologies into process, large-batch, and small-
batch (or unit) technologies.

Pure process technologies are not represented in our
sample, although a small proportion of the steelworkers
have jobs in such technologies.   Auto assembly firms,
steel mills and shipyards in our sample are sufficiently
homogeneous and different from other plants to merit separate categories.   As described in Appendix 1, four
large firms of each type are represented here.   On the
basis of the nature of their production, the remaining
thirty-six firms are divided into two classes, large-
batch firms and small-batch (or unit) firms.   Firms with
small-batch technologies, on average, have a considerably
higher proportion of skilled workers than firms with
large-batch technologies.   The small-batch as well as the
large-batch firms differ in size.   We thus end up with a
classification of our firms into the following types,
based on the predominant technologies;   (i) Large-batch
firms (small, medium and large);   (ii) Auto assembly firms;
(iii) Steel mills;   (iv) Small-batch firms (small, medium
and large);   and (v) shipyards.

It must be remembered, however, that there often is a
considerable technological variation within the firms.
In this large-scale, anonymous survey of metal-workers it
was not possible to map the intra-firm variation in technology by any 'objective' descriptions of the respondents'
own particular technological environment.   In order to
describe different aspects of this environment, we thus
had to rely on information given by the respondents themselves.   As in chapter 4, we will characterize the respondent's work by indicators referring to skill requirements, freedom of movement, degree of autonomy, attention
requirements, 'hectic-ness', the extent to which the job
is machine-paced and the degree of intrinsic job satisfaction.

Two additional indicators of the technologically structured work environment among our metal-workers will also
be used.   One indicator refers to the extent to which co-
operation with other workers is required for the successful performance of works tasks, something that can be expected to structure social interaction.   An index of
required co-operation at work is constructed on the basis
of the following two questions: 'Do you have to co-
operate with others when you perform your own work?' and
'Do you and your workmates have to talk and discuss with
each other in order to get the job done?'   (Cf. Appendix
2.)

Another aspect is the degree of internal stratification within a department or shop. This affects the extent to which the workers have similar or different economic interests as well as the conditions for interaction between them. An index of *internal stratification in the department* has been constructed on the basis of the following three questions: 'Are the differences in wages between various workers in your department/shop small or large?'; 'Are the differences in responsibility between various workers in your department/shop small or large?'; and 'Do you think that there are workers in your department/shop who think that they have better or more respectable jobs than the others?' (Cf. Appendix 2.)

2   THE FLOW OF TALK

This section and the three that follow examine different aspects of social relationships around work among Swedish-born men and women. The situation of immigrants will be analysed in a separate section. We begin with an elementary but basic form of social behaviour - the flow of verbal communication. The frequency with which workers talk to each other at the place of work can be assumed to depend on their opportunities and needs to communicate with other workers. Opportunities are affected by the extent to which the job provides the possibility to talk, e.g. while taking a break, but also by the extent to which other workers are found within hearing. Talking may be either instrumental, to get the work done, or expressive, to satisfy social needs.
The amount of talking with other workers at the place of work is measured by three questions in the survey: 'Does it happen that you talk with other workers when you take a break, e.g. to smoke, to go to the toilet or to take a rest?'; 'Does it happen that you talk with other workers at meal breaks?'; and 'Do you have an opportunity to talk with other workers while you attend to your own work?' This last-mentioned question thus refers to an opportunity for talking rather than the actual realization of it. On the basis of these three questions, an additive index of *frequency of talking with workmates* is constructed. Somewhat more than one-third of the metalworkers in our population responded 'very often' or 'fairly often' to all three of the above questions, while somewhat less than one-third did so to none or only one of these questions (cf. Appendix 2).
Figures not given here indicate that, between firms with different production technologies, there are only

minor differences in the average level of talking with
workmates.   The frequency of talking, however, is clearly
related to the technologically structured immediate work
environment and to the nature of the respondents' work
tasks.   A path analysis indicates that, with decreasing
attention requirements of the job, i.e. when work can be
performed even while thinking of something else, the frequency of talking increases (Figure 6.1).   Talking at
work may thus sometimes be a relatively superficial activity.   As might be expected, freedom of movement also
increases the frequency of talking, as does the extent to
which the worker has to co-operate with others in performing his job.   With increasing age, however, frequency of
talking decreases.   These four factors can account for
15 per cent of the variance in the frequency of talking.

3 WORKGROUP MEMBERSHIP AND COHESIVENESS

To what extent are the metal-workers in our population
members of informal workgroups, and how common are cohesive workgroups on the shopfloor?   These questions are
relevant for the hypothesis that modern industrial workers
have a predominantly instrumental orientation to work and
therefore have a low emotional involvement in shopfloor
social relations.   When asked 'Do you have a feeling that
you belong to a tightly knit group or gang in your depart-
ment/shop?', 48 per cent affirmed that this was the case.
The feeling of personal attachment to one's current workmates was also gauged by the following question: 'Suppose
that there is to be a large-scale reorganization at this
firm so that many workers must move to new places of work.
Which ones would you then most prefer to have as closest
workmates?'   In such a situation 42 per cent would have
preferred their present workmates, whereas most others
stated that it did not matter or that they did not know.
    On the basis of the above two questions, an index of
workgroup membership was formed (cf. Appendix 2).   About
one-third of the workers in our population have neither a
feeling of belonging to a tightly knit workgroup, nor a
preference for their present workmates in case of a
departmental organization.   Somewhat less than one-third,
however, feel both that they belong to such groups and
that they would prefer their present workmates.
    Two questions in the survey gauge to what extent the
metal-workers perceive that there are cohesive workgroups
in their departments.   On a direct question, 'Is it
common that the workers in your department/shop stick
together to the extent that one could speak about tightly

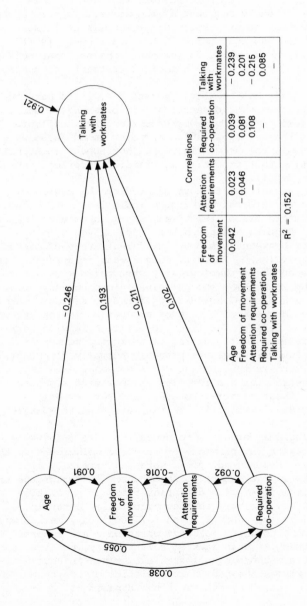

	Freedom of movement	Attention requirements	Required co-operation	Talking with workmates
Age	0.042	0.023	0.039	− 0.239
Freedom of movement	—	− 0.046	0.081	0.201
Attention requirements		—	0.108	− 0.215
Required co-operation			—	0.085
Talking with workmates				—

Correlations

$R^2 = 0.152$

FIGURE 6.1 Path diagram indicating effects of age, freedom of movement, attention requirements and required co-operation in job on frequency of talking with workmates at the place of work (Swedish-born workers only)

knit groups or gangs?', 37 per cent stated that this was
'fairly common' or 'very common'. When asked, 'Do you
have a feeling that the unity among the workers in your
department/shop is good or bad?', 56 per cent state that
it is 'fairly good' or 'very good'. On the basis of
these two questions an index of perceived *group cohesiveness* was formed. The marginal distribution of this
index shows that 29 per cent of the workers in our population think that tightly knit workgroups are at least
fairly common and that unity in the department is at
least fairly good, while 33 per cent consider that neither
of these conditions holds in their department (cf Appendix
2).

On the basis of the above percentages, it is not easy
to evaluate the level of emotional involvement of our
metal-workers in informal workgroups on the shopfloor.
In view of the relatively high turnover among these workers, however, the above figures do not appear to support
an assumption that primarily superficial shopfloor social
relations prevail.

An analysis of the factors related to the degree of
membership in informal workgroups indicates that technological factors are of relatively small importance in this
context. Figures not given here show only negligible
differences between firms with different types of production technologies. Further, only a weak relationship is
found between the technologically structured work situation of the respondent and perceived group cohesiveness.
Workgroup membership, however, is found to decrease with
age but to increase with time of employment in the present
firm (Figure 6.2). The frequency of talking with workmates is related to the degree of workgroup membership,
and these two variables are probably mutually dependent.
Workgroup membership also increases somewhat with the
degree to which the job requires co-operation with other
workers. These factors, however, account for only a
relatively small proportion in the variation in workgroup
membership.

Technological factors also appear to have relatively
weak effects on the presence of cohesive workgroups on the
shopfloor. Figures not given here indicate only minor
differences in the extent to which cohesive workgroups are
reported from firms with different types of production
technologies. Nor are the technologically determined
aspects of the respondent's job related in any marked way
to the extent to which cohesive workgroups are reported in
the department. This lack of relationship, however, can
be in part a methodological artefact, since in heterogeneous departments the job characteristics of the respondent
need not be shared by others in the department.

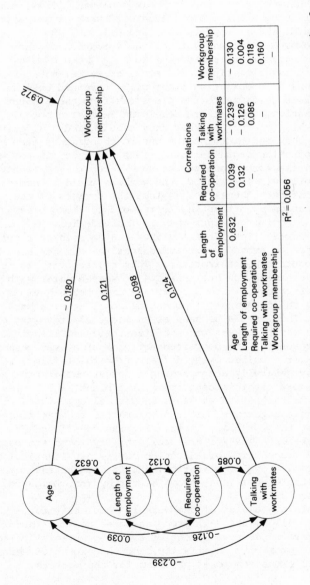

	Length of employment	Required co-operation	Talking with workmates	Workgroup membership
Age	0.632	0.039	− 0.239	− 0.130
Length of employment	−	0.132	− 0.126	0.004
Required co-operation		−	0.085	0.118
Talking with workmates			−	0.160
Workgroup membership				−

Correlations

$R^2 = 0.056$

FIGURE 6.2 Path diagram indicating effects of age, length of employment, required co-operation in job and frequency of talking with workmates on degree of membership in an informal workgroup at the place of work (Swedish-born workers only)

4   THE WORKERS' COLLECTIVITY

It has often been observed that, among the rank-and-file
participants in organizations (Etzioni, 1961), social
norms tend to develop which to some degree oppose the
norms that the organizational leadership stands for and
wants to uphold.   For instance, such counter-norms have
been observed in prisons, schools (Coleman, 1961), military training camps (Korpi, 1964) and work organizations
(Lysgaard, 1961; Lipset, Trow and Coleman, 1956).

A comprehensive analysis of the formation of such
counter-norms in work organizations has been made by
Lysgaard (1961).   In a case study of worker-management
relations in a Norwegian paper mill, Lysgaard observed
that, as a response to the pressures from the production
organization, the workers developed defensive social
norms which prescribed that they should find collective
rather than individual solutions to the demands made by
the production organization.   Thus, as subordinated members in the work organization upon which they were dependent for their livelihood, the workers could to some
extent protect themselves against the demands of the
organization by attempting to respond to these pressures
as a collectivity rather than as individuals.

The workers' collectivity thus can be seen as a buffer
developed to protect workers against the demands made by
the production organization.   This collectivity lacks
formal organization but consists of shared norms with related sanctions, which specify the expected behaviour of
workers in situations of potential conflict with management.   Thus it can be seen as an informal organization
through which workers can mobilize their small individual
power resources for concerted action against management.
The workers' collectivity differs from the informal workgroup by generally encompassing a larger membership, e.g.
the workers within a department or a plant, and by involving norms that stand at least in partial opposition to the
norms of management.   It can be seen as the manifesta-
tion, on the workplace level, of class consciousness of
the workers.   The workers' collectivity forms the basis
for the trade union organization but is not identical with
the formal union organization, and to some extent may even
oppose the higher level union hierarchy (cf. Lysgaard,
1965, pp. 99ff.).

In his discussion of the workers' collectivity,
Lysgaard (1961, chs 7-9) proposes three general factors
which favour the development of a strong workers' collectivity: proximity, similarity, and the extent to which
the work situation poses problems for the workers.

Proximity refers the conditions that facilitate interaction between workers in a plant or department, e.g.
working conditions affecting the opportunities for spon-
taneously selected interaction and turnover of personnel.
Similarity is related to the possibilities of the workers
to identify with each other, e.g. the absence of status
demarcation among workers.   The extent to which the work
situation poses problems for the workers, in Lysgaard's
view, depends primarily on the degree of pressures exerted
by management, on the degree to which workers are dependent
on the firm for employment, and on the leadership style in
the firm.

The hypotheses that similarity and proximity facilitates the development of workers' collectivities appears
well founded, while the hypothesis that, the greater the
problems that workers must face, the stronger the collectivity, requires qualification.   It appears that the
strength of the workers' collectivity both reflects and
affects the difference in power resources between management and workers.   We can expect that the more the balance of power resources favours management, as indicated
e.g. through a high level of unemployment, the weaker is
the workers' collectivity and the more problems do the
workers have to cope with in the work situation.   The
extent to which problems posed for the workers are amenable to collective rather than individual solutions also
appears relevant.   Where problems can or must be solved
collectively, collective solutions more probably will be
attempted, leaving a residue in the form of a stronger
workers' collectivity.   On a more general level, the
strength of the workers' collectivity would appear to be
dependent on factors that facilitate 'voice' rather than
'exit' in dissatisfying situations (Hirschman, 1970).

In the metal-workers' study the strength of the workers' collectivity is measured at the level of the department or shop.   The department, generally a relatively
well-defined and homogeneous unit which workers can be
expected to know fairly well, is often a natural basis for
collective action.   The respondents were asked to indicate the probability of mobilization for collective action
in four hypothetical situations of conflict affecting
worker-management relations.

A typical situation of breach against the norms of the
workers' collectivity is outlined in the following question: 'Suppose that a worker in your department/shop is
trying to get in good with his superiors.   Would you bet
that the other workers can get together and see that he
changes?'   Somewhat less than half, 44 per cent, of the
respondents answered 'yes, definitely' or 'yes, perhaps'

to this question.   Another situation is the following:
'Suppose that a new man comes to your department/shop and
works entirely too hard.   Would you bet that the other
workers can agree to seeing that he slows down?'   A somewhat larger proportion, 55 per cent, responded affirmatively to this question.

No less than 70 per cent responded affirmatively to the
question, 'Suppose that the superiors treat a worker in
your department/shop in a way that most think is unfair.
Would you bet that the other workers can agree to seeing
that he receives a fair treatment?'   The affirmative proportion is even higher (80 per cent) on the following
question: 'Suppose that there is a foreman or time-study
man in your department/shop who is trying to do the workers a bad turn and lower their earnings.   Would you bet
that the workers can agree on doing something to put an
end to it?'   A greater probability of mobilization thus
is expected in situations where action is to be taken
against management representatives rather than against
workmates.   The above four questions are combined into an
index of *strength of the workers' collectivity* (see Appendix 2).

What factors affect the perceived strength of the workers' collectivities among our metal-workers?   Two measures regarding characteristics of the department as perceived by the respondent are related to the strength of
the workers collectivity (Figure 6.3).   Both refer to
the degree of heterogenity in the department.   An increasing proportion of immigrants in the department is

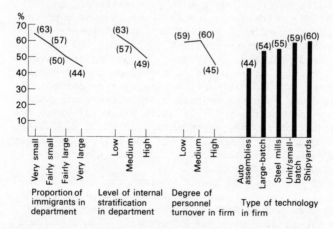

FIGURE 6.3 Percentage reporting strong workers' collectivity in department among Swedish-born metal-workers in
different types of departments and firms

related to a decreasing strength of the workers' collectivity. An increasing level of internal stratification within the department also tends to decrease the strength of the workers' collectivity.

On the basis of information supplied by the firms, we can classify them according to the degree of personnel turnover during the two years preceding the study.   Firms with the highest level of turnover are found to have weaker workers' collectivities than the others.   The predominant type of technology in the firm is also related to the strength of the workers' collectivity.   As might be expected, the workers' collectivity is weakest in auto assembly plants.   Steel mills and plants with large-batch production have moderately strong workers' collectivities while the strongest collectivities are found in firms with small-batch or unit production, including the shipyards. Figures not given here indicate that size of firm is not related to the strength of the workers' collectivities.

The survey among the metal-workers also provides some opportunities to analyse how worker-management relations are affected by variations in the strength of the workers' collectivity.   Two questions in the survey are used as a basis for an index of the *selective power of immediate superiors*: 'Do your immediate superiors have any possibilities to give favours to a worker whom they approve of strongly?' and 'Do your immediate superiors have any possibilities to "get at" a worker whom they dislike?' (see Appendix 2).   With increasing strength of the workers' collectivity the proportion reporting high selective power of superiors tends to decrease, at least when we move from weak to medium strength of the collectivity (Figure 6.4)   This finding is in line with the assumption that the collectivity tends to function as a buffer or protective net in relation to management.

But an increasing strength of the workers' collectivity should also result in, from the workers' point of view, more satisfactory worker-management relations.   Three questions in the survey are combined into an index of *managerial consideration in department*: 'Do you find it easy or difficult to get management to correct something that creates dissatisfaction in your department/shop?';   'Do you think that management attempts to take into consideration what the workers think about different conditions in your department/shop?'; and 'Do you think that planning and preparation of work in your department/shop is good or bad?' (cf. Appendix 2).   When we move from weak to medium-strong workers' collectivities, the proportion reporting high managerial consideration in the department increases.

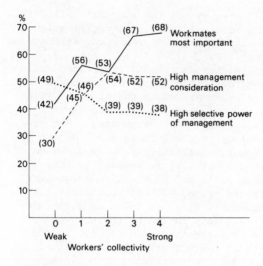

FIGURE 6.4 Percentage reporting high selective power of
management, high management consideration in department
and other workers as having the most important sanctions
among metal-workers, by strength of workers' collectivity
(Swedish-born only)

The strength of the workers' collectivity can also be expected to affect the relative importance of sanctions from
workmates and from management.   The relative importance
of the sanctions was measured by a single question:
'Which would you bet would be worst in your department/
shop, to be on bad terms with management or to be on bad
terms with the other workers?'   The proportion indicating
that workmates have the most important sanctions tends to
increase when we move from weak to strong workers' collectivities. (1)

5   TECHNOLOGY AND SOCIAL RELATIONSHIPS

The foregoing analysis indicates that the role of technology in shaping social life within the firms in our sample
is important in some respects but insignificant in others.
Generally the technologically determined work tasks and
work roles are of great significance for structuring the
more superficial aspects of social relationships, primarily the extent of talking with workmates.   They appear to
be considerably less important, however, for determining
more enduring aspects of social relationships like integration into workgroups, cohesiveness of workgroups and

the strength of workers' collectivities.   Our data, however, indicate that firms with small-batch or unit technologies with jobs having rather high skill requirements
provide more favourable opportunities for the development
of strong workers' collectivities than do firms with
large-batch technologies, where the majority of the jobs
have low skill requirements.

Although the firms in the metal-working industry cover
the most prevalent types of technologies found in manufacturing, the entire range of technologies is not represented in our sample of firms.   Thus for example process
technology is only partially represented by the steelworks
in our sample.   Process technology may in some respects
provide more favourable opportunities for the formation of
social relationships among workers (Wedderburn and Crompton, 1972;   Gardell, 1971), although it need not lead to
the high degree of vertical integration between workers
and management as claimed by Blauner (1964) among others.

Within the range of technological variation found in
our sample of firms, only the extreme case of assembly-
line technology tends markedly to affect workgroup membership, cohesiveness of workgroups and strength of workers'
collectivities (Table 6.1).   Among Swedish-born men those

TABLE 6.1 Percentage reporting high workgroup membership,
high group cohesiveness and strong workers' collectivity
among workers on assembly lines and on other types of
jobs, by sex and ethnicity

	Type of job	Swedish-born		Foreign-born	
		Men	Women	Men	Women
High work-group membership	Assembly line	22	26	22	25
	Other	31	18	20	15
High group cohesiveness	Assembly line	19	10	31	26
	Other	31	20	26	19
Strong workers' collectivity	Assembly line	51	38	48	63
	Other	56	49	49	39

working on assembly lines thus report less favourable conditions in all these respects than those in other types of
jobs.   The limitations of the technological factor, however, is indicated by the fact that foreign-born women on
assembly lines actually report more favourable conditions
in these respects than other foreign-born women.   This is
probably related to the fact that in our sample the
foreign-born women on the assembly lines work in ethni-

cally more homogeneous environments than do other immigrant women.

6   OFF-THE-JOB SOCIAL RELATIONSHIPS

In the present context off-the-job social relationships
of workers are of interest since they can reinforce or
weaken the effects of the encounters and influences among
workers at the place of work.   One relevant aspect here
is the extent to which contacts with other workers from
the firm are maintained during leisure.   The more that
social relationships off the job overlap with those at
work, the more we would expect them to reinforce work-
related interests and provide informal channels for influences and information between workers.

In the survey among the metal-workers, a set of questions was aimed at ascertaining the extent and type of
off-the-job social relationships.   Two of these questions
were combined into an index of *off-the-job contacts with
workers from the firm*: 'Does it happen that you visit
other workers *who work in this firm* at their homes or that
they visit your home?' and 'With whom do you mostly associate in your leisure time, with people *who work here
at this firm* or with *other* acquaintances?'   Not less than
two-thirds of the respondents indicate that they meet with
other workers from the firm at each others' homes at least
a few times a year, and 40 per cent indicate that they
associate at least as much with workers from the firm as
with other acquaintances during leisure (cf. Appendix 2).
Among our metal-workers the level of off-the-job contacts
with other workers from the firm thus appears to be relatively high.

The structure of the local community can be expected
to influence the pattern of off-the-job contacts of workers, including the extent to which contacts established
at work are continued at leisure.   In our sample widely
different types of communities are represented.   On the
one hand there are industrial communities, where manual
workers comprise a clear majority of the economically
active population.   Some of these industrial communities
are dominated by a single firm.   On the other hand we
have communities where the economy is based primarily on
services and commercial activities and where the population is more mixed in terms of socioeconomic status.   The
three largest cities in Sweden belong to this category,
as do some of the smaller communities represented in our
study.

If off-the-job social contacts were made randomly, we

would expect the frequency of contacts with workers from
the same firm to increase with the size of the firm and
to decrease with the size of the community.   In fact,
such trends can be observed among the metal-workers in
our population.   The proportion reporting a high level
of off-the-job contacts with other workers from the firm
thus tends to increase with size of firm;   it is smallest
in the big cities and greatest in communities where the
firm dominates on local labour market, i.e. in one-plant
communities or in small communities (Table 6.2).

TABLE 6.2 Percentages with a high level of off-the-job
contacts with workers from the firm, by size of firm and
type of community (Swedish-born only)

Type of community	Size of firm		
	Small	Medium	Large
Big cities	14	23	36
One-plant towns			65
Other industrial communities	33	48	48
Mixed communities		37	
Small communities	47		

   Although structural factors thus appear to affect the
extent of off-the-job associations with workmates, there
is considerable variation between individuals in this
respect.   This variation depends partly on the extent to
which the individual has other bases for social contacts
such as the family and the community, which offer alternatives to the social contacts at work.   This is evident
when we relate contacts with workmates to marital status
and length of time in the community (Figure 6.5).   The
frequency of off-the-job contacts with workmates is generally lower among married as compared with unmarried
persons, and it decreases with the length of time one has
lived in the community.   The place of work is thus of
greater importance as a basis for social relationships
for those who do not have a conjugal family and for those
who have not had the time to build up a social network in
the community.
   To a considerable degree, work-related social contacts
tend to overlap with kinship relationships.   No less
than 40 per cent of our metal-workers indicate that they
have at least one close relative who is a worker in their
firm, and 13 per cent indicate that they have a close
relative among their firm's white-collar employees.   As
one might expect, the extent to which respondents' rela-

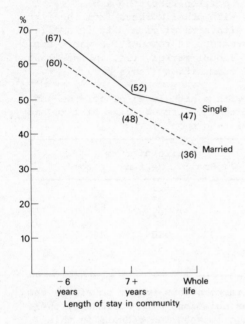

FIGURE 6.5 Percentage indicating high level of off-the-
job contacts with workers from the same firm, by marital
status and length of stay in community (Swedish-born
workers only; standardization for age)

tives are employed in the same firm varies with community
type and size of firm in the same way as does the frequency of off-the-job contacts with workmates.   Among
workers in big firms in industrial communities, every
second employee has a close relative who is a worker in
the same firm, while about every fifth respondent has a
close relative who is a white-collar employee in the firm.
   The social relationships of our metal-workers are
dominated by contacts with other workers. Only 12 per
cent of the Swedish-born metal-workers indicate that they
'visit any white-collar employees or someone with his own
business', or that such persons visit their home 'often'
or 'fairly often'. This proportion appears quite constant regardless of differences in types of communities.
Industrial workers in the big cities and in the 'mixed'
communities would thus appear to have as homogeneous

working-class social contacts as workers in communities
dominated by industry.   The differences between community
types are related primarily to the extent to which workers
associate with other workers from the same firm at leisure
as well as to the proportion of industrial workers in
these communities.

7   THE IMMIGRANTS

As a result of language difficulties and a higher degree
of mobility between firms and communities, we would expect
immigrant workers to be less involved in social relationships at the place of work than the Swedish-born workers.
This assumption is partly borne out by our study, where
the foreign-born workers show a somewhat lower level of
integration into workgroups and a somewhat lower frequency
of talking with workmates than the Swedish-born workers
(Figure 6.6).   The foreign-born workers, however, have a
higher frequency of contact with other workers from the
firm during leisure than the Swedish-born workers.   For
the   immigrants the place of work is thus generally the
main basis for social contacts in the new country.

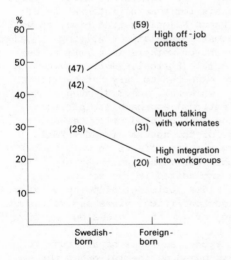

FIGURE 6.6 Percentage reporting high frequency of off-
the-job contacts with other workers from the firm, high
frequency of talking with workmates and a high level of
integration into workgroup among Swedish-born and foreign-
born metal-workers (standardization for age, sex, marital
status and length of residence in community)

Foreign-born workers are a relatively small minority
in the Swedish labour force.   To some extent they tend
to be concentrated into certain types of firms and jobs.
Thus among the metal-workers, only 12 per cent of the
Swedish-born workers but 27 per cent of the foreign-born
men and 49 per cent of the foreign-born women indicate
that they work in departments with a very large proportion
of workers of foreign descent.   The immigrants, however,
are a heterogeneous minority and we find few signs of
ethnically based cohesive subgroups among them.   Thus,
the extent to which immigrants are integrated into workgroups is not clearly related to the proportion of immigrants in the department.   Among foreign-born women,
however, who are clustered into relatively few firms and
departments, ethnicity appears to be the basis for strong
workers' collectivities and good workgroup integration,
which as we have seen also can overcome such adverse
working conditions as assembly-line technology.

8   THE FIRM AS AN EMPLOYER

Conflict of interest, inherent in the relationship
between sellers and buyers of labour power, makes normative integration of workers in a firm problematic.   There
appears to be no solid basis for a moral integration of
the type assumed in the Human Relations tradition, as well
as much of mainstream industrial relations writing.   Generally we expect involvement of workers in a firm to be
calculative rather than moral (Etzioni, 1961).   Views on
the firm, however, can be expected to vary between firms
and between categories of workers.   As indicated above,
the 'technological implications' approach to industrial
sociology assumes that the type of production technology
is of crucial importance for the nature of industrial
relations within the firm via its effects on work tasks
and work roles.   Attitudes and values that workers bring
to the place of work are emphasized in the action
approach.   Also, from a wider sociological point of view,
we would expect general sociopolitical views and values of
the workers to affect and reflect their views on the firm
in which they work.
    In the metal-workers' study, an index of *attitude to
the firm as an employer* is based on the following three
questions: 'Do you think that the workers in this firm
consider it to be, on the whole, a good place to work in
or a bad place to work?'; (2) 'Do you sometimes have a
feeling that the firm puts pressures on the workers in an
uncomfortable way to get out as much as possible from

them?'; and 'Do you sometimes have a feeling that the
firm treats the workers like machines?'   In our population of metal-workers 71 per cent perceive that their
firm is considered to be a 'very good' or a 'rather good'
place to work in.   Every second respondent, however,
states that they feel 'very often' or 'rather often' that
the firm puts unreasonable pressures on the workers; and
45 per cent feel that 'very often' or 'rather often' the
firm treats workers like machines (Appendix 2).

Another aspect of the relationship of the workers to
the firm concerns the perception of 'distributive justice'
in the wage-effort bargain.   More than half (58 per
cent) of the metal-workers in our population do not think
that workers in their firm 'receive a decent share of the
money which the firm takes in', and 51 per cent say that
the workers in the firm cannot come up to 'decent earnings
without having to drudge and toil in an uncomfortable way'
(cf. Appendix 2).   The responses thus indicate that the
level of normative integration with the firm is not very
high.

A multiple-classification analysis indicates that satisfaction with one's own wage has the strongest effect on
satisfaction with the firm (Table 6.3)   Intrinsic job
satisfaction, however, also is clearly related to the
views on the firm as an employer.   This finding again
contradicts assumptions of widespread and strong instrumental orientations to work among our metal-workers which
would colour their whole situation as employees, including
the views on the employer.   While age is not systematically related to satisfaction with the firm, the longer
the term of employment, the more likely a worker is to be
dissatisfied with the firm.   General sociopolitical views
of the respondent are also related to his attitude towards
the firm.   With a decreasing awareness of class differences in society (see Appendix 2), satisfaction with the
firm increases.   Satisfaction also tends to increase when
we move from left to right on the political spectrum.   To
a rather large extent, then, the views on the employer are
coloured by the general sociopolitical outlooks of the
workers.

Technological factors appear to be of some relevance to
the workers' views on their employer.   For instance, with
an increasing freedom of movement, attitudes to the firm
tend to become more positive.   In the auto assemblies we
find the most negative views on the firm, while the most
positive views are found in the steelworks, where especially workers in jobs with low skill requirements have
markedly positive views of the employer.   In firms with
unit or small-batch technologies, however, views on the

TABLE 6.3 Multiple-classification analysis of views on firm as an employer (57% 'positive' in population; N = 3996)

Independent variable; category			Positive Unadjusted %	Adjusted %	Eta	Beta
Sex	Men		56	57	0.038	0.011
	Women		62	55		
Ethnicity	Swedish-born		55	56	0.056	0.019
			62	58		
Satisfaction with wage	Very satisfied	1	70	68	0.216	0.195
		2	66	64		
		3	63	63		
		4	44	45		
	Very dissatisfied	5	41	43		
Perceived class differences	Low	0	69	65	0.197	0.140
		1	62	61		
		2	53	54		
	High	3	40	45		
Intrinsic job satisfaction	Low	0	45	47	0.156	0.138
	Medium	1	57	57		
	High	2	65	65		
Length of employment	Less than 6 months		73	74	0.132	0.134
	6-12 months		64	63		
	1-3 years		63	63		
	4-7 years		55	54		
	8-15 years		57	56		
	15+ years		50	50		
Production technology and size of firm	Large-batch	small	63	63	0.131	0.127
		medium	53	53		
		large	53	54		
	Auto assemblies		52	49		
	Steel mills		71	70		
	Unit/small-batch	small	70	70		
		medium	51	56		
		large	53	56		
	Shipyards		59	58		
Skill requirements in job	Low	0	62	63	0.101	0.121
	Medium	1	55	54		
	High	2	48	47		
Party preferences	Communists		45	54	0.114	0.064
	Social	Left	51	53		
	Democrats	Centre	59	58		
		Right	64	61		
	Bourgeois		61	62		
	Unknown		58	56		

Independent variable; category			Positive		Eta	Beta
			Unadjus-ted	Adjust-ted		
			%	%		
Freedom of	Low	0	47	49	0.083	0.062
movement	Medium	1	55	56		
	High	2	60	59		
Workers'	Weak	0	48	49	0.075	0.057
collectivity		1	52	55		
		2	58	57		
		3	57	57		
	Strong	4	61	60		

$$R^2 = 0.144$$

firm are only slightly more positive than in firms with
large-batch production.   Workers in the smallest firms
tend to have the most positive views about the employer.
With an increasing level of skill, attitudes towards the
employer tend to become more negative. (3)   By and large,
however, general sociopolitical views appear to be of
greater importance than technological factors for the
workers' views on their employer.

The nature of social relationships with other workers
appears to be of small importance for views on the firm
as an employer.   Figures not given here show that the
degree of integration in an informal workgroup is unrelated to views on the firm.   This indicates that 'horizontal' social relationships among the workers tend to be
independent of the 'vertical' relation between the worker
and management.   The fact that views on the firm tend to
become more positive with an increasing strength of the
workers' collectivity underlines its role as a protective
buffer in relation to management.

As we have noted above, workers in the iron and steel
works, especially the semi-skilled ones, have very positive views of their employer.   The iron and steel works
in our sample are examples of one-company towns
(brukssamhälle) that have played an important role in the
early industrialization of Sweden.   The iron industry
and also the wood and paper industry was and is largely
concentrated in these relatively small communities on the
countryside, characterized by a very high concentration
of manual workers, dependence for employment on a single
company, a rather rigid status hierarchy structured around
the dominating firm and often old, patriarchal relationships between workers and the employer.

It is possible that the patriarchal traditions continue
to be important for the pattern of expectation towards the
employer in these communities.   Disappointment when such
expectations were frustrated was voiced in spontaneous
comments in the questionnaires by a couple of our respondents in these communities.   A young repairman thus explained that the reason he had been so critical of the
firm was that

> we have now such an ill willed and unreasonable works
> manager.   With the profits the company now makes, they
> should be able to do more for the workers, e.g. decent
> housing, some party or perhaps a trip.   What I react
> most against is that persons who have worked during
> perhaps 50 years for the company are not even thanked.
> ...   For my part I hope that these conditions will
> improve when the present works manager retires in two
> years.

In another old steelworks taken over by a multinational
corporation, a man said that 'this company has become a
really tyrannical company when we received a new manager
after Mr N.N.'   The expectations of benevolence from
management and the tendency to interpret worker-management
relations in terms of personalities are apparent in these
comments.

9   TECHNOLOGY, COMMUNITY AND ORGANIZATIONAL POTENTIAL

The preceding analysis.indicates that the key role often
accorded production technology for the shaping of social
relationships among workers, as well as between workers
and management, must be qualified.   In the metal-working
industry it is primarily assembly-line technology, which
tends markedly to inhibit the development of cohesive
workgroups and strong workers' collectivities.   There
is, however, no evidence that an increasing proportion of
the industrial workforce is found in jobs that constrain
workers to the same extent as does assembly-line technology.   In fact, where 'protest' reactions like, for
example, high turnover and absenteeism are possible, managements are pressured to find alternatives to this type
of technology, something that can be witnessed in the
Swedish auto industry.

Our analyses throw doubts on the assumption that the
production technology of a firm is a crucial determinant
of the quality of its industrial relations.   Although
process technologies in some respects may offer more
favourable opportunities for the creation of good social
relationships among workers than technologies on the

medium level of mechanization, there is no solid basis for the assumption that process technologies can overcome the conflicts of interest between workers and employers, and thus to provide possibilities for a stable 'vertical' integration in the firm.   Further, only a limited proportion of the workforce can be expected to find jobs in firms where process technology predominates.   In the foreseeable future technological developments would thus appear not to be about to affect crucially the organizational potential of the working class.

The hypothesis that, in contrast the the 'traditional' workers, markedly instrumental orientations to work among modern industrial workers will lead to limited and primarily superficial social relationships between workers (Goldthorpe et al., 1968a, 1969), does not receive support in our data.   Although our data are relatively weak in these respects, social relationships between our metalworkers do not appear to be markedly superficial, or restricted to the place of work.   Our data also point to the importance of community structure for the extent to which social relationships created at work are continued during leisure.   It is thus possible that the extensive overlap between social contacts on and off the job that are assumed to characterize 'traditional' workers (like miners, steelworkers and longshoremen), rather than being based in specific work orientations, reflect primarily the fact that they live in communities dominated by a single firm.   If overlap between social relations on and off the job are decreasing, this may thus be a result more of changes in community structure than of changing work orientations.

The decreasing importance of one-plant communities need not have primarily adverse effects on the organizational potential of the workers.   In communities dominated by a single employer, workers are highly dependent on this employer, something that tends to undercut their power resources.   Patriarchal traditions may also tend to prevail in such communities.   For workers on the move, the job assumes central importance and tends to provide an important base for the creation of new social relationships in the local community.   It is thus possible that the migrating workers come to have more homogeneously working-class social contacts than 'stable' workers among whom kinship is more important in structuring social relations.

7 The union at the workplace

Together with the political party, the labour union is the main power resource of the working class. Of these two, the union is in many ways closest to the everyday life of the worker, representing his interests in relation to the employers. For understanding the position of the working class in an advanced industrial society, it is therefore crucial to analyse the functioning of the union as a potential class organization of the workers. In this and the two subsequent chapters, we will look at different aspects of the relationship between workers and their union, focusing on the Metal Workers' Union, the largest union in Sweden.

This chapter begins the analysis of the union organization at its grass roots, the workplace. In contrast to several other countries, such as Britain, workplace unionism in Sweden is incorporated into the formal union organization, which usually has its smallest sub-organizations at the workplace level. It is thus at the workplace that Swedish workers have their closest experiences of the union. After outlining the formal structure of the union, we will here consider the meaning that workers give to union membership, especially regarding the extent to which the traditional solidaristic commitment to the union as part of a class-based popular movement is retained. As in all voluntary organizations, the problems of participation and influence of the rank-and-file union members are vital. In this chapter we are concerned specifically with participation and influence in the workplace union. The bases of internal conflicts about union policy are also explored, as is the bargaining power of the workplace union.

1   UNION ORGANIZATION

The Swedish Metal Workers' Union is an industrial union, founded in 1888.   Even before the First World War, it had become the largest union in the LO.   With 458,000 members in 1976, it has more than doubled since 1950. (1)   The basic organizational structure of this union follows the general pattern within LO unions, and is outlined in Figure 7.1.   The highest decision-making body of the union is the congress, which meets quadrennially.   Between congresses the union council, meeting at least twice a year, is the formal decision-making organ.   The executive board of the union, meeting bi-weekly, has the final decision-making power in collective bargaining.   The contract council, separately elected, serves as an advisory

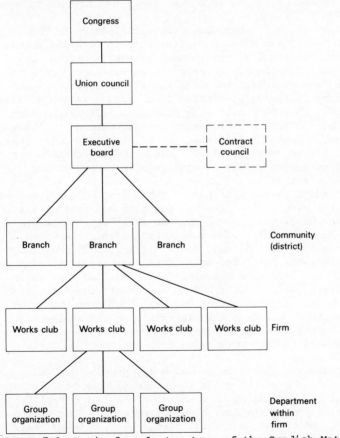

FIGURE 7.1 Basic formal structure of the Swedish Metal Workers' Union

body to the executive board in wage negotiations.   The
chairman of the union usually plays an important role in
directing the day-to-day affairs of the union.   In 1976
about 40 elected representatives and 130 administrative
personnel were employed at the union headquarters in
Stockholm.

The union operates through geographically delineated
branches, which are the sub-organizations of the union.
In 1977 the union had 203 branches.   The branch, in turn,
has works clubs in all except the smallest workplaces. (2)
Branches as well as works clubs are governed by separate
boards, elected by the members.   In most of the larger
branches the membership meeting has been replaced by an
assembly of elected representatives.   Branches with more
than one thousand members usually employ one or more full-
time 'ombudsmen'.   In 1976 the number of branch ombudsmen
was 105.

Being the only independent sub-organization of the
union, the branch plays a central role in internal union
affairs.   Several factors, however, contribute to give
the works club the key role in the day-to-day representation of member interests vis-à-vis the employer.   Since
the firms in the metal-working industry are rather heterogeneous, they have differing problems.   It is therefore
difficult and often unnecessary to find common solutions
to them.   Instead, problems have to be solved where they
arise, i.e. at the workplace.   Thus the branch need not,
and often can not, play a major role in co-ordinating
workplace activities.

According to the statutes of the union, the purpose of
the works club is 'to prepare, organize and deal with all
the demands of the workers on, and their interrelations
with the employer'.   The combination of minimum wages in
the industry-wide contract and the traditional prevalence
of piece rates have lead to a lively workplace unionism
related to piece rate bargaining.   According to dispute
procedures laid out in the Main Agreement, the works club
can ask for assistance from the branch or from the union
headquarters to aid in negotiations with the employer.
In the metal-working industry, however, branch ombudsmen
have had to ask for permission from employers to visit
firms.

The union statutes do not give any precise guidance
concerning the way in which the works club is to fulfil
its tasks.   Depending on local conditions and traditions,
different procedures have been worked out.   Size of the
firm is, of course, a crucial factor here.   Union statutes provide the possibility for the works club to decentralize its activities; it can for example form auxiliary

'group organizations' in the firm's main departments,
which at the first stage serve to deal with problems arising within the department.   There are also informal ways
of decentralizing activities and reaching out to different
parts of the firm, e.g. through 'contact men' in the departments.   In our sample of firms, the majority of the
small works clubs do not have a decentralized structure.
In the medium-sized clubs, however, 'contact men' or group
organizations are common, and in the large clubs group
organizations are the rule.

The statutes of the union prescribe that the works club
shall have membership meetings at least four times per
year, and that the board of the works club shall meet at
least once a month.   Interviews with representatives from
the works clubs in our sample, however, indicate that,
during the preceding year, one-third of the small works
clubs did not hold the stipulated number of membership
meetings, and that the majority of them did not have the
stipulated number of board meetings.   About half of the
medium-sized clubs had had less than the stipulated number
of board meetings, and a few held less than four membership meetings.   The large clubs, as a rule, fulfilled
these basic requirements.

Based on information received from our informants, some
aspects of the relationship between the works club and the
branch and the works club and the union headquarters can
be described.   We find that, while the majority of the
works clubs in the small firms are in contact with the
branch on an average of, at most, once a month, in the
large firms daily contacts are the rule.   In the medium-
sized firms the frequency of contacts with the branch is
high only where the chairman of the works club is a member
of the branch board.   Contacts between the works club and
the branch concern a variety of issues.   A considerable
part relates to activities of the national union, e.g.
participation in study courses arranged by the union.
The main part, however, appears to concern the daily activities of the works club, e.g. such issues as interpretation of the contract, regulations concerning overtime work
and work safety, requests from the employer to hire
foreign labour (3) and economic issues including the pay-
ment of membership dues to the branch.

In large firms, initiative for contact appears to come
about as often from the branch as from the works club.
With decreasing size of the firm, however, it is more
often the club that takes the initiative.   Satisfaction
with the outcome of contacts between the club and the
branch also appears to be higher, the smaller the firm.
In spite of a higher frequency of contacts with the

branch, the big works clubs thus appear to be less dependent on the branch than the small clubs.

Most of the contacts between the works club and the
union headquarters are mediated through the branch. This
formal channel, however, appears to be bypassed quite
often. The frequency of direct contacts between the
works clubs and the union headquarters varies with the
size of the firm. In the majority of the large and
medium-sized firms, the board of the works club had com-
municated or exchanged visits with the union headquarters
at least once during the preceding year, while in the
small firms this was the exception.

2   UNION INVOLVEMENT

In Sweden union membership is voluntary and the closed-
shop system is illegal. Union dues are high: in the
Metal Workers' Union 1.5 per cent of gross earnings. Yet
only 4 per cent of the metal-workers in our population
indicate that they do not belong to the union. The
young, recently employed, women and immigrants are over-
represented among the few non-members. (4)   Once a worker
is more permanently included in the labour force, however,
union membership is practically universal.

What motivates Swedish workers to belong to unions?
The emotional-evaluative orientation or involvement of
members in their organization can be expected to reflect
important aspects of the nature of the organization.
Etzioni (1961, pp. 3-21) shows how differences in types of
organizational involvement tend to be related to differences in the bases of compliance and loyalty, and to differences in the types of power resources - normative, re-
munerative or coercive - that typically are available for
the organizational leadership in relation to the rank-and-
file members.

The union is a voluntary organization of a rather mixed
nature. As an economic interest organization it has a
basic instrumental role. But in Sweden, as in most other
European countries, unions are a part of a socialist labour movement encompassing working-class-based political
parties and often also consumers co-operatives. To be a
union member, to vote for the workers' party, to read the
labour newspaper and to shop in the local 'co-op' have
been significant characteristics of traditional working-
class culture. As part of a popular movement, union
leaders thus also command normative power resources and
have been able to rely upon a self-sacrificing spirit
among the members.

We have attempted to tap the types of organizational
involvement among the metal-workers in our population
through the following question: 'People are members of
the union for many different reasons.   Which would you
say is the *most important* reason for yourself being a
member?'   The following summarizes the responses to the
alternative reasons presented to the sample:

	%
I am not a member of the union	4
I felt obliged to join	8
I was not very interested but joined none the less	9
I personally benefit from being a member of the union	37
I think that one should be solidaristic with the labour movement	41
(Other reasons or no answer)	2
	Total 101

In the following analyses we will combine those who
were not members, those feeling themselves obliged to join
and those joining without much interest into a category of
workers *reluctant* to join the union.   Workers stating
that personal benefit was their primary reason for membership can be said to have an *instrumental* involvement in
the union, whereas workers indicating solidarity with the
labour movement as their main motive can be said to have a
solidaristic union involvement.   This is admittedly a
crude classification of motives for union membership and
of types of union involvement, unreflective of the relative importance of the different types of motives present
among most union members.   Yet the question appears to
tap the major alternatives in a meaningful way.   The responses indicate that the great majority of all workers
have a positive involvement in the union;   i.e. their involvement is solidarist, or instrumental or a combination
of these motives.   The reluctant workers, among whom we
find those lukewarm or negative to the union, comprise
only about one-fifth of our population of metal-workers.
The meaning of the different types of union involvement
as measured by the above question can be illuminated by
relating these responses to indicators describing support
for the labour movement and participation in union
affairs.   In the metal-workers' study, a simple index of
labour movement support, relevant to everyday life of the
workers, is based on preference for buying the LO-owned
Social Democratic evening paper rather than its bourgeois
competitor, and preference for shopping in a co-operative
store rather than in a privately owned store (Appendix 2).
As we go from the reluctant to the solidaristic Swedish-
born workers the proportion of labour movement supporters

increases whereas the proportion of union 'outsiders',
i.e. workers who do not participate in the affairs of the
works club, tends to decrease (Figure 7.2).   The reluctant workers deviate most from the others in these respects, whereas the differences between the instrumental
and the solidaristic workers are smaller.   Thus the
latter two types of union involvement may indicate differences in feelings and moral overtones attached to union
membership, rather than, under normal circumstances, distinctly different behaviour in union affairs.

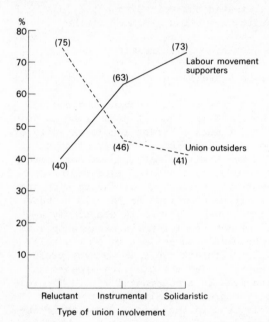

FIGURE 7.2 Percentage of labour movement supporters and
union outsiders by type of union involvement (Swedish-
born only)

3   IS UNION SOLIDARITY ERODING?

Large differences in types of union involvement are found
between older and younger workers.   Among Swedish-born
workers the proportion with solidaristic union involvement
is much lower in the younger birth cohorts (Figure 7.3),
while the proportion of reluctant and instrumental workers
tends to be greater.   The proportion of labour movement
supporters is also clearly - though not as drastically -
lower in the younger birth cohorts.

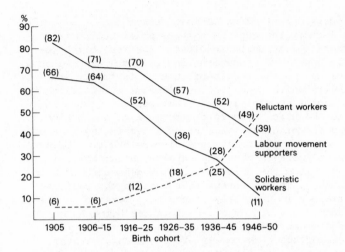

FIGURE 7.3 Type of union involvement and labour movement
support by birth cohort (Swedish-born only)

Why is there less solidaristic union involvement and less
support for the labour movement among the younger birth
cohorts of metal-workers? Is it a question of age differences or generational differences; that is, with time,
will the now-young metal-workers acquire roughly the same
views which the elderly workers currently possess, or will
the overall level of solidaristic involvement and labour
movement support decrease as the older generations retire?
Since orientation to the union movement is a relationship
between two entities, the workers and the union movement,
the factors accounting for differences between birth cohorts can logically rest either in the union movement or
in the workers, or in acombination of these two.

Broadly speaking, orientations to the union and the
labour movement can be acquired at three different periods
in the life of a worker. Early socialization in the
family of origin may thus inculcate a union orientation in
a working-class youth. The second crucial period is the
years around his twenties, when he comes of working age
and enters into the labour force. Thirdly, it is possible that socialization in these areas continues in the
later stages of his working life.

Studies of political socialization indicate that political preferences and party allegiances tend to be formed
mainly from experiences during youth and in early adult-
hood (when reaching voting age). Changes in political
outlook later in life tend to be less common (Butler and
Stokes, 1969; Hyman, 1959). The level of voting tends,
however, to increase up to a somewhat later stage in life.

If the development of union involvement can be expected
to follow largely the same pattern as political socialization, differences in union involvement between birth cohorts would appear to be generational. Such generational
differences can be the result of changes in family and
community life which generate instrumental orientations to
work (Goldthorpe et al., 1968a). We must, however, look
not only to the union members for sources of generational
differences in union involvement; changes in the role of
the union movement in society are also relevant. Later
generations of workers thus may enter a union that differs
significantly from the union an earlier generation met in
its own youth. To the extent that this is the case, and
that experiences in the early stages of a working career
are important, we would expect differences between cohorts
to be generational differences. If socialization in
later stages of the work career are important, however,
the differences can be interpreted as age differences.

To explore the social bases of differences in types of
union involvement among our workers, two multiple-classification analyses have been carried out. First, the dichotomy of reluctant versus other workers was taken as the
department variable; then the dichotomy of solidarist
versus other workers (Table 7.1). (5) The results indicate that, with the exception of age, demographic factors
are largely irrelevant to type of union involvement.
Differences in early socialization also appear to have
relatively small independent influences on union involvement. Thus a father's occupational status, his party
preference and level of union activity, as well as the
respondent's own experiences of economic hardship, are
relatively weakly related to union involvement. On the
other hand, early socializing experiences tend to affect
the respondents' party preference (cf. chapter 10), which
is of importance for union involvement. Social Democrats
have the smallest proportion and the bourgeois supporters
the largest proportion of reluctant workers. There is a
decrease in solidaristic union involvement from left to
right, with the largest proportion of solidaristic workers
found among the Communists and the left-wing Social Democrats.

At first sight, the decreasing proportion of solidaristic union members, and the corresponding tendency towards an increasing level of instrumental union involvement, would appear to fit hand in glove with the hypothesis of increasingly instrumental orientations to work
among modern industrial workers (Goldthorpe et al., 1968a,
1969). Again, however, our data fail to indicate the
presence of the mechanisms assumed to underlie such a

development.   The degree of solidaristic union involvement, for instance, is not related to skill requirements
of the job.   It is not markedly low among the better paid
workers, nor are married persons less solidaristically
oriented than single ones.   Figures not given here indicate that, among workers on jobs with low skill requirements, those with high wages have a solidaristic union
involvement as often as others.   Nor is solidaristic
union involvement related to intrinsic job satisfaction or
to relative affluence in terms of car and home ownership
in the direction that this hypothesis would predict.

The relatively high level of solidaristic involvement
among the materially better-off workers also indicates
that our data can not be interpreted in terms of an increasing *embourgeoisement* among workers based on increasing standards of living.   The high proportion of reluctant union members among the lowest paid workers deserves
attention.

Previous studies indicate that the character of the
local community and of the region can be of relevance for
political behaviour (Butler and Stokes, 1969; Janson,
1961; Tingsten, 1937; Gustafsson, 1974).   It is therefore also possible that the local community is of some
importance in the formation of orientations to the labour
movement.   In our study different types of communities
are represented.   On the one hand we have industrial communities, where the socialist parties dominate the political scene.   On the other hand we have 'mixed' communities, where services and commerce are important in the
local economy, and where the bourgeois parties often successfully compete with the socialist parties.   As discussed in chapter 5, however, the frequency of 'cross-
class' contacts off-the-job among our metal workers is
relatively low also in the mixed communities.   Our data
indicate only small differences in the type of union involvement between workers living in different types of
communities.

The social climate at the workplace can also be of
relevance for union involvement.   The strength of the
workers' collectivity reflects one important aspect of
this climate;   another is the presence of workmates who
function as informal activists in union-related issues.
An index of *density of union activists* at the workplace
is here based on three questions.   These explore the extent to which there are workers in the department or shop
to whom others can turn for advice concerning how to correct unsatisfactory conditions at the place of work;   information on issues being discussed on union meetings;
and the interpretation of the contract (Appendix 2).

TABLE 7.1 Multiple-classification analyses of types of union involvement among metal-workers (reluctant workers constitute 20% and solidaristic workers 41% of the population; N = 3986)

Independent variable; category		Reluctant workers				Solidaristic workers			
		Unad-justed %	Adjus-ted %	Eta	Beta	Unad-justed %	Adjus-ted %	Eta	Beta
Sex	Men	19	20	0.034	0.040	43	42	0.147	0.077
	Women	24	15			20	30		
Age cohort	- 1905	7	11	0.320	0.206	65	60	0.357	0.273
	1906-15	6	10			63	59		
	1916-25	12	16			50	46		
	1926-35	18	18			34	35		
	1936-45	31	28			25	29		
	1946-50	49	36			10	20		
Ethnicity	Swedish	17	18	0.135	0.068	44	41	0.146	0.025
	Foreign-born	30	25			27	38		
Marital status	Married	14	18	0.215	0.051	47	41	0.178	0.035
	Other	32	23			28	41		
Father's socio-economic status	Middle class	29	24	0.100	0.045	35	42	0.088	0.038
	Farmer	25	22			33	37		
	Working class	18	19			43	41		
Father's union activity	Unknown or low	22	21	0.091	0.053	39	40	0.085	0.057
	Medium	16	18			40	38		
	High	10	14			54	49		

Father's party preference	Bourgeois	28	25	0.172	0.051	38	43	0.150	0.281
	Unknown	26	19			32	39		
	Socialist	13	19			48	41		
Early economic hardships	Low	25	18	0.108	0.047	30	38	0.182	0.049
	Medium	19	20			43	41		
	High	14	23			55	45		
Unemployment experience	No	23	20	0.114	0.024	35	40	0.175	0.017
	Yes	14	20			54	42		
Party preference	Communist	17	20	0.318	0.223	54	49	0.266	0.154
	Social Democrat Left	7	13			56	49		
	Centre	14	16			45	43		
	Right	9	9			42	42		
	Bourgeois	43	36			23	31		
	Unknown	34	30			24	30		
Skill requirements of job	Low	21	20	0.043	0.014	38	40	0.058	0.012
	Medium	20	20			41	40		
	High	16	19			46	42		
Wage level	Low 1	47	37	0.204	0.135	18	36	0.164	0.106
	2	23	23			39	40		
	3	15	16			46	43		
	4	18	20			41	39		
	5	18	19			36	35		
	High 6	14	14			54	53		

$R^2 = 0.185$ $R^2 = 0.183$

   Figures not given here indicate only small differences
in type of union involvement between workers living in
different types of communities.   An increasing strength
of the workers' collectivity, however, tends slightly to
decrease the proportion of reluctant workers but is not
systematically related to the proportion of solidaristic
union members.   On the other hand, as shown in Figure
7.4, an increasing density of union activists not only

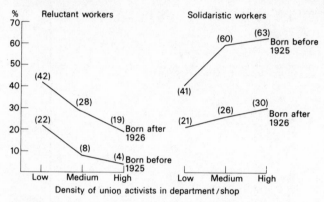

FIGURE 7.4   Type of union involvement by age cohort and
density of union activists in department/shop

decreases the proportion of reluctant workers but also
leads to some increase in the proportion of solidaristic
workers.   The proportion of labour movement supporters
tends to increase with an increase both in the strength of
the workers' collectivity and in the density of union activists (Figure 7.5).   It is also higher in industrial
than in mixed communities.

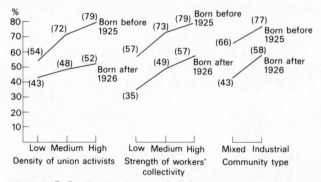

FIGURE 7.5   Percentage of labour movement supporters by
age cohort and density of union activists, strength of
workers' collectivity and community type

Thus our data indicate that socialization at the workplace and in the local community can affect the degree of
labour movement support and the reluctance to join the
union movement. This implies that, when the now-young
metal-workers grow older, we can expect reluctance to the
union movement to decrease among them, while labour movement support can be expected to increase. Only a limited
amount of 'adult socialization', however, can be expected
with respect to the degree of solidaristic union involvement.

The marked differences between birth cohorts in the
level of solidaristic union involvement would appear to
be largely generational differences and thus the results
of factors that have affected different birth cohorts differently, but the same birth cohorts in similar ways.
A political interpretation of these differences in terms
of the changing role of the labour movement in society
therefore appears appropriate.

The views of the metal-workers who came of working age
before 1932 were formed in a climate of manifest class
conflict, where union strength and solidarity were tested
in frequent and often bitter strikes and lockouts; where
the members could participate in the making of vital decisions through contract referendums; and where the long-
term strategy of the labour movement was often subjected
to intensive political debate.

After the Social Democratic government came to power in
1932, the strategy of the labour movement changed in ways
that probably affected the workers' roles as union members.   In the postwar period the union became more of an
anonymous and complex organization; it requested dues as
well as support for the Social Democratic government in
the general elections; but it did not mobilize members in
referendums or on picket lines.   The goods were deliv-
ered through legislation in the Riksdag, or through wage
increases brought about after top-level, nationwide negotiations, where the members were informed but not engaged.   Instead of a militant class struggle, there were
attempts at co-operation between union and management to
increase productivity; and technical discussions concerning what wage increases were permitted by the growth of
productivity without concomitant high inflation.   This
type of union did not generate the same type of loyalty
among its members as the early union did.

Metal-workers who came of working age in the postwar
period thus entered into a union movement that was significantly different from the union that the prewar generations of metal-workers grew up with.   The changing role
of the union in society would thus appear to be the most

important factor accounting for the decline in the level
of solidaristic union involvement among the younger generations of metal-workers.   This decline indicates that
the younger generations of metal-workers probably have a
more critical and questioning attitude to the union than
their elders.   As we have seen, however, this more conditional orientation to the union is congruent with a very
high level of union membership and reliance on collective
action through the union.

4 PARTICIPATION IN UNION GOVERNMENT

The almost exclusive reliance on representative forms of
government on the branch and national levels of the Metal
Workers' Union, and the absence of referendums in recent
decades, have left few opportunities to the rank-and-file
members for direct participation in decision-making at the
higher levels of the union organization.   The meetings of
the works club and of the group organizations, however,
provide a natural forum for membership participation in
decision-making on workplace issues, and in the governing
of the workplace union organization.

In our population of metal-workers, 47 per cent claim
to have attended at least one meeting of the branch, the
works club or the group organization during the preceding
twelve-month period.   The attendance lists circulated on
the meetings of the workplace union (usually two meetings
in a four-month period preceding the survey) were signed
by 12 per cent of the members. (6) Three per cent of the
metal-workers in our population held some kind of an elected union office.   In the 1968 Level of Living Survey of
a random sample of the Swedish population, 41 per cent of
workers employed in the metal-working industry claimed to
have attended at least one union meeting during the last
twelve months.   A follow-up study in 1974 indicated no
change in this figure, although the percentage claiming
to have attended a union meeting during the last three
months increased from 20 to 26 per cent.

On the basis of the data from both the questionnaire
and the attendance lists, a five-level index of *union participation* was constructed (Appendix 2).   In this index,
chairmen and board members of a works club or branch as
well as chairmen of a group organization are classified as
local leaders.   Delegates to the branch assembly, representatives to the joint shop committee, safety representatives, deputy members, etc. are classified as *marginal
office-holders*.   The *regular participants* attended the
union meetings where attendance lists were circulated but

held no elected office. *Marginal participants,* consti-
tuting 36 per cent of our population, reported that they
attended at least one union meeting during the preceding
year, but are not included on the attendance lists.   The
remaining workers, 52 per cent of our population, are
classified as *outsiders*.

The index of union participation is more or less
strongly correlated with other union-related activities.
Some of these activities, e.g. regular reading of the
union journal, are carried out also by the 'outsiders' to
a relatively large extent (Figure 7.6);   figures not given

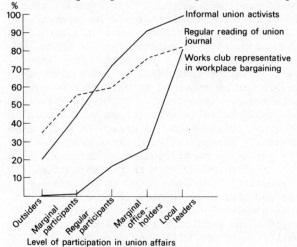

FIGURE 7.6 Percentage of informal union activists, regular readers of union journal and works club representatives in workplace bargaining by level of participation in
union affairs

here indicate that basic knowledge of the collective contract is also diffused relatively widely among workers.
In some other respects, however, differences between the
various categories of our participation index are strikingly large.   This is the case for instance with regard
to informal union activism, based on frequency of initiation of discussions with workmates on union issues and
efforts to interest other workers in attending union meetings (Appendix 2).   Participation in union study circles
and knowledge of national union affairs also show the same
sharp differences between levels of union participation.
Some activities, e.g. representing the union in workplace
bargaining, are carried out primarily by the local
leaders.   It is primarily the local leaders also who
spend part of their working time in union work, who are

engaged in union work at leisure, and who attend the information conferences and congresses of the union.   In
the large firms the club chairmen, but sometimes also one
or two other members of the board of the works club, actually spend all of their working time in union activities. (7)

Previous analyses of participation in union affairs
have largely focused on the correlates of participation
(Kyllönen, 1951; Spinrad, 1960; Tannenbaum, 1965).   In
attempting to understand differences in union participation, it appears fruitful to view participation as a form
of mobilization of power resources.   Participation thus
can be expected to increase the better a union member perceives both the possibility of his own influence over
decisions of the union, and the capacity of the union
itself to affect conditions at the workplace or in society.   Workers with larger individual or collective power
resources therefore can be expected to participate more
than workers with smaller resources.   In this context the
level of occupational skills is thus relevant.   According
to the 'technological implications' approach we would also
expect technologically structured work tasks and roles to
be of importance for union participation.   Informal
social relations created around work in the form of an
'occupational community' have been found to mediate between the worker and the union (Lipset et al., 1956).

The results of a multiple-classification analysis,
where the level of union participation is dichotomized so
that regular participants and office-holders form the
category of participants, are given in Table 7.2.   Women
and foreign-born workers have a lower proportion of participants than others, but this difference is mediated
through other variables included in the analysis.   The
level of participation increases with age, declining only
among workers above the age of sixty.   Single workers
participate somewhat less than married ones.   As expected, the level of union participation tends to increase
with an increasing level of perceived membership influence in the works club.   Participation is also somewhat
higher among workers who feel that the works club has a
high bargaining power in relation to management.

If the union is seen as limited to an 'economistic'
role of interest representation in relation to management,
we would expect the main motives for participation to reflect the quality of worker-management relationship.   Our
data do not support this assumption, however.   Figures
not given here, for instance, indicate that participation
is not related to views of the firm as an employer.   Instead, the level of political interest comes out in our

TABLE 7.2   Multiple-classification analysis of union participation (propor- tion union participants in population = 12%;   N = 3995)

Independent variable; category	Union participants		Eta	Beta
	Unadjusted	Adjusted		
	%	%		
Sex Men	13	12	0.093	0.042
Women	3	11		
Age -20 years	1	8	0.189	0.076
21-30	6	16		
31-40	11	13		
41-50	16	11		
51-60	21	11		
61+	12	9		
Ethnicity Swedish-born	13	12	0.101	0.011
Foreign-born	5	11		
Marital status Married	15	13	0.150	0.074
Other	5	8		
Political Low 0	4	7	0.308	0.225
interest 1	11	11		
2	13	11		
High 3	36	31		
Perceived Low 0	9	12	0.270	0.148
membership 1	6	9		
influence 2	13	11		
in works club High 3	35	25		
Skill Low 0	7	8	0.183	0.142
requirements 1	12	12		
of job High 2	24	21		
Size of firm Small	35	33	0.124	0.120
Medium	16	17		
Large	11	11		
Bargaining Low 0	10	10	0.187	0.088
power of 1	8	9		
works club 2	7	9		
3	8	12		
4	18	17		
5	22	13		
High 6	25	16		

Independent variable; category			Union participants		Eta	Beta
			Unadjusted	Adjusted		
			%	%		
Party	Communist		17	15	0.163	0.056
preference	Social Democrats	Left	16	10		
		Centre	16	14		
		Right	12	11		
	Bourgeois		6	11		
	Unknown		4	10		
Density of	Low	0	5	9	0.135	0.043
union activists		1	10	12		
in department		2	15	12		
	High	3	17	13		
Workgroup	Low	0	11	12	0.044	0.025
membership		1	11	11		
	High	2	14	13		
Off-the-job	Low	0	13	12	0.045	0.023
contacts with		1	12	11		
workers from	High	2	9	11		
firm						

$$R^2 = 0.190$$

data as the major determinant of union participation.
Whereas only about one out of every twenty workers with a
low level of political interest participates regularly in
union affairs, every third worker with a high level of
political interest is a participant.   Figures not given
here indicate that the relationship between political interest and union participation holds irrespective of party
preference.   The low level of participation among bourgeois workers partly reflects their lower level of political interest.   The strong relevance of political interest for union participation thus points to the markedly
political nature of the union as part of a class-based
labour movement.

As might be expected, the level of union participation
increases with skill requirements of the job, and is
especially high among the skilled workers.   The level of
participation decreases with increasing size of the firm.
Technologically structured work roles appear to have some
significance for union participation.   The level of participation is thus low in the auto assemblies.   The extensive use of shift work in the steel industry presumably
accounts for part of its low level of union participation.

The aspects of the informal social structure at the
workplace of direct relevance for union affairs (for
instance the density of union activists in the department), are of some importance for union participation.
Our data indicate, however, that mere social integration
into workgroups, or frequent off-the-job contacts with
other workers, do not tend to increase union participation. Union participation thus appears to be a markedly
goal-oriented activity, and as already noted the union
does not appear to function as a 'social club'.

Close at hand, it appears to interpret the higher level
of union participation among skilled workers as resulting
from fairly constant personality characteristics, such as
general competence. Alternatively, it can be seen as
reflecting the relative advantage of individual power resources of skilled workers, which makes mobilization more
attractive. If this was the case, the participation of
skilled workers would not be especially high in situations
where they do not enjoy this advantage. To elucidate the
background to the high participation of skilled workers,
we can look at the level of participation among persons
with different occupational skills working in shops with
differing levels of internal stratification, measured in
terms of differences in wages, responsibility and status
(see Appendix 2).

In departments with a low level of stratification,
where generally the majority of workmates share the skill
level of the respondent, very small differences in the
level of union participation are found between workers on
jobs with different skill requirements (Figure 7.7).
With increasing heterogeneity and stratification, however,
the level of participation of skilled workers tends to
increase, while participation of the semi- and unskilled
workers to some extent decreases. The increase in participation is especially marked among the elderly skilled
workers.

Where workers are together with their equals, i.e.
where the workers in the shop include predominantly
skilled workers or predominantly low-skilled workers, the
differences in the level of participation between the
various skill levels are thus insignificant. If, however, workers of different skill levels are mixed in the
same department, participation of the skilled workers increases markedly, while to some extent it decreases among
the semi- and unskilled workers. The elderly skilled
workers especially then come to assume the role as spokes-
men for their workmates in the department. Our data thus
point to differentials in resources and perhaps also
status rather than personality characteristics as the most

important factors behind the higher participation of
skilled workers.

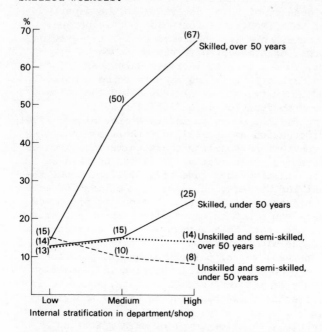

FIGURE 7.7 Percentage of union participants by level of
internal stratification in department, skill requirements
in job and age (Swedish-born men only)

The lower rate of union participation in the larger firms
indicates that participants in the large firms are a more
select category than those in the smaller firms.   This
higher selectivity in the large firms is based partly on
the level of political interest (Figure 7.8).   While the
level of political interest among the outsiders is not
related to size of firm, political interest increases
markedly with size of firm among those active in union
affairs.   In the large firms the difference in the level
of political interest between the average rank-and-file
members and the more active workers is thus greater than
the corresponding difference in the small firms.   The
works clubs in the large firms would thus appear to be
more 'politicized' than those in the small firms.   Figures not given here indicate also that knowledge of
national union affairs among the active union participants
increases with size of firm.

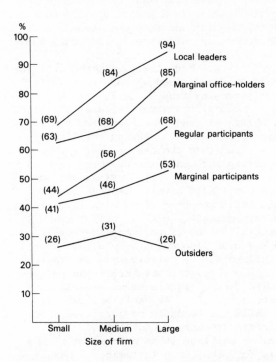

FIGURE 7.8 Percentage with a high level of political interest by level of union participation and size of firm (Swedish-born men only)

5   MEMBERSHIP INFLUENCE

To what extent do our metal-workers perceive that they, as rank-and-file members, can influence the policy of the works club?   When asked, 'Do you and the workmates you know best here at this firm have enough to say about how the works club handles negotiations with the firm?' almost half of the workers in our population responded in the negative.   To the question, 'Do you think that the board of the works club takes into enough consideration what the members think?' however only 27 per cent said no.   A question presented various degrees of centralization of decision-making: 'In some clubs a single person makes most of the decisions.   In other clubs there are many who participate in the decision-making.   How do you think that it is in your club?'   About one-third of our metal-workers thought that one or a few persons decide in their club, while another third said that many or rather many participate in decision-making (and the others did not know).   The above three questions were combined into an index of perceived *membership influence in the works club* (Appendix 2). (8)

The percentage reporting a high level of membership influence in the works club as defined by our index varies greatly between firms, ranging from 23 to 86 per cent. Our data show that structural characteristics of the plant and of the works club are of some importance for the level of perceived membership influence.   Taking the firms as units of analysis, we find that the average percentage reporting a high membership influence in the works club is highest in the small firms (Table 7.3).   Firms with unit and small-batch technology also have a somewhat higher perceived membership influence than firms with large-batch production and the steelworks.

The degree of centralization of the organizational structure of the works club also appears to affect perceived membership influence.   A relatively decentralized organizational structure characterizes large- and medium-sized works clubs with groups organizations as well as small clubs with 'contact men'.   As Table 7.3 indicates, greater membership influence tends to be perceived where the internal organization is more decentralized.   The frequency of membership meetings is an expression of the formal possibilities for membership influence.   Large- and medium-sized works clubs with more than four membership meetings per year and small clubs with more than three meetings are considered to have a relatively high frequency of meetings.   Our data (Table 7.3) indicate that the level of membership influence is seen to be somewhat higher in firms with a high frequency of membership meetings.   The differences are pronounced among the small firms. (9)

A multiple-classification analysis of perceived membership influence in the works club indicates that, of the demographic characteristics, only age has an independent relationship to membership influence, which is perceived as highest by workers above fifty years of age (Table 7.4).   The informal structure and social relationships among workers in the department/shop appear to be key factors in mediating membership influence within the workplace union.   The stronger the workers' collectivity, the higher is membership influence seen to be.   The density of union activists in the shop, i.e. the presence of workmates whom others can turn to for advice in union-related issues, also considerably increases the feeling of membership influence.   It is also greater, the higher the level

TABLE 7.3   Average percentage of workers in the firm reporting a high degree of membership influence in works club, by size of firm, type of production technology, organizational structure of works club and frequency of membership meetings

| | | Size of firm | | | | | |
		Small %	No. of firms	Medium %	No. of firms	Large %	No. of firms
Type of production technology	Large-batch and steel	43	(8)	34	(8)	35	(13)
	Unit or small-batch	50	(6)	38	(4)	42	(9)
Organizational structure of works club	Centralized	43	(11)	34	(8)	31	(4)
	Decentralized	59	(3)	37	(4)	40	(18)
Frequency of membership meetings	Low	37	(5)	34	(8)	36	(8)
	High	51	(9)	37	(4)	40	(14)
Total		46	(14)	35	(12)	38	(22)

TABLE 7.4 Multiple-classification analysis of perceived membership influence in works club (38% 'high influence' in population; N = 3994)

Independent variable; category			High influence		Eta	Beta
			Unadjusted	Adjusted		
			%	%		
Sex	Men		39	38	0.078	0.003
	Women		27	38		
Age	-20 years		24	35	0.178	0.102
	21-30		30	34		
	31-40		40	38		
	41-50		38	35		
	51-60		50	46		
	61+		50	57		
Ethnicity	Swedish-born		39	37	0.049	0.025
	Foreign-born		33	40		
Workers' collectivity	Weak	0	17	22	0.261	0.198
		1	18	23		
		2	33	35		
		3	44	43		
	Strong	4	53	49		
Level of union participation	Local leaders		87	76	0.275	0.189
	Marginal office-holders		71	61		
	Regular participants		60	54		
	Marginal participants		47	43		
	Outsiders		26	30		
Density of union activists in department	Low	0	21	30	0.230	0.122
		1	35	37		
		2	38	35		
	High	3	54	47		
Party preference	Communist		39	36	0.192	0.099
	Social	Left	43	37		
	Democrats	Centre	45	43		
		Right	49	46		
	Bourgeois		23	31		
	Unknown		26	33		
Wage level	Low	1	21	31	0.141	0.063
		2	31	34		
		3	37	38		
		4	39	38		
		5	42	39		
	High	6	50	43		

$$R^2 = 0.166$$

of union participation.   While skill level is not important in this context, membership influence is perceived to
be higher by those receiving high wages.

The strong relationship of political interest to union
participation indicates that party preference, too, can be
related to perceived membership influence.   As compared
with the Social Democrats, supporters of minority parties,
i.e. Communists and bourgeois workers, generally see more
limited possibilities for membership influence.

Participation in union affairs further increases the
feeling of membership influence considerably faster among
Social Democrats than among other workers.   The difference between Social Democrats and others regarding perceived membership influence thus becomes greater, the
higher the level of union participation (Figure 7.9).
This presumably reflects the greater ease with which active supporters of the political majority group can have

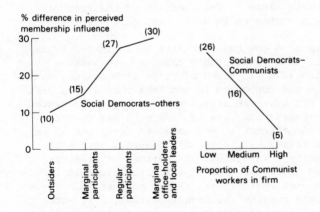

FIGURE 7.9 Difference in perceived membership influence
in works club between Social Democrats and workers with
other party preferences by level of union participation
and proportion of Communist workers in firm (Swedish-born
only)

their point of view considered in policy-making within the
works club.   Similarly, where a political minority group
is relatively strong, one can expect its possibilities of
influencing works club policy to increase, which will
affect perceived membership influence among its supporters.   As Figure 7.9 indicates, this is the case for the
Communist workers.   The difference in perceived membership influence between Social Democrats and Communists
decreases markedly with an increasing proportion of Communist workers in the firm. (10)

6   INTERNAL CONFLICTS

To what extent do differences of opinions on works club
policy lead to internal conflicts?   We can expect dissension on works club policy to be reflected in the frequency of contested elections to positions on the board
of the works club.   These boards consist of five to nine
persons elected on two-year terms, half of whom stand for
re-election every year.   Candidates for chairman and
treasurer are nominated separately, and may not simultaneously run for other positions on the board.
   In the mid-1960s the frequency of contested elections
to positions within the works clubs was low.   A questionnaire sent out in 1965 to works clubs in firms with
more than fifty workers indicates that the election to at
least one seat of the board was contested in about 6 per
cent of the works clubs.   The election of chairman or
treasurers were contested in 4 per cent of the works
clubs.
   The results of a new questionnaire sent out ten years
later indicate that considerable changes have taken
place.   In the 1975 elections of works club boards, at
least one seat was contested in not less than 41 per cent
of all works clubs.   The relative frequency of contested
elections increases with size of firm - 38 per cent in
small firms, 46 per cent in medium-sized firms and 53 per
cent in large firms.   It does not, however, vary with
size of community.   Elections of chairman or treasurer
were contested in 15 per cent of all works clubs in 1975.
In only 3 per cent of the works clubs, however, did elections take place outside the annual meeting, i.e. with
polling at the place of work and usually a complete slate
of alternative candidates to all positions.   In the
branches, the election of at least one board member was
contested in about one-third of the branches.   This increase in the proportion of contested union elections
probably largely reflects the increasing political

activity of groups to the left of the Social Democrats as well as of the Centre Party, which have attempted to break into the Social Democratic strongholds at the workplaces.

As a result of the sampling procedures used in the metal-workers' study, works clubs with a relatively high level of internal conflict probably are over-represented in our sample of firms (cf. Appendix 1). A relatively large proportion of our metal-workers thus belonged to works clubs where contests in elections were common and where the level of internal conflict on works club policy was rather high. (11) Our data thus provide possibili-ties to analyse situations of internal conflicts which subsequently have become common.

In the survey, an attempt was made to ascertain the extent of dissension on works club policy. When asked, 'Would you say that the workers in your department/shop are in agreement or disagreement about what the works club should do?' 28 per cent of the respondents indicated 'very much' or 'rather much' disagreement. In response to the question, 'Does it ever happen that workers in your department/shop have heated arguments over what the works club should do?', 47 per cent stated that this occurred 'very often', 'rather often' or at least 'rather seldom'. On the basis of the above two questions an index of aware-ness of *internal conflicts on works club policy* was con-structed (cf. Appendix 2). This index shows that two-thirds of the metal-workers were aware of at least a min-imum level of internal conflicts on works club policy in their department. The differences between firms in the level of internal conflicts on works club policy are rela-tively small, the major part of the variance found within rather than between firms. The level of internal con-flicts increases slightly with size of firm, however.

A multiple-classification analysis of internal con-flicts on works club policy indicates that differences in political views are the most important factors underlying dissension on works club policy (Table 7.5). With in-creasing heterogeneity of political opinions within the department, the proportion reporting a high or medium level of internal conflict increases markedly. The level of conflict also clearly increases with the frequency of political discussions in the department. Party pref-erence is not strongly related to perceived internal con-flicts. Awareness of internal conflict is lower among workers who have been employed in the firm for less than three years, indicating that it may take some time to learn about the opinions of workmates. The perceived level of internal conflict tends to increase with increas-ing union participation, and is especially high among mar-ginal office-holders.

TABLE 7.5 Multiple-classification analysis of conflicts in department on works club policy (56% medium and high conflict in population, N = 3993)

Independent variable; category		Reporting high and medium internal conflicts		Eta	Beta
		Unadjusted	Adjusted		
		%	%		
Sex	Men	59	57	0.149	0.069
	Women	35	46		
Age	-20 years	38	55	0.125	0.036
	21-30	54	54		
	31-40	59	58		
	41-50	62	57		
	51-60	57	57		
	61+	59	54		
Ethnicity	Swedish-born	58	55	0.057	0.049
	Foreign-born	51	61		
Political opinions in department	Very heterogeneous	73	70	0.337	0.209
	Rather heterogeneous	68	63		
	Rather homogeneous	55	53		
	Very homogeneous	55	55		
	Don't know	26	39		
Frequency of political discussion in department	Almost every day	75	67	0.281	0.125
	A few times a week	70	63		
	A few times a month	61	57		
	Almost never	47	52		
	Don't know	23	43		
Length of employment in firm	Less than 6 months	29	42	0.212	0.118
	6-12 months	41	46		
	1-3 years	47	52		
	4-7 years	60	59		
	7-15 years	67	63		
	15+ years	62	58		
Union participation	Local leaders	71	60	0.203	0.093
	Marginal office-holders	78	68		
	Regular participants	69	63		
	Marginal participants	65	60		
	Outsiders	47	52		
Internal stratification within department	Low 0	51	50	0.118	0.090
	1	57	58		
	2	53	55		
	High 3	69	65		
Party preference	Communist	66	60	0.156	0.073
	Social Democrats Left	62	56		
	Centre	49	51		
	Right	63	60		
	Bourgeois	61	62		
	Unknown	46	55		

$$R^2 = 0.168$$

A high level of occupational and economic differentiation among workers can be expected to form the bases for
internal dissension on works club policy, since collective
decisions through the works club will have different consequences for workers differently situated in the socioeconomic structure of the firm (Lipset et al., 1956).
Data in Table 7.5 showing that increasing internal stratification within the department tends to increase the
level of internal conflicts give some support to this
hypothesis.

7 BARGAINING POWER

The bargaining power of the works club in relation to
management is of course of central importance for union
members.   In the metal-workers' study the respondents
were asked to evaluate some aspects of the bargaining
power of the club.   Our data indicate considerable doubts
among metal-workers about the efficacy of the works club
in pushing member demands.   Only one-third of the metal-
workers indicate that the works club does 'much' or
'rather much' to increase wages of the workers;   and only
one-fifth of them think that the works club had been able
to push through 'very large' or 'rather large' wage increases during the preceding year. (12)   Two-thirds indicate that the works club would get 'rather little' or
'almost nothing' if in piece rate negotiations it demanded
considerably more than what management was willing to
give.   Somewhat more than one-third think that the negotiators from the works club are 'rather weak' or 'very
weak' when compared with management representatives.   The
six questions dealing with these issues have been combined
into an index of *perceived bargaining power of the works
club* (Appendix 2).

The variation between firms in perceived bargaining
power is great: the proportion reporting a high bargaining power of the works club ranges from 12 to 98 per cent.
The metal-workers thus find themselves in widely differing
contexts with respect to how much support they can count
on from the works club in their dealings with management.
Quantifiable structural factors referring to the works
club and the firm, however, can account for only a small
proportion of the variation between firms in this respect.
For instance, perceived bargaining power of the works club
is not related to the size of firm.   Works clubs in large
firms with unit or small-batch production - especially the
shipyards - however are seen as having a higher bargaining
power than clubs in large firms with standardized produc-

tion.   The state of the local labour market during the
preceding two-year period shows no clear relationship with
the bargaining power of the works club;   nor does the organizational structure of the works club.   This suggests
that the bargaining power of the works club may be the
result of historical and other factors not reflected in
our indicators, e.g. characteristics of management.

The frequency of membership meetings in the works club,
however, does seem to be related to the perceived bargaining power of the works club.   Among small- and medium-
sized clubs, perceived bargaining power is considerably
higher in those with a high frequency of membership meetings than in those with a low frequency (Figure 7.10).

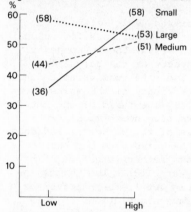

FIGURE 7.10   Average percentage reporting a high bargaining power of works club by frequency of membership meetings and size of firm

This relationship, however, does not hold in the large
firms.   Thus, while the weakness of works club in the
smaller firms is manifested both in a low frequency of
membership meetings and in low bargaining power, the works
clubs in the large firms generally have formal organizations efficient enough to fulfil minimum requirements in
terms of membership meetings even if they are not strong
in relation to the employers.   Figures not given here
indicate that, in firms with a high wage level relative
to the distribution of skill requirements among the workers,   the bargaining power of the works club is perceived
to be somewhat higher than in firms with a relatively low
wage level.

The results of a multiple-classification analysis of
perceived bargaining power of the works club are shown in
Table 7.6.   Age and length of employment in the firm show

TABLE 7.6 Multiple-classification analysis of rated
bargaining power of works club among metal-workers (N = 3996;
proportion in population reporting high bargaining
power = 51%)

Independent variable; category		Reporting high bargaining power		Eta	Beta
		Unadjusted	Adjusted		
		%	%		
Sex Men		50	50	0.055	0.054
Women		59	59	0.143	0.080
Age -20 years		67	60	0.143	0.080
21-30		43	47		
31-40		48	48		
41-50		49	53		
51-60		56	53		
61+		59	54		
Ethnicity Swedish-born		50	51	0.042	0.001
Foreign-born		55	51		
Perceived Low 0		13	19	0.432	0.371
membership 1		51	51		
influence 2		64	63		
in works club High 3		85	81		
Satisfaction Very satisfied		66	62	0.228	0.177
with own wage Rather satisfied		65	61		
Neither satisfied nor dissatisfied		52	52		
Rather dissatisfied		43	45		
Very dissatisfied		31	35		
Length of Less than 6 months		77	73	0.169	0.130
employment 6-12 months		61	59		
in firm 1-3 years		48	52		
4-7 years		42	46		
8-15 years		46	47		
15+ years		54	49		
Party Communist		33	39	0.202	0.130
preference Social Left		50	51		
Democrats Centre		59	55		
Right		63	58		
Bourgeois		32	38		
Unknown		53	54		

Independent variable; category		Reporting high bargaining power		Eta	Beta
		Unadjusted	Adjusted		
		%	%		
Wage level Low 1		65	64	0.118	0.097
2		47	49		
3		47	50		
4		49	48		
5		56	54		
High 6		50	46		
Union participation	Local leaders	91	71	0.121	0.075
	Marginal office-holders	74	64		
	Regular participants	62	59		
	Marginal participants	50	51		
	Outsiders	48	49		
Strength of workers' collectivity	Low 0	42	44	0.147	0.069
	1	37	46		
	2	51	52		
	3	53	50		
	High 4	59	55		

$$R^2 = 0.281$$

a curvilinear relationship with bargaining power: it is
perceived to be low by middle-aged workers with a relatively long employment.   Evaluation of membership influence and bargaining power in the works club are strongly
associated.   Taken together with the earlier finding
that, in the small- and medium-sized firms, the frequency
of membership meetings is related to a higher estimated
bargaining power of the club, this indicates that works
clubs where the leadership is responsive to the members
is also seen as being relatively strong in relation to
management.

Perceived bargaining power also increases with level
of union participation.   It is especially high among the
local leaders, who carry out most of the negotiations with
management.   An increasing satisfaction with one's own
wage is also strongly related to perceived bargaining
power of the works club, indicating that workers see their
wages at least partly as the result of the intervention of
the club.   Strength of the workers' collectivity is
positively related to perceived bargaining power.   Social
Democrats rate the bargaining power of the works club
higher than do the supporters of the other parties.

8   THE WORKPLACE UNION

The presence of only one industrial union within the metal-working industry, and the inclusion of workplace unionism in the formal structure of the union organization, are of crucial importance for the functioning of the union at the workplace.   The everyday activity of the works club in safeguarding and promoting the interests of the workers at the place of work thus has become an integrated part of the efforts of the national union and of the whole labour movement.

In comparison with most other countries, the level of union membership in Sweden appears incredibly high. (13) To belong to the union has gradually come to be taken for granted.   But force of tradition is not the sole or the primary reason that Swedish workers continue to pay high union dues.   Motivation for union membership must be recreated for every new generation of workers, and maintained through the activities of the union and the labour movement.   Our data indicate that, while a feeling of moral obligation and of solidarity with the labour movement was the ultimate motive for union membership in the older generation of metal-workers, the younger generation tends to have a somewhat more conditional union involvement, making support for the union more dependent on its utility for the individual.   This generational difference appears to be the result primarily of the changing strategy of class conflict of the labour movement, reflected in the move from an earlier situation of a 'zero-sum' type of relatively open class conflict, to a 'positive-sum' type of conflict strategy based on the formula of increased economic growth.   This shift in conflict strategy has changed the role of the union movement in society as well as the demands which the unions makes on its members and the opportunities it offers.   The common situation of wage-earners having to sell their labour power on the labour market, however, continues to force them to act collectively through the union.   The considerably increased level of organization in the postwar period implies also that workers who in earlier periods would have stayed outside the union are now, perhaps sometimes reluctantly, members of the union.

The active cadre of workers who keep the union going at the shopfloor level is relatively small: about one out of eight metal-workers belongs to this active category. About half of the metal-workers are largely out of touch with the internal government and activities of the union. Although the union performs a central function in representing the interests of workers in relation to manage-

ment, it is not primarily dissatisfaction with management
or with workplace conditions that motivates workers to
become active in the union.   Nor is the union a social
club, where friendship relations are important for maintaining membership and cohesiveness.   Our data indicate
that, instead, political interest is the most important
factor contributing to active participation in the union.
The central importance of politics for union activity
gives a vivid illustration of the reality behind the
traditional concept of the union and the party as two
wings of a unified labour movement.   The political function of the workplace union is especially pronounced in
the large firms.

The majority of metal-workers appear to regard possibilities for membership influence in the works club as
relatively good.   A decentralized and open organizational
structure of the works club facilitates membership influence.   The informal social structure at the workplace in
the form of a strong workers' collectivity and the presence of union activists play a central role in mediating
the influence of the rank-and-file members within the
works club.   Because of the marked political tone of
union activity, the supporters of minority parties easily
feel themselves outside the channels of influence within
the workplace union.

In the late 1950s and early 1960s the level of internal conflicts within the works clubs was relatively low.
Since 1970, however, the level of conflict about works
club policy has increased.   This has been manifested in
a marked increase in contested union elections.   While
dissension over works club policy is based to some extent
on internal differentiation among workers in terms of
wages and skill, it results mainly from divergent political views.   The increase in the level of dissension thus
probably reflects the intensified political activity at
the workplace level of the parties to the left as well as
to the right of the Social Democrats.   The political activity of these groups, however, has been largely unsuccessful and has not weakened the Social Democratic dominance among the workers.

Although great variation is found in the extent to
which our metal-workers perceive that they can expect
effective support from the works club in dealing with
management, our data indicate that the metal-workers generally feel their works club is weak in relation to management.   This is probably a correct perception of the
fact that, at the place of work, the dominating part of
the power resources has continued to rest with management.
Collective action limited to the place of work is thus not

enough.   It is only by becoming a movement encompassing
the whole working class that the union can be an effective
organization for pressing the demands of the workers.
This task is also greatly facilitated by the co-operation
with the political wing of the labour movement.   In the
latter half of the 1970s, legislation has thus been enacted which can considerably improve the power resources
of the wage-earners at the workplace.

8 Union democracy and membership influence

Being major power resources of the workers, a central
function of the unions is the articulation of the interests of wage-earners on the labour market and in society.
The interests of workers often come into conflict with
those of other collectivities and classes.   Also, between
various categories of workers differences in interests can
be found.   These conflicts of interest are generally re-
solved through some kind of compromises.   In these processes of interest aggregation, the workers are usually
represented by the elected officials of their organizations.   The way in which the power resources of the working class come to be used in class conflict depends
therefore partly on the form of union government.

For the debate on the position of the working class in
capitalist industrial society, two aspects of the internal
decision-making procedures in unions become crucial.   One
aspect refers to the problem of 'horizontal' integration
between workers: how can co-ordination between different
groups of workers be achieved so as to increase their combined power resources and make class action possible?
The other concerns the 'vertical' integration within the
union organization: how can union leaders be held responsible to the members so as to assure that rank-and-file
interests are represented and that the goals of the union
are not diverted?   The debate on union government has
traditionally focused on the latter problem, i.e. internal
union democracy, while the problem of co-ordination of
action on a class basis largely has been overlooked.   The
development of the internal decision-making procecures
within the Swedish union movement, however, cannot be
understood unless it is viewed also in relation to the
search for organizational forms to express the interests
of workers as a class.   The issue of decision-making procedures within unions becomes closely intertwined with the
role of unions in class conflict.

This chapter is devoted to an analysis of how changes in union rules and procedures have affected the possibilities of rank-and-file members to participate and influence decision-making in the Swedish Metal Workers' Union. These changes are discussed against the background of attempts to achieve co-ordination between different sectors of the working class and the changing strategies of class conflict in the Swedish labour movement.

1   GOVERNMENT FOR THE PEOPLE OR BY THE PEOPLE?

Although the problems of democracy at the union level in many respects differ from those at the national level, some key issues are shared.   One of these concerns the extent to which participation in decision-making by the members-citizens is desirable and necessary.   In classical democratic theory, originating in Rousseau, the idea of participation of all citizens in decision-making plays a vital role.   Democracy is seen not only as a means, but also as an end in itself.   In 1861, J.S. Mill (1952) thus argued that, by allowing for extensive citizen participation in decision-making, democracy contributes to the making of good citizens, who thereby learn to feel responsible not only for themselves but for the whole society.   Participation also trains citizens to defend their interests, and only universal participation in decision-making can assure that the interests of all citizens are taken into account.   Thus, in the classical tradition democratic government is government *by* the people.

In recent decades, however, democracy increasingly has been defined as government *for* the people: it is seen only as a method, not as an end in itself.   This revision of democratic theory is expressed in Schumpeter's (1947, p. 269) well-known definition of democracy as 'that institutional arrangement for arriving at political decisions in which individuals acquire the power to decide by means of competitive struggle for the people's vote'. According to this view the central feature of democracy is the competition for votes by different party elites.   The participation of the citizenry, in general, is of secondary importance.

This revision of the classical democratic theory was partly inspired by the crises for democracy that came in the 1930s and was evidenced, for example, in rather widespread support for fascist parties in several countries. Advocates of this revision also saw it as supported by election studies, indicating that the average citizen is often not as active and informed as classical democratic

theory would imply. (1)   Findings from survey studies
also have been interpreted to suggest that widespread
participation in political decision-making is not even
desirable, since the entry of a more passive and ill-
informed mass of citizens into politics can be associated
with crises in democracy: apathy thus serves a positive
function for stable democracy.   As Johansson (1971b,
p. 13) has pointed out, the people were seen as a security risk for democracy.   Democratic theory was therefore
revised to stress the important functions of elites in the
democratic process.

Against these 'revisions' of classical democratic
theory, an 'orthodox' interpretation of the classical
tradition has reasserted the central role of participation
by the people in the decision-making process.   In recent
years a lively debate has taken place between these two
divergent interpretations of democratic theory. (2)

A central issue underlying this controversy has been
the question of the distribution of power resources between different categories of citizens.   The orthodox
interpretation of democratic theory implies a relatively
equal distribution; the revisionist interpretation is
congruent with much greater inequality in the distribution
of power resources.   This is because the extent of participation in the decision-making system both reflects and
affects the distribution of power resources in society.
With increasingly unequal distribution of power resources,
aspirations as well as expectations of success by weaker
groups can be expected to decrease, thereby decreasing the
likelihood of participation (cf. chapter 2).   Decreasing
participation in the decision-making processes will also
lessen the likelihood of their interests being adequately
represented in the aggregation of interests.   To empha-
size participation as a basic element in democratic theory
is thus to stress the goal of equality in the distribution
of power resources in society.

In the Swedish debate on the conceptualization of democracy, the issue of the participation in decision-making
by the people has played an important role.   Political
scientists have been primarily interested in the consequences of participation and have tended to define democracy in terms of the effects of participation.   Westerståhl (1971) has thus stressed the representativity of the
elites and the agreement in opinions between the elites
and the people as the basic elements of democracy.   Lewin
(1970) accords the participation by the people a considerably greater role in democratic decision-making.   In his
definition of democracy as well as in his empirical
studies of the functioning of democratic organizations,

however, he takes the consequences of participation in terms of the development of a 'public spirit' among the citizens as the key factor (Lewin, 1977).   Sociologists, on the other hand, have stressed the potential and actual participation by citizens in decision-making as the fundamental aspect of democracy (Johansson, 1971b).

The views of the citizens as well as the correspondence in outlooks between the citizens and the elites can be affected also by factors other than citizen participation. It is therefore more fruitful to make the potential and actual participation by the citizens in decision-making the central aspect of democracy.   One can then study the consequences of participation, e.g. on the views of the citizens and on the representativity of the elite.

2   COLLECTIVE DECISIONS AND UNION DEMOCRACY

Decision-making procedures within unions become problematic to the extent that there are lines of cleavage among members, which structure and differentiate effects of collective decisions made by the union on behalf of all its members.   Where collective decisions have objectively different consequences for different categories of members, or are differentially evaluated, they may become the focus for internal conflict and require democratic forms for decision-making.   Two different types of such cleavages are of relevance here.   One is based on differentiation between workers in terms of positions on the labour market, the other on the organizational hierarchy within the union.

Internal differentiation between workers in terms of market capacities and location in the economy structures the effects of a union's collective decisions.   Level of skill and branch of industry are probably the most important lines of cleavage here;   unions have often been based on a branch of industry and level of skill, thereby increasing homogeneity within the decision-making unit. Such cleavages thus can be obstacles to class-based collective action and organization among workers.

The main part of the collective decision-making of a union refers to different aspects of work in the labour market where the union members are found.   The   internal union hierarchy structures the effects of these decisions, since the full-time union officials, as employees of the union, are not in the same labour market as the other members. (3)   This introduces a potential cleavage between union officials and rank-and-file members, thereby posing a problem for union democracy.

It is important to remember, however, that union
leaders are dependent on rank-and-file members, who constitute their 'power base'.   Union leaders thus cannot
become a 'new class' in society, since they do not command
independent power resources.   If the situation of the
working class in society deteriorates, and if rank-and-
file support for the union declines, the position of the
union leaders as a group, in the long run, will be undercut.   In the short run, however, the consequences of the
compromises made through collective decisions by the
unions are differentiated along the internal union hierarchy.   Internal means therefore have to be devised
whereby the rank-and-file members can hold union leaders
responsible for decisions they make on behalf of the membership.

The debate on union democracy in some ways has been a
less sophisticated version of the general discussion on
democratic theory.   As is well known, Michels (1970)
denied the possibility of democracy in organizations like
trade unions; he postulated 'an iron law of oligarchy',
according to which decisive power in such organizations
tends to be held by a few full-time officials,   This pessimistic view has been shared by others (e.g. Lipset,
Trow and Coleman, 1956; Goldstein, 1952).

Allen (1954) has argued that democratic procedures
within unions are not necessary to ensure that union
leaders are responsive to member interests; the threat of
a declining membership is an effective alternative for
maintaining responsiveness among the leaders.   This
assumption that 'exit' can be an effective alternative to
'voice', however, is questionable.   For dissenting union
members, the alternative to continued membership is
generally not to join another union but to remain unorganized.   Quite unrelated to the degree of leadership
responsiveness, unions fulfil important functions for
their members, for instance by hindering the underbidding
of wages and by offering unemployment insurance.   Thus in
the short run, union membership can not be expected to
decline as a result of dissatisfaction among members.

It has also been argued that, since unions are organizations for conflict, internal democracy and the factions
associated with it 'are a luxury most unions cannot
afford' (Taft, 1954, p. 239).   Apparently the actuality
and possibility of conflict requires a considerable degree
of centralization of power within a union.   But the difficulties facing democratic organizations in conflict situations, be they nations or unions, are not a sufficient
argument for throwing out democracy from the system.
Rather, organizational arrangements are needed for more
effective decision-making in such situations.

Definitions of union democracy suggested in previous
research reflect the distribution of power resources
within the decision-making unit to various degrees.
Union democracy has been defined in terms of the presence
of an institutionalized party system (Lipset, Trow and
Coleman, 1956);   in terms of the   closeness of outcome in
elections to top union office (Edelstein, 1967;   Edelstein
and Warner, 1976), and in the extent to which opposition
within the union is tolerated and survives as a recognized
form of political activity (Martin, 1968).   The first of
these definitions is extremely restrictive, and does not
do justice to actual variation in the distribution of
power resources found within unions. (4)   The second
definition reflects better the actual internal distribution of power but mixes opposition with democracy.   The
third definition is based on the assumption that even the
presence of an unstructured faction within a union, by
providing potential means for its overthrow, limits the
ability of the executive to disregard rank-and-file opinion.   This definition is thus related to the actual distribution of power resources within the union.

We define union democracy here in terms of the potential for membership influence in the decision-making process.   This potential is a function of the distribution
of power resources between various groups of actors in
the union.   The potential for membership influence is a
continuous variable, which can be dichotomized at some
point to separate democratic unions from oligarchic ones.
A democratic union organization must provide its members
with *legitimate possibilities for the overthrow of the
union executive*.   Union democracy is thus defined in institutional terms in a way that leaves room for significant variation in the potential for membership influence
among unions classified as democratic.

The distribution of power resources within a union organization is a function of the constitutional rights of
different groups of actors within the union, and of their
capacity to mobilize members.   The rights of different
groups are to a large extent codified in union statutes
through specification of the legitimate participants in
and forms for decision-making.   Also of importance, however, is the degree to which a constitution is open to
different interpretations, and the extent of the areas it
leaves unregulated.   In addition, availability of other
power resources, such as number of personnel and possibility for dissemination of information, are significant
since they affect the capacity for member mobilization.
The nature and frequency of opportunities for membership
intervention in the decision-making process is also of

importance.   Thus, the meaning and significance of constitutional rights in practice depends to a large extent
on the capacity and opportunity of different groups to
mobilize members.   Changes in the distribution of power
resources within a union thus can occur not only through
explicit changes in formal rights but also, and often in
more subtle ways, through changes in decision-making procedures which affect the capacity and opportunity for
member mobilization.

Like other Swedish trade unions, the Metal Workers'
Union clearly fulfils the fundamental requirements of a
democratic union. (5)   It provides a system of representative democracy, where alternative slates of candidates
to elected offices can freely compete for the support of
the rank-and-file members.   Elected representatives
assemble at the union congress, which constitutes   the
supreme decision-making authority within the union.   Members can belong to political clubs which may sponsor candidates to offices at all levels of the union.   Democracy
has been limited neither by corruption, nor by other un-
ethical practices.

The distinction between democratic and undemocratic
unions is of course crucial, but leaves considerable room
for variation in decision-making procedures and in the
distribution of power resources among democratic unions.
A pattern of centralism, where decisive power in the union
is delegated to the elected representatives, has long
traditions in the Swedish union movement (Hansson, 1938,
pp. 115-24).   Important changes in decision-making procedures and in the distribution of power resources, however, have occurred in the LO unions during this century.

In the first place there was a drive for increasing
centralization in LO unions during the 1930s. (6)   This
drive was reflected in the new statutes recommended in
1935 by the board of the LO to its member unions.   More
important, however, was the initiation of central negotiations between the LO and the SAF, leading to the conclusion of the Main Agreement in 1938, (7) the intervention
of the LO in wage negotiations of member unions in 1937
and work leading to the adoption of the new constitution
for the LO and its member unions in 1941.   A second
period of centralization came in the 1950s, with the institutionalization of top-level wage negotiations between
the LO and the SAF.   In the 1960s, finally, came a wave
of amalgamations of unions and branches.

3   FACTORS AFFECTING UNION POWER STRUCTURE

Different types of factors combine to shape the distribution of power resources within unions.   Attention has
been focused on the formal structure of the union (Edelstein, 1967);   the characteristics of union leaders and
members (Michels, 1970;   Pearlin and Richards, 1960);   the
structure and technology of the industry in which the
union operates (Lipset, Trow and Coleman, 1956;   Martin,
1968);   the extent to which the union becomes the forum
for competing political groups (Craig and Gross, 1970);
and on influences from the state (Sunesson, 1974, ch. 2).
Some factors of importance for shaping the internal power
structure in Swedish unions are briefly reviewed below.

Informal social structure

The distribution of power resources within a union depends
partly on the level of occupational skills among members,
and partly on the extent to which the industrial environment provides for the development of an informal social
structure that can resist tendencies towards centralization.   Factors assumed to favour the growth of strong
informal structures include the predominance of large
firms in the industry, firms located in working-class-
dominated communities, and a production technology that
does not hinder formation of social bonds between workers.
Where bargaining power is based on the skills of the workers rather than in the number of members, the independence of local organizations will be enhanced.   Such
factors have been found to be associated with differences
between unions in the degree of centralization of power
(Sunesson, 1974, ch. 6).

Sectional conflicts

The need to prevent any single group of members from using
an unduly large share of the common resources for their
own benefit tends to promote centralization.   This problem is generally solved by delegating responsibility for
union funds to the executive board, an organ 'above' the
competing members.   The right to decide on strikes, as
well as important functions in collective bargaining, are
often to be delegated to this board.

Employer organization and tactics

Highly centralized employers' organizations also tend to
result in increased centralization within unions, since
employers then must be dealt with centrally rather than
locally. The early development of central organizations
of employers in Sweden and their militant tactics, including use of large-scale lockouts, necessitated a considerable centralization of union power and the active intervention of the LO in the bargaining process already during
the first decade of this century. The SAF has favoured
centralized wage bargaining with the LO (Meidner, 1973),
and has actively discouraged splinter unionism.

State intervention

For a long period the state was used in attempts to curb
the growth of the labour movement through legislation re-
stricting the rights of unions and socialist parties
(Eklund, 1974). The coming to power of the Social Democratic government in 1932, however, changed this pattern.
In the following decades intervention from the state was
mainly indirect, through pressures on the parties on the
labour market to regulate their affairs in a desired
direction. In 1935 the Nothin Commission, headed by a
former Social Democratic member of government, argued
that, to avoid legislation and increase the possibilities
for industrial peace, the unions should centralize their
decision-making procedures; in particular, they should
abolish referendums on contract proposals (SOU, 1935, nos
65-6, pp. 108-10).

The strategy of class conflict

From 1932, when the Social Democratic government came to
power, one cannot consider the role of state intervention
apart from the labour movement's strategies of class conflict. What we have called the economic growth strategy
of class conflict became increasingly important for the
labour movement during the 1930s; it involved an attempt
to increase the efficiency of production so as to make
possible a positive-sum type of conflict between labour
and capital, where both parties could improve their positions even if their relative shares did not change much
(cf. chapter 4). This new strategy implied some measure
of accommodation and co-operation with employers and was
of relevance for internal decision-making procedures
within the unions.

The gradually increasing strength of the labour movement in the 1930s also implied that increasing efforts
could be made to co-ordinate the actions of unions on the
basis of class rather than branch and occupation.   Such
a co-ordination implied an expanding role of the union
leaders.

4   CHANGING DECISION-MAKING PROCEDURES: COLLECTIVE BARGAINING

Let us now consider how changes in decision-making procedures in the LO unions during this century have been reflected in the Swedish Metal Workers' Union and how they
have affected the potential for membership influence.   We
will begin with the most important area, collective bargaining.

The distribution of power resources within a collective
bargaining system depends partly of the number of units
concerned by the decisions, and on the type of wage predominant in the industry.   The early change from local to
industry-wide bargaining in the metal-working industry
placed a greater area of decision-making in the hands of
the executive board.   The predominance of piece work in
combination with minimum wages, however, left the metal-
workers with considerable opportunities to affect their
own earnings.

The desirability of centralized control over the strike
weapon is well illustrated by the case of the Metal Workers' Union.   Even the first statutes of the union stated
that only strikes approved by the executive board could
receive economic support from the union.   This rule
became important when the 1897 congress decided to increase the strike funds.   Already at that time, the dis-
cipline wielded by the executive board was so strong that
local strikes were not called except with its permission.
This practice was written into the union constitution at
the congress of 1909.   The new 'normal statutes' accepted
by the LO in 1935 recommended that all unions incorporate
this rule into their constitutions.   In 1941 this became
a requirement for membership in the LO.   Also the LO executive was then given the right to veto strikes - the so-
called 'double veto power'.

The control over the right to strike, and the final
authority in accepting or rejecting contract proposals,
was thus acquired by the executive board at an early
stage.   Under the able leadership of Ernst Blomberg,
member of the executive board and chairman of the union
from 1893 until his death in 1911, the power of the

executive board was used for frequent militant actions;
but these were always cautious and disciplined, calculated
not only to achieve victory in the specific dispute, but
also to strengthen the union organization.   Centralized
leadership thus coexisted with a high level of industrial
conflict, and appears to have been essential for the
strengthening and stabilizing of the union in its early
period of growth.

At the congress in 1919, a major fight over forms of
decision-making in collective bargaining took place.   A
proposal to increase membership influence with respect to
strikes, and to put the decisive authority for the conclusion of contracts in membership referendums, was carried
by a narrow majority but lost about as narrowly in a subsequent referendum.

The history of the Metal Workers' Union, however, also
illustrates that centralized control in collective bargaining can be combined with effective membership consultation.   The two main forms of membership consultation
have been advisory referendums and contract conferences.
The contract conferences, in operation up to 1961, were
relatively large bodies of elected representatives in each
sector of the metal-working industry, the largest ones
being engineering and steel.   From among its members the
conference elected a bargaining committee where union
officials were in a minority.   For about half a century
bitter internal conflicts raged over whether referendums
should supplement contract conferences as a form of membership consultation in collective bargaining.   Constitutional rules in this area, being compromises between
different interests, often have been somewhat ambiguous.
The majority on the executive board have wanted to limit
the use of referendums.   It would appear that it has
occasionally stretched the words of the constitution to
permit practices that it deemed desirable.

Advisory referendums first ceased to be used with
regard to the termination of contracts.   While the congress in 1922 decided that, at their expiring, termination
or prolongation, contracts should be submitted to the
members for consideration, the executive board soon interpreted this to mean that contract conferences rather than
referendums should be used.   The last referendum on the
termination of contracts was held in 1924. (8)   The right
of the executive board to decide on termination of contracts was explicitly conceded by the congress in 1929.

For many years, contract proposals were customarily
submitted to the metal-workers in advisory referendums.
For internal and political reasons the executive board
could hardly afford to disregard membership opinion ex-

pressed in such referendums. (9)   In 1935 the congress
formalized this procedure through the important decision
that contract proposals 'shall be submitted for consideration to the members concerned', whereafter the final decision is to be made by the executive board.

This pattern changed, however, in 1937, when the LO
intervened in wage negotiations to forestall termination
of contracts and strikes during the sensitive period of
negotiations with the SAF over what later became the Main
Agreement.   With the consent of the contract conference,
negotiations with employers began in the steel sector in
advance of the expiration of the contract. Because the
proposal for the new contract was negotiated before termination of the previous contract, the executive board did
not consider it necessary to subject it to a referendum,
but signed it after consultation with the contract conference.   (In the engineering sector, however, the contract was terminated and the proposals for the new contract accepted in a referendum.)   The use of advance negotiations of this type was not regulated in the constitution, but the union had previously made a couple of con-
troversial attempts to use them.   In 1938, however, the
system of advance negotiations was recommended by the LO
(Lind, 1938b), and later became standard practice.

After the conclusion of the 'frame agreements' between
the LO and the SAF at the outbreak of the Second World
War, the union agreed to contracts after advance negotiations, and without referendums.   In 1945 referendums
were held again, playing a crucial role in the big engineering strike that year (chapter 9).   The latest referendums in the union were held in 1947.   In that year the
congress explicitly excluded use of referendums in contract proposals based on advance negotiations, while retaining them as a requirement in other cases.   After wage
freezes in 1949 and 1950, only advance negotiations were
used and contract proposals were considered by contract
conferences alone.   The union participated in the 'co-
ordinated' bargaining between the LO and the SAF, which
was introduced in 1952, becoming the general pattern after
1956.   Only after the decision by the congress of 1969
that referendums could be used at the discretion of the
executive board did the board notify employers about the
termination of contracts, however without submitting the
new contract proposal to a referendum.

In 1961 the contract conference was replaced by a
permanent *contract council* common to all sectors of the
union.   This council is elected directly by the members
for four-year terms.   The council has only advisory
functions, but elects the bargaining committee.   To

improve communication between members and the union
leadership with respect to collective bargaining, local
information conferences have been held in connection
with wage rounds since the late 1940s.   In 1969 this
practice was written into the union constitution.   In
these conferences, union officials and members of the
contract council meet to exchange views with worker representatives.   All firms with at least five union members
have the right to be represented at these meetings.
During the 1970s, about six thousand members a year participated in these conferences.

Recently, improved communications between the rank-and-
file members and the union leadership have also been
attempted through *consultations* centring around specific
problems like wages and working time.   These consultations are arranged in the form of local 'study circles',
where union members discuss material prepared at the
national union headquarters and express the views of the
group in replies to questions which are then returned to
union headquarters.

The prolonged struggle over forms of membership consultation in collective bargaining indicates that, although
formally they have the same advisory status, referendums
differ in important respects from representative institutions such as contract conferences.   The crucial difference appears to be that referendums offer considerably
greater possibilities for oppositional groups to mobilize
union members.   Participation in referendums has been
high, on the average close to 70 per cent in this union
(Westerstähl, 1945, p. 132), while it is very low in election of conferences, which usually take place at branch
meetings.   This difference is partly a result of the
greater clarity of issues in the referendums.   Another
factor is the publicity given to the various stages of
the bargaining rounds which function somewhat like 'election campaigns' for increasing the interest of the rank-
and-file.   Representatives to the contract conferences,
on the other hand, were elected before the wage rounds, at
a time when rank-and-file interest was often low.   This
difference is even more pronounced in comparison with the
new contract council, since expiration of the four-year
terms need not coincide with the years for the expiration
of contracts.   Discontinuation of advisory referendums
has therefore decreased membership influence, primarily
by decreasing the possibilities for mobilization of
members.

The 'risks' inherent in referendums are illustrated by
the relatively frequent defeats of proposals sponsored by
the executive board.   Between 1920 and 1947, close to

half of the referendums on contract proposals in the engineering and steel sectors of the union were thus defeated.   In comparing rejected contract proposals with final
contracts within all Swedish trade unions up to 1945,
Westerståhl (1945, pp. 117-18) concluded that rejections
generally have resulted in improvements for the workers.
In his view, 'it is an unquestionable fact that the members in many situations by voting "no" have succeeded in
gaining larger or smaller concessions in addition to those
that the delegates at the preceding negotiations had
reached.'
    The probable reason for the improvements following a
negative outcome of a contract referendum is that the
union negotiators thereby are given an irrevocable commitment and are publicly bound to reject a settlement in
terms of the original proposal, something that increases
their bargaining strength in relation to the employers.
The referendum thus provides the union negotiators with a
type of a bargaining tactic for publicly binding themselves to an outcome better than the one voted down in the
referendum.   Such tactics have been recognized as important elements in the strategy of conflict.   According to
one analyst of the strategy of conflict (Schelling, 1960,
p. 22),

    the essence of these tactics is some voluntary but ir-
    reversible sacrifice of freedom of choice.   They rest
    on the paradox that the power to constrain an adversary
    may depend on the power to bind oneself; that, in
    bargaining, weakness is often strength, freedom may be
    freedom to capitulate, and to burn bridges behind one
    may suffice to undo an opponent. (10)

5 CENTRALIZATION IN OTHER AREAS

Tendencies towards a centralization of power within the
union can be noted also in other areas, but in addition
there have been some changes in the opposite direction.
The most important changes are reviewed below.

Control over membership

Expulsion of a member is a union's final sanction.   While
membership was originally granted by the union branches,
in 1913 the congress transformed the branches into sub-
organizations of the national union, and membership has
since been granted and withdrawn by the executive
board. (11)   In the politically tainted conflicts around

1930, some representatives of the left-wing minority were
expelled.   In 1940, the rights of Communists to hold
elected positions within the union were limited upon
recommendation of the LO, but these limitations were
dropped a few years later.

Congress representation

Historically, opposition within the union has had its
strongholds in the big branches of the union.   The relative representation of large and small branches at the
union congress therefore can affect the possibilities for
an opposition to mobilize support.   In the early years
the focus was on the representation of branches rather
than members, and small branches had more than their pro-
portionate share of delegates to the congress.   Against
the resistance of the executive board, the congresses of
1909, 1913 and 1916 gradually eliminated this over-rep-
resentation, adopting a rule that stipulated that the
number of delegates from each branch be in direct proportion to its membership (with the smaller branches forming
election districts).   (12)

Congress intervals

The possibility of oppositional groups to mobilize the
membership depends to some extent on reactions of members
to external factors, e.g. recessions, inflation or wartime deprivations.   With more frequent congresses there
is greater probability that elections to the congress take
place in a climate where rank-and-file members are dissatisfied with union policy.   After a period of irregular
intervals between congresses, the three-year congress
period was institutionalized in 1909.   Since 1953, however, the congress has met only every fourth year.

The executive board

Full-time union officials have always been in a minority
on the executive board of the union, where lay or 'working' members form the majority.   The working members of
the executive board are generally chairmen of large works
clubs or branches, and are therefore engaged on a full-
time basis in union work.   The congress of 1965 introduced bi-weekly meetings of the executive board, inter-
spersed with 'preparatory meetings' for the full-time

officials on the board.   Possibly, the full-time officials may therefore come to function as an informal
'working committee' within the board.

Appointment of officials

Officials of the union are elected by the congress.
Since the vacancies in the office of the chairman during
this century have almost without exception occurred between the congresses, the union council has appointed the
new chairman, subject to confirmation by the following
congress.   While the council has provided the branches
with an opportunity to recommend candidates to this position, the full-time officials have played a crucial role
in the selection procedures.   In 1925 and in 1932, for
instance, the Communist vice-chairman of the union was bypassed by the council, primarily because of resistance
from the full-time officials (Back, 1963).
    Until 1935, the full-time officials had to stand for
re-election at every congress.   While only one ombudsman
failed to be re-elected, (13) the number of votes given in
support of each candidate could be interpreted as an informal way of 'grading' the union officials.   The congress in 1935 adopted the 'normal statutes' for the LO
unions, including the principle that, after being elected
for the first time by the congress, officials were to
serve until further notice.
    Ombudsmen at the branch level were for a long time
elected directly by the branch members.   In 1953, however, the executive board was authorized to evaluate and
rank the applicants.   The next step, taken in 1962, was
to limit the choice of the branch to three rank-ordered
candidates.   In 1969 the congress authorized the executive board to appoint branch ombudsmen after consultation
with the branch board.   The main arguments of the executive board were that demands on the branch ombudsmen had
increased, that the branches tended to limit their choice
to local candidates, and that 'momentary opinions' often
affected the elections in the branches.   The arguments
by the executive representatives also indicated a desire
to control the recruitment process in order to retain
'promising' young men within the union by placing them in
branch offices (Svenska Metallindustriarbetareförbundet,
1969, pp. 165-72).   This change may increase the attention paid by prospective candidates and branch ombudsmen
to the views of the union leadership, since promotion possibilities depend on the executive board rather than on
the members whom the ombudsman serves.   The branch

ombudsmen have important functions at the branch level,
and are frequently permanent members of the branch boards.

Number of officials

In the early 1940s the relative number of full-time officials in the national union headquarters and in the
branches of the LO unions was roughly one official per
1800 members (Westerståhl, 1945, pp. 92-3).   The density
of full-time union officials has increased somewhat since
then: it was about one official per 1400 members in 1967
(Carlsson, 1969, pp. 105-8), and one official for roughly
1200 members around 1970 (LO, 1974). (14)
   In comparison with the other LO unions, the Metal Workers' Union has relatively few full-time officials.   Excluding administrative personnel, whose appointment is not
subject to confirmation by the congress or the union council, the union since 1950 has had one official for somewhat less than 3000 members.   Even as early as 1909, the
relative number of full-time officials (a total of nine)
was almost as high as in 1950.   The number of ombudsmen
on the branch level, having increased from 56 in 1950 to
106 in 1976, has approximately kept pace with the increasing membership, with one branch ombudsman per 4000 members
during most of the postwar period.   In this sense, then,
no 'bureaucratization' has taken place in the union.   The
relatively low number of full-time officials in the union
reflects the fact that the works clubs are in charge of
most of the day-to-day negotiations with the employer.
In fact, in the larger firms one or more of the elected
works club officials are engaged on a full-time basis in
union work.

The branches

In the Metal Workers' Union the branch is more important
than the works club for the internal functioning of the
union, since it is the principal independent decision-
making unit under the executive board. (15)   Two developments have affected the role of the branch as a channel
for communication of membership opinions to, and influence
on, the union executive.
   The congress in 1929 authorized branches with more than
5000 members to replace the branch meeting, open to all
members, with an assembly of elected representatives. (16)
Members may attend the meetings of this assembly, but they
do not have a voice in the decision-making.   Apart from

the argument that no suitable localities were available to
accommodate a full-scale membership turnout, the new
system is seen as a way of ensuring that all sub-units of
the branch are represented, and of introducing stability
in the working of the branch.   'There is no lack of examples where momentary opinions have been created before a
meeting and that it has later been necessary to change
decisions then taken' (Bengtsson, 1971, pp. 41-2).   Since
alternative slates of candidates are relatively infrequent, the branch assembly often elects not only the
branch board but also representatives to both the congress
and the contract council.

Another factor of some importance in this context is
the recent policy of combining smaller, contiguous
branches into one 'big' branch for the whole area, in
order to create units large enough to support an ombudsman.   The former branches usually become sections of the
larger branch.   Generally a branch assembly is introduced
in these amalgamated 'big' branches.   This policy has almost halved the number of branches in the union, from 364
in 1960 to 203 in 1977.   In the LO as a whole, the decrease in the number of branches has been even greater
(Eriksson, 1973; Hadenius, 1976).   More than three-
fourths of all branches disappeared between 1960 and 1975
as a result of amalgamations of unions and branches.   By
1975 the branch meeting that was open to all union members had practically disappeared as a decision-making instrument in LO unions.   While dictated by practical considerations, as well as by an interest in supplying members with more effective services, these changes also have
had the indirect consequence of making it more difficult
for oppositional groups to mobilize union members.   Among
the rank-and-file members, the amalgamation of branches
has met rather widespread criticism on the grounds that it
decreases membership influence and makes contacts between
the branch board and the members more difficult (Lewin,
1977, pp. 171-3).

Some organizational changes have decreased centralization.   The best example concerns efforts to decentralize
the organization of works clubs by stimulating the development of group organizations in different departments of
large and medium-sized firms.   The strong increase in the
study activities of the union in recent years has provided
union leaders with additional channels of communication
with the membership, but probably also has increased the
resources of the members. (17)

6   THE MEMBERS' VOICE AT THE UNION CONGRESS

At the congress of the union, formally its supreme decision-making institution, the interests of the members are
articulated through elected delegates as well as through
motions.   It is therefore of interest to analyse the pro-
ceedings of the congresses to see how the articulation of
the members' voice has changed over time, and to what
extent it has reflected the trend towards centralization
of union power structure noted above.

Motions

Branches as well as works clubs and individual members may
initiate motions to the congress.   Motions initiated by
members and works clubs are presented to the branch meeting, which may accept the motion as its own or forward it
to the congress as a motion from one of its sub-organizations or from an individual member.   Together with recommendations from the union council, the motions are
printed and put on the agenda of the congress.   Since the
1930s, roughly 75 per cent of all motions have come from
the branches of the union although they usually have been
initiated by individual members or works clubs.   In the
sixteen ordinary congresses from 1913 to 1961 the number
of motions has averaged around 115 per congress.   At the
congresses since the 1960s, however, the number of motions has increased, reaching 377 motions at the 1973
congress (Figure 8.1).   To the 1977 congress a record of
620 motions were submitted.

To give an overview of the issues raised in the motions, these have been roughly grouped into nine categories for three different periods, as given in Table 8.1.
The three congresses from 1929 to 1935 appear typical of
the congresses in the period between the world wars.
One-fourth of the motions (categories 1 and 2) raise
issues related to the power structure of the union, and to
forms of decision-making in collective bargaining.   About
one-half of the motions concern union administration, a
large proportion pertaining to fees and eligibility for
unemployment benefits.   In sum, the motions reflect a
union torn by internal strife, but in the process of developing internal working procedures.

The motions since 1950 give a picture of a more settled union.   The bulk of motions concern social policy
issues, reflecting the presence of far-reaching social
policy programmes, some of them resulting from agreements
between the parties on the labour market which members

TABLE 8.1 Contents of motions to the congresses of the
Swedish Metal Workers' Union in three different periods

Motions related to	1929-35	1953-7	1969-73
	%	%	%
1 Rules and practices concerning membership and elections	11	6	4
2 Rules and practices concerning decision-making in collective bargaining	14	2	3
3 Rules and practices concerning internal administration, dues, benefits and relations to other unions	49	24	10
4 Studies, union information (internal and external) and union journal	5	3	9
5 Content of contracts and wage policy	7	11	21
6 Legislation and agreements concerning social security, public and union insurance, social policy, vacations, working time, health, workers' protection, and work environment	5	38	36
7 Legislation and agreements concerning influence in relation to employers, industrial democracy, industrial policy, and goals of union	4	13	11
8 Foreign policy and international relations	2	2	5
9 Other issues	3	1	2
	100	100	100
(No. of motions)	(378)	(184)	(556)

want to perfect and extend.   A large proportion of the
motions focus on activating the union as a political
pressure group via the Social Democratic government in
legislation concerning social policy and also, to some
extent, economic and industrial policy.   The proportion
of issues related to specification of clauses in contracts
has been increasing in the motions, especially since
1969.

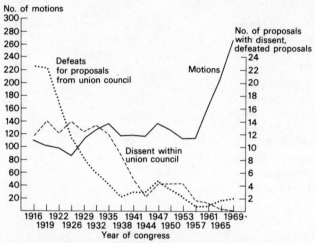

FIGURE 8.1   Number of motions, number of proposals from
union council with recorded dissent and number of defeated proposals from union council at congresses of the
Swedish Metal Workers' Union, 1913-73 (three-year moving
averages)

Challenges to the union executive

When oppositional groups had a foothold in the union
council, this council played a relatively active role in
union affairs.   Its importance, however, appears to have
declined in recent decades.   For instance, the number of
recommendations to the congress in which dissenting views
within the supervisory board is recorded has been decreasing.   In such cases, some members of the supervisory
board, sometimes joined by members of the executive
board, have written reservations to the recommendations
adopted by the majority.   The number of such splits

averaged around thirteen in the congresses from 1913 to 1938, dropped to an average of three in the congresses from 1941 to 1961, and have been practically absent in the congresses since 1965 (Figure 8.1).

The number of total or partial defeats for recommendations by the supervisory board show a marked decline in the 1930s, reaching a very low level after the 1950 congress.   This change thus also points to an increase in the power of the executive board.

The fading voice of the members

The shifting balance of power within the union is also indicated by the degree of activity of different categories of delegates at the union congresses.   Since 1929, congress minutes have given relatively good verbatim records of speeches.   By measuring the amount of space in the minutes taken up by different speakers, we are provided with an estimate of the relative distribution of speaking time between different categories of speakers at each congress, and thus also given an indication of the direction of the communication flow.

Up to the congress of 1944, representatives elected by the members dominated the deliberations of the congress: they used, on an average, somewhat more than half of the total speaking time recorded in congress minutes, with full-time officials at the union headquarters using about a third of the total time (Figure 8.2).   In the following congresses, however, the proportion of speaking time used by the elected delegates decreased while that of the union officials increased.   A watershed came at the congresses of 1947 and 1950, when the time used by the union officials was roughly equal to that of the elected delegates. At the congresses since 1953, union officials have used roughly half of the total speaking time, while the proportion used by elected delegates has been considerably lower.   In the congresses since 1965, however, the elected delegates have increased their proportion of speaking time. (18)

Lay members on the executive board and in the union council have generally been less active than full-time union officials on these boards and have increasingly tended to be silent at the congresses.   This again points at the decreasing importance of the union council, and the increased power of full-time officials.

The guest speakers, invited by the executive board, have been prominent members of the Social Democratic government and the LO executive, and have addressed the con-

gress on general and political issues. Thus, to some
extent, the congresses have become political manifestations in support of Social Democratic policies.

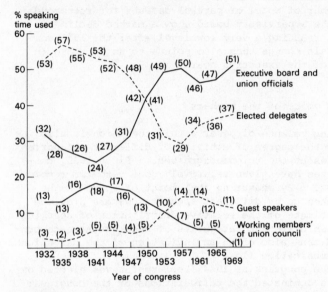

FIGURE 8.2 Relative distribution of speaking time used by
different categories of speakers at the congresses of the
Swedish Metal Workers' Union, 1919-73 (three-year moving
averages)

Thus, in contrast to the situation before the Second World
War, elected delegates to congresses since 1950 have more
often listened to officials of the labour movement than
presented rank-and-file views to these officials. The
decline in the activity of the elected delegates at the
congresses after 1950 coincides with the defeat of the
Communist opposition within the union. This, however,
does not appear to be the major explanation of the trend,
since the pattern of speaking time in the congresses of
1929, 1938 and 1941 - where the Communists had only a few
representatives - does not differ much from that of other
prewar congresses. The change in the direction of the
flow of communication at the congresses in the postwar
period, instead, would appear to reflect the generally
strengthened position of the full-time officials within
the union. As already noted, however, elected delegates
have increased their activity somewhat at the congresses
since 1965.

7   UNION POWER STRUCTURE VIEWED FROM BELOW

What do the rank-and-file members think of their opportunities for influencing the governance of the Metal Workers' Union?   Three questions in the metal-workers survey
pertain to the relationship between the union leadership
and rank-and-file members: they serve as rough indicators
of perceived membership influence in the union.   The
questions and the distribution of responses among our
metal-workers are as follows:

			%
(a)	Do you think that the common members have enough say within the Metal Workers' Union?	Yes, certainly	5
		Yes, perhaps	18
		No, perhaps not	30
		No, certainly not	26
		Don't know	21
			100

			%
(b)	Do you think that those in the union leadership know enough about how it is to be a worker nowadays?	No, certainly not	25
		No, perhaps not	27
		Yes, perhaps	23
		Yes, certainly	12
		Don't know	13
			100

			%
(c)	Do you think that the union leadership has good or bad contact with the workers?	Very good contact	3
		Fairly good contact	30
		Fairly bad contact	34
		Very bad contact	12
		Don't know	21
			100

Our metal-workers thus have a rather pessimistic view of
the possibilities for rank-and-file members to influence
union affairs at the national level, and generally tend to
feel that the union leadership is rather distant from the
members.   Only about one-fourth affirm that the rank-and-
file members have enough say within the union; only a
third indicate that the national union leadership is in
sufficient touch with, and has a good grasp of, the situation of the workers.
    The above three questions have been combined into an
index of *perceived membership influence in the union*
(Appendix 2).   A multiple-classification analysis with
twelve independent variables, accounts for 22 per cent of

the variance in perceived membership influence in the
union, indicating that demographic characteristics are
relatively unimportant in this context (Table 8.2).   The
works club appears to play a major role in mediating membership influence within the union.   Workers satisfied
with the degree of membership influence within the works
club also generally tend to perceive a high degree of membership influence in the national union. (19)   A high
density of union activists in the department/shop also
contributes to a feeling of membership influence in the
union.

Perceived membership influence in the union has little
relationship to the level of union participation.   Dissatisfaction with the level of membership influence
apparently is not attributable to ignorance, since it does
not vary much with the respondent's knowledge of national
union affairs.   Relations with the employer as well as
more general sociopolitical views, however, are reflected
in perceived membership influence.   It decreases, the
more negative the worker's view of the firm as an employer
and the more dissatisfied he is with the workers' share of
the profits of the firm.   Workers more strongly aware of
class differences in society tend to perceive low membership influence in the union.   Perceived membership influence has a curvilinear relationship to party preference.   Bourgeois workers especially are critical of membership influence in the union, and perceived influence
increases as we move from Communists to right-wing Social
Democrats.

Although level of participation in the affairs of the
works club has little relationship to perceived membership
influence in the union, data not given here indicate that
particularly local leaders in the large works clubs regard
the level of membership influence in the union as very
satisfactory.   Among the metal-workers in our sample in
elected positions within works clubs, we can discern three
different works roles: the full-time works club officials, who spend more than thirty-five hours per week in
union work;   the part-time officials, spending between
four and thirty-five hours in union work;   and the marginal officials, with only three hours or less per week in
union work (cf. Appendix 2).   Data in Figure 8.3 indicate
that regular participants and marginal works club officials perceive membership influence in the national union
almost in the same way as the average rank-and-file members and that part-time works club officials are only
somewhat more optimistic about the possibilities of rank-
and-file influence in the union.   Full-time works club
officials, however, have an extremely positive view of

TABLE 8.2 Multiple-classification analysis of perceived
membership influence in national union (proportion perceiving
high membership influence in popu-lation = 34%;   N = 3996)

Independent variables; category			Reporting high membership influence		Eta	Beta
			Unadjus-ted	Adjus-ted		
			%	%		
Sex	Men		35	35	0.044	0.052
	Women		28	27		
Age	-20 years		39	39	0.060	0.053
	21-30		33	36		
	31-40		34	34		
	41-50		32	33		
	51-60		38	34		
	61+		33	29		
Ethnicity	Swedish-born		33	33	0.065	0.052
	Foreign-born		40	39		
Perceived membership influence in works club	Low	0	9	20	0.340	0.208
		1	32	32		
		2	44	40		
	High	3	65	55		
Perceived bargaining power of works club	Low	0	10	26	0.360	0.177
		1	22	30		
		2	29	30		
		3	33	30		
		4	53	45		
		5	64	52		
	High	6	60	44		
Views of firm as an employer	Negative	0	15	24	0.229	0.114
		1	27	31		
		2	36	35		
	Positive	3	47	41		
Density of union activists in department	Low	0	24	30	0.178	0.112
		1	29	30		
		2	45	44		
	High	3	44	37		
Party preference	Communists		25	32	0.172	0.089
	Social Democrats	Left	35	35		
		Centre	43	38		
		Right	45	40		
	Bourgeois		20	25		
	Unknown		30	32		

Independent variable; category			Reporting high membership influence		Eta	Beta
			Unadjusted	Adjusted		
			%	%		
Fairness of workers'	Low	0	24	30	0.220	0.084
share of firm profits		1	34	34		
	High	2	51	41		
Level of union	Local leaders		54	24	0.041	0.072
participation	Marginal officials		40	23		
	Regular participants		36	28		
	Marginal participants		34	33		
	Outsiders		34	37		
Perceived	Low	0	44	37	0.173	0.064
class		1	40	38		
differences		2	30	32		
	High	3	21	30		
Knowledge of	Low	0	35	35	0.080	0.047
national		1	33	33		
union affairs		2	28	31		
		3	36	34		
	High	4	49	42		

$$R^2 = 0.220$$

possibilities for rank-and-file members to exert influence within the union, and of the relationship between the national union leadership and the rank-and-file members: practically all of them feel rank-and-file influence in the national union is high.

Because of the key role full-time works club officials play in the union, these views are especially significant. These officials fill the majority of the positions in the representative system within the union, and thus speak for the rank-and-file members as delegates to the union congresses and as members of the contract council, the union council and the executive board of the union.   Ombudsmen at the branch and national level are also recruited from among them.   They have frequent contacts with the national leadership, and can be expected to function as 'informants' to the leadership regarding rank-and-file views. At the local level they often perform important functions in other branches of the labour movement and sometimes also in local government.   Our data indicate that, in their role as full-time elected officials, they tend to some extent to be set apart from the rank-and-file members in a way that can potentially influence their functioning as member representatives.

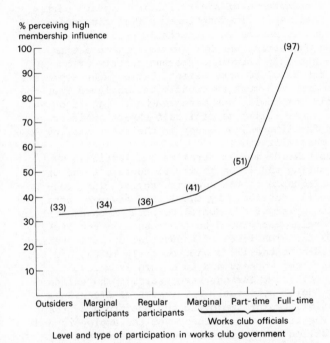

FIGURE 8.3 Percentage perceiving high membership influence in Swedish Metal Workers' Union by level and type of participation in government of works club (standardization for age, sex and ethnicity)

8   WHY INCREASING CENTRALIZATION?

Collective decision-making in conflict situations requires that elected representatives wield relatively strong decision-making power. As we have seen, a considerable centralization of power developed at an early stage in Swedish unions and accelerated markedly in the 1930s and in the postwar period. A complicated set of factors appears to underlie this development. The most important ones relate to the changing strategies of class conflict adopted by the labour movement. Others reflect the differing

positions of union leaders and rank-and-file members.
Increasing size of the organizations and an increasing
complexity of issues faced by the union also contribute
to this trend.

We have seen that full-time union officials generally
favour more centralization than rank-and-file members.
Their higher acceptance of centralization appears partly
to reflect their specific functions.   Full-time union
officials come to assume an essentially political role in
the union organization, which requires them to act as
'mediators' not only between different sectors of the
membership but also, to some extent, between the employers
and the members, who must eventually be convinced that the
best possible compromise has been reached.   It is only
natural that many full-time officials expect their functions to be facilitated, at least in the short run, by
increasing centralization.

The drive towards more centralization initiated by the
LO leaders during the 1930s, however, appears to be primarily a consequence of the new strategy of class conflict, gradually developed by the labour movement after
the coming to power of the Social Democratic government in
1932.   A partial background to the change in conflict
strategy was the high level of industrial disputes taking
place in Sweden in the 1920s and the early 1930s, and the
hardships that the workers had to endure as a result of
the high unemployment during these years.   The unions
saw the new Social Democratic government as offering a
crucial possibility for improving the positions of the
workers.   The continuing dominance of the employers and
the groups allied with them, however, necessitated the
development of a strategy of compromise founded on
attempts to increase the efficiency of production (see
chapter 4).

This economic growth strategy was based on Social Democratic control of the government.   Previously, the frequent strikes had been necessary but primarily defensive
measures.   Now legislation, not industrial action, was to
be used to improve the share of labour in the growing production.   The new strategy necessitated the co-ordination
of union action on the basis of class rather than on the
basis of industry or occupation.   As long as the labour
movement had been outside the government, the unions could
and had to act relatively independently in attempting to
defend and to improve the situation of their members;
they required co-ordination primarily for defensive purposes, to avoid draining the strike funds.   The new
strategy, however, required that all sectors of the union
movement accept the same major guidelines for action,

which was partly intended to increase productivity.   The
maintenance of the Social Democratic government became an
overriding goal.
   Institutional factors can partly explain why the initiative for this drive towards increasing centralization
of decision-making came from the LO leadership.   The
leaders of the LO were the only ones in organizational
positions in which the interests of the whole union movement could be considered.   In contrast to the leaders of
member unions and their sub-organizations, keyed to represent the interests of an industry, an occupation or a
group of workers, only the LO leaders were in organizational positions where they both had to - and could -
represent the interests of the workers as a class.
   The key role of the growth strategy of class conflict for the ensuing changes in the internal decision-
making procedures within the LO unions, and the complicated interplay between compromise and advance in this new
strategy, is well illustrated by the development of the
'solidaristic wage policy' of the LO.   The concept of a
solidaristic wage policy was introduced in the 1930s
(Lind, 1938b), but the meaning of this policy was partly
ambiguous and its accent has changed over time.   A long-
time goal of this policy, however, has been to decrease
'unwarranted' differences in wages between workers in
different sectors of the economy and, especially, to improve the wages of the lowest paid workers.   Since the
most visible differences in wages were found between
rather than within unions, an expanded role of the LO in
wage negotiations was seen as necessary.   The solidarity
of the better-off workers, channelled through the LO,
could help to improve the position of the weaker groups.
Solidaristic wage policy was an important argument for
shifting power from members union to the LO.   It was
stressed in connection with the acceptance of new union
statutes in 1941, and again in the mid-1950s, when co-
ordinated collective bargaining was established, involving
top-level negotiations between the LO and the SAF.
   From the beginning, however, the proponents of the solidaristic wage policy also emphasized economic growth in
the context of the long-term stability of the economy as
central elements in this policy (e.g. Lind, 1938b, p. 13).
In the internal union debate preceding the co-ordination
of wage negotiations under LO leadership in the 1950s,
stability of the economy and avoidance of inflation were
actually emphasized much more than the need to decrease
wage differentials (Meidner, 1973, pp. 145-6).
   Because the solidaristic wage policy implied that wage
demands were not to be based on the profitability of the

firm or branch of industry, but to be directed towards decreasing wage differentials among LO members, it came to
have two different types of effects. On the one hand, it
allowed for high profits in firms and branches with already high wages.   These profits could be used for investment and expansion, and this wage policy thus greatly
facilitated economic growth.   On the other hand, it also
helped to improve the position of the lowest paid workers
and introduced co-ordinated, class-based action into wage
negotiations.   But it was not until the end of the 1960s
that this policy became really effective in equalizing
wages within the LO.   Eventually, however, concern over
'excess' profits and the increasing inequality of wealth
resulting from this policy and other measures intended to
provide expansive firms with good possibilities to finance
investments, led to the very radical LO proposal of 'wage
earners' funds (see chapter 11).

The way in which the union hierarchy has structured and
differentiated the consequences of the efficiency strategy
of class conflict appear also to have had an effect upon
internal decision-making procedures.   Increasing the
efficiency of production has involved some negative consequences for rank-and-file members, e.g. a more intensive
utilization of working time, rationalization, mechanization, shift work, and control methods, which deprive workers of possibilities to derive intrinsic job satisfaction.   The union officials, however, are not directly
affected by these consequences.   Compared with the
latter, then, it was therefore more difficult for the
rank-and-file members to accept the new growth strategy.
The union leaders may have favoured greater centralization to overcome this source of internal resistance.

The greater centralization of decision-making within
the unions had also a specific political function - to
make it more difficult for the Communist opposition to
mobilize rank-and-file members against the new strategy.
During the 1920s and 1930s the Communists made several
attempts to strengthen their positions within the union
movement by advocating a militant strategy against the
employers.   Left-wing groups were able to mobilize widespread rank-and-file support for their strategy, for
example through large strikes in the mining industry in
1928, the paper industry in 1928 and 1932, the building
sector in 1933-4 and among the seamen in 1933.   In several referendums connected with these strikes, the members
defied the advice of the Social Democratic leadership in
their unions and in the LO.   The strike in the building
sector, in particular, was seen to hinder the Social Democratic government in its efforts to get the economy going;

it required the active intervention of the LO before it
could be brought to an end (Kupferberg, 1972).   The upsurge of Communist support towards the end of the Second
World War, and the crucial role played by referendums on
contact proposals in the big engineering strike in 1945,
probably underlined the desirability of decision-making
procedures, which would decrease opportunities for the
oppositional groups to mobilize rank-and-file members
against policies favoured by the Social Democratic leaders
(see chapter 9).

'Embourgeoisement' is an often suggested explanation of
the preference of labour leaders for accommodation with
employers, and for the growth strategy of class conflict.   This type of explanation is often supported by
arguments that union leaders come from 'the labour aristocracy' (e.g. Hentilä, 1974);   that an increasing proportion of labour political leaders come from middle-class
backgrounds (Parkin, 1971, pp. 128-36);   and that 'de-
radicalization' among union leaders has resulted from
changing styles of life and improved standards of living.

Such interpretations, however, do not appear to provide
a good explanation of the actions of Swedish union
leaders.   The selection processes involved in becoming
active in the union and in abstaining from moving over to
'the other side' by becoming a foreman (an option open to
a high proportion of union members active at the works
club level) tend to ensure that those who reach top
leadership positions are closer to the traditional radical
ideology of the labour movement than the average rank-and-
file members.   The salaries of the full-time union officials in the LO unions are also relatively modest, roughly
one and a half to two times the average wages of manual
workers. (20)   As argued in the debate on the embourgeoisement of the working class, an increased standard of
living also need not be de-radicalizing.   The standard
of living of union leaders probably has a very limited
effect upon the degree of union militancy.   For instance,
American union leaders, by Swedish standards, receive extremely high salaries;   at the same time the level of industrial disputes in North America is one of the highest
in the world.

While it can be argued that unions, because they are
organizations for conflict, require a relatively high
degree of centralization, this cannot explain the increasing centralization within the LO unions since the late
1930s.   On the contrary, increasing centralization was
accompanied by a marked decrease in industrial conflict. (21)

Our explanation of the increasing centralization of

decision-making within LO unions since the 1930s is primarily political.   The changes in the internal decision-
making procedures - as well as the decrease in industrial
conflict - can be viewed largely as consequences of the
new strategy of class conflict, which was gradually developed by the labour movement in a situation where employers and their allies were still dominant, but where
the labour movement had improved its position through
control over the government.   Our evidence thus again
speaks against the thesis of the independence of indus-
tiral and political conflict in 'post-capitalist' societies proposed by Dahrendorf (1959, pp. 267-72) and others.

9   FOR THE MEMBERS OR BY THE MEMBERS?

The Metal Workers' Union has been and remains a democratic
union.   As shown above, however, important changes in the
internal power structure in this and other LO unions have
taken place since the 1930s.   Actual decision-making
powers have tended to become concentrated to the LO, the
executive boards of the unions and the full-time officials.   Thus the LO unions are increasingly governed *for*
the members rather than *by* the members.
   Changes in decision-making procedures in the Metal
Workers' Union have affected membership influence not primarily by limiting the formal rights of the rank-and-file
members but by limiting the possibilities for oppositional
groups to mobilize the membership.   The single most important limitation of the latter type is probably discontinuation of advisory referendums on contract proposals.
Of the formal limitations on membership participation in
decision-making, the executive boards' appropriation of
the right to appoint all full-time union officials may
embody the greatest long-term significance.   Participation of the rank and file members in decision-making at
the national level is now limited to the quadrennial
elections of delegates to the congress and the advisory
council.
   The inclusion of 'working members' on the executive
board and the union council is apparently not a very
effective way of ensuring that the views of rank-and-file
members are adequately represented.   The relative passivity of the working members at the congresses of the
union, and the absence in recent years of dissension
within the union council, appear to indicate that the
outlook of working members does not differ much from that
of full-time union officials.   The role of the working
members as full-time works club officials may in some

measure account for this.   Moreover, the congress, formally the supreme decision-making institution within the
union, has only limited possibilities to effectively guide
union actions: it meets only every fourth year.   The
recent increase in the number of motions to the congresses, however, and the tendency towards a somewhat more
balanced flow of communication there, may indicate that it
is regaining some of its earlier importance in the conduct
of union affairs.

On the other hand, in the quadrennial elections to the
congress and to the advisory contract council, it is exceedingly difficult for oppositional groups to mobilize
membership support for candidates not acceptable to the
branch leadership.   The introduction of information conferences and 'membership consultations' helps to increase
communication from the rank-and-file members to union
leaders.   Yet their contribution to union democracy is
limited, since they leave initiative and interpretation at
the discretion of the union executive.   Of crucial importance in this context, however, is that the explicit and
well-known association between the Social Democratic Party
and the LO has made labour leaders sensitive to possible
political repercussions that can result from dissatisfaction with and within the LO unions. (22)

The leaders of the LO unions have undoubtedly strived
to take the interests and opinions of union members into
account in their decisions, and to articulate member
interests on a class basis.   Yet the present structure
of power within the unions brings to the fore central
issues in the general debate on democracy.   In view of
the objective differences in life situations between full-
time union officials and rank-and-file members and the
ensuing differences in the consequences of collective
decisions, can the interests of the rank-and-file members
be adequately represented without their own active participation in collective decision-making?   Is it necessary
to deprive rank-and-file members of the positive aspects
of self-government, central to classical democratic tradition, in order that the union movement effectively represent their interests as a class?

A high degree of centralism contains dangers of both a
decline in the responsiveness of union officials to rank-
and-file views, and a feeling among rank-and-file members
that important decisions are made above their heads.   It
can hardly be argued that the former risk has already
become a reality in the LO unions.   Our data indicate,
however, that the latter danger is no longer only a theoretical risk.   We have thus found relatively widespread
feelings of powerlessness and distance from national union

leaders among the rank-and-file members in the Metal
Workers' Union.

Once organizational forms have been developed that make
it possible for the union movement to act on the basis of
class rather than branch of industry or occupation, it
would appear easier to work out methods for rank-and-file
participation in decision-making that are conducive to
class action.   The new stress of the LO on industrial
democracy and on increasing the possibilities for workers
to participate in decision-making at work should also have
as its natural counterpart a search for ways to increase
opportunities for the rank-and-file members to participate
in the governing of the union movement.   Advisory referendums on contract proposals covering not merely a single
union but, for example, the whole LO-SAF area could be an
important step in this direction.

9 The internal union opposition

The debate on the working class in capitalist industrial society has not been limited to researchers. The research object itself has carried on a lively 'inner monologue' where its various factions have voiced differing and often conflicting views on the proper direction of the labour movement. Although the Swedish labour movement, since its beginning, has manifested a high degree of unity, it has continually contained at least an embryo of internal opposition to its Social Democratic leadership.

Initially, this internal opposition came from the right. The liberal opposition within the LO unions, however, was defeated already towards the end of the nineteenth century, although for some years it remained significant in a few craft unions. (1)   Since the beginning of this century the challenge to Social Democratic dominance within the labour movement has come from different groups to its left. The 1917 split in the Social Democratic Party formalized the cleavage between 'reformist' and 'revolutionary' tendencies within the labour movement, represented in the political sphere by the Social Democratic and the Communist Parties. In some periods, the Communist Party has defined itself as being a 'friendly prompter' in relation to the Social Democrats. The major tactical goal of the Communist Party, however, has been to break the Social Democratic dominance in the labour movement. For obvious reasons this led to attacks against the Social Democrats in and through the unions.

The Metal Workers' Union, which organizes the most advanced sectors of the working class, has been a forum where oppositional groups have been stronger than in most other Swedish unions. In the present chapter we will concentrate our discussion on this opposition, focusing on its nature and the factors affecting its strength. On

237

the basis of survey data we will also analyse the pattern
of criticism of union policy and the members' views on
unofficial strikes, an issue on which union leaders and
rank-and-file members often take opposite positions.

1   THE LEFT-WING OPPOSITION

In the union movement the conflicts between the Social
Democrats and the left-wing opposition have centred around
the tactics to be used against employers and, in a broader
sense, the strategies to be adopted in class conflict.
The economic growth strategy of class conflict, involving
some measure of co-operation between labour and capital
in an effort to increase the efficiency of production and
thereby the total product to be shared, has been the main
target for attack.   The opposition has viewed this strategy as 'class collaboration', which strengthens capitalism.
    Many of the controversies between the opposition and
the union leadership, however, have been primarily tactical, related to the fight for power within the union.
The controversies concerning the degree of centralism in
decision-making are part of these struggles.   The opposition has favoured decentralization, which facilitates
membership mobilization, while the union leadership has
been more in favour of centralism.   Separation between
political parties and unions has also been an issue of
tactical relevance;   the opposition has wanted to weaken
the relation between the Social Democratic Party and the
unions.
    The proceedings of the congresses of the Metal Workers'
Union give a flavour of the debate between the union
leadership and the left-wing opposition pertaining to the
growth strategy of class conflict.   A central area has
concerned union policy with regard to the rationalization
of work by time studies;   for instance, such issues were
debated at the congresses of 1929, 1932 and 1938.   While
the union leadership tended to accept and support various
measures aimed at increasing productivity, the opposition
was more critical, pointing out the double-edged character
of such measures.   At the congress in 1938, several motions thus criticized time studies on the basis that they
were arbitrary and 'aimed at achieving a frenzied and un-
normal speed of work, which in the long run will wear out
the worker'.   The union council, however, argued (Svenska
Metallindustriarbetareförbundet, 1938, pp. 174-5):

    Time studies are in many cases an instrument for
    achieving a rational production.   The increased

efficiency of production is a condition for the workers to receive higher wages and thereby to increase their standard of living.   To work against rationalization and time studies associated with them is thus to counteract the prerequisites for increased wages for the workers.

In the postwar period, differing views between the union leadership and the opposition about strategies of class conflict have been evidenced on the question of the extent to which the state of the national economy should be considered in the making of union wage policy.   The period of wage freezes, 1949-50, evoked motions to the 1950 congress criticizing union wage policy.   For instance, the Communist-led Göteborg branch stated (Svenska Metallindustriarbetareförbundet, 1950, p. 223):

> From the point of view of the working class the wage freeze policy must be condemned, since it is only in favour of the employers, as is the talk that workers and employers are in the same boat.   From this false starting point influential union leaders recommend an erroneous and basically deceitful wage policy.   Due to wage freezes and a restrictive wage policy in a pronounced boom period, the capitalists have stabilized their economy, while the workers continue to live in the same economic insecurity.   The capitalist society can never create social or economic security for the working people.   This is a fact which should be the guiding star in the present wage policy as well as when it comes to the fight for a socialistic society.

To such motions the union council replied (Svenska Metallindustriarbetareförbundet, 1950, p. 225):

> The question about the wage policy is considerably more complicated than what is stated in the motions.   The trade union movement can not only demand increased wages without thinking of the different types of consequences this will have on the economy of the society. It is fully evidenced that, if general wage rounds had taken place during the last few years, this would have created such changes in the level of prices and costs that the resulting wage increases would not have created better real wages.   The present wage policy has contributed to the stability of the economy of the nation and should have laid the ground for improvements in the standard of living in coming years.

As the examples given above indicate, union leaders have tended to see the sound development and stability of the total economy as a prerequisite for the improvement of the lot of the workers.   The left-wing opposition, however, has not seen economic growth and stability as

necessarily contributing to the advancement of the position of the working class;   consequently, it has recommended industrial action and militant policies more often
than has the union leadership.   The union leadership has
for a long time advocated a solidaristic wage policy,
where efforts were directed primarily to help to advance
the lowpaid workers while the highpaid ones were to be
held back.   The opposition has criticized the solidaristic wage policy, arguing that the highpaid workers should
be used as a spearhead for the lowpaid ones.

The opposition within the unions has been closely related to the parties and groups to the left of the Social
Democrats, and these political groups have made various
attempts to organize an opposition within the unions.
These attempts have not been very successful.   The internal opposition has been very strong only when important
segments of the Social Democratic union members have
joined with the left-wing groups to oppose policies of the
union leadership.   Internal union opposition can thus be
ranged along a continuum: at the one end has been basic
resistance to Social Democratic union policy on a broad
spectrum of questions;   at the other end opposition has
been focused around a specific issue.   Membership in organizations sponsored by left-wing political parties or
groups indicates what one might call *fundamental opposition*, involving a broad and basic resistance to reformist
policies.   This type of opposition has received only
limited support.   Opposition on specific issues, which
can be referred to as *issue opposition*, however, often has
been of considerable importance in the history of the
Swedish trade union movement and has had a much broader
political base.

2   OPPOSITION IN THE METAL WORKERS' UNION

The following sections will focus on changes over time in
the strength of the internal left-wing opposition within
the Metal Workers' Union.   In view of its loose and
changing organization, however, the delineation of the
opposition becomes problematic.   To trace the changes in
its strength we rely on minutes from the congresses and,
to some extent, from the contract conferences.   In each
assembly one or a few key issues in which the left-wing
opposition has been strongest and voting done on roll
calls can be taken as bases for a rough delineation of
the opposition. (2)   We can thereby follow variations
over time in opposition strength and study its sources of
strength.   The opposition thus defined will include not

only the 'fundamental opposition' based on the parties to
the left of the Social Democrats but also, and to a somewhat varying extent, the 'issue opposition', with a
broader political base.

At the early congresses of the Metal Workers' Union,
proposals of the executive board were rather frequently
defeated.   The basis for the opposition, however, appears
to have fluctuated from issue to issue and did not arise
from organized groups either within or outside the union
(Lindgren et al., 1948, pp. 297-304, 398-405, 549-54).
The early opposition thus appears to have been largely an
issue opposition.   Especially at the congresses of 1909
and 1916, however, an opposition based upon syndicalists
and the Socialist Youth Organization appeared but its influence was rather weak.   In 1908-9, a few branches of
the union (among them the Stockholm branch) discontinued
membership in the Social Democratic Party when the Socialist Youth Organization broke with the party (Schiller,
1967, p. 261).   In the decade before the First World War
and especially in 1916 the growing split within the Social
Democratic Party also manifested itself at the congresses.
Of the twenty founders of the Swedish Union Opposition,
ten were metal-workers, among them a future chairman of
the union, Fritiof Ekman.

In this early period of militant trade unionism, the
policies adopted by the union leadership appear to have
been congruous enough with the problems faced by the
union members so that they did not provide a basis for a
prolonged or significant opposition in the union.   At
any rate the bases of cleavage had not yet become stabilized.   The break in the Social Democratic Party in
1917, however, made manifest the lines of cleavages, and
from then on we can clearly distinguish a left-wing opposition within the union.   The variation over time in the
strength of this opposition, as defined in terms of voting
on key issues at each congress, is given in Table 9.1.

The breakthrough for the left-wing opposition came at
the congress of 1919 (Lindgren et al., 1948, pp. 644-95).
The election of delegates to the congress had been pre-
ceded by intensive party agitation, where the Union Propaganda Association was active.   The different oppositional groups won a narrow majority of the 200 delegates to
the congress.   The largest oppositional group, comprising
about 70-80 delegates, was connected with the Social Democratic Left Party.   In addition, 20-30 delegates - syndicalists or Social Democrats - joined the opposition
against the union leadership on some of the key issues.

Together these different oppositional groups won a
majority for a motion that, in the spirit of the Union

TABLE 9.1 Approximate strength of the left-wing opposition at the congresses of the Swedish Metal Workers' Union, 1919-73

Year of congress	Approximate proportion of delegates supporting the opposition	Content of proposals on the basis of which opposition strength is estimated*
	%	
1919	55	Membership influence in collective bargaining, collective membership in political parties
1922	32	Membership influence in collective bargaining, collective membership in political parties
1926	19	Collective membership in political parties
1929	<5	Activity of the Committee for Union Unity
1932	25	Membership influence in collective bargaining, criticism of executive board concerning the handling of wage negotiations
1935	22	Acceptance of new 'normal statutes', criticism concerning the forms for appointment of the new chairman in 1932
1938	<5	
1941	11	Expelling of Communists from elected positions
1944	42	Return of expelled Communists, membership influence in collective bargaining, editing of union journal
1946	44	Vote of confidence for the executive board for the handling of the 1945 engineering strike
1947	29	Membership influence in collective bargaining, socialization of metal-working industry
1950	<5	

Year of congress	Approximate proportion of delegates supporting the opposition	Content of proposals on the basis of which opposition strength is estimated*
	%	
1953	<5	
1957	<5	
1961	<5	
1965	<5	
1969	<5	
1973	<5	

* Where two or more issues are used, the mean vote for the opposition on the issues is given.

Propaganda Association, required that the final decision concerning contracts should be made by members in a referendum, and that the executive board of the union could not overrule a strike proposal, which was supported by three-quarters of the members in a secret vote. The motion was sponsored by the Stockholm branch of the union, the chairman of which was Fritiof Ekman. It was defeated in a subsequent referendum, however, and the opposition thus did not manage to achieve any crucial changes in the statutes of the union.

The ideology of the Union Propaganda Association was also manifested in other decisions at the congress. According to the new statement of purpose accepted by the congress, the union was to foster the workers for the struggle for reshaping society on a socialist basis, and to direct its work towards the socialization of production. The congress decided to establish a 'socialization committee' to work out proposals in this direction, and to set up a 'register of employers' - which was to include information on working conditions, wages, etc. in different firms - to be used for example in secret blockades. It further recommended that the branches not join political parties. These measures, however, turned out to be of small practical significance.

Probably the most important consequence of the congress in 1919 was that a set of opposition representatives attained leading positions in the union. These men were to remain active in key roles in the union for up to the

next three decades.   In the party splits in 1921, 1924,
1929 and 1937, however, most of them returned to the
Social Democratic Party.   At the congress in 1919 the
opposition received a majority on the executive board as
well as on the union council.   Since it was not united,
however, all full-time officials except one were re-elected.   Owing to substitutions the opposition lost its
majority in the executive board before the next congress.
Union policy thus was not drastically changed during these
years.
    Partly as a result of criticisms at the congress, the
chairman and treasurer of the union resigned shortly
afterwards.   In 1920 Johan-Olov Johansson was appointed
chairman of the union; he had become the first ombudsman
in the iron and steel sector of the union in 1908, and was
a member of the Social Democratic Party.   Because of his
independence and radicalism he came to function as a unifying link between the newly elected radicals and the
older union officials, thereby easing the tensions in the
union leadership.   Five years later Johansson became the
treasurer of the LO. (3)
    Two of the opposition representatives who attained
leading positions in the union in 1919, Fritiof Ekman and
Oscar Westerlund, came to play especially important roles
in the union.   In many ways these two men personify the
drama and fate of the internal union opposition.
    Fritiof Ekman, one of the founders of the Swedish
Union Opposition and a leading representative of the
Social Democratic Left Party, defeated an incumbent ombudsman in the elections at the congress in 1919.   After
the split in the Left Party in 1921 he went over to the
Social Democratic Party a few years later.   In 1925
Ekman defeated Westerlund in the contention for the
chairmanship in the union, primarily because of politically based resistance against Westerlund from among full-
time officials in the executive board.   As chairman of
the union Ekman was often criticized.   He became an
ardent opponent to the Communists as well as a convinced
spokesman for the efficiency strategy of class conflict
(Back, 1963, p. 210).   In 1932 he became minister of
commerce in the Social Democratic government, and a few
years later he assumed a position in the public bureaucracy.
    Westerlund was elected to the union council in 1919,
became secretary of the union in 1920 and vice chairman in
1922.   The roads of Westerlund and Ekman parted when
Westerlund joined the Communist Party in the party split
in 1921, as he later stated 'after a three months period
of consideration'.   As vice-chairman of the Metal

Workers' Union, Westerlund was the most prominent representative of the left-wing opposition in the LO unions
during the following years.   In this capacity he was
often subject to strong attacks.   Westerlund remained in
the Communist Party after the break in 1924, but in the
1929 split he joined the Communist Party outside the Comintern.   In 1932 he was expelled from this party when, as
a member of the bargaining committee of the Metal Workers'
Union, he finally accepted wage cuts demanded by the employers during the depression.   Although several of the
leaders of the party were in sympathy with Westerlund's
point of view, it was against the more militant party
line.   At the meeting where Westerlund was expelled a
friendly atmosphere prevailed, and he himself declared
that in spite of what had happened, he would not become
'an enemy of our movement' (Kennerström, 1974, p. 51).

As in 1925, Westerlund was bypassed in the appointment
of union chairman in 1932, again largely owing to politically based opposition from other full-time union officials.   Soon after his expulsion from the Communist
Party, he joined the Social Democratic Party, and was then
unanimously appointed chairman of the union in 1936.   A
decade later he was to lead Social Democratic attacks
against the Communists in connection with the 1945 engineering strike.   After Westerlund's death in 1952, his
successor to the chairmanship of the union, Arne Geijer,
said that the experiences during this strike '[have] shortened Westerlund's life by several years' (Svenska Metallindustriarbetareförbundet, 1953, p. 8).

The oppositional tide within the union began to recede,
and at the congress of 1922 the strength of the opposition
had decreased, a tendency that continued at the following
congresses.   At the congress in 1926 the opposition received support only from about one-fifth of the delegates.
To the first conference of the Committee of Union Unity in
the same year, only about 17 per cent of the metal-workers
were represented.   A low point was reached at the congress in 1929, where only a handful of delegates represented the opposition.   In comparison with the preceding
congress elections, the vote for the oppositional candidates increased but the opposition did not manage to get a
majority in any of the big branches.   The breaks in the
Communist Party in these years partly explain the decline
in opposition strength.   At the congresses during the depression in 1932 and 1935, representation of oppositional
groups increased to almost one-quarter of the delegates.
At the conferences arranged by the Central Committee for
the Unemployed in 1930 and 1933, however, the representation from the Metal Workers' Union was small - only 1-2
per cent (Kennerström, 1974, p. 54).

When Oscar Westerlund joined the Social Democrats in
the middle of the 1930s, the opposition lost its leading
representative in the union.   The great Social Democratic
victory at the communal election in 1938, when the party
for the first time received more than 50 per cent of the
total vote, was reflected in the very low representation
of the opposition at the union congress of the same year.
At the congress of 1941, following the LO's decision to
disqualify Communists from elected union positions, the
oppositional groups were very weak.

The Second World War, however, was accompanied by a
strong upsurge for the opposition within the Metal Workers' Union.   The opposition returned to the congress of
1944 with the support of close to half of the delegates.
The following year the opposition was also manifested in
the big engineering strike, which became a dramatic con-
frontation between the union leadership and the internal
opposition.

3   THE BIG ENGINEERING STRIKE

In the history of the Swedish labour movement, the 1945
engineering strike ranks second only to the general strike
in 1909 in terms of length and involvement.   These two
strikes also have other similarities.   In both cases reluctant union leaders felt themselves forced by militant
members and oppositional groups to declare a strike, which
they judged unjustified and apparently also doomed to
failure.   The union leaders, however, were in political
situations where a strike was perceived as necessary to
prevent the more militant factions from gaining an advantage within the labour movement (Westerståhl, 1945, pp.
144-50; Schiller, 1967, pp. 226-35; Treslow, 1972).
The engineering strike thus turned into a three-cornered
fight between the employers, the union leadership and the
left-wing opposition.   According to Social Democratic
interpretations, this strike is often seen as caused by
Communist machinations.   This, however, is too simplistic
a view.   Instead the engineering strike illustrates the
complicated processes that can bring a majority of the
rank-and-file members in opposition to the policy of the
union leaders.

Sources of the 1945 strike must be sought in the deprivations resulting from the defence effort as well as in
the social dislocations during the Second World War.   The
'frame agreement' concluded by the LO and the SAF at the
end of 1939 tied wages to the cost of living index, aiming
at a 75 per cent compensation for price increases.   In

the agreements of the next two years the compensation
level was reduced to 50 per cent.   As prices rose real
wages thus decreased very considerably. (4)
At the end of 1942 a price freeze was introduced.
Combined with a wage freeze, it was to allow some wage
increases among the lowest paid workers but, in practice,
was also to allow for some wage drift.   Furthermore, the
labour shortage during the war had apparently led to increased efforts to rationalize industry.
The Social Democratic policy during the war was to
'distribute the burdens according to capacity', and to
avoid an inflationary development of the type that had
occurred during the First World War.   The wage and price
freezes were thus seen as essential elements in the anti-
inflationary policy.   The Communists claimed that the
workers suffered more than others, and that inequalities
in wages and property were increasing.   Such claims,
however, were not easy to substantiate (Hirdman, 1974,
pp. 190-209;   Rehn, 1945).   In the wartime years the increases in money wages were in fact slightly higher for
industrial workers than for the white-collar groups in
industry.   Workers in agriculture and forestry, with low
wages, improved their relative position considerably,
while the wage for construction workers, a high-wage category, developed least as favourably (LO, 1951, p. 112).
The critics, however, claimed that the construction of the
cost of living index did not fully reflect the impact of
increasing prices.   Prolonged periods of military service
also tended to decrease the standard of living (Abukhanfusa, 1975).
The fact that prices were fixed to allow profits even
in the least efficient firms, however, could be expected
to result in high profits being made in the more efficient
parts of industry.   In sectors of importance for the
defence effort, e.g. the metal-working industry, profits
were relatively high.   In recognition of such possibilities, the government introduced an extra tax on dividends
from war profits that favoured the investment of profits
in the firms.   Income taxes generally were made more progressive during the war.   Thus the Social Democrats
apparently went to considerable length in their efforts
to 'distribute burdens according to capacity'.
The main disagreements, however, developed around the
question of how long the restrictive policies were to be
maintained.   In the beginning the war burdens were generally accepted by the workers.   From the summer of 1943,
however, the Communists argued for an end to the wage
freeze.   The new postwar programme of the Social Democrats, accepted in the spring of 1944, postponed a return

to the 1938 standard of living until the immediate postwar
period.   At the union congress in 1944 the opposition had
strong support;   even some Social Democrats accused the
union leadership of passivity in its wage policy.

Up to 1944 contracts were agreed upon in advance negotiations before their termination, and thus without referendums.   In the elections to the contract conference
in the engineering sector in September 1944, the oppositional groups won a majority among the delegates.   Anti-
cipating opposition at the conference, the executive board
suggested that the contract be terminated.   Because of
the danger of inflation, however, the policy of wage restraint had to continue.   The executive board outlined a
proposal for a contract that would slightly increase minimum wages.   While in line with the restraint policy,
according to the union executive the proposal provided
ample margins for bargaining and could not be expected to
be fully achieved.

The contract conference, however, raised the bid considerably by asking for higher wage increases as well as
improved possibilities both to check the bases for time
studies and to bargain on piece rates set by time studies.
The LO representative to the conference backed the chairman of the union, Oscar Westerlund, who denounced these
demands as totally unrealistic and harmful, since they
would break the wage freeze and lead to inflation.   The
opposition, however, received a majority among the delegates in the bargaining committee of the union.   In the
ensuing negotiations the union leaders thus had to work
for demands to which they were personally opposed.

The counter-proposal from the employers' association in
the engineering sector demanded a status quo in terms of
wages, and a considerable concession from the workers in
other respects, e.g. with regard to their potential influence on time studies.   The employers felt their position was strong: they feared no foreign competition since
practically all foreign trade was discontinued.   Thus
they refused to consider the proposal made by the contract
conference.

When the attempts at conciliation failed, the union
arranged a referendum where the alternatives were to continue negotiations in order to get the best possible
agreement, or to go on strike in support of the demands
already made.   The union journal made it clear that the
executive board wanted to continue negotiations on the
basis of a considerably modified proposal, and hinted at
political disagreements in the bargaining committee.   The
outcome of the referendum (in which 77 per cent of the
members participated) was 72 per cent in favour of the

strike alternative.   Although not necessitated by the
union constitution, the political situation was such that
the executive board chose not to go against the vote of
the members.   Nor did the LO leadership use its recently
acquired constitutional veto power.   The strike started
on 5 February 1945.

The politically based disagreements among the union
negotiators soon became public.   The LO leaders gave full
support to the restrictive policy of the union executive.
The three-cornered fight was thus a fact.   At the end of
March the executive board tried to get support directly
from the members in a referendum on its original contract
proposal, which had been turned down by the contract conference.   With a 73 per cent participation rate, the proposal was turned down by 59 per cent of the voters.   At
the second meeting of the contract conference in the
middle of May, August Lindberg, chairman of the LO and
one-time member of the Union Propaganda Association, declared that, although the strike from the beginning had
been doomed to failure, it had been necessary to accept it
in order not to give the Communists an advantage.   Referring to lost strikes in the 1920s and 1930s, unsupported
by the union leaders but in which the Communists had been
very active, he said (Svenska Metallindustriarbetareförbundet, 1945, p. 48):

> After long and severe months the workers had to go back
> [to work].   These were very hard experiences, but it
> appears that one has to have these experiences as new
> cadres come to the branches.   There is nothing one can
> do to it, one just has to go ahead and try to make the
> best possible of the situation ... it would appear that
> we are forced to do this at least once for every gen-
> eration.

In the middle of May the board of conciliation arranged
the third referendum on the basis of a proposal that was
not supported by the union executive.   With a participation rate of 73 per cent, the proposal was turned down by
77 per cent of the voting members.   At the third meeting
of the contract conference in May a proposal from the executive board, which contained not insignificant improvements over its original proposal, won a narrow majority
and was accepted by the employers with only minor modifi-
cations.   The Communists, however, were divided over its
acceptance (Olsson, 1976b, pp. 37-8).   In the fourth referendum, at the end of June, 66 per cent of the members
participated and 55 per cent voted against the proposal.
When the employers threatened to enlarge the conflict the
executive board used its veto power, signed the contract
proposal on 6 July and thus ended the five-month strike.

The final contract included the increase in minimum wages
originally proposed by the executive board, as well as
some additional improvements demanded by the opposition.
    The engineering strike highlights some of the differ-
ences between the union leadership and the oppositional
groups: problems of internal communication, and the role
of politics in decision-making within the union. The
leaders of the union as well as the LO appear to have
decided their wage policy as much from considerations of
what they saw as required by the total Swedish economy as
from considerations of the sectional demands by the union
members. If anything, the benefit of doubt when judging
the basis for the demands appears to have been given to
the societal interests. In an uncertain situation the
union leadership thus chose to continue the wage freeze
rather than to support the wage claims of the majority of
the members. The oppositional groups, on the contrary,
gave a higher priority to members' sectional interests.
    It appears doubtful if the union leaders would have
continued support of the wage freeze policy after 1944 had
they been fully aware of the massive membership resistance
to this policy. Possibly they were unaware of the momentum that the opposition to the restrictive policy has acquired when the end of the war was in sight, and the
spirit of sacrifice and the danger of an invasion had
faded into the background. Because of the absence of
contract referendums the union leaders had lost a valuable
channel for contact with rank-and-file opinion in this
extraordinary situation. The union chairman, Oscar
Westerlund, especially appears to have underestimated the
militancy and dissatisfaction among the rank-and-file
members. (5) What the union leaders may have initially
regarded as primarily Communist-instigated dissatisfaction
turned out to have won the support of a large proportion
of the Social Democratic rank-and-file members. Probably
roughly 60-70 per cent of the Social Democratic metal-
workers supported the oppositional alternative in the
first referendum.
    When the lines of cleavage had been drawn at the first
meeting of the contract conference and were made public in
connection with the first referendum, an important objective of the Social Democratic union leaders probably
became to prove that the more militant policy advocated by
the Communists was wrong. Even the Communist members of
the bargaining committee, however, gave the executive representatives credit for working in accordance with the
decisions of the majority at the contract conference
(Svenska Metallindustriarbetareförbundet, 1945, p. 19).
But the publicity given to the original proposal of the

executive board, the continued adherence of the board to
this proposal (made evident e.g. in the second referendum)
and the negativism of the LO leaders to the strike all
worked against the policy of the opposition.

The employers were encouraged to continue resistance:
they rightly perceived that the executive board of the
union exercised strong pressures upon the recalcitrant
members of the bargaining committee, and that the LO
leaders were strongly against this strike.   The resistance from the employers' organization also reflected
their wish not to play into the hands of the Communists.
This strong negativism actually made it easier for the
union opposition to defend its position to the general
public.   It was internally criticized within the SAF,
which would have preferred a less negativist approach in
the beginning of the negotiations (Treslow, 1972).

The tenacity of the rank-and-file metal-workers in
their resistance to the solutions favoured by the union
executive (as indicated by the outcome of the four referendums) deprived the Social Democratic leaders of the
opportunity to demonstrate the obvious failure of militant Communist union policy.   Neither could the Communists claim, however, that the outcome of the strike was a
success.

It has often been assumed that the outcome of the
strike was detrimental to the Communist Party.   For example, according to Peterson (1954, p. 496), 'the 1945
strike almost ranks with Prague as a cause of Communist
decline in Sweden'.   Such interpretations appear unfoun-
ded.   At the extra congress in 1946, demanded by the
opposition to discuss the activity of the executive board
in connection with the strike, the opposition received
almost half of the delegates - slightly more than at the
1944 congress.   In the 1946 communal elections the Communists achieved the record support of their history.

The great decline in Communist support came in connection with the Communist takeover in Czechoslovakia in
1948 and the subsequent Cold War atmosphere.   Since the
1950s only a handful of delegates at most have offered
more systematic opposition at the congresses of the Metal
Workers' Union.   As we have seen, however, the extent of
opposition has increased at the firm level in recent
years, although it has not been strong enough to win a
sizable representation at the congresses.

4   OPPOSITION STRONGHOLDS

Sociological theory in addition to previous studies would
lead us to expect that opposition strength will vary by
type of community as well as by size of firm (e.g. Lipset
et al., 1956; Lindblad, 1960; Ingham, 1970).   The congress minutes contain information on the election district
and branch of all delegates.   The oppositional delegates
can thus be located on branches and communities but not on
firms.   Some information on the structure of firms in the
communities is, however, available.   An analysis of variation in the local strength of the opposition is here
based on voting patterns on the two occasions when opposition strength was at its maximum, i.e. 1919 and 1944-6.
Branches (election districts) are classified according to
community type as well as the size distribution of firms
within them. (6)
    Roll calls at the congress in 1919 on the proposal con-
cerning greater membership influence in collective bargaining are used to measure the bases and strength of the
opposition.   The delegates are identified by the branches
or election districts that they represented. (7)   Contiguous smaller branches had been combined into election districts.   As is shown in Table 9.2, the opposition was

TABLE 9.2 Percentage of votes cast for the opposition at
the congress in 1919, by type of branch/election district

Type of branch/ election district	Votes for opposition %	(No. of delegates)
1 Three big cities	74	(57)
2 Mill towns with large firms (700+ workers) or branches with high average size of firms (120+)	73	(51)
3 Branches with medium average size of firms (50-120)	36	(56)
4 Branches (election districts) with small average size of firms (-50)	25	(36)
Total	54	(200)

strong in the three largest cities (Stockholm, Göteborg
and Malmö). The opposition was also strong in communities where one or a few big firms dominated the labour
market, i.e. in mill towns (generally with relatively
large iron or steelworks), or in communities with a high
average size of firms in the metal-working industry. In
the remaining branches opposition strength was considerably lower but tended to increase with increasing average
size of firms.

In the period 1944-6 the opposition is delineated on
the basis of roll calls at the congresses in 1944 and
1946, as well as at the first contract conference in connection with the wage negotiations in 1944-5. Oppositional delegates are identified at the congress in 1944
as those supporting motions concerning expelled Communi-
nists, a proposal for increased membership influence in
collective bargaining, and/or criticism of the editing of
the union journal; at the extra congress in 1946 as
those voting against the proposal of confidence for the
executive board, and at the contract conferences as those
voting against the original wage proposals by the executive board. During this period the opposition received
almost unanimous support from the three big-city branches,
which contributed somewhat more than one-fourth of the
delegates to these assemblies (Table 9.3). Opposition
strength was considerably lower in other types of branches
and communities, but again tended to increase with the
extent to which large firms were found in the
branches. (8)

The role of big cities and large firms as opposition
strongholds is further illustrated if we look at voting
patterns of the four largest branches of the union -
Stockholm, Göteborg, Malmö and Eskilstuna (9) (Table 9.4).
Of the three big cities, the Göteborg branch has most
often been in the hands of the opposition, while the Malmö
branch generally has been held by the Social Democrats.
As we have seen, the Göteborg branch played a central role
in attempts to organize the union opposition in the period
between the wars. In Eskilstuna, a medium-sized community with the fourth largest branch in the union, the
union opposition has traditionally been very weak. (10)

The same pattern is also revealed when we look at the
relative strength of the parties to the left of the Social
Democrats in these four communities. In Göteborg, the
left-wing parties have been strong since 1917. In 1934
a left-wing group in the Social Democratic Party in Göteborg joined the Socialist Party. Eskilstuna, on the contrary, has been a Social Democratic bastion. In fact,
the third and only loyal youth organization of the Social

TABLE 9.3 Percentage of votes cast for the opposition at the congresses in 1944 and 1946 and the contract conferences in 1944, by type of branch/election district

Type of branch/election district	Congress 1944 %	(N)	Congress 1946 %	(N)	Contract conferences 1954* %	(N)	All three assemblies %	(N)
1 Three big cities	90	(73)	100	(72)	100	(39)	96	(184)
2 Branches dominated by large firms with 1400+ workers	40	(30)	40	(30)	32	(25)	38	(85)
3 Branches having over 25 per cent of workers in plants with 700–1400 workers	26	(50)	22	(49)	31	(36)	26	(135)
4 Other branches/election districts having at least one firm with 200–700 workers	22	(64)	15	(65)	17	(53)	18	(182)
5 Branches/election districts with smaller firms only	15	(33)	18	(34)	13	(24)	15	(91)
Total	44	(250)	44	(250)	40	(177)	43	(677)

TABLE 9.4   Strength of the left-wing opposition in the four largest branches of the Metal Workers' Union in 1919 and 1944-6 and selected characteristics of the communities where these branches are located

Branch in	Votes cast for opposition		Votes for left-wing parties as percentage of Social Democratic vote		Metal-workers in firms with over 1000 workers		Industrial workers of population	
	1919	1944-6	1920	1944	1919	1944	1920	1945
	%	%	%	%	%	%	%	%
Stockholm	75	100	12	39	14	22	10	10
Göteborg	89	100	10	61	55	57	11	13
Malmö	17	73	2	16	29	•38	15	15
Eskilstuna	9	0	6	11	19	20	22	25

Democratic Party was initiated from Eskilstuna in 1917 and
had had its seat there up to 1930.

When these four communities are compared in terms of
the structure of firms in the metal-working sector, we
find that four or five big firms, three of them shipyards,
dominate Göteborg, whereas the other communities each have
only one relatively large firm from the metal-working
sector.   Eskilstuna especially is noted for an old tradition of small-scale metal manufacturing firms.   Thus two
factors appear to be of importance for the strong oppositional traditions in Göteborg: the big-city factor, and
the domination of the city of big firms with large proportions of skilled workers.   Stockholm, the capital of the
country, also has been the natural headquarters for all
political groups, and oppositional groups have traditionally been strong there.

The organizational ties between the internal union opposition and political groups to the left of the Social
Democrats leads us to expect a correlation between the
strength of the left-wing parties and union opposition.
As is shown in Figure 9.1, there is such a correlation
over time.   The upsurge in the electoral support for
parties to the left of the Social Democrats at the end of
the First and Second World Wars as well as during the mid-
1930s is reflected in a simultaneous increase of opposition strength at the congresses of the Metal Workers'
Union.

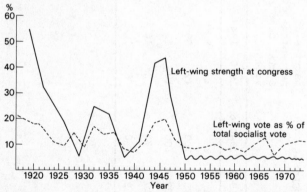

FIGURE 9.1 Approximate strength of left-wing opposition
at the congresses of the Swedish Metal Workers' Union,
1919-73, and proportion of left-wing party vote of total
socialist vote in general elections, 1917-76

The relative strength of parties to the left of the
Social Democrats on the community level also tends to co-
vary with the strength of the internal opposition.   For

the larger branches (with over 200 members), we can take
the relative strength of the Social Democratic Left Party
in the elections to the Riksdag in 1920 in the area of
the branch as a measure of relative Left Party strength
in the branch one year earlier.   The results indicate
that, with increasing relative strength of the Left Party
in the area, the opposition strength in the branch tends
to increase (Table 9.5).   A similar relationship is also

TABLE 9.5 Percentage of branches with strong left-wing
opposition at the congress in 1919, by relative strength
of the Social Democratic Left Party in the area of the
branch (only branches with at least 200 members included)

Relative strength of Social Democratic Left Party in area*	% of branches with strong opposition**	(No. of branches)
	%	
Low	38	(21)
Medium	47	(17)
High	89	(19)

* Votes for the Left Party as % of Social Democratic
party: weak = below 14%; medium = 14-28%; and
strong = 25+%.
** At least one-third of the votes for the opposition.

found in the period 1944-6: given the structure of the
branch, the proportion of delegates supporting the opposition covaries with the relative electoral strength of
the Communist Party in 1944 in the area of the branch
(Table 9.6).
     As noted above, some of the larger branches like those
in Göteborg and Eskilstuna have had long patterns of
either opposition or loyalty to the executive board of
the union.   But a more detailed analysis of the forty-
seven large branches in the union, the voting patterns
of which can be traced in 1919 as well as in 1945-6, indicates that such traditions are exceptional (Table 9.7).
In these branches no overall association is found between
opposition strength in 1919 and in 1944-6.   The weakness
and disarray in the organizational basis of the opposition
have apparently inhibited the formation of more lasting
local patterns of opposition within the union.

TABLE 9.6 Percentage of votes cast for the opposition at the congresses in 1944 and in 1946 and the contract conference in 1946, by type of branch/election district and relative Communist voting strength in the area in 1944 (election districts composed of smaller locals excluded)

Type of branch	Relative Communist strength in area*					
	Low		High		Total	
	%	(N)	%	(N)	%	(N)
1 Three big cities	73	(26)	100	(158)	96	(184)
2 Branches dominated by one big firm with 1400+ workers	17	(24)	46	(61)	38	(85)
3 Branches with over 25 per cent of workers in firms with 700-1400 workers	16	(69)	36	(60)	25	(129)
4 Branches with at least one firm with 200-700 workers	2	(41)	42	(31)	19	(72)

* Communist vote below or above 23% of the Social Democratic vote

TABLE 9.7 Percentage of branches in the Swedish Metal
Workers' Union with strong opposition in 1944-6, by
strength of the opposition in the branch in 1919 (larger
branches only)

Opposition strength in branch in 1919	% of branches with strong opposition in 1944-6	(No. of branches)
Low	43	(26)
High	46	(21)

5 OPPOSITION AND DEPRIVATION

The covariation over time as well as on the community
level between the strength of left-wing political parties
and the internal union opposition might serve as a take-
off for 'conspirational' theories: the internal opposition could be seen as having been engineered from the outside by more or less 'foreign' forces.   Such a theory
leaves unexplained, however, why the strength of the parties to the left of the Social Democrats has varied.

The covariation over time between the strength of internal union opposition and left-wing political parties
can be interpreted as the results of their common dependence on the same factors.   Because of the close alliance
between the Social Democrats in politics and in the LO
unions, worker dissatisfaction with policy in one area can
be reflected in the other; since party lines are more
established in politics than in union elections, we would
expect the effects of variation in worker dissatisfaction
to be more pronounced in union elections than in general
elections.

The peaks of opposition strength came at the end of the
two world wars and in the first half of the 1930s.   These
were periods when the increase in the standard of living
of the working class was interrupted and reversed.   After
the beginning of the First World War, real wages in manufacturing decreased up to 1917, and reached the prewar
level only in 1919 (Bagge et al., 1933, ch. 13).   The
years 1917 and 1918 were also marked by a shortage of food
and hunger demonstrations (Klockare, 1967).   Unemployment
within the metal-working industry was relatively low
during the first part of the war, but increased somewhat
towards its end (Svenska Metallindustriarbetareförbundet,
1919, p. 6).   Also, the first part of the 1930s was

characterized by decreasing real wages and high unemployment.   During the Second World War unemployment was relatively low while real wages dropped (see above).

It thus appears that the increase in opposition votes
in the union elections as well as in the general elections
during these three periods resulted from an *increasing
absolute deprivation of the working class*.   A partial
exception to this pattern is the depression after the
First World War, but this was relatively short and real
wages decreased only during one year, 1922 (SOS, 1942,
p. 79).   Opposition strength was also relatively high at
that time.

6   CRITICISM OF UNION POLICY

Let us now.move over to study the pattern of criticism
and disagreements between the rank-and-file members and
the union leadership that were found in the late 1960s.
Two questions in the survey among the metal-workers can
be taken as an index of *criticism of union policy* (Appendix 2).   The questions refer to aspects of union policy
upon which the internal opposition traditionally has been
focused.   One concerns the degree of militancy against
the employers: 'Do you ever have the feeling that the
union leadership yields too easily to the point of view
of the employers?'   The other question concerns the
relative stress of sectional versus societal interests
in union policy: 'Do you think that in wage negotiations
the union leadership pays too much attention to the opinions within the government?'

A multiple-classification analysis with eleven independent variables can account for 31 per cent of the variance in criticism of union policy (Table 9.8).   Criticism shows a curvilinear relationship with age and is
highest among persons in their forties.   The perceived
bargaining power of the works club emerges as the variable
most strongly related to criticism of union policy.
Since the rated bargaining power of the works club in turn
is related to other important aspects of how the works
club is perceived to function, this indicates that if the
works club is not perceived to function in a satisfactory
way, criticism of union policy is pronounced.   Dissatisfaction with the workers' share of the profits of the
firm also increases dissatisfaction with union policy.
As can be expected, criticism of union policy clearly increases with increasing dissatisfaction with membership
influence in the union.   Criticism of union policy cannot
easily be ascribed to passivity or ignorance.   If any-

TABLE 9.8 Multiple-classification analysis of criticism of union policy (proportion in population indicating high or medium criticism = 40%; N = 3996)

Independent variable; category		Critical of union policy		Eta	Beta
		Unadjusted %	Adjusted %		
Sex Men		42	41	0.108	0.055
Women		25	32		
Age -20 years		14	28	0.190	0.117
21-30		36	35		
31-40		44	43		
41-50		50	45		
51-60		43	45		
61+		40	40		
Ethnicity Swedish-born		41	38	0.051	0.062
Foreign-born		35	46		
Perceived bargaining	Low 0	78	66	0.430	0.289
power of works' club	1	58	52		
	2	41	40		
	3	23	29		
	4	25	31		
	5	20	25		
	High 6	18	25		
Perceived membership	Low 0	67	56	0.408	0.238
influence in union	1	32	35		
	.2	23	31		
	High 3	15	25		
Participation	Local leaders	29	41	0.157	0.095
in works' club	Marginal office-holders	48	48		
government	Regular participants	49	46		
	Marginal participants	48	44		
	Outsiders	33	36		
Party preference	Communists	65	52	0.218	0.092
	Social Left	47	42		
	Democrats Centre	30	36		
	Right	31	38		
	Bourgeois	44	40		
	Unknown	35	38		
Perceived fairness	Low	55	45	0.273	0.082
of workers' share	Medium	37	39		
of firm profits	High	20	34		

Independent variable; category			Critical of union policy		Eta	Beta
			Unadjusted	Adjusted		
			%	%		
Perceived class differences	Low	0	29	38	0.211	0.059
		1	32	37		
		2	44	42		
	High	3	58	44		
Knowledge of national union affairs	Low	0	34	38	0.127	0.037
		1	43	42		
		2	49	40		
		3	50	43		
	High	4	42	39		
Size of workplace	Small		40	37	0.022	0.013
	Medium		43	41		
	Large		40	40		

$$R^2 = 0.309$$

thing, critical views are more widespread among regular participants and marginal office-holders than among outsiders, and they do not decrease with an increasing knowledge of national union affairs.

Opposition to union policy is embedded in a wider political context. Communist workers especially are more critical of union policy than others. Left-wing Social Democrats and bourgeois workers are also relatively critical. Awareness of class differences in Swedish society colours the views on union policy among the metal-workers. We find that among both Social Democratic and bourgeois workers criticism of union policy increases with an increasing awareness of class differences (Figure 9.2). Among Communist workers the criticism tends to be high irrespective of awareness of class differences. In sum, however, in the late 1960s the criticism of union policy as reflected in these questions came largely from the left. This pattern may of course change with changes in union policy. In the mid-1970s, the union leaders have sometimes been accused of being too radical, for example on the issue of wage earners' funds (chapter 11).

The level and type of participation in works club government is also of relevance for the views on union policy. We find that the extent of criticism has a curvilinear relationship to participation in works club government. Criticism is thus highest among the marginal

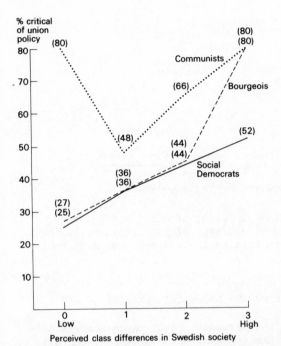

FIGURE 9.2 Percentage critical of union policy among metal-workers, by party preference and perceived class differences in Swedish society (Swedish-born men only)

and regular participants on the grass-roots level; it is lower among the outsiders and above all, among the part-time and full-time works club officials (Figure 9.3). Again therefore we find that the full-time works club officials, who play a central role in the articulation of rank-and-file interests within the national union organization, have views on union affairs that in important ways differ from those of the rank-and-file members.

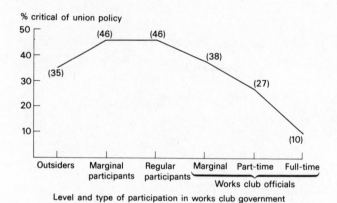

% critical of union policy

Level and type of participation in works club government

FIGURE 9.3 Percentage critical of union policy among metal-workers by level and type of participation in works club government (standardization for sex, age and ethnicity)

7   THE UNION HIERARCHY AND UNOFFICIAL STRIKES

The differences in the perspectives of union members differently placed in the internal union hierarchy can also be illustrated by the views of the members of unofficial strikes.   The Law on Collective Agreements from 1928 makes strikes during the term of the contract illegal. In breaches against this law unions and individual workers are liable to damages. (11)   Unofficial strikes are also against the union constitution, which gives the executive board the final say in questions concerning industrial conflict.   Through the union journal, study material and in other ways, the leadership of the Metal Workers' Union has attempted to promote a negative view on unofficial action in the postwar period.   Yet there has been some amount of unofficial action throughout this period, with a rather dramatic increase in strike rates in the 1970s. In recent years, the issue of unofficial strikes is probably the most important area in which the union leadership and the rank-and-file members have had diverging opinions.

In the survey among the metal-workers acceptance of unofficial strikes was ascertained through an index with five questions sketching situations of conflict between management and the workers in their own department.   In

these conflict situations bargaining procedures were assumed to have been exhausted and the question was posed,
whether or not the respondent accepted unofficial action
in order to put additional pressure on management.   The
conflict situations concerned piece-rate bargaining, behaviour of foremen, employer marks of individual workers,
internal transfers of workers and sacking (Appendix 2).
On average, the proportion supporting the idea of unofficial action in these situations was somewhat greater than
the proportion disapproving of it.

Acceptance of unofficial action shows a markedly curvilinear relationship to the level and type of participation in the government of the works club (Figure 9.4).
It is thus highest among workers who participate regularly
in the meetings of the works club but do not have elected
positions in the union.   The level of acceptance decreases among workers less active in the works club, the
marginal participants and the outsiders, but above all
among those with part-time or full-time engagement in
union work.

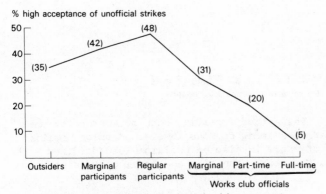

% high acceptance of unofficial strikes

FIGURE 9.4 Percentage with high acceptance of unofficial
strikes among metal-workers, by level and type of participation in works club government (standardization for sex,
age and ethnicity)

Workers entering elected union positions appear to undergo
some kind of a socialization process that decreases their
acceptance of unofficial action.   Those who have spent

between three and five years or more in union office at
the works club level are thus considerably less accepting
of unofficial strikes than those who have recently been
elected into office (Figure 9.5).

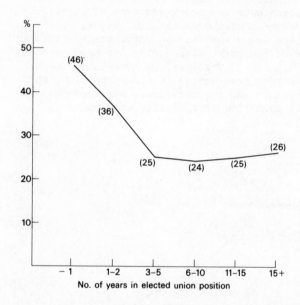

FIGURE 9.5 Percentage reporting high acceptance of unofficial strikes among persons in elected union position,
by number of years in elected position (standardized with
respect to age, sex, ethnicity and level of present union
position)

Basically, the reliance of the rank-and-file workers on
unofficial action reflects the fact that, at least in the
short run, such action can be instrumental for achieving
their goals.   The workers often find themselves in situations where the possibilities to bargaining have been exhausted or where negotiations appear doomed to failure.
The main alternative to acceptance of management decisions
is thus unofficial action.   This poses a problem for collective decision-making, since in such situations the
union hierarchy differentially structures the consequences
of decisions.

The relatively low acceptance of unofficial action among workers in elected union positions has also been observed among shop stewards in British industry (Donovan, 1968, p. 114; McCarthy, 1967). Probably the most important factor accounting for this relatively low acceptance derives from the position of the elected men as representatives of the other workers in relation to management. Unofficial action is generally beyond their control. Yet it presents a potentially powerful challenge to management and may lead to serious conflicts between management and the workers. It would appear difficult for union officials to accept that initiation of conflict, crucial for the fulfilment of their own tasks, is left outside their control. Unofficial action is also generally attempted as a solution to problems of only one section of the membership and may thus create tensions with other sections.

The illegal nature of unofficial strikes and the liability of the union to damages if it supports unofficial action have probably also contributed to the more negative attitude to such action among the union officials. This more negative view does not however appear to be a simple reflection of information or normative pressures. Figures not given here indicate that acceptance of unofficial strikes is not strongly related to knowledge of union affairs, reading of the union journal or participation in union study circles.

8 THE ROLE OF THE LEFT-WING OPPOSITION

In attempting to specify the role of the left-wing opposition within the labour movement it is instructive to ask why the support for the political parties and organization to the left of the Social Democrats has been considerably weaker than the support for oppositional candidates in union elections on the national and the local level. As indicated in Figure 9.1 above, the relative strength of the left-wing parties has never exceeded one-fifth of the total socialist vote in the general elections, and the Social Democrats have probably received 70-80 per cent of the working-class vote. Yet at the end of the two world wars about half of the metal-workers voted for oppositional delegates to the congresses, and an even larger proportion supported the oppositional alternatives in the crucial referendums in connection with the 1945 engineering strike. At least in these periods, but probably also during the first half of the 1930s, a considerable proportion of the vote for oppositional candidates in elections to the higher organs of the unions

as well as at the workplace level must have come from
Social Democratic workers.

Membership in the Communist Party or in an organization
sponsored by the Communists can be taken to reflect a
lasting dissatisfaction with, and a fundamental opposition
to, the policies of the Social Democrats. A vote for an
opposition candidate in union elections, however, often
appears to indicate only temporary dissatisfaction with
Social Democratic policies on more specific issues; it
may be seen as a way of inducing more militancy in situations where the growth strategy of class conflict has
perhaps led to a toothless union policy.

In this context it is worth noting that Communist
voting in the general elections also appears to a significant extent to reflect temporary dissatisfaction with the
Social Democrats. This is indicated by the fact that a
sizable proportion of Communist supporters actually report
identification with some other party, usually the Social
Democrats (Petersson and Särlvik, 1974, pp. 48-9). Support from workers for Communist candidates in union elections, and to a considerable extent also in general elections, thus appears to have functioned as a safety valve
for temporary dissatisfaction with Social Democratic policies and perhaps was intended to be a spur to radicaliz-
ing these policies.

In an article in the party journal in 1952 Linderot,
in some ways the most successful leader of the Communist
Party, confirmed that the major tactical goal of the Communist Party has been 'to isolate the right-wing Social
Democratic leaders from the masses, to take the leadership
in the struggle of the masses and to create a hegemony for
the [Communist] party in the labour movement'. He cer-
tified however (Linderot, 1972, p. 338) that

in a period of 35 years, the party has not been able
to solve its major tactical task. The Social Democrats are still dominating the labour movement....
[And] all attempts to capture the leadership in the
union movement through organizations like the Committee for Union Unity and the Red Union Opposition have
failed. Why? Because there was not within the party
any unified conception with regard to the tactical
problems.

After more than half a century the Communist Party is
still as far from achieving its major tactical goal as
before. Linderot's explanation of this failure in terms
of erroneous tactics smacks more of an idealistic interpretation than of a materialistic explanation. He
appears to have gone one step further towards an explanation when, in the same article, he states that the failure

of the party should not be interpreted to mean that the
masses are generally hostile to socialism or to the
actual policies represented by the party.   But it means
that 'the masses do not think that the Communists have as
good qualifications as the Social Democrats to represent
their wishes and demands in relation to the capitalists.
Therefore they support the Social Democrats' (Linderot,
1972, p. 340).

Internal disagreements and tactical mistakes of the
parties to the left of the Social Democrats have contributed to their relative weakness.   But the strength of the
Social Democrats within the Swedish labour movement cannot
be explained merely in terms of tactical errors of their
competitors or in terms of 'false consciousness' of the
workers.   Instead, it would appear that the material
basis of Social Democratic strength must be sought in the
way in which its own policies have improved the situation
of the working class and have held out a realistic promise
of future improvements.

In the three peaks of opposition strength discussed
above, the periods of deprivation and dissatisfaction do
not appear to have lasted long enough to sustain a search
for more permanent alternatives to the reformist Social
Democratic policies.   Towards the end of the First World
War, for instance, the LO and the Social Democrats undertook more militant actions, which resulted in rising real
wages.   The gaining of universal suffrage in 1918 and the
eight-hour working day in 1920 were also clear victories
for the working class.   In the same way, the formation or
the Social Democratic government in 1932 and the activities this government undertook to relieve distress and to
introduce social reforms led to a strong increase in
Social Democratic support in the elections in 1936 and
1938.   The Second World War was followed by a period of
full employment and social reforms which, aided by the
Cold War atmosphere, also kept the Communists on the
defensive.

10 Working-class politics and the union

In reformist strategies for the transcendence of capitalism, a crucial step is to win the support of the electorate for policies increasing the power resources of the
wage-earners as well as for an ideology questioning the
legitimacy of capitalism.   A prerequisite for a reformist
strategy appears to be that the gap between people's roles
as wage-earners and their roles as citizens is bridged,
i.e. that in the citizen role action is influenced by the
interests in the wage-earner role.   Via a close alliance
with a party, a union can bring resources, considerations
and influences from the sphere of work closer to politics.
Where the union and the political party act as two wings
of a unified labour movement the worker-citizen roles tend
to overlap.

We have seen that in Sweden the ties between the LO and
the Social Democratic Party have historically been very
close.   The inter-connectedness between politics and the
union is also indicated by our finding that political interest is the most important single factor accounting for
variations in the level of participation in the affairs of
the workplace union.   The workplace receives its importance in the political context, since it can be seen as a
prism which refracts the competing value systems of society.   It is also a forum where political power resources
of the labour movement are created and maintained.

This chapter focuses on the bases of party preferences
among workers, and on the role of the workplace and the
union in influencing their political views and activities.
We begin by analysing the class basis of voting in Sweden.

1 THE CLASS BASIS OF VOTING

Voting can be seen as a rational choice between parties on
the basis of the relative utility to the voter of the policies the parties are likely to carry through in the
future (Downs, 1957; Barry, 1970; Key, 1966). Voting
is thus future-oriented action. The choice between parties reflects how the voter perceives his own interests,
and what he thinks are the likely consequences of the policies offered by the parties. The past programmes and
policies of the parties as manifested in the political
struggle provide the main bases for the voters' conception
of what the parties stand for. Changing patterns of
voting can indicate changing policies of the parties as
well as changes in the voters' interests and their perception of these interests. As is well known, however,
there is a certain inertia in voting patterns. Party
preferences tend to be established at a relative early
stage in a person's life and then to remain fairly stable.

In Sweden more than in most other countries, the class
structure is the dominating generator of differences in
political choice between various societal groups (Rose,
1974, pp. 16-17). This partly reflects the fact that
Sweden does not have important alternative bases for cleavages such as ethnic, religious or regional differences.
It is however also a result of skilful Social Democratic
leadership, which until the mid-1970s has managed to keep
issues related to the welfare and interests of the wage-
earners in the centre of the political debate. It has
avoided 'cross-class' issues like religion, the monarchy,
nuclear armament and membership in NATO or the European
Economic Community, which have shaken the labour parties
in Norway, Denmark and Britain, for example. In 1976,
however, a 'cross-class' issue - nuclear energy - was
allowed to become the dominating issue in the election
campaign.

Position on the labour market is the main expression of
the class structure, and occupation thus forms the major
dimension of cleavage in the Swedish electorate. In the
dominating occupational or class dimension, workers and
employers are placed at opposite poles. The Swedish pattern of social mobility, however, illustrates that the
Swedish class structure is not completely uni-dimensional
(Carlsson, 1958; Erikson, 1971). Of the occupational
groups that fit only partially into this uni-dimensional
structure, farmers comprise the largest one. In Sweden,
as in other Nordic countries, farmers have been represented by agrarian parties. As response to the rapidly
diminishing proportion of farmers in Sweden, the agrarian

party was renamed the Centre Party in 1956 and has since then been relatively successful in broadening its electoral base to urban occupational groups.

Where the class structure of society creates exploitative relationships between societal groups, a major problem for the dominant groups becomes the maintenance and legitimation of the existing social order. Political parties, representing those in the lower end of the class structure, constitute potential threats to the stability of this structure. Different value systems, buttressed by power resources of varying importance, e.g. in the mass media, affect the way in which citizens come to perceive both their own interests and the policies offered by the parties.

Following Parkin (1971, pp. 81-2), we can distinguish three major value systems through which the class structure and the accompanying pattern of social inequality tend to be interpreted. The dominant value system is based in the 'upper-class' groups in society. Backed by the superior power resources of the dominant groups, this value system promotes endorsement and acceptance of existing inequalities, and deference to the upper class or aspiration to upward social mobility among the subordinate classes. The subordinate value system, which is generated by the informal working-class community, tends to promote accommodation to existing conditions. The radical value system, the main proponent of which is the mass political party representing the working class, can provide an oppositional interpretation of class structure and inequality. In practice, however, these value systems tend to be mixed and the values subscribed to in different social groups can often appear inconsistent (Mann, 1970).

Theories of democracy that view the policies offered by political parties as a result only of their competition for votes (e.g. Downs, 1957) cannot explain why the centre of gravity in the electorate of countries like the United States, France and Sweden are differently located on the left-right continuum, and why the choices offered by the party system thus also come to differ. In the United States, for instance, the two dominant parties are on the whole more or less conservative, while in Sweden on the average even the bourgeois parties are comparatively 'liberal'. This differential location of voters and parties on the left-right continuum can be seen as the result of an interaction between the class structure and the social consciousness of the voters. Partly mediated through the value systems, the power structure in society is reflected in the voters' perception of their interests.

The distribution of power resources in society thus determines the base line for the competition between the
parties.

While the LO has been able to organize the overwhelming
majority of workers in its unions, the bourgeois parties
have continued to receive support from a sizable minority
of the workers.   This apparent paradox points to an interesting fact.   The unions operate in a clearcut relationship of opposition with a stable base in societal
structure: that between wage earners and employers, between sellers and buyers of labour power.   While the organizations on the labour market thus are based on the
class structure of society, political parties primarily
reflect its stratification system.   On the political
arena, the lines of cleavage are less incisive and depend
on attempts by the parties to win the votes of the inter-
mediary groups in the occupational hierarchy.   Partly by
gradually accepting large parts of Social Democratic welfare policies, the bourgeois parties have been able to
retain some political support also among workers.   They
have, however, had to allow Social Democratic initiative,
rooted in the union wing of the labour movement, to move
the political centre of gravity to the left.

The close relationship between occupation and party
preferences in the Swedish electorate has been previously
observed (e.g. Särlvik, 1974).   We will here analyse this
relationship on the basis of data from a large random
sample of the Swedish population in 1974, and shall look
especially at the persons in the labour force. (1)   Among
workers in occupations normally organized in the LO
unions, close to three-fourths of those expressing party
preferences choose the Social Democratic or Communist
Party (Table 10.1).   The socialist proportion is somewhat
higher among men than among women, and increases slightly
with the skill requirements of the occupation, something
that partly reflects differences between sectors of the
economy. (2)   Among persons in white-collar occupations
normally organized in unions of salaried employees, somewhat more than one-third indicate a preference for the
socialist block.   The white-collar groups, however, are
greatly differentiated according to skill requirements.
Among persons in the higher white-collar occupations (requiring at least five years of training beyond the nine
years of compulsory schooling), about three-fourths indicated their preference for bourgeois parties.   Also among
the entrepreneurs, especially those who employ labour, the
proportion of socialist preferences is relatively low.
It is lowest, however, among the farmers.

Although the differences in party preferences between

TABLE 10.1 Percentage of Social Democrats and Communists of two-bloc vote among persons in the labour force in 1974, by sex and occupational category

		Men		Women		Total	
		%	(N)	%	(N)	%	(N)
Workers	Unskilled	72	(64)	67	(138)	69	(202)
	Semi-skilled	73	(154)	70	(101)	72	(255)
	Skilled	76	(201)	76	(21)	76	(222)
	All	74	(419)	69	(260)	72	(679)
White-collar	Lower	39	(61)	47	(134)	45	(195)
	Intermediate	40	(131)	36	(56)	39	(187)
	Higher	27	(79)	25	(32)	26	(111)
	All	36	(271)	41	(222)	38	(493)
Farmers		7	(41)	4	(23)	6	(64)
Entrepreneurs	Without employees	31	(39)	23	(17)	29	(56)
	With employees	13	(39)	10	(21)	12	(60)

occupational groups are large, it is noteworthy that the
support for socialist parties, primarily the Social Democrats, is not limited to the workers.   Even among high
white-collar groups and the self-employed, one out of four
votes supports the Social Democratic Party.   This contrasts with the situation in such countries as Britain and
Finland, where a lower proportion of the socialist vote
comes from the white-collar groups (Butler and Stokes,
1969, pp. 136ff.;   Rose, 1974, p. 502;   Uusitalo, 1975b;
Korpi, 1972).

Among workers, preference for socialist parties varies
to a significant extent by sector of economy (Table 10.2).
Our analysis of survey data from a random sample of the
Swedish population (3) indicates that in 1970 preference
for the socialist parties was higher among workers in the
metal-working industry than in other parts of the secondary sector.   Socialist preferences are lower in the
tertiary sector, and lower still in the primary sector of
the economy.   These sectional differences in party preferences among workers may reflect differences in the industrial and community environments of the workers, e.g.
differences in relationship to the employer, size of workplace and exposure to influences via the union and the
community.   These differences thus partly reflect the
extent to which workers are exposed to different types of
value systems.

The 1970 survey contains information on taxed income
taken from the tax registers.   Among male workers, the
level of income is not strongly related to party preference (Table 10.2).   The tendency that bourgeois workers
more often than other workers live in the countryside
contributes to the tendency for bourgeois preferences to
be somewhat more frequent among workers with low incomes.
The proportion of Communists is also higher in the low-
income groups.   The proportion with an income below
30,000 kronor was thus 54 per cent among the Social Democrats, 57 per cent among the bourgeois workers, but
65 per cent among the Communists. (4)

The close relationship between voting and the occupational structure also emerges in the voting patterns of
union members.   Data from a survey in 1973 indicate that
at least three out of four members of the LO unions voted
for the socialist parties, primarily the Social Democrats (5) (Table 10.3).   Among the members of the TCO
unions somewhat less than 40 per cent supported the socialist bloc, which also had support from one-quarter of
the members of the SACO-SR unions.

Because of changes in the occupational structure as
well as in the policies of the parties, we can expect the

TABLE 10.2 Party preference among workers in 1970 by sector of economy and annual income (men only)

Party preference	Metal-working Income			Other manufacturing construction, mining Income			Services Income			Agriculture, forestry, fishing Income		
	-30	+30	All	-30	+30	All	-30	+30	All	-30	+30	All
	%	%	%	%	%	%	%	%	%	%	%	%
Bourgeois	20	17	18	29	27	28	34	39	36	50	36	42
Social Democrat	70	79	75	64	69	66	62	58	60	45	64	56
Communist	10	4	7	7	5	6	4	3	4	5	0	2
Total	100	100	100	100	100	100	100	100	100	100	100	100
(N)	(143)	(145)	(288)	(374)	(283)	(657)	(218)	(207)	(425)	(44)	(58)	(102)

TABLE 10.3 Percentage of votes in 1973 general elections among economically active men and women by union membership

Voted for	Membership in union in		
	LO	TCO	SACO/SR
	%	%	%
Communists	6	3	3
Social Democrats	71	35	22
Centre Party	16	33	18
Liberal Party	4	12	10
Conservative Party	1	14	42
Other	2	3	5
Total	100	100	100
(N)	(555)	(321)	(69)

relationship between occupation and voting patterns to vary over time. Surveys carried out in connection with the general elections in the period 1956-73 provide data for describing these changes in recent years (Petersson and Särlvik, 1974). If we include lower-placed salaried employees in public service among manual workers, (6) we find that, after a peak in the elections in 1960, the proportion voting for the socialist bloc shows a slight decrease in the elections of 1970 and 1973 (Figure 10.1). In the non-manual category, the proportion voting for the

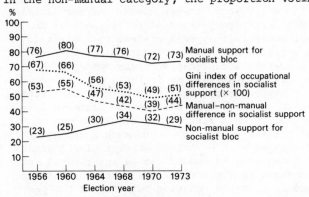

FIGURE 10.1 Percentage of manual and non-manual support for the socialist parties, manual-non-manual differences in support for socialist parties and the Gini index (× 100) of occupational differences in socialist support in Swedish elections, 1956-73

socialist bloc increased markedly up to 1968, whereafter
it showed some decrease. The difference between the percentage of manual and non-manual categories supporting the
socialist bloc, which is often taken as an index of class
voting (Alford, 1967), thus tended to decrease during this
period. The Gini index, which can be used to describe
differences in socialist support between several occupational groups (Korpi, 1972), also showed a decrease in
this period. (7)

The above changes in the voting patterns of different
occupational groups has led to some changes in the occupational composition of party support. The proportion of
manual workers showed a decrease among the Social Democrats - frcm 56 per cent in 1956 to 52 per cent in 1973 -
and a very marked decrease among the Communists - from
over 70 per cent before 1964 to about 50 per cent in 1973.
The proportion of manual workers supporting the bourgeois
bloc varies around 25 per cent in this period: it tended
to increase for the Centre Party but to decrease for the
Liberal Party.

The changes over time in the voting patterns of manual
and non-manual groups can also be elucidated by an exam-
ination of the voting patterns of different birth cohorts
(Table 10.4). The difference in support for the socialist bloc between manual and non-manual categories is
generally higher among men than among women. The difference is highest in the oldest cohorts and lowest in the
youngest cohorts, primarily as a result of increasing support for the socialist bloc among the younger non-
manuals. (8) This tendency is especially marked among
women.

Although the difference between manual and non-manual
support for the left-wing parties often is taken as an
index of class voting, it appears misleading however to
describe the decrease in this index during the last two
decades as indicating a decrease in class voting in
Sweden. This is because persons in the non-manual occupations are so heterogeneous that they hardly constitute a
class in any basic sense; and because the decrease in
this index primarily is a result of increasing support for
the socialist parties in the lower non-manual groups.

The above changes in the voting patterns of different
occupational categories in Sweden can be interpreted both
in terms of changes in the occupational structure of the
electorate and in terms of changing policies of the parties. (9) An important intellectual tradition assumes
that, with the development of industrial society, the
occupational structure will change so as to decrease the
base for socialist support (see chapter 1). It is

TABLE 10.4 Percentage of votes for socialist parties of two-bloc vote in the 1970 elections among persons in the labour force by sex, occupation and age cohort

Year of birth	Men			Women			All		
	Manual	Non-manual	Difference	Manual	Non-manual	Difference	Manual	Non-manual	Difference
	%	%	%	%	%	%	%	%	%
-1920	73	31	42	65	30	35	70	31	39
1921-30	68	38	30	61	39	22	65	39	26
1931-40	66	33	33	66	39	27	66	35	31
1941-	71	43	28	65	50	15	69	47	22
Total	70	35	35	64	39	25	68	36	32
(N)	(1472)	(1094)		(836)	(619)		(2308)	(1713)	

however apparent that, at least in Sweden, several factors
have instead worked in the opposite direction.

One significant change in the postwar period is the
continuing decrease of the independent farmers, which has
diminished a strongly bourgeois occupational group in the
'non-manual' category.   Also, agricultural workers, among
whom socialist support has been relatively weak, have decreased markedly.   While the expansion of the white-
collar categories has increased the proportion of salaried
employees the proportion among them who are in positions
of special trust in relation to the employers has probably
decreased.   This expansion has thus contributed to make
the position of the great majority of the salaried employees more like that of common wage-earners.   The salaried employees have also increased primarily in the
public sector, where they, in principal at least, are servants to the public rather than to capital.

Of long-term significance furthermore is the fact that
a greatly increasing proportion of married women has entered the labour force and found employment, primarily in
lower white-collar jobs in the public sector. (10)   As a
result of their experiences in the role as wage-earners,
employed women can be expected to be more inclined to
support socialist parties than housewives.   The large
category of women working in domestic service, difficult
to reach for socialist influences, has also practically
disappeared in the postwar period.   Although the Swedish
employees are still a heterogeneous category, their
common role as wage-earners thus appears to have come increasingly to the foreground, something that is reflected
in their pattern of unionization.

The decrease in manual support for the Social Democrats
in the first part of the 1970s is probably partly a reaction to the 'stagflation', with a rapid inflation and
increasing unemployment, which was also reflected in markedly increased social assistance rates in these years.
The Swedish experience however indicates that political
change is not a mere reflection of social and economic
change.   Party preference are also moulded and changed by
the issues that come into focus in the political
struggles.   Thus in the late 1950s the question of social
justice, manifested in the supplementary pensions issue,
increased Social Democratic support, especially in the
white-collar groups.   The Social Democratic election campaign in 1968, centring around equality and full employment, probably contributed to the record high non-manual
support for the Social Democrats.   Of importance also is
the fact that for a long time the Social Democrats have
managed to avoid 'cross-class' issues from coming to the

centre of the political debate.   This tradition was
broken, however, when the question of nuclear energy
became a major political issue in the mid-1970s.

2   THE SOCIAL ROOTS OF PARTY PREFERENCES AMONG METAL-
WORKERS

While the cleavages generated by the class structure provide the basis for the strong socialist support in the
working class, the above data indicate that considerable
variations in party preferences are found among workers.
Of our population of metal-workers, the majority support
the Social Democrats, while the Communists on the one
hand and the bourgeois workers on the   other hand comprise
minority groups of about equal strength (Table 10.5).

TABLE 10.5 Party preferences among metal-workers in population by ethnicity and sex

Party preference	Swedish-born Men	Women	Foreign-born Men	Women	Total
	%	%	%	%	%
Communist	12	7	2	3	10
Social Democrats	60	47	57	47	47
Bourgeois	10	11	15	14	10
Not indicated	17	36	25	36	23
Total	99	101	99	100	100

Communist preferences are stronger among the Swedish-born
(especially among Swedish-born men) than among the
foreign-born.   Preference for the bourgeois parties are
slightly more common among the foreign-born.   The proportion not indicating party preferences is relatively large,
especially among the women.   In the following, we shall
analyse the social basis of these differences in party
preferences, concentrating on the Swedish-born men in our
population.
     As is well known, young people tend to assume the party
preference of their parents, partly through processes of
political socialization, partly because they tend to
occupy similar positions in the class structure as their
parents.   The relationship between the party preference
of the Swedish-born male workers in our population and the
party preference of their fathers (as recalled by the

sons) is given in Table 10.6.   By far the greatest inter-
generational stability in party preference in this population is shown by the sons of Social Democratic fathers:
three-fourths of them remain Social Democrats.   Among
sons of Social Democrats who have changed party preferences, the majority have become Communists.   The probability that a son of a Social Democratic father will become a
Communist is almost three times higher than the probability that he will prefer a bourgeois party.   The relative
size of these 'outflow' percentages can be taken as indicators of the relative distance between parties.   In this
core group of the working class, the left-wing alternative
is thus considerably closer at hand than the bourgeois
one.   This is also indicated by the choice of 'second-
best' party: among the Social Democratic metal-workers,
the Communist party is thus chosen as 'second-best' party
almost twice as often as any of the bourgeois
parties. (11)

The attrition rate among sons of Communist fathers is
relatively high.   Only about half of them remain Communists, while the others generally have become Social Democrats.   The attrition rate among sons of bourgeois
fathers, however, is even greater.   Only about one-fourth
of them retain the bourgeois preferences of their fathers,
while more than half have become Social Democrats or Communists.   Our data thus indicate that the environment of
the metal-workers is especially uncongenial to bourgeois
political views, while it tends to be supportive of Social
Democratic preferences.

The political origin of the sympathizers for a given
party in terms of the party preferences of their fathers
is given in Table 10.7.   Two-thirds of the Social Democratic men had Social Democratic fathers.   Close to half
of the men with bourgeois party preferences had bourgeois
fathers.   Only about one-tenth of the Communist metal-
workers, however, report that their fathers had the same
party preference.   These figures thus indicate that the
process of becoming a Communist metal-worker is quite different from that of becoming a Social Democratic or a
bourgeois one.   Among the 'deviant' bourgeois workers,
party preferences have been inherited to a much greater
extent than among the Communists. (12)

TABLE 10.6 Political destiny of sons by recalled party preference of father (Swedish-born men only)

Party preference of son	Party preference of father				
	Communist	Social Democrat	Bourgeois	Unknown	Total
	%	%	%	%	%
Communist	46	11	7	14	12
Social Democrat	46	78	48	37	60
Bourgeois	7	4	27	10	9
Unknown	1	7	18	40	18
Total	100	100	100	100	100

TABLE 10.7 Political origin of sons according to recalled party preference of father (Swedish-born men only)

| Party preference of father | Party preference of son | | | | Total |
| | Communist | Social Democrat | Bourgeois | Unknown | |
	%	%	%	%	%
Communist	11	2	2	0	3
Social Democrat	46	67	23	20	46
Bourgeois	9	12	43	14	14
Unknown	35	19	32	66	36
Total	101	100	100	100	99

The communist workers

It has often been assumed that communist party preferences
among workers are expressions of non-rational behaviour.
Thus Lipset (1960, chs 2 and 4) maintains that communist
party preferences reflect working-class authoritarianism;
while Allardt (1964a, b) assumes that communist preferences are partly an expression of anomie.   In another context, I have argued that working-class communism need not
be regarded as non-rational, and that communist party
preferences among workers in postwar Western Europe can be
interpreted in terms of a rational model of voting (Korpi,
1971).

The main assumptions of such a model are that voters
are motivated primarily by material self-interest;   that,
more than other parties, the communist parties generally
stress the desirability of a thoroughgoing redistribution
of rewards in their programmes and propaganda;   and that
working-class voters therefore perceive of the communist
parties as standing for a more thoroughgoing restructuring
of the distributive process than the other parties.   The
Communist Party can therefore be expected to appeal especially to the lower sections of the working class.
Available data on party preferences among workers in
Sweden and in other western European countries indicate
that, in comparison with the Social Democrats, the Communist supporters tend to be somewhat more disprivileged;
e.g. they have experienced greater economic insecurity.
Communist workers also tend to be somewhat more aware of
inequalities in their society than the Social Democratic
workers (Korpi, 1971).

In our population of metal-workers we can take the
dichotomy between the Communists on the one hand and those
expressing other party preferences on the other as the
dependent variable in a multiple-classification analysis
(Table 10.8).   The battery of variables describing the
metal-workers' demographic characteristics, social ori-
gins, formative experiences and present socioeconomic
position can explain only a relatively small proportion -
12 per cent - of the variation around the Communist-non-
Communist dichotomy. (13)   The Communist proportion is
higher among men than among women, but has no consistent
relationship with age.   As previously indicated, however,
the party preference of the father is relevant.   Socially
downward mobile persons, especially those of farm origin,
are Communists less often than others.   The Communist
proportion tends to be slightly higher in industrial communities and big cities than in the more mixed communities.

TABLE 10.8 Multiple-classification analysis of party preferences among metal-workers dichotomized as Communists v. others and as bourgeois v. others (Swedish-born only; of workers indicating party preferences Communists constitute 14% and bourgeois workers 12%; N = 3008)

Independent variable; categories	Communists v. others Communists				Bourgeois v. others Bourgeois			
	Unadjusted	Adjusted	Eta	Beta	Unadjusted	Adjusted	Eta	Beta
Sex Men	15 %	15 %	0.087	0.081	12 %	12 %	0.069	0.034
Women	3	4			20	16		
Age -20 years	7	12	0.062	0.056	25	19	0.228	0.196
21-30	15	16			22	22		
31-40	13	15			15	14		
41-50	15	15			10	11		
51-60	17	14			4	5		
61+	13	9			4	5		
Father's party Communist	44	40	0.212	0.191	7	8	0.325	0.261
preference Social Democrat	11	10			5	6		
Bourgeois	8	14			35	30		
Unknown	22	21			17	16		
Perceived class Low 0	7	8	0.163	0.143	12	11	0.018	0.025
differences 1	12	12			13	13		
2	17	16			12	13		
High 3	23	23			12	12		
Wage level Low 1	5	8	0.099	0.104	27	22	0.132	0.106
2	15	19			16	16		
3	15	16			11	12		
4	15	13			10	11		
5	15	12			10	10		
High 6	14	13			11	8		

Standard of living	Owns home and car	9	11	0.112	0.100	19	22	0.079	0.122
	Owns home or car	12	12			12	12		
	Owns none of these	19	19			11	9		
Traditional cultural values	Church-goer, member of free church and/or temperance organization	5	8	0.135	0.097	19	16	0.107	0.058
	None of these	17	16			10	11		
Fathers' socioeconomic position	Middle-class	12	12	0.088	0.070	27	23	0.227	0.101
	Farmer	8	9			25	13		
	Working-class	16	16			8	11		
Unemployed for more than one month?	No	12	13	0.096	0.061	16	13	0.129	0.009
	Yes	19	17			7	12		
Formal education	Compulsory only	15	15	0.067	0.053	10	11	0.185	0.099
	Occupational training	12	12			17	14		
	Higher	12	11			33	24		
Early economic deprivation	Low	8	12	0.117	0.050	20	14	0.173	0.036
	Medium	16	15			11	11		
	High	19	16			5	13		
Community type	Big cities	16	16	0.049	0.034	14	16	0.103	0.076
	Industrial communities	14	13			10	10		
	Mixed communities	10	10			23	14		
Skill requirement of job	Low	16	16	0.049	0.034	13	13	0.016	0.013
	Medium	14	13			12	12		
	High	10	14			12	12		
Size of firm	Small	10	11	0.020	0.018	11	9	0.025	0.021
	Medium	14	14			15	13		
	Large	14	14			12	12		
				$R^2 = 0.115$				$R^2 = 0.195$	

Our data also give some support to the interpretation
of Communist voting in terms of a rational model.   With
respect to standard of living, Communist supporters among
the metal-workers tend to be less well off than others.
The proportion of Communist supporters among those who own
neither a car nor a home is thus about twice as high as
among those who are home- and car-owners.   Workers having
only compulsory formal education are Communists slightly
more often than those having received some additional education.   The Communist proportion also tends to increase
with early economic deprivation, as indicated by long-term
unemployment of father and economic difficulties in the
childhood home.   Workers who have themselves experienced
long-term unemployment also tend to be Communists somewhat
more often than others.   Differences in wage level or in
the level of skill requirements of the job, however, are
not of major importance in this context.   It thus appears
that workers who have had a relatively difficult start in
life, or who for various reasons cannot uphold as high a
standard of living as other workers, tend to support the
Communist Party more often than other metal-workers.   The
Communist proportion also clearly increases with an increasing awareness of class differences in society.

Moral values associated with religion, and to a lesser
extent with the temperance movement, have been observed to
counteract socialist party preferences (Gustafsson, 1969).
In our population of metal-workers, the Communist proportion is halved among workers who attend church services
frequently and/or belong to a separatist church or a temperance organization.

Large firms have been assumed to increase left-wing
party preferences (e.g. Lipset, 1960, p. 237).   We have
found evidence that, at the end of the two world wars,
large firms became strongholds of the internal opposition
in the Metal Workers' Union (see chapter 9).   The large
firms in our sample, however, do not have considerably
higher proportion of Communist supporters than the small-
and medium-sized firms. (14)   Even if the proportion of
Communist or oppositional workers is not very high in the
large firms, these firms can play a crucial role in periods of general crisis and dissatisfaction among workers.
They tend to become natural targets for the activities of
oppositional organizations.   The oppositional activities
in the large firms is facilitated by the fact that in them
a minimum number of oppositional workers are assembled who
can form the nucleus of an organization.   The possibilities for mobilization are therefore better in the big
firms than in the smaller places of work.   Under normal
circumstances, however, the proportion of oppositional
workers in large firms need not be especially high.

The bourgeois workers

Dichotomizing party preferences between bourgeois workers
on the one hand and socialist workers on the other, we
find that our battery of independent variables explains a
larger proportion, 20 per cent, of the variance around the
bourgeois-socialist dichotomy (Table 10.8). Women have
bourgeois preferences somewhat more often than men.
Bourgeois preferences are considerably more common among
the younger workers than among the older ones. Downward-
ly mobile persons, and those whose fathers had bourgeois
or unknown party preferences, support the bourgeois parties more often than others. (15)   Religious workers and
teetotallers have bourgeois party preferences more often
than others. Early economic deprivation, experiences of
unemployment and perceived class differences are, however,
not important in this context. Bourgeois party preferences are somewhat less frequent in industrial communities,
but do not vary with size of firm.

Our data give somewhat contradictory evidence concerning the importance of relative standards of living for
bourgeois party preferences. Such preferences are most
common among the lowest paid workers. Skill requirements
of the job, however, are unrelated to bourgeois party preference. Workers with a relatively high standard of
living, as indicated by ownership of home and car, have
bourgeois preferences more often than others. Also, workers with formal education above the compulsory level have
bourgeois preferences more often than others. Data on
British workers indicate the same type of relationship between a high standard of living, formal education and conservative party preferences (Rose, 1974b, pp. 504-7).

Together with our previous data on Communist Party preferences, these figures indicate that the internal socioeconomic stratification within the working class is reflected in party preferences on the left-right continuum
with the better-off workers inclined somewhat more to the
bourgeois parties and the more disadvantaged ones to the
Communists. It appears, however, that these data can not
be interpreted in developmental terms as supporting the
thesis of the increasing 'embourgeoisement' of the workers
with increasing absolute levels of income and standard of
living. The fact that, with increasing wages, bourgeois
party preferences tend to decrease indicates that the
sources of the higher standard of living related to bourgeois party preferences might be at least partly found
outside the sphere of work, perhaps related to social
origin.

3   THE POLITICAL ROLE OF THE WORK ENVIRONMENT

The inter-generational attrition of bourgeois party preferences and the increase in socialist party preferences
with age among our metal-workers noted above indicates
that the work environment is of political significance.
The political effects of the work environment are partly
results of explicitly political activities at the workplace. The environment at work may also have indirect
political effects by exposing or insulating workers from
certain types of experiences. Employers, however, do
not allow political parties to disseminate information or
to arrange meetings within the premises of the firms.
    One explicitly political activity is informal political
discussion on the shop floor. When asked, 'Does it
happen that you discuss politics at your department/shop?'
28 per cent of the metal-workers in our population indicate that this occurs 'almost every day' or 'a few times
per week', 30 per cent 'a few times per month' and 35 per
cent 'almost never'. The political views of workmates,
however, are not perceived as highly homogeneous. Only
one-quarter of the metal-workers in our population indicate that the political views of their workmates are
'rather' or 'very' similar, while more than half of them
indicate that they are 'rather' or 'very' dissimilar. (A
rather large proportion are also unaware of the political
views of their workmates.)   As can be expected, those
belonging to the political 'majority' group among the
metal-workers, i.e. the Social Democrats, perceive the
political environment as more homogeneous than others.
Only about half of them indicate that the political views
in the department are 'very' or 'rather' dissimilar, as
against about two-thirds among Communist and bourgeois
workers.
    The proportion reporting heterogeneous political views
among their workmates tends to increase with size of firm,
from 40 per cent in the small firms to 51 per cent in the
medium-sized firms and 53 per cent in the large firms.
In the politically heterogeneous departments the frequency
of political discussions tends to increase with the size
of the firm.   The proportion reporting a high frequency
of political discussions is thus 31 perccent in the small
firms, 37 per cent in the medium-sized firms and 40 per
cent in the large firms.   In the politically homogeneous
departments, the frequency of political discussions is
lower and not consistently related to size of firm.   This
indicates that in the larger firms with a greater choice
of alternative social relationships, political heterogeneity may stimulate the political debate and allow for a

greater degree of political conflict than in the smaller
firms, where potentially divisive political issues may
become de-emphasized to avoid disruption of workplace
social relationships (cf. Lipset, Trow and Coleman, 1956,
pp. 223-6).

The size of the firm is also related to the level of
organized political activity and competition among the
workers.   One aspect of this is the presence of Social
Democratic and Communist political clubs in the firm.
The purpose of these clubs is to influence workers politically and to affect the policy of the works club, e.g.
via union elections.   In the small- and medium-sized
firms political clubs are an exception, whereas they are
found in most of the large firms (Table 10.9).   In our
sample of firms, the Social Democratic political clubs
outnumber the Communist clubs by three to two.

TABLE 10.9 Number of firms with political clubs and with
different levels of political competition, by size of firm

| | | Size of firm | | |
		Small	Medium	Large
Political clubs	None	13	10	6
	Social Democratic only	1	0	9
	Social Democratic and Communist	0	2	17
	No. of firms	14	12	22
Political competition within works club	Low	11	9	5
	Medium	3	2	11
	High	0	1	6
	No. of firms	14	12	22

The level of political competition in the works club in
the years preceding the study was estimated on the basis
of information from the two bargaining representatives of
each works club concerning the presence of politically
identified candidates in the union elections, politically
coloured debates at the works club meetings, workers identified with the Communist or the bourgeois parties on the
board of the works club and Communist political clubs at
the work place (cf. Appendix 2).   Works clubs classified
as having a high degree of political competition all had

Communist club chairmen. The level of political competition is clearly related to size of firm (Table 10.9)   In
the small- and medium-sized firms political competition
has been an exception, whereas at least some degree of
competition has been the rule in the large firms in our
sample. Among the large firms with unit and small-batch
production political competition is somewhat more frequent
than in those with a standardized production. We have
seen in chapter 7, the level of internal conflicts in the
works clubs has increased in the 1970s, presumably largely
as a result of attempts from left and right to break the
Social Democratic dominance at the work places.

4 WORK ENVIRONMENT AND INTER-GENERATIONAL POLITICAL CHANGE

One way of attempting to trace the political effects of
the work environment is to look at the pattern of inter-
generational change in the party preferences of workers in
different types of political settings.   In a cross-sectional study this involves some obvious difficulties.
One difficulty arises from the fact that the effects of
the political milieu can be expected ·to come only gradually.   Since a considerable proportion of workers shift
departments, firms and communities in the course of their
work career, the characteristics of their current sur-
roundings can only partly reflect the political influences
to which they have been exposed.   The methodological
problems in analysing such contextual effects are also
considerable (Hauser, 1970; Schuessler, 1971, pp. 229-
38), and we have to make largely arbitrary assumptions
about the causal ordering among the variables.
    A strong indication of the political importance of the
work environment for the metal-workers is the effect of
the length of exposure to influences from the industrial
environment upon the likelihood that their party preferences will 'deviate' from those of their fathers.   As an
indicator of length of exposure we can take the number
of years worked in industry.   Figure 10.2 indicates that
the proportion of socialist party preferences tends to increase with length of time worked in industry, even after
standardization for age.   The increase is very strong for
workers whose fathers had bourgeois or unknown party preferences, but is found also among those whose fathers were
Social Democrats.   The figures indicate, however, that it
may take about a decade before the effects of the work
environment become pronounced. (16)
    On the shop floor level the informal union activist is

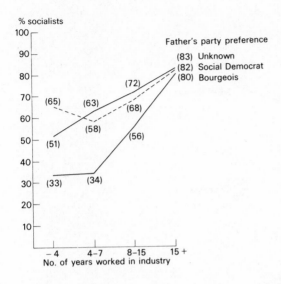

FIGURE 10.2   Percentage indicating socialist party preferences by party preference of father and number of years
worked in industry (standardization for age;   Swedish-born
men only)

the mainstay of the union.   The dominance of the Social
Democrats within the union movement implies that the great
majority of the informal union activists are Social Democrats.   Of the Swedish-born men in our population who
tend to function as informal union activists, 73 per cent
are Social Democrats, while 16 per cent are Communists and
only 5 per cent have bourgeois party preferences.   An increasing density of informal union activists in the department thus implies increasing Social Democratic influences.   An indication of the potential effects of these
influences is provided by the inter-generational change in
party preferences of workers located in departments with
differing densities of informal union activists.   The
proportion of those with Social Democratic Party preferences increases markedly, among sons of both bourgeois and
Social Democratic fathers, when the density of informal
union activists in the department increases (Figure 10.3).
Among those whose fathers had Communist or unknown party
preferences, however, no marked increases in Social Democratic preferences can be observed.
    With an increasing level of political competition in
the works club, the   dominance of Social Democrats among
the informal union activists can be expected to decrease.
Communist activists especially can be expected to become

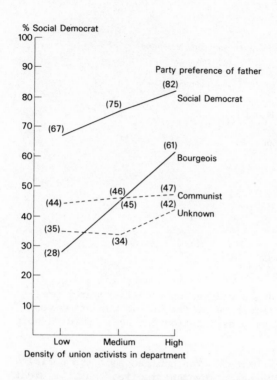

% Social Democrat

Party preference of father

(82) Social Democrat

(75)

(67)

(61) Bourgeois

(46)   (47) Communist

(44)   (45)   (42) Unknown

(35)

(34)

(28)

Low   Medium   High

Density of union activists in department

FIGURE 10.3 Percentage with Social Democratic Party preferences among metal-workers, by party preference of
father and density of union activists in department
(Swedish-born men only)

more frequent when the level of competition increases; in
firms where political competition is relatively vivid,
they can be expected to exert a political influence that
countervails that of the Social Democrats.

These countervailing influences appear to be reflected
in the pattern of inter-generational political change.
The proportion of sons of Communist fathers who have retained the Communist Party preference of their father thus
tends to increase with an increasing level of political
competition in the firm (Figure 10.4).   The proportion of
Communist sons to non-Communist fathers is only weakly
related to the level of political competition in the works
club.   The proportional reduction of error in predicting
the party preferences of the son with, rather than without, knowledge of the party preferences of the father is
not large but increases with increasing strength of the
political competition. (17)   The data would thus appear

to indicate that political opposition at the level of the
works club can be of importance for preserving Communist
Party preferences between generations.

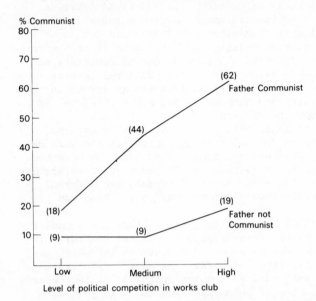

% Communist

FIGURE 10.4 Percentage of Communists among metal-workers,
by party preference of father and level of political competition in works club (Swedish-born men only)

5   POLITICAL INTEREST AND WORKPLACE SOCIAL CLIMATES

It appears that our metal-workers have a rather lively
interest in politics. For instance, 53 per cent of them
indicate that they are 'very' or 'rather' interested in
politics. About 40 per cent indicate that they read
editorials or other political articles in the newspapers
'almost every day' or at least 'a few times per week',
and 17 per cent had attended at least one political meeting during the preceding election campaign. These three
questions form the basis for an index of *political interest* (Appendix 2). A related index on *informal political activism* is based on questions concerning initiation
of political discussions with workmates, attempts to
interest workmates in reading political articles, viewing
election programmes on television or voting for a specific
party, as well as the frequency of advice to workmates on
issues discussed in the election campaign (Appendix 2).
A multiple-classification analysis indicates that, as

expected, men take considerably greater interest in politics than women (Table 10.10). Political interest increases markedly with age. Degree of labour movement
support is strongly associated with political interest.
Workers with a solidarist union involvement are more interested in politics than others. This again indicates
that the tie between politics and the union is at the core
of the labour movement. Left-wing Social Democrats and
Communists have considerably higher political interest
than other workers. Political interest is lowest in the
mixed communities and highest in the big cities, but is
not related to size of firm.

Level of informal political activism is related to
these independent variables in approximately the same way
as political interest, but some differences can be noted.
Political activism does thus not increase quite as strongly with age. Left-wing Social Democrats are informal
political activists considerably more often than are
others.

The factors in the work environment that are supportive
of socialist party preferences but inimical to bourgeois
political views can be expected to vary in intensity between different places of work. Strength of the workers'
collectivity and density of union activists in the department are variables of potential importance in this context. Their effects on party preferences can be expected
to be mediated partly via influences on the level of political interest and the informal political activism of the
workers.

When we relate the level of political interest to the
perceived strength of the workers' collectivity in the
department, we find that among Social Democrats and Communists it tends to increase with an increasing strength
of the workers' collectivity (Figure 10.5). Among bourgeois workers, on the contrary, the level of political
interest drops markedly when the strength of the workers'
collectivity increases. The same differential effects of
the workers' collectivity are evident with respect to the
level of informal political activism; where the workers'
collectivity is weak, bourgeois workers show a considerably higher level of informal political activism than the
Social Democratic and Communist workers. Increased
strength of the workers' collectivity however tends to
stimulate the informal political activity of the socialist
workers somewhat while bourgeois workers become markedly
de-politicized.

The above figures indicate that a strong workers' collectivity is generally supportive of socialist party preferences, of both Communists and Social Democrats. We

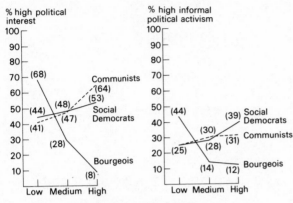

FIGURE 10.5 Percentage with high political interest and high informal political activism, by strength of workers' collectivity in department and party preference (Swedish-born men only)

have seen however that informal union activists on the shop floor are largely Social Democrats.   For Social Democratic workers, then, both the workers' collectivity and the informal union activists tend to have supportive effects.   Communist workers however can be caught in cross-pressures here, supported by the workers' collectivity but generally discouraged by the informal union activists.

While the strength of the workers' collectivity and the density of union activists to some extent is associated, there are many departments that combine a relatively high density of union activists with a rather weak workers' collectivity and, conversely, there are departments combining a low density of union activists with a strong workers' collectivity.   It is therefore of interest to analyse the combined effects of the workers' collectivity and the union activists upon the level of political interest and informal political activism of Social Democrats and Communists.

We find that, given the strength of the workers' collectivity in the department, the political interest of the Social Democrats increases with the density of union activists, but that the reverse holds true for the Communists (Figure 10.6).   While an increasing density of union activists thus markedly counteracts the effects of the

TABLE 10.10 Multiple-classification analyses of political interest and informal political activism among metal workers (proportion in population with high political interest = 38% and with high informal political activism = 34%; N = 3996)

Independent variables; categories		Political interest High interest				Informal political activism High activism			
		Unadjusted	Adjusted	Eta	Beta	Unadjusted	Adjusted	Eta	Beta
		%	%			%	%		
Sex	Men	41	40	0.169	0.124	37	35	0.126	0.074
	Women	14	20			17	24		
Age	−20 years	14	26	0.242	0.125	12	25	0.206	0.082
	21–30	31	36			26	32		
	31–40	31	33			35	38		
	41–50	45	40			43	37		
	51–60	50	44			43	37		
	61+	57	49			44	34		
Ethnicity	Swedish-born	40	38	0.100	0.013	38	35	0.130	0.002
	Foreign-born	28	39			23	33		
Labour movement support	Low	24	28	0.294	0.200	20	25	0.324	0.228
	Medium	39	38			34	32		
	High	59	53			59	52		
Party preference	Communists	48	45	0.262	0.134	40	38	0.352	0.254
	Social Democrats Left	55	46			58	51		
	Centre	41	38			31	28		
	Right	38	36			41	39		
	Bourgeois	28	38			34	43		
	Unknown	19	28			9	17		

Type of union involvement	Reluctant	22	33	0.216	0.069	20	31	0.208	0.064
	Instrumental	35	38			31	32		
	Solidaristic	49	41			45	38		
Community type	Big cities	40	42	0.066	0.071	34	37	0.026	0.046
	Industrial	38	36			35	33		
	Mixed	26	33			30	34		
Size of firm	Small	37	39	0.004	0.007	36	35	0.010	0.006
	Medium	38	39			36	35		
	Large	38	38			34	34		
		$R^2 = 0.154$				$R^2 = 0.192$			

workers' collectivity for the political interest of the
Communists, it increases the political interest of the
Social Democrats.   Figures not given here indicate that a
similar pattern of relationships between party preference,
strength of workers' collectivity and density of union
activists prevails also with respect to the informal political activism of Social Democratic and Communist workers.

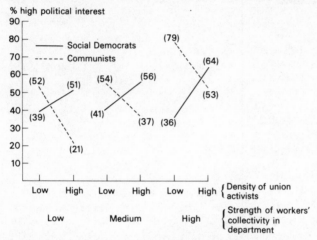

FIGURE 10.6 Percentage with high political interest among
Social Democratic and Communist metal-workers, by density
of union activists and strength of workers' collectivity
in department (Swedish-born men only)

6   WOMEN AND IMMIGRANTS

We have seen that the social relationships and organization created around work have powerful effects upon the
political views and activities of the metal-workers.   A
'counter-culture' is thus created around work and this
counteracts the pressures mediated via the dominant value
system in society.   Young workers, women and immigrants
on the fringes of this counter-culture, however, are less
strongly affected by it.   Among them, bourgeois party
preferences are more common than among other metal-workers, and their political interest is relatively low.
   When women and immigrants are exposed to the effects of
the work-related political culture, their political views
tend to be modified in much the same way as those of the
Swedish-born men.   With an increasing length of time in
industrial work, socialist party preferences thus tend to
become more common among them.   As the figures in Figure

10.7 indicate, an increasing density of union activists in the department is associated also with an increasing proportion of Social Democrats in both these groups.

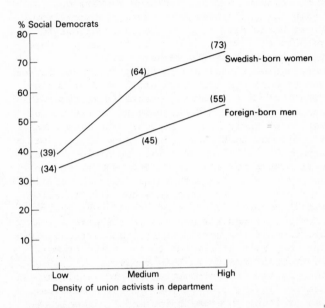

FIGURE 10.7 Percentage of Social Democrats among Swedish-born women and foreign-born men, by density of union activists in department

7   THE UNION AND THE SOCIAL DEMOCRATIC PARTY

The close relationship between the LO unions and the Social Democratic Party dates back to the early history of the labour movement.   On the organizational level this relationship is evidenced in the collective membership of a sizable proportion of the union branches in the party, the heavy economic support that the LO unions give to the party and the high frequency with which elected union representatives simultaneously hold elected positions in the party, or are party representatives in local government. In this section we will describe some of these interrelationships, and the metal-workers' views of them.

The collective affiliation of the members of union branches to the local Social Democratic Party organizations has been a hotly debated issue inside as well as

outside the labour movement throughout this century.
Since the requirement for party membership of all LO
unions was waived in 1900, union branches have had the
option of collectively affiliating their members to the
local party organization. This occurs through a majority
decision at the branch meeting. Branch members not
willing to join the party have the right of abstention.
Since the First World War, roughly one-third of the LO
members have been collective members of the party, consti-
tuting about 70 per cent of its membership.

Of the metal-workers included in our population, 52 per
cent belonged to branches that were affiliated with the
local organizations of the Social Democratic Party. The
level of awareness among the metal-workers of the collective affiliation of their branch is low: not less than
43 per cent indicated that they did not know whether or
not their branch was affiliated. The proportion believ-
ing that their branch had affiliated its members to the
party was 55 per cent in firms that were actually affiliated and 36 per cent in firms that were not affiliated.
In the latter firms only 18 per cent stated that their
branch had not affiliated its members to the party. A
sizable proportion of the metal-workers thus erroneously
believed that they were affiliated to the party or were
uncertain about their status in this respect.

As can be expected, the proportion of the metal-workers
in our population having elected positions in political
organizations or local government increases markedly with
level of participation in works club government (Figure
10.8). Elected positions are more common in political
organizations than in local government. Of workers with
elected positions in the works club, 45 per cent have
elected positions in political organizations and 19 per
cent in local government. Of the Social Democratic
metal-workers with elected positions in union government,
46 per cent have elected positions in political organizations and 21 per cent in local government. The corresponding figures for the Communists are 49 per cent and
17 per cent and for the bourgeois workers 9 per cent and
0 per cent. For the bourgeois workers it is apparently
more difficult than for Social Democrats or Communists to
combine political and union activity. Size of firm is
important in so far as workers in elected positions in the
works club also hold elected positions in political organizations: it increases from 21 per cent in the small
firms to 35 per cent in medium-sized firms and 51 per cent
in the large firms.

The extensive participation of elected union representatives in local politics meets with some criticism among

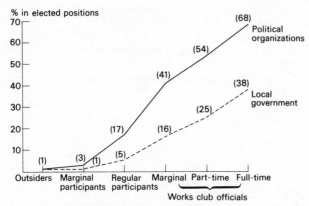

FIGURE 10.8 Percentage of metal-workers with elected
positions in political organizations or local government,
by level of participation in government of works club

the metal-workers.   Close to 40 per cent of the metal-
workers stated that they would prefer the club chairman
not to be politically active.   Almost half of them indicate that they would vote for a candidate to the works
club board even if they knew that he did not have the same
political views as they themselves.   When asked if they
thought that their branch should affiliate with the party,
only about one-fourth opposed it and others would not take
a stand.   About one-third of the metal-workers also dis-
approved of the economic support of their union to the
party.
     As might be expected, support for a close relationship
between the Social Democratic Party and the union increases with level of participation in works club affairs.
Positive views on economic support to the party are very
common among workers having elected positions in the works
club (Figure 10.9).   It is noteworthy, however, that only
somewhat more than one-half of workers in elected positions explicitly supported the collective affiliation of
the branch to the party. (18)
     Naturally, the Communist and bourgeois workers are
highly critical of mixing politics with union affairs.
Among Social Democrats, resistance to the political involvement of the union tends to increase with an increasing level of manifest political conflict in the works
club (Figure 10.10).   Comments from the workers indicate
that intensive political fights tend to be seen as weaken-

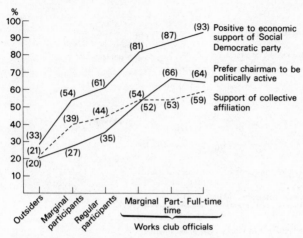

FIGURE 10.9 Percentage of metal-workers who are positive
to economic support of the Social Democrats, prefer works
club chairman to be politically active and support collective affiliation of branch to the Social Democratic Party,
by level of participation in works club government
(Swedish-born men only)

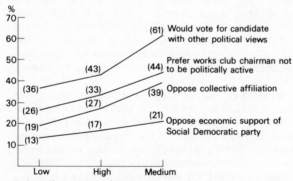

FIGURE 10.10 Percentage of Social Democratic metal-workers, who oppose collective affiliation to the party,
prefer works club chairman not to be politically active,
would vote for candidate to works club board with other
political views and who oppose economic support to the
Social Democratic Party, by level of manifest political
conflicts in works club (Swedish-born men only)

ing the works club.   A plater at a shipyard, where the
political fights were especially harsh, summarizes these
views:
    Banish politics from works club meetings so that Social
    Democrats and Communists will stop fighting each other
    instead of helping each other! When e.g. a Communist
    gets up and makes a proposal concerning something which
    he thinks is wrong, as soon as he sits down a Social
    Democrat gets up and criticizes the previous speaker so
    that it fits Social Democratic policies.   This is done
    exactly the other way around when a Social Democrat ex-
    presses his views.   Then the Communists have to resist
    it.   So it goes on meeting after meeting.   Small
    wonder that members, who are not politically interes-
    ted, find no reason to attend the meetings.
    While some level of politically based competition in
the works club often may function as a spur to democratic
process, it appears that the political fights between the
Social Democrats and the Communists can sometimes become
so intensive that they are perceived as detrimental also
by the Social Democrats.

8   WORKING-CLASS POLITICS IN PERSPECTIVE

The electoral success of the Social Democratic Party in
Sweden is largely a reflection of the fact that the party
not only has managed to build up and maintain strong support among manual workers, but also gradually has been
able to enlarge its support within the white-collar
groups.   Historical, structural and political factors
have made this development possible.   The growth of a
socialist labour movement prior to the extension of suffrage, and the relatively small importance of religion,
have meant that the party has had no heavy conservative
heritage to overcome among the working-class electorate.
The structural changes that have contributed to increase
unionization in the white-collar groups have also been of
importance in enlarging the electoral base of the Social
Democrats.
    In discussions of working-class politics, party pref-
erences have generally been seen as reflections of positions in the stratification system.   The thesis of 'embourgeoisement' thus has been criticized for assuming too
simplistically that an increased standard of living among
workers will decrease their propensity to vote for socialist parties (Goldthorpe et al., 1968a, b, 1969).   Discussions on changes in the degree of class voting are also
often limited to changes in the stratification system.

It must be kept in mind, however, that party choice is
generally a choice between policy packages, which are
posed as alternatives in political conflict. Of crucial
importance for the electoral success of the Swedish Social
Democrats has been that for a long time they have managed
to make issues of welfare, employment and social justice
the central lines of cleavage in politics. These issues
polarize the electorate along class lines, making it possible to organize the wage-earners for unified political
action.

Ongoing structural changes in the Swedish occupational
structure need not threaten the continued political
strength of the Social Democratic Party. As we have indicated, many of these changes have actually increased the
possibilities for the Social Democrats to enlarge their
support.

A powerful threat to the Social Democratic electoral
future would appear to come, instead, from the type of
issues focused upon in the political conflicts. In recent years, for instance, the economic growth strategy of
class conflict has placed the Social Democrats on the
defensive regarding issues such as regional development
and protection of the environment. The growth strategy
of class conflict also led the party leadership to support a programme for the development of nuclear energy,
which did not have the support of the electorate. In the
mid-1970s, then, a largely 'moral' question, nuclear
energy, has become a major political issue, cutting across
party and class lines. This issue crucially contributed
to the narrow victory of the bourgeois block in the 1976
elections. In the early 1970s, however, issues of industrial and economic democracy also came into political
focus. The political balance of power in the country
through the 1980s therefore appears dependent on which of
these themes becomes the most important in the political
struggles.

The 'classical' split within the labour movement between its 'revolutionary' and 'reformist' wings appears
based at least to some extent on differences of relative
positions within the stratification system. To a somewhat larger extent than the Social Democrats, Communist
workers appear to have experienced early economic deprivation and to have a low standard of living. This probably partly explains why they have come to perceive society, and the means to change it, in ways different from
the Social Democrats. The Communists have been even more
disadvantaged in comparison to the Social Democrats in the
union leadership, where the skilled workers traditionally
have dominated. For the metal-workers - the core group

of the working class - the Communist Party appears as a
closer alternative to the Social Democrats than do the
bourgeois parties.   Bourgeois party preferences are
largely 'inherited', and partly reflect downward social
mobility.   Although its total effect is small, religion
tends to counteract Communist Party preferences and to
support bourgeois preferences.
The radical value system among Swedish workers is to a
large extent mediated through the industrial work environment.   This environment tends to counteract bourgeois
party preferences.   It also contributes to a relatively
high class awareness among Swedish workers (Scase, 1977).
The workers' collectivity and the informal union activists
at the place of work are central parts of this environment.   The informal union activists are important links
between the Social Democratic Party and the union members.
The left-wing Social Democrats tend to function as informal activists more often than other Social Democrats.   In
our sample, variation in the work environment appears to
be more important than type of community for providing a
background for and mediating the political influences on
the metal-workers.   While the large firms need not, under
normal circumstances, have more radical or oppositional
workers than smaller firms, mobilization of the workers
appears easier there since they often have an embryo of an
oppositional organization and a somewhat higher level of
political conflicts at the workplace.
The bourgeois value system is mediated to workers
largely through the mass media.   More than half of the
metal-workers in our population thus regularly read bourgeois newspapers.   The bourgeois dominance in the mass
media has become more important in the 1970s as a result
of a lowering of the voting age to eighteen years and the
increasing proportion of the young persons that continue
their schooling.   This means that, while in the 1960s the
first-time voters usually had their own experiences as
wage-earners for about five years, the first-time voters
in the 1970s have little or no work experience.   They
have thus not been subjected to the 'counter-culture' at
the workplace to the same extent as other voters.
The immigrants, which now constitute a relatively large
proportion of workers, could weaken the political
strength of the working class.   By increasing restrictions on immigration and by attempts to ensure equal
rights to the immigrants, the Social Democrats have partly
avoided the creation of important ethnic cleavages within
the working class.   The granting of suffrage to immigrants in local and regional elections in 1976 is a significant step in this direction.   In the mid-1970s, how-

ever, about one-tenth of the LO members were not entitled
to vote in elections to the Riksdag.

The historically close connection between the unions
and the Social Democratic Party has been crucial in preserving it as a party of and for the working class.
Until state support to the political parties become important in the 1970s, the party received its main economic
support from the LO unions.   Via the system of collective
affiliation of branches, LO members have constituted more
than two-thirds of the party membership.   This has given
the workers and their representatives a strong power base
within the party.   The close connection between the party
and the unions is strongly supported by Social Democratic
workers active in union affairs.   Also among them, however, the system of collective affiliation receives relatively weak support.   It thus appears that new formal
ways are needed to preserve the close relationship between
the party and the unions, and the dominance of union members within the party.

11 The labour movement in welfare capitalism

Let us now again face our original question: have the workers, as Disraeli anticipated, matured as conservative angels in the marble of welfare capitalism, or are they still the grave-diggers of capitalism as Marx and Engels foresaw? Will the domination of men by men cease in the economic sphere, or will democracy halt at the factory gate and office entrance? This final chapter will not attempt to summarize all the evidence presented in the previous chapters of relevance in this context. Against the background of these previous analyses, however, it will point at conditions and processes of major significance in a considered response to the question on the possibilities to achieve economic and industrial democracy in our 'test' country, Sweden. The analysis of the background to the postwar political developments in Sweden will also be continued and the changes in the political scene up to the late 1970s will be discussed.

1 PROBLEMS GENERATING CHANGE

The starting point for our analysis of the future development of society is the assumption that structural change is generated by a process through which social collectivities, confronted with problems, attempt to solve them (cf. chapter 1). This problem-solving process is comprised of various stages: recognition of the problem, definition of alternative solutions and choosing among the solutions. Taking place within the framework of the societal power structure, this process is influenced by the social consciousness of citizens; it can also be marked by social conflict. In the following we examine some major problems which can prompt citizens to consider alternative solutions which can move the economic system away from capitalism, in a socialistic direction.

309

Economic security and production

Although the development of capitalist societies has led
to a record high average standard of living, especially in
the decades since the Second World War, periodic economic
crises continue to characterize the capitalist system.
The hope that economic policy could provide effective
cures has proved too sanguine. In most capitalist countries sizable sectors of citizens are unemployed or in-
securely employed. A lower class remains, often consisting of immigrant workers or minority groups. The capitalistic system thus appears unable to relieve significant
sectors of the population from the insecurity connected
with the material conditions of life. This fact was
underscored by the economic crisis sweeping the western
countries in the 1970s.

With the development of capitalism the social nature of
production has become increasingly pronounced. Production processes thus have become more complex and interdependent. They require increasingly larger collective
contributions to the reproduction and maintenance of the
labour force as well as development of an infrastructure
which can make production possible. (1) The increasingly
social nature of production also makes more acute the contradiction between rationality at the level of the firm
and rationality at the societal level. Decisions concerning production, rational according to the criteria established for management of a capitalist firm, may have
important negative consequences and costs for society.
This generates a need for societal planning.

In some countries a tendency for falling profit rates
in recent years has made it increasingly difficult for
private firms to sustain a level of investment which makes
possible a sufficient rate of economic growth and a high
level of employment. This has necessitated various types
of public measures to channel taxpayers' money to the
firms, creating thereby latent tensions around issues of
distributive justice and economic power in society.

Finite resources

The other side of the tremendous increase in productivity
in capitalistic industrial society has been the increasing
destruction of the environment and consumption of finite
natural resources. In the 1960s, attention focused on
the environmental disasters which threatened the industrialized countries, as well as the limits to our natural resources, including food, for an increasing world popula-

tion.   The oil crisis in the early 1970s heightened
awareness of the looming depletion of the world's energy
resources.

The survival of a firm in a capitalistic system depends
on its ability to accumulate profit.   Keyed to the pursuit of profit, it has been neither necessary nor possible
for it adequately to consider the external effects of its
activities.   It is also difficult to re-define the action
parameters of the capitalist firms by political means to
increase resource economizing and consideration of the
environment.   Since the national economy depends on the
successful operation of these firms, governments are reluctant to restrict them.   The firms tend to use their
power to counteract and evade rules which limit their opportunities for profit-making.   Societal attempts to
economize on finite resources and to protect the environment thus tend to generate solutions which increase the
role of planning and limit the sphere of operation of capitalist principles.

Inequality

The belief that all men were created equal is a persistent
warp in the web of human thought.   In comparison with the
agrarian societies, industrialism generated a long-term
decrease in the degree of inequality.   The winning of
universal suffrage and the right of organization have
marked important points in this development.

In the decades since the Second World War, however, inequality of opportunity and of result have proved highly
resistant to social reform, much more so than liberal re-
formers had expected.   Distributions of income and property have not become significantly equalized in these
decades.   While political democracy has introduced formal
equality among citizens, actual as well as formal inequality prevails in industry.   Individuals who sell their
labour power to the capitalist firm become subordinated in
a power structure where power is derived from the owners
of capital.   Inequality of opportunity and of result thus
appears inherent in the capitalist system.   This inequality is also a restriction on the freedom of citizens.   To
the extent that the distribution of power in society becomes more equal, the basis for this restriction will be
questioned.

Meaningful work

In human life the nature of work has important consequences.   It significantly affects a person's mental as well
as physical health.   The long arm of the job also influences the 'effective scope' of the citizen: his levels of
aspiration, his view of himself, the objects of his pur-
suits.   A person's work can provide him with a potentially important base for a meaningful life.   Our data
indicate that the desire for a satisfying job is important
among Swedish workers.

In comparison with craft production, processes of mechanization have decreased the possibility of manual workers
finding intrinsic job satisfaction.   Technological developments connected with automation may somewhat improve
these possibilities.   The nature of jobs, however, are
determined primarily by the structure of power in the context in which technology and the work organization are
developed.   In a capitalist economic system the development of technology and the work organization is guided
basically by the profit interests of the employers.   To
the extent that employers are satisfied with the latent
and manifest consequences of technology and work organization, they generally will not be greatly concerned with
job satisfaction for workers.   Thus, in a capitalist
system large sectors of the employees have only limited
possibilities for intrinsic job satisfaction.

The above problems are common to most capitalist industrial societies. (2)   The extent to which they become
recognized as important societal problems and the directions in which solutions for them are sought, depends on
several factors.   In the following sections we will discuss the most important of them as they have become evident in Sweden.

2   CHANGING CLASS STRUCTURE

Position in the class structure defines important 'objective' or 'latent' interest of a citizen.   Changes in the
class structure therefore can affect the overall balance
of interests in society and thus are important for its
future development.   Contrary to what is often assumed,
the relative size of the working class in Sweden has remained quite stable throughout the present century, at a
level somewhat above 50 per cent of the economically
active population. (3)   Middle-class groups have not increased their relative size but drastic changes have taken
place in their composition.   The most important change

has been a rapid decrease in the farm population and an increase of salaried employees, the 'new' middle class. In the mid-1970s, the number of salaried employees equalled about half the number of workers.

As a result of the changing composition of middle-class groups, the overwhelming majority of the economically active citizens now earn their living by selling their labour power on the market. The drastic increase in the proportion of married women in the labour force is another indication that a large and increasing majority of the population share the positions and experiences of wage-earners.

The argument that the working class will become innocuous to capitalism by merging with the middle class is based on the assumption that the middle class already is integrated into the capitalist system. This argument passes lightly over the fact that the salaried employees, which constitute the bulk of the middle class, share the basic condition of the workers: they are forced to sell their labour power to earn their living. The growth of the number of salaried employees results from the increasing density of salaried employees in industry and from the swelling public sector. It thus partly reflects the increasingly complex and social nature of production. The largest increase has taken place in the public sector, where the majority of the white-collar groups perform some type of administrative or service functions. In industry the majority of the salaried employees are engaged in administrative or technical work.

A decreasing and by now relatively small minority of the 'new middle class' is thus directly involved in the line of authority which reaches down from the level of employers, to the manual workers. As a result of mergers and rationalization, salaried employees, especially those new on the labour market, have become threatened by unemployment and insecurity more often than previously. Their growing number also has made salary costs an increasing proportion of a firm's expenditures, thereby stimulating collective bargaining in the white-collar sector.

Difference in wages between manual workers and salaried employees probably has decreased during the postwar period, but the distribution of pre-tax income among adult men has remained relatively stable, partly because working time has been shortened more for workers than for white-collar groups (Spånt, 1975). Some narrowing of differences between the working class and the middle class has also occurred because legislation on improved pensions, health insurance, vacations and employment security has been of greater significance for workers.

Although the salaried employees still have more favourable work and status situations than the workers and although some of them share the function of the employers in
framing and enforcing rules for other employees, the developments pointed to above have underlined the similarities in class position between white-collar and blue-collar employees. These developments have also contributed
to make the market position for the majority of the salaried employees more like that of workers, forcing them to
rely increasingly on collective action to protect their
interests vis-à-vis the employers. (4)

3 MOBILIZATION POSSIBILITIES

The 'latent' interests of citizens, derived from their
positions in the class structure, cannot, in themselves,
generate collective action. They provide, instead, a
potential basis for such action. Several factors can be
assumed to affect the possibilities to mobilize wage-
earners in support of problem-solving which results in a
movement away from the capitalist system.
   Social change within the working class inducting an
increasing proportion of workers into more anonymous and
impersonal relationships with employers has facilitated
such mobilization. This, however, does not result primarily from an increase in the proportion of workers in
very large places of work, but instead from the gradual
decline and disappearance of particular branches and types
of jobs, e.g. agricultural workers and domestic servants.
The marked increase in employment among the married women
is also significant. Generally, increasing standards of
living, economic security, leisure and educational levels
have considerably facilitated the mobilization of
workers.
   A factor significantly decreasing the possibility to
mobilize workers is the growing proportion of immigrants
among them. Immigrants generally have not the right to
vote in elections to the Riksdag. We have seen that
among the metal-workers, the presence of a sizable proportion of immigrants tends to weaken the workers' collectivity. Immigrants also tend to form part of a lower class
in Swedish society. As a result of Social Democratic
efforts, however, this tendency is much less pronounced in
Sweden than in most other industrialized countries of
western Europe. Important measures have been undertaken
in an attempt to give immigrants largely the same position
as other citizens. (5)   Legislation giving immigrants
universal suffrage after, say, three years of residence in

Sweden, would also, directly and indirectly, overcome the most significant hinders for their mobilization.

In the late 1960s, the increase in the proportion of employment in manufacturing tended to stagnate. This was a result of the marked decrease of employment in some branches, e.g. textile and clothing, while employment increased in other branches, e.g. in the metal-working industry. The stagnation largely reflects the international division of labour in advanced capitalist economies, where labour-intensive branches tend to become located in low-wage, developing countries. It need thus not herald the beginning of the 'post-industrial' or 'service' society. Nevertheless this trend may have long-term significance for the mobilization of workers, since union organization tends to be weaker in the increasing tertiary sector. Our analyses indicate, however, that technological change within manufacturing may have more limited consequences for the strength of the workers' collectivities and for the possibilities to mobilize workers than what many have believed.

It is often assumed that recent changes in community structure and housing patterns have tended to decrease the possibilities of mobilizing workers on a class basis. These hypotheses are based on the assumption that stable, working-class dominated communities tend to diminish cross-class pressures, and to reinforce social influences from the working class through intra-class contacts and class-based organizations. The breakup of homogeneous working-class communities, combined with an increase in geographical mobility are assumed to facilitate a privatized and consumption-oriented style of life.

We must avoid, however, the interpretation that changes in community structure, geographical mobility and patterns of housing generally have tended to counteract the possibilities to mobilize workers. Instead, increasing urbanization probably has greatly facilitated the mobilization of the working class by breaking up the more conservative rural and small-town styles of life. It further appears that the stability of the working-class communities in the period before the Second World War often has been over-estimated. Swedish figures indicate that movements across parish boundaries, i.e. short-distance mobility, was at least as high in the first four decades of this century as in the postwar period (Jacobsson, 1970, p. 97). Long-distance geographical mobility, as indicated by the proportion of different age cohorts living in more than one community during childhood (up to fifteen years of age), has increased, however, beginning with cohorts born around 1930 (Erikson, 1971). (6)   Social segregation in

housing in the larger Swedish towns may have decreased
somewhat in the postwar period (Janson, 1965). (7)

There is surprisingly little empirical evidence to support an assumption that changes in community structures,
housing patterns and geographical mobility rates have had
substantial negative effects on working-class mobilization. Communities in Sweden traditionally regarded as
most typically working class - i.e. the one-company towns
- have characteristics which hinder mobilization, primarily paternalistic worker-management relations and great
dependence on the dominant employer in the community.

Our empirical study among the metal-workers gives only
limited support for hypotheses about the effects of community structure on the pattern of union and political
activities of the metal-workers. Although the frequency
of off-the-job contacts with workers from the same firm
depends on ·the relative size of the firm in the local
labour market, the degree of contacts with middle-class
persons is low among all metal-workers and does not vary
much among community types. Party preferences appear
somewhat less socialistic and political interest somewhat
lower in mixed communities as compared with either big
cities or industrial communities, but differences are not
very large. The extent of labour movement support (evidenced e.g. in preference for Social Democratic rather
than bourgeois newspapers and in shopping at a co-op
rather than in a private store) is somewhat higher in communities strongly dominated by the working class than in
other communities. Significantly enough, however, these
differences do not affect the extent of solidaristic and
instrumental orientations to the labour movement. The
decrease in solidaristic orientations to the union movement among the younger workers evidenced in our data can
thus not be explained in terms of changes in patterns of
housing and in community structures.

Our data further indicate that geographical mobility is
not strongly related to union activity or political interest. For geographically mobile workers, the place of
work functions as the first basis of social contacts in
the new community. Thus geographically mobile workers
actually may have more class-homogeneous social relations
than the stable workers, for whom kinship is a more important factor structuring social relations. In communities
with a large proportion of migrants, however - most typically the new suburbs with multi-family housing - the
Social Democratic party organization obviously faces at
least temporary difficulties.

It is thus apparent that community structure and geographical mobility are related to possibilities for

mobilizing the working class.   Important changes in
these areas in recent decades have tended to facilitate
mobilization while those changes hindering mobilization
appear to have had more limited effects than what is often
assumed.

4   POWER RESOURCES

The probability of changes in the economic organization
of society depends basically on changes in the distribution of power resources between the contending classes.
The power resources of the bourgeoisie are primarily based
on capital.   The concentration of capital in Sweden is
very high and has been increasing in the postwar period.
The competition between different interests has not hin-
dered the development of a web of interlocking organizations among capital owners.   Since the beginning of this
century Swedish employers have been organized to a very
high degree.   The high level of organization among employers in Sweden reflects the need for a more effective
utilization of their power resources in the face of the
increasing organizational strength of the labour movement
and attempts by the unions to utilize the splits among the
employers. (8)   The role of capital is also strengthened
by other circumstances.   Some of the largest Swedish
firms are multinational corporations, which increases
their independence.   To a very high degree, the Swedish
economy depends on exports, which makes the country potentially sensitive to international economic conditions and
pressures.   Foreign multinationals, however, are relatively unimportant.
     The relatively close contact between the representa-
tives of capital and some of the bourgeois parties is also
significant in this context.   This relationship is mediated partially through control over the mass media.   In
modern societies control over the mass media is an important power resource, which markedly affects the formation
of social consciousness of the citizens and thereby the
potential for collective action.   Newspapers in Sweden
represent political parties or political blocks, taking
explicit editorial positions on a left-right continuum.
The socialist share of the press has decreased during the
postwar period, largely as a result of selectivity in the
distribution of economic resources through advertising.
In the mid-1970s, the Social Democrats had only 20 per
cent of the total volume of daily newspapers, and a considerably smaller proportion of the politically important
morning newspapers.   To a small degree this strong bour-

geois dominance is counterbalanced by labour union jour-
nals.   Publicly owned, non-commercial radio and television also provide, by international standards, informative
programmes.   The bourgeois dominated newspapers, however,
largely define the limits of the public debate also in
radio and television.

The power resources of the wage earners are channelled
through unions and political parties.   As we have seen,
unions in Sweden have been growing gradually but continuously, reaching a level with about 80 per cent of the
labour force organized in the mid-1970s.   Equally important is the changing nature of unionism.   Workers are now
organized on the basis of class in industrial unions under
a unified leadership in the LO.   The white-collar organizations are also largely based on the principle of industrial unionism and have become more militant.   A marked
tendency toward increasing co-operation between the two
main union organizations, the LO and the TCO, is also evident since the 1960s.   A close relationship between the
TCO and the LO is of strategic importance for political
development in Sweden.

The high level of unionization and the dominance of
industrial unions also in the white-collar sector underlines that numbers rather than specific market capacities
are the main power resources for the great majority of
the wage earners.   Therefore we can expect that the
level of unionization as well as the size of union collectivities will continue to increase, since it is the main
way to improve the position of wage earners in relation
to the employers.   The marked increase in the level of
unionization among workers during the Social Democrats'
period in government indicates the importance of political
action for the process of organization and generation of
power resources when power depends on numbers.

The political party is the other important power resource for the wage earners.   It is of crucial importance
for the position of the Swedish working class that it is
represented by unified organizations in both the political
and in the economic spheres.   Close ties between the organizations in these spheres - the two wings of the labour
movement - have helped to bridge the gap between the roles
as citizen and as wage earner.

The power resources of wage earners also have been directly and significantly improved through political measures.   The most important factor has been maintenance of
a high level of employment in the postwar period.   The
development of good social insurance systems, e.g. in the
areas of health, unemployment and pensions, has also markedly increased the economic independence of the workers.

Pension funds under public control, created in the 1960s, potentially can counterbalance the dominance of private capital. So far, however, they have been invested in industry only to a limited extent.

5   POLITICS OF NECESSARY COMPROMISE

As previously indicated the dominant assumption among political sociologists has been that the electoral difficulties of the social democratic parties in postwar Europe have resulted from changes in the structure of class and community, which have decreased the structural base for socialist policies among the voters and made it more difficult to mobilize support for such policies. The weakness in this interpretation becomes apparent when it is applied to the Swedish case. Such an interpretation is not congruent with the fact that the greatest Social Democratic election victories came as late as in 1960, 1962 and 1968. Nor can structural changes explain the increasing volatility of election outcomes with serious Social Democratic setbacks in 1966 and 1976, close to the great victories. The analysis in the previous sections also indicates that the prevailing orthodoxy is wrong in its basic assumptions of a gradual contraction of the structural base for socialist support and of increasing difficulties to mobilize this support. Although changes in Sweden in the class structure, the stratification system and the structure of communities during the postwar years have been partly contradictory, on balance they have tended to improve the possibilities to find support for social democratic policies.

The alternative interpretation argued for here focuses on the content of politics as much as on the conditions for politics given by the social structure. In my view the electoral difficulties of the Social Democrats result primarily from the restrictions which the dominance of capital and the capitalistic economic system have placed on Social Democratic policies, restrictions which have necessitated compromise politics with dualistic consequences for potential socialist voters.

In this context it is important to remember that party choice is essentially future-oriented action. When choosing between parties, the citizen ideally evaluates the utility of their future policies on the basis of his perception of their programmes and past performance. Party choice, however, is not a direct reflection of 'latent interests' or of structural change. The citizen must become conscious of his interests and to be convinced that one party is more likely than others to promote these interests. The voters' perceptions of the likely consequences of what the parties stand for are to an important extent formed by political struggles in connection with the elections, by the policies which parties become identified with in government position as well as by the interpretation of political action provided by the mass media.

The Social Democratic Party is part of a popular movement and is thus an instrument for mobilization of power resources based on numbers. In this process, a pronounced future orientation, manifest in a promise of a better and equitable society plays a key role for raising and directing the aspirations of workers and for creating political loyalties. There is a complicated interaction between practice and promise in the process of mobilization. Promise is essential but, in the end, practice prevails.

In spite of adverse mobilization possibilities, the labour movement was able gradually to change social consciousness and increase the capacity for collective action among workers. Lacking a policy to solve the severe unemployment problems in the 1920s, however, the weak Social Democratic minority governments in those years could not increase the electoral support of the party. The crucial break-through for the party came first in the crises in the 1930s, when it was able to hold out a realistic promise of change in the life situation of the workers. This promise stood in stark contrast to their actual conditions of living as well as to the future perceived to be connected with the bourgeois parties.

Since the mid-1930s, the policies of the Social Democratic government came to be dominated by what we have called the historical compromise between labour and capital made possible, as well as necessitated, by the fact that political power had become separated from economic power. As we have seen, the historical compromise resulted in a shift from a 'zero-sum' conflict situation to a 'positive-sum' strategy of class conflict. It was based on a formula of co-operation between the labour movement and the representatives of capital to increase economic growth. Decision-making in the sphere of production was largely left to capital. The labour movement undertook responsibility for affecting distribution of the increasing product by political means, through the government, according to criteria of social justice. This strategy was also seen as speeding up the maturation of capitalism and thereby as facilitating the movement towards socialism.

The growth strategy of class conflict implied, in a
sense, collaboration between classes.   But it was not
'class collaboration' deriving from ideological or moral
weakness among the leaders of the labour movement.   This
compromise, instead, was necessitated by the structure of
power prevailing in Swedish society at that time.   It
offered possibilities but also contained risks.   This
type of compromise seems to be an inescapable step in the
maturation of capitalism.   Since the 1960s, the mass Communist Parties of Western Europe appear to be realizing
the impossibility of the revolutionary strategy associated
with the Third International.   The political strategies
labelled Eurocommunism, which have been developed by the
parties in Italy, France and Spain in the 1970s, appear in
several ways to resemble the approach adopted by the
Swedish Social Democrats in the 1930s.

The historical compromise was an achievement for the
Swedish labour movement, made possible by the increased
political support for the Social Democratic Party.   This
compromise therefore provided the base for policies which
were to have important positive consequences for the wage
earners.   Of crucial importance were the economic and
labour market policies which made it possible to decrease
unemployment in the 1930s and to maintain a very high
level of employment in the inflation-unemployment dilemmas
facing governments in the west in the postwar period and
up to the 1970s.

A high level of employment not only improved the economic situation of the workers.   It had crucial indirect
effects by improving the power position of workers in the
labour market and at the workplace.   Although the forms
of industrial democracy were absent, the bargaining position of the workers was so improved that they in different
ways could affect the decision-making of managements.
The full employment policies relieved significant numbers
of workers from debasing experiences and removed the
threat of unemployment from the centre of their consciousness.   The greatly improved social policies increased
economic security.   The policies based on the compromise
also contributed to economic growth and thereby facilitated an increasing standard of living as well as the acceptance of redistribution policies.   Beneficial consequences of policies based on the historical compromise helped
to increase the support for the Social Democrats and the
LO.

But we must not forget that the historical compromise
was necessitated by the still inferior power resources of
labour.   The policies deriving from this compromise
therefore also came to embody negative consequences for
wage earners.

A major circumstance generating negative consequences
for workers was that the initiatives to increase economic
growth were largely left to the representatives of capital.   Private profit, therefore, became the over-arching
decision-making criterion in the restructuring of the
economy.   Technological changes and rationalizations initiated by managements probably increased monotony and
stress at work.   The compromise allowed for the concentration of industry to the urbanized areas and accelerated
the migration of sometimes reluctant workers to these
areas. (9)   The concentration of capital increased.   The
growth strategy was probably also significant in the centralization of decision-making in the unions beginning in
the late 1930s.

The strong reliance by the Social Democrats on the
growth strategy made the leaders of the labour movement
sometimes appear as parts of the techno-structure, having
economic growth as their main goal.   Combining compromise politics with a pronounced future orientation also
proved difficult for the labour movement.   Its leadership
became absorbed with day-to-day political responsibili-
ties.   The party faced difficulties in developing programmes for continued societal change in the direction of
economic democracy.   In the eyes of many voters, the
Social Democrats gradually became identified with the compromise and growth policies.   They also tended to defend
most aspects of these policies, often also those that
caused dismay among potential supporters.   As we have
seen the gradual decline in the popular movement characteristics of the unions were reflected in changing union
orientations among the metal-workers, from a solidaristic
orientation among the older workers to a more instrumental
and conditional orientation among the younger generations.

The bourgeois parties' gradual acceptance of welfare
measures once enacted made the Social Democrats seem but
one among several reform parties competing for the right
to administer existing society.   By focusing on some of
the negative aspects of the compromise policies, especially rapid urbanization, regional inbalance, centralization
and problems with the environment and with nuclear energy,
since the late 1960s the bourgeois parties were able not
only to maintain but also to increase their political
support.

The interpretation suggested here is thus that electoral difficulties of the Social Democrats have arisen
largely from the continued superiority of the power resources of the capitalist class, which has constrained
Social Democratic policies, necessitating compromises with
dualistic consequences for potential supporters.   The

traditional view with its stress on changes in class and
community structures underestimates the importance of
popular movements and the role of political action and
political goals for the mobilization of people.

It would appear that the interpretation suggested here,
derived from the Swedish experience, also can help to explain electoral difficulties of social democratic parties
in other European countries in the postwar period. Fal-
tering Labour support in Britain, for instance, seems to
be explainable largely in terms of the type of economic
policies which the Labour government was forced to apply
in attempts to improve Britain's economic position - even
at the costs of record high unemployment and a partial
stagnation of the living standards of workers. It would
not appear necessary to invoke explanations in terms of
changes in class and community structures which affect the
mobilization possibilities and the latent interests of the
workers. In Norway and Denmark, social democratic leaders felt it necessary to seek entry into the European
common market in order to maintain economic growth, a
policy which split and severely weakened these parties.

6   REORIENTATION OF POLICY

Our theoretical analysis of the relationship between
changes in power resources and relative deprivation indicates that levels of aspiration can be expected to grow
with increasing power resources. It is thus improbable
that workers can be 'bought off' with an increased standard of living to accept the subordination inherent in the
institution of wage labour. If their power resources
continue to grow, aspirations will eventually extend to an
influence over decision-making at work and in production.

Why did the Social Democratic Party in the postwar
period tend to avoid advancing programmes and taking
action in the direction of economic democracy? One important reason for this reluctance was the labour movement's continued inferiority with respect to power resources. The years following the Second World War witnessed
a resurgence of the power of capitalism, marked by the
American dominance on the international scene. The
powerful attacks against the Social Democratic postwar
programme and the subsequent weakening of the party was
indicative of this. Advances in the direction of economic democracy would have been risky, subject to misrepre-
sentation in the mass media and misinterpretation among
the voters.

The issue of Social Democratic postwar strategy also

raises questions about the responsiveness of labour
leaders to the demands of the rank-and-file members, and
about possibilities for the members to affect policies
and strategies of the organizations. Our analysis indicates that the economic growth strategy of class conflict
was associated with the centralization of decision-making
procedures within the Swedish union movement. Collective
decision-making within the labour movement is naturally
affected by the differences in perspectives between leaders and the rank-and-file, as well as by the differing
consequences of collective decisions for members differently placed in the internal organizational hierarchy.
The Swedish experience, however, indicates that these organizations have not been subject to 'the iron law of
oligarchy'.
In the late 1960s the Social Democratic Party began to
reorient its policy back to its original and radical direction. This reorientation followed the strengthening
of the Social Democrats in connection with the political
struggles over pensions reforms of the late 1950s, and it
had several sources. In the mid-1960s, information
became available indicating that contrary to what was
generally assumed, income inequality had not continued to
decrease. It was also argued that significant aspects
of Social Democratic economic and fiscal policies had
tended to maintain and even to increase income inequality
(e.g. Bergström, 1965). Increasing attention was drawn
to the negative consequences which industrial rationalization had for workers. In 1965, the Social Democrats initiated a commission to probe into the background and
extent of low incomes and low levels of living.
The Social Democratic setback in the communal elections
in 1966 underlined the need for a reconsideration of policies. The strike by highly paid members of SACO in 1966
- the most dramatic strike since 1945 - stimulated the
debate on equity with respect to the distribution of
income and welfare in society. To this was added the
gradually increasing awareness that economic growth did
not automatically lead to improved welfare of the population but contained, instead, threats of destruction of the
environment, depletion of natural resources and increasing
risks as well as pressures on the workers. The basic
insecurity of wage earners inherent in welfare capitalism
was underlined when a long boom period reaching a peak in
1965 was converted to a severe recession in 1968.   A
change in the intellectual climate in the country can also
be traced back to the mid-1960s.   Works of art reflected
an increasingly critical view towards Swedish society as
well as an increasing awareness of the third world prob-

lems.   The war in Vietnam came to serve as an important
catalyst for this development.
The extra party congress of the Social Democrats in
1967 attempted to reorient policy.   The guiding principle
became the stress on 'greater equality'.   Together with
the widespread faith in the ability of the Social Democrats to maintain employment in the deepening recession,
this reorientation crucially affected the record victory
of the Social Democrats in the 1968 elections: they won
over 50 per cent of the votes and the largest proportion
ever of the electorate.   The wave of unofficial strikes
in the winter of 1969-70 brought an abrupt end to the
often celebrated calm on the Swedish labour market.
After some hesitation the leaders of the labour movement
interpreted this outburst as indicating the need for far-
reaching reforms in the area of working life.
The LO played a leading role in the reorientation of
Social Democratic policy.   It thus broke with the tradition established in the 1930s that the developments on
the labour market should be guided by agreements between
the labour market organizations with the state as a 'neutral' third party.   On the initiative of the LO, the
Social Democratic government established commissions in
the early 1970s to propose legislation to increase the
influence of wage earners in working life.   In the following five years legislation was enacted improving the
employment security of the wage earners, giving them
minority representation on company boards, enlarging the
authority of the elected safety officers of the workplace
union, and improving possibilities for workplace union
representatives to carry out their work.
At the end of the 1960s the international wave of
'stagflation' hit Sweden.   Prices, especially on housing
and food, increased rapidly.   Unemployment increased.
Among men, the proportion in the labour force decreased in
all age groups.   The proportion of the population having
to rely on means-tested social assistance increased,
reaching a postwar record in 1972.   The Social Democratic
campaign for 'greater equality' was outflanked by strong
left-wing criticism of Swedish society, based partly on
the new organizations leading the protest movement against
the American war in Vietnam.   This protest movement developed largely outside the political parties but resulted
in the establishment of small groups to the left of the
Communist Party.   The Social Democratic Party was placed
on the defensive.   Restrictive economic policy contributed to high unemployment in 1972-3.
Public opinion polls indicate that the probably
strongest asset of the Social Democrats, the belief in the

electorate that a Social Democratic government was the
best safeguard for full employment, was depreciated in
these years.   Before the 1968 elections the Social Democrats had a lead with 20 percentage points over the bourgeois parties in terms of which government was best able
to safeguard employment in the country.   This shifted to
a lead for the bourgeois block with 6 per cent before the
1970 elections and with 10 per cent before the 1973 election (SIFO, 1976).   The elections in 1973 resulted in a
stalemate in the Riksdag.   The Social Democrats remained
in power but sought compromise solutions to the major political issues.

An important step in legislation to enlarge the power
resources of wage earners and their unions was taken in
1976, when the managerial prerogatives in hiring and
firing and in leading and directing work were formally
abolished. ˙The increased influence of the wage earners
was to be channelled not through the creation of new
organs for co-determination according to the West German
model but rather through enlarging and improving the possibilities of the unions to bargain with the employers. (10)   The new legislation made all subjects, including the nature and type of production, negotiable between
unions and managements.   It improved the power resources
of the unions basically by increasing their possibilities
to delay the implementation of management decisions.   The
law thus required managements to initiate negotiations
with the workplace union in advance of important changes
in the firm, a demand which was made effective by requiring the firm to give the union access to the firm's internal information.   The workplace union also received the
right to continue negotiations at the central level before
management is authorized to undertake proposed changes.
In cases of disagreement, the union representatives were
given the prerogative to interpret the contracts.   If the
national unions failed to come to an agreement with the
employers' organizations on the forms and extent of the
enlarged influence of wage earners, the union retained the
right to strike on these issues during the term of the
contract.

We have seen that in the mid-1960s, the criticism of
union policy among the metal-workers came primarily from
the left, tending to increase with an increasing awareness
of inequality in Swedish society.   The initiatives taken
by the union leaders in the following years thus can be
seen as a response to this criticism.   The union leaders,
being more directly dependent on the workers, were apparently more sensitive than the party leadership to the
opinions among the workers.   In 1975 the Social Democra-

tic Party accepted its new and relatively radical party programme, which underlined the commitment of the party to economic democracy.   The most important concrete proposal in the direction of economic democracy, however, came from the LO.   This proposal reflected the fact that the economic growth strategy, the efforts to maintain full employment and the solidaristic wage policy of the unions had generated problems, the solution of which prompted the unions to question crucial aspects of the capitalist economic system.

7   THE GROWTH-EQUALITY PREDICAMENT AND WAGE EARNERS' FUNDS

In the growth strategy of class conflict, policies to enable and encourage private firms to finance investments from their profits occupied a central place.   In the 1960s, as costs of investment increased and profit rates tended to fall, this became increasingly difficult. Schemes for the direct and indirect support to private industry were developed on a massive scale. (11)   The solidaristic wage policy, which did not base wage claims on the profitability of the firm or industry, contributed to increase profits in the most expansive sectors of industry.   Both these circumstances facilitated the concentration of capital in industry.   The rate of industrial mergers has increased drastically since the 1950s.

For a long period the increasing concentration of an already highly skewed distribution of capital in Swedish industry was accepted by the labour movement as an unavoidable consequence of otherwise sound policies.   In the 1970s, however, this acceptance withered away.   The tendency of compromise policies and the growth strategy to increase inequality with respect to the distribution of capital and economic power gradually gained recognition as a major problem.

At the LO congress in 1971, several motions - the most important ones emanating from the metal-workers - criticized these aspects of the compromise policies.   They demanded that the LO act to channel excess profits from the most expansive sectors of industry to organs under control of the wage earners or the public, if possible in ways which would increase the influence of the wage earners in the firms.   The congress authorized a working group within the LO to develop a proposal which was to complement the solidaristic wage policy, to counteract the concentration of capital and to increase the influence of the wage earners in economic life.   The proposal should further ensure that full employment and good

investment possibilities were maintained but it should not
affect costs for the firms, nor wages and prices (LO,
1976, pp. 9-19).

The working group, led by Rudolf Meidner, presented its
reports to the LO congress of 1976 (Meidner et al., 1975;
LO, 1976).   The group rejected increased company taxation as a method to achieve the goals.   A high rate of
profits must be accepted to facilitate the investments
necessary for economic growth.   Instead it proposed the
creation of 'wage-earners' funds', which would shift the
economic control over the firms from the previous shareholders to collectivities of wage earners.   This was to
be achieved by requiring privately owned companies above
a certain size to emit shares to wage-earners' funds pro-
portionate to their gross profits.   These funds should
not be limited to a single company but should encompass
a number of·firms.   The report discussed the possibility
of creating regional funds but ended up by proposing funds
based on branches of industry, which was seen as facilitating industrial development.

Depending on the profitability of the firms and on the
proportion of profits to be emitted to the wage-earners'
funds - the working group proposed 20 per cent - the funds
would achieve dominating control of firms in large sectors of industry within about ten to twenty years.   The
wage-earners' funds, however, should not be seen as the
centres of large business concerns.   Their purpose was
rather to break the opposition of the previous shareholders to the influence of employees in the running of the
firm.   A firm controlled by the funds would thus be
relatively independent.

According to the proposal by the working group, a wage-
earners' fund was to be governed by a board where about
one-half of the members would come from the unions in the
industry and another half from other unions.   The boards
would also have minority representation of the state.
When the funds increased their proportion of shares in a
firm, they would gradually receive the right to representation on the board of the firm.   The workplace union
organization were to elect board members representing the
first 20 per cent of the shares of the firm.   With increasing control over shares, the wage-earners' fund would
appoint additional board members, subject to the consent
of the workplace union organizations. (12)   The LO-con-
gress accepted the basic ideas behind the proposal on
wage-earners' funds but did not commit itself to any
specific institutional arrangements concerning the funds.

Significantly enough, within the TCO thinking on these
problems had developed in very much the same way as in

the LO. At the TCO congress in 1976 a working group presented a report discussing various aspects of 'wage-
earners' capital' (TCO, 1976). The starting point of
this report, too, was that economic growth to maintain
full employment and rising standards of living necessitated a high rate of investments in industry. Yet, direct
and indirect economic support to private firms, combined
with a solidaristic wage policy, was seen as increasing
inequity with respect to the distribution of capital and
wealth to an unacceptable degree. Since this wealth was
largely created by state support with taxpayers' money
as well as by the solidaristic wage policy of the unions,
wage earners were entitled to share this new wealth.

The TCO report saw the creation of some type of wage-
earners' funds based on shares emitted by firms in relation to their profits as the best solution to the problem
of enabling private industry to maintain a high level of
investment capacity, while avoiding increasingly unacceptable inequalities in the distribution of capital. The
TCO report did however not identify increased economic
influence of wage earners as a major goal of the funds.
While approving the increased influence made possible by
these funds, the report regarded legislative change as the
main way to increase the power of wage earners in the economy. The TCO report discussed various forms of wage-
earners' funds. It favoured collective funds rather than
funds based on single firms, but left open the possibility that employees can have individual shares in the funds
which can be cashed in after some period of time. The
TCO-congress remitted the report to further investigation
and studies among the members.

The Federation of Swedish Industries together with the
SAF authorized a group of prominent industrialists and
economists to draft a report discussing business profits,
investment capital and wage-earners' funds (Sveriges
Industriförbund, 1976). This report strongly criticized
the LO proposal of wage-earners' funds. The creation of
such funds would change the economic system of society.
The capital market would break down. Business profits
would no longer be the criterion for investment. Gradually, a planned economy would be introduced. This would
lead to centralization, bureaucratization and inefficiency
much as if the firms were nationalized. The requirement
that profits be given in the form of shares to a new category of owners was interpreted as a form of expropriation,
probably incompatible with fundamental principles of justice in society. (13)

The proposal of wage-earners' funds rapidly became a
significant political issue. The Social Democratic

leadership expressed general sympathy for the LO proposal but did not come out in clear support of it. Instead a parliamentary commission was established to work out alternative proposals concerning wage-earners' funds. The bourgeois parties strongly criticized the LO proposal, labelling it a socialistic proposal which threatened pluralistic, democratic society.

8   THE SOCIAL DEMOCRATIC DEFEAT IN 1976

The 1976 election is a historical landmark because it ended the 44-term of Social Democratic dominance of the government. The campaign in this election started in early 1976 when the mass media focused long and intensive attention on a series of 'scandals' within the labour movement. ·Several of these affairs would probably hardly have been noticed had they not taken place in Sweden and involved representatives of its labour movement. The attention in the mass media on these affairs, however, gave the Social Democrats an exceedingly difficult start in the 1976 election campaign. (14) As a result of successful efforts to maintain a high level of employment in the deepening international recession, the Social Democrats this time had a lead over the bourgeois block with 11 per cent in terms of being seen as the party best able to safeguard employment in the nation (SIFO, 1976).

The last two weeks of the election campaign were dominated by the issue of nuclear energy. The Social Democrats were the only party explicitly to support a programme for limited build-up of nuclear power stations. At this stage the Centre Party made opposition to nuclear energy the central issue in its campaign. An opinion survey carried out during the two weeks preceding the election indicates that a clear Social Democratic lead in the beginning of this period dwindled into a minority before election day. In this period, when the issue of nuclear energy dominated the election campaign, the Centre Party at the same time clearly increased its support, while the other parties remained relatively stable. (15) Another opinion poll indicates that the issue of nuclear energy increased in importance among those who made up their minds towards the end of the election campaign. The proportion saying that nuclear energy was a 'very important' issue for their final party choice, increased from 23 per cent among those who had come to their decision already three months before the election day, to 30 per cent among those who decided in the intermediate period, and to 39 per cent among those who made up

their minds in the week preceding the election day. (16)
Attacks against the LO proposal on 'wage-earners' funds'
also played a considerable role in the campaign.   The
defeat of the Social Democrats was narrow, however, and
the party was not discredited. (17)
   The indications thus are that nuclear energy was the
single most important issue for the defeat of the Social
Democratic government in the 1976 election.   The Social
Democratic leadership viewed access to cheap energy as a
necessity for continued economic growth.   Nuclear energy
would also counterbalance the strong dependence of the
Swedish economy on oil.   Its opponents were able to
utilize the widespread fear for nuclear power for their
purposes.   In this way the Social Democratic government
finally became the victim of the economic growth strategy
in class conflict.   The relative success of the 'scandals
campaign', however, also illustrates that the labour movement has become vulnerable to charges of bureaucracy and
autocracy.   Such charges could probably not become politically highly effective if they did not have the increasingly centralized forms of decision-making in the unions
as well as in politics as a soundingboard.   As we have
seen already in the late 1960s, there was a widespread
feeling among the metal-workers that the distance between
the union leadership and the rank-and-file members had
become too great.

9   TOWARDS ECONOMIC DEMOCRACY

In advanced industrial societies the demise of capitalism,
if and when it comes, most probably will not occur in a
revolutionary form.   It is more likely to be slow and
gradual, reflecting the changes in the distribution of
power resources in society which tend to accompany the
'maturation' of capitalism (for opposite views, see e.g.
Mann, 1973, p. 73).   Institutional changes which gradually extend the principle of 'one man, one vote' into the
spheres of work and production will likely result from
attempts to find solutions to important societal problems
in accord with the values and aspirations of organized,
powerful collectivities of wage-earners.
   From the point of view of the labour movement, our analysis of the trends in the development of power resources
in Swedish society is basically optimistic.   On balance,
ongoing structural changes in society have tended to facilitate the mobilization of wage-earners for collective
action.   Unions can be expected to continue to grow,
basing their action increasingly often on class interest

rather than on more narrow occupational or sectional interests. With the strengthening of the collective power
resources of wage-earners, their levels of aspiration
will increase, extending to issues of control over work
and production.

In this context we must remember that the aspirations
of collectivities at the base of the societal hierarchy
change only slowly.   It thus took decades to mobilize
workers for demands that are now taken for granted, the
right of organization and universal suffrage. For the
generations of workers who entered the labour market in
the 1920s and 1930s, the welfare state with full employment, social security and high living standards was a
dream.   Their grandchildren have grown up in this dream,
sensing it as a reality with important deficiencies. The
growth of aspirations thus partly reflects generational
change.

Central among these deficiencies are problems connected
with the four areas we referred to in the beginning of
this chapter: economic security and production, finite
resources, inequality and meaningful work. If the power
resources of the wage earners continue to increase, their
social consciousness and levels of aspiration will probably extend from a focus on the daily economic problems
to concern with the wider aspects of equality and control
in the sphere of work and production.   'Trade union consciousness' can thus develop into a questioning of the
basic capitalistic principle that legitimate power in the
sphere of work and production must be derived from ownership of capital. (18)

In retrospect, the LO proposal on wage-earners' funds
may mark a turning point in the strategy of the Swedish
labour movement.   This proposal indicated that the collective power resources and social consciousness of the
workers had developed to a point where the dominance of
capital in the sphere of production was no longer accepted.   The issues of power and control in the economy had
received top priority on the agenda of the union movement.
This proposal, if realized, would be the crucial step in
the direction of economic democracy.

The great strength of the LO and TCO proposals for
wage-earners' funds is the idea that private firms, in
proportion to their profits, emit shares to collectively
controlled funds.   This principle allows for a gradual
transferring of economic power from private capital to
democratically governed collectivities in ways which will
minimize disturbances in the economy.   Legislation for
this purpose implies that work as well as capital can give
legitimate power in the economic sphere.   Such a prin-

ciple of justice will probably find widespread support
among wage-earners. The emission of shares to collective
funds in proportion to profits therefore can be a tool
which can break the resistance of the representatives of
capital to economic democracy.

The proposals on wage-earners' funds, however, have
dealt with the organization and operation of the funds in
incomplete and partly unsatisfactory ways. Let us
briefly point at some interrelated problems concerning the
government of the funds, the participation by the employees in the decision-making in the firm, and the role
of the union. The basic issue is how the enormous economic power, now in a few private hands, should be re-dis-
tributed and democratically controlled.

According to the LO and TCO proposals, only part of the
citizens, the wage-earners, are entitled to participate in
the governing of the collective funds. The proposals
further leave control over the governing of the funds to
the internal processes within the unions. It can, however, be argued that the 'franchise' in the governing of
the funds should be extended to all citizens. The specific interests of the employees, derived from their work in
the production organizations, can be satisfied through
rules and legislation assuring their influence within the
firm. Such a change of the 'wage-earners' funds' into
'citizens' funds' would also make it possible to use the
established party system for democratic control over the
funds.

A system of competing parties is suited for the articulation and aggregation of interests in decision-making on
economic issues involving multiple, heterogeneous interest
groups. Union are less adequate for such purposes since
they are basically organizations for conflict with relatively homogeneous memberships and therefore have developed centralized decision-making structures. The basic
features of the LO and TCO proposals, however, can be
maintained if the funds are converted into 'citizens'
funds'. The political parties can then nominate candidates to the boards of the funds and elections can e.g.
take the form of an additional ballot in the general election. The board of a collective fund should be kept
separate from political bodies as well as from the state
apparatus. Its task would be to administer the funds and
to appoint part of the members to the firms' board. A
democratic decision-making system and a pluralistic power
structure thereby could be assured. In the political
struggles which will precede the introduction of the
funds, such a strategy would draw the line of cleavage on
this issue between, on the one hand, the minority which

supports the present capital owners and, on the other
hand, the vast majority of the employees.

As the collective funds increase in size, a system
like the one sketched above would introduce democratic
principles into decision-making in the economic sphere
and increase pluralism in the distribution of power in
society.   At the same time it would retain the unions in
their traditional role representing the collective interests of the wage-earners.   On the national level, the
unions would have an important role in shaping wage policy
according to the principles of solidarity.   At the level
of the firm independent and strong union organizations are
necessary to counterbalance the expert power of management.

The proposals on wage-earners' funds illustrate how
structural change in advanced industrial societies can
result from attempts to find solutions to problems which
have become increasingly acute for powerful collectivities
of wage-earners: in this case the growing inequality in
the distribution of capital, resulting from public support to private industry in order to maintain full employment and economic growth, as well as from the solidaristic
wage policy reflecting efforts to class-based action among
the wage-earners.   That the LO and the TCO arrived at
largely similar conclusions on the nature of the problems
and on the principles for their solution indicates that
the working class need not find itself alone in supporting
solutions implying a gradual move to economic democracy.
The majority of the white-collar groups may come to see
the problems in much the same way as the workers and to
support similar solutions.

In the latter part of the 1970s, the Swedish labour
movement finds itself in a paradoxical situation.   The
organizational strength of the LO unions and their capacity to act on the basis of class is higher than ever
before.   With considerable success, the LO has attempted
to establish alliances with the rapidly growing unions of
the salaried employees, which also act primarily in terms
of collective interests of their members as wage-earners.
To solve problems emanating partly from compromise policies, to which the power of capital has constrained the
Social Democratic government, the unions have invented a
tool, the collective wage-earners' funds, which is a key
to economic democracy.   At the same time, the Social
Democratic Party has lost its long-term hold over the
government, largely as a result of the opposition to the
negative aspects of its compromise policies.

The Social Democratic Party is now at a crossroads.
It can attempt to win back government power with a pro-

gramme of welfare policies based on compromises with capital.   It could do this on the basis of greater competence in administering such policies, but would then again
be drawn into the vicious circle of gradually discrediting
compromise policies.

The other alternative is to adhere to its distinctive-
ness.   As stated in its first party programme, 'the
Social Democratic Party differs from other political parties by wanting to totally restructure the economic organization of bourgeois society.'   The 1975 party programme
reaffirms that the Social Democratic Party wants to re-
mould society so 'that the right of determination over
production and its distribution is placed in the hands of
the whole people, that the citizens are freed from dependence on any kind of power groups outside their control
and that a social order based on classes gives place to a
community of people co-operating on the basis of freedom
and equality.'

This latter alternative would imply that the party
accepts the challenge of economic democracy.   It must
therefore become the political wing of a popular movement
for economic democracy, stimulating and channelling the
aspirations of wage-earners towards self-determination in
work and production.   The analysis in this book indicates
that such a political strategy can strengthen loyalties
among the workers to the labour movement and also has a
good possibility of gaining the support of the salaried
employees.   The links between the LO and the Social Democratic Party induce the labour movement to choose a course
leading toward economic democracy.

In conclusion, then, our analysis shows that the working class in the advanced industrial societies continues
to pose a challenge to the capitalist economic system.
The Swedish case indicates that the development of capitalism engenders societal problems which cannot be solved
within the framework of capitalism.   It can also generate
the conditions for the solution of these problems on the
terms of the sellers of labour power, that is, strong,
class-based organizations which span the labour market and
the political arena.

The Manifesto urged the working men to unite.   The
materialization of unity is organization.   The Swedish
experience attests to the crucial role of organization
among the wage-earners in changing the power structure of
society.   In the advanced industrial societies the rule
of capital can only be challenged through all-encompas-
sing, class-based organizations.   Where the competition
among the wage-earners ceases, the foundation of capitalism has eroded.

Appendix 1

A EMPIRICAL DATA

The metal-worker survey

A main source of data for this study is a survey among
Swedish metal-workers which the author carried out in the
period October 1966 to March 1967. This survey was
undertaken as part of an investigation commissioned by the
Swedish Metal Workers' Union to probe into the background
of unofficial strikes in the industry. The employers'
organizations in the metal-working industry asked their
member firms to facilitate the carrying out of the study.
   The questionnaire to be used in the study was gradually worked out and tested in interviews, which the
author and a research assistant carried out in six firms
of different types in the metal-working industry. About
30 workers as well as representatives for the union and
management were interviewed in each firm. The final
questionnaire was pre-tested with a sample of 60 workers.
   The survey involved a two-stage sampling procedure.
In the first stage a purposive sample of firms was selected. On the basis of information to the union of unofficial strikes in different firms provided through reports from the employers in the period since 1949, the
fifteen most 'strike-prone' firms in the metal-working
industry, especially those with recent strike experiences,
were selected. The majority of these were large firms.
For each one of these firms a 'twin firm' was selected,
as similar as possible in size, type of production technology and proportion of skilled workers, but characterized by a low level of reported unofficial strikes.
Additional firms were included to ensure variation in
size, production technology and community type. Since
practically no strikes were reported from firms with less

than about fifty workers, however, the firms with less
than this number of workers were excluded.

Of the selected firms all but one small firm with about
fifty workers agreed to participate in the study.   The
sample therefore came to include forty-eight firms ranging
in size from about 40 to 4300 workers.   These firms employed altogether 53,000 workers or about one-sixth of the
membership of the union at that time.   This population,
however, differs from the total metal-working industry in
some significant respects.   Firms with less than fifty
workers, which constitute 80 per cent of the firms in the
metal-working industry and employ 17 per cent of all
metal-workers, are thus excluded.   Since unofficial
strikes were most common in the large firms, these firms
are markedly over-represented in our population.   Limiting comparisons to firms with fifty or more workers we
find that, while somewhat less than 50 per cent of all
metal-workers work in firms with over 1000 workers, not
less than 87 per cent of the workers in our population are
employed in such large firms.   The sample includes 14
small firms (40-170 workers), 12 medium-sized firms (250-
635 workers) and 22 large firms (870-4280 workers).   (For
a distribution of workers according to size of firm, type
of technology and type of community see Appendix 2.)
Steelworks, shipyards, auto assemblies, electro-technical
firms and metal manufacturing firms as well as different
type of engineering firms are represented in the sample.
These firms are located in different types of communities:
small service and commercial towns, heavily industrialized
communities and the three largest cities in the country.
As it later turned out, however, the reports on the frequency of unofficial strikes in the firms were incomplete.
A relatively large proportion of strikes had not been reported by the employers to the union.   The differences
between the 'strike-prone' firms and those without reported strikes in this respect were not very large.

The population was defined to include all workers employed under the collective agreement in the selected
firms at the time of the study.   Workers absent from work
for more than six months (e.g. owing to military service
or illness) as well as immigrants not able to read Swedish
or Finnish were excluded.   In the second stage, a strati-
fied random sample of workers was selected within each
firm.   The firms provided lists of employed workers and
these lists were used as sampling frames.

Based on level of union activity, workers were divided
into three strata.   The first stratum consisted of the
members of the boards of the works clubs (5-9 persons),
who were all included.   On the basis of attendance lists

on union meetings, kept especially for the purpose of this
study during roughly a six-month period preceding the data
collection, a second stratum of active union members was
defined and densely sampled. The third stratum consisted
of the other workers within the firm. Within each plant
a maximum of about 100 workers were sampled. Where possible up to 45 workers in the second stratum and about 50
workers in third stratum were selected. The respondents
were asked to complete a questionnaire on the premises of
the firm and during working time paid by the union.

The respondents selected were usually informed by the
works club representatives that they had been randomly
selected as participants and were given a leaflet providing essential information on the general nature and practical details of the study. Depending on the circumstances, the questionnaires were filled in by groups of
10-30 workers at a time. A brief standardized introduction was given by a member of the project staff (usually
a sociology student) in which the voluntary nature and
importance of participation was underlined. The questionnaires were anonymous and were put by the respondents
into envelopes which were sealed and handed to the representative of the project staff, who ticked off the respondent on the list of participants. The great majority of
the participants filled in the questionnaire in about
fifty to seventy minutes. Of the respondents, 84.5 per
cent filled in the questionnaire during working time. A
mailed questionnaire was sent to workers absent from the
firm at the time of the study. The number of usable
questionnaires received was 3999, a response rate of not
less than 97.2 per cent.

In each firm generally two management representatives
and two leading representatives of the works club were
also interviewed as informants on union-management relations in the firm.

Since the probability for being included in the sample
varies greatly between the three strata as well as between
large and small firms, the number of respondents in the
sample on which percentages are computed often differs
considerably from the weighted number of respondents in
respective categories. Because of the size of the
sample, the number of respondents in each category usually
is large. I have therefore not given the N's in the
tables based on the metal-workers survey. Where the
basis for percentages is less than 30 respondents, this
is indicated in notes.

B   PATH ANALYSIS

Where it appears reasonable to make assumptions about the causal ordering of the variables, the technique of path analysis provides an instructive and convenient way of presenting a set of quantitative data relevant to inferences about potential causal relationships between variables and of analysing to what extent a relatively complex set of proposed interpretations is consistent with the observed data.   The technique of path analysis assumes that the direction of causality between different factors has been established, and that there is no two-way or reciprocal causality between the variables.   The relationships between variables are assumed to be linear and additive.   The effects of the variables not considered in the causal model are assumed to be uncorrelated.   Variables are also assumed to be measured at least through interval scales, although the consequences of violations against this requirement often appear to be relatively small (Labovitz, 1967, 1970;   Mayer, 1972).

In the path diagram representing the causal system assumed to operate in the population, the exogenous or independent variables are placed to the left.   Two-headed curvilinear arrows connecting the independent variables indicate that the relationships between these factors are taken as given and remain unanalysed.   The correlations between them are indicated on the two-headed arrows.

From the independent variables, one-headed arrows denoting one-way causality are drawn to the endogenous or dependent variables.   Such arrows indicate that there is a *direct* causal effect between the variables, the direction of which is given by the arrow.   The relative size of the direct effects is indicated by path coefficients, which are standardized regression coefficients.   A path coefficient denotes the fraction of the standard deviation in the dependent variable for which the independent variable is directly responsible in the sense of the fraction that would be found if the independent variable would vary to the same extent as in the observed data, while all other variables, including those outside the causal system, were constant.

The path diagram also indicates different chains of *indirect effects* on the dependent variables.   The indirect effects of a particular independent variable can be located on the diagram by starting from the dependent variable of interest and tracing back its immediate and remote causes.   In isolating such a chain of indirect effects (or a compounded path), we are allowed to move once, but only once, against the direction of causality

as indicated by an arrow.   The two-headed arrows between
the exogenous variables can be traced in either direction,
but only one pair of exogenous variables can be included
in each compounded path.

The size of the total indirect effect of a variable on
the dependent variable is given by the difference between
the coefficient of correlation between the variables and
the direct path coefficient between them.   The indirect
effect via a particular chain or compounded path is found
by multiplying the path coefficients and/or the correlation coefficient along this particular chain.   A minimum
test of the adequacy of the proposed causal model is provided if the observed correlations between variables are
satisfactorily reproduced by the effects - both direct and
indirect - of the independent upon the dependent variables
in the hypothetical causal model.   Comprehensive accounts
of the path analytic technique can be found in the methodological literature.

C MULTIPLE-CLASSIFICATION ANALYSIS

Multiple-classification analysis (Andrews et al., 1973;
Blau and Duncan, 1967, pp. 128-40) provides a convenient
way of analysing and summarizing the relationship of a set
of 'independent' variables on a 'dependent' variable, when
the independent variables are known to be correlated and
are measured on a nominal level.   The dependent variable
is assumed to be dichotomous or measured on an interval
scale.   It is based on a model, where each category of
each independent variable is assigned a coefficient, indicating how membership in this particular category
'affects' the dependent variable.   The score or position
of an individual on the dependent variable is assumed to
be the sum of the coefficients assigned to the categories
on the independent variables characterizing him, plus the
average for all individuals and an error term.   The
extent of a relationship between an independent variable
and the dependent variable, or the 'effect' of an independent variable, is indicated by the differences between
means for individuals in different categories of the independent variables.   The empirical or 'unadjusted' mean on
the dependent variable for all individuals in a specific
category of the independent variable is complemented with
an *'adjusted' mean*, which indicates what the mean on the
dependent variable would have been if the individuals in
this category of the independent variable were exactly
like the total population with respect to its distribution
on all other independent variables.

The effect of an independent variable can be summarized in terms of the proportion of the total variance in the dependent variable, which is accounted for by differences between the weighted means of the categories of the independent variable. The eta coefficient gives the square root of the proportion of variance explained by the unadjusted means; the beta coefficient gives the square root of the corresponding proportion of variance explained by the adjusted means. The square of the multiple-correlation coefficient, R^2, gives the proportion of the variance in the dependent variable which is accounted for by all the independent variables. Since this technique assumes that independent variables are measured only at the nominal level, it is not sensitive to the order of the categories of the independent variables. The nature of the relationship between the dependent variable and an independent variable, which is measured on an ordinal or higher level, must therefore be determined by looking at the trend of the means in the categories of the independent variable.

To facilitate the reading and understanding of the results of multiple-classification analyses presented here, the dependent variable is treated as a dichotomy. Differences between categories can thus be read as percentage differences.

Appendix 2
Scales, indices and questions

Wherever possible the variables introduced into the analyses have been measured with more than one question. Two or more questions have thus been combined into indices or scales on the basis of the intercorrelation (Yule's Q) between questions. Response alternatives to the questions have generally been dichotomized. Where it has been logically reasonable and practically feasible the 'don't know' and 'no response' categories have been placed into alternately the 'positive' and the 'negative' dichotomy to avoid extreme index values for individuals not taking a stand on several questions in the same index.

The homogeneity of an index has been evaluated on the basis of the pattern of intercorrelations between the questions included in an index, the mean intercorrelation for each question and the total mean correlation between all questions in the index. Some of the indices can be regarded as approximately cumulative scales. To evaluate the degree of reproducibility of the response patterns on the basis of the total 'score' on the index for the respondents, an index of reproducibility (Rep), giving the proportion of correctly reproduced responses of all respondents on the basis of their scale score, has been computed. Also, the index of reproducibility assuming independence between responses to the questions within the scale (Rep_I) has been computed and is related to the observed reproducibility through the 'index of consistency', I, (cf. Green, 1956), where $I = (Rep - Rep_I)/(1 - Rep_I)$.

In the following the questions/items included in each index are presented and the estimated response distribution in our population of metal-workers is given for each question. For each question the response alternatives designated as 'positive' and the total percentage of 'positive' respondents are given. For each index score, the estimated percentage in the population with this score

as well as the actual (unweighted) number of respondents
in the sample having this score are given.   For scales
with three or more questions the cut-off points for scale
scores designated in the text as 'low', 'medium' or 'high'
are given.

Also, single questions used in the analyses are listed
here.

1   INTRINSIC JOB SATISFACTION

				%
(a)	Do you think that your work is on the whole varied or monotonous?	1	Very monotonous	9.0
		2	Rather monotonous	29.3
		3	Rather varied	46.9
		4	Very varied	13.3
		5	Don't know	1.5

				%
(b)	People perform some jobs only for the money. Other jobs give not only money but also a feeling of personal satisfaction. What kind of job is the one you have now?	1	I do it for the money only	51.3
		2	It gives a feeling of personal satisfaction as well	38.9
		3	Don't know	9.8

Item	Positive response alternatives	% positive
a	3,4	60.2
b	2,3	48.7

Correlation between items = 0.577

Index score and cut-off points	% in population	No. of respondents in sample
Low 0	28.0	1,147
Medium 1	35.2	1,357
High 2	36.8	1,495
	100	3,999

2   SKILL REQUIREMENTS OF JOB

				%
(a)	About how long do you think it takes a beginner without training and experience	1	Less than two weeks	10.3
		2	Two-three weeks	13.6
		3	One-three months	17.5

	in industry to learn about your job?	4	Four-twelve months	13.5
		5	One-three years	19.2
		6	Four-six years	9.5
		7	More than six years	5.1
		8	Don't know	11.3

(b)	Could just about anybody learn to do your job well?	1	No, certainly not	15.5
		2	No, perhaps not	14.5
		3	Yes, perhaps	30.0
		4	Yes, certainly	33.5
		5	Don't know	6.5

Item	Positive response alternatives	% positive
b	1, 2, 5	36.5
a	5, 6, 7	33.8

Correlation between items = 0.395

Index score and cut-off point	% in population	No. of respondents in sample
Low 0	46.4	1,709
Medium 1	36.8	1,473
High 2	16.7	817
	100	3,999

3   FREEDOM OF MOVEMENT AT WORK

				%
(a)	Do you work on an assembly line	1	No	83.4
		2	Yes	14.4
		3	No answer	2.2

(b)	Are you tied to a definite place (station) during working time or can you move around freely within the department/shop	1	Can move around freely	19.1
		2	Can move around rather freely	35.8
		3	Am rather tied	25.7
		4	Am very tied	19.7
		5	Don't know	1.5

Item	Positive response alternatives	% positive
a	1, 3	85.6
b	1, 2	54.2

Correlation between items = 0.662

Index score and cut-off point	% in population	No. of respondents in sample
Low 0	11.2	329
Medium 1	37.0	1,474
High 2	51.8	2,196
	100	3,999

4   REQUIRED CO-OPERATION AT WORK

			%
(a)	Do you have to co-operate with other workers in doing your job?	1 Very seldom	27.1
		2 Rather seldom	15.2
		3 Rather often	24.6
		4 Very often	32.0
		5 Don't know	1.2
(b)	Do you and your work-mates have to talk with and consult each other in order to accomplish the job?	1 Very seldom	33.7
		2 Rather seldom	19.6
		3 Rather often	27.3
		4 Very often	17.7
		5 Don't know	1.7

Item	Positive response alternatives	% positive
a	3, 4, 5	57.8
b	3, 4	45.0

Correlation between items = 0.808

Index score and cut-off point	% in population	No. of respondents in sample
Low 0	40.7	1,629
Medium 1	23.8	953
High 2	35.4	1,417
	100	3,999

5   INTERNAL STRATIFICATION AMONG WORKERS IN DEPARTMENT/ SHOP

				%
(a)	Are differences in earnings between different workers in your department/shop great or small?	1	Very great	9.1
		2	Rather great	30.6
		3	Rather small	39.1
		4	Very small	13.1
		5	Don't know	8.1
(b)	Are differences in responsibility between different workers in your department/shop great or small?	1	Very small	20.8
		2	Rather small	40.0
		3	Rather great	23.8
		4	Very great	7.0
		5	Don't know	8.4
(c)	Are there any other workers in your department/shop who in your opinion think that they have better or higher-class jobs than the others?	1	Yes, certainly	21.9
		2	Yes, perhaps	26.6
		3	No, perhaps not	13.8
		4	No, certainly not	25.8
		5	Don't know	11.9

Correlations between items a		Item	Positive response alternatives	% positive
0.366 b		c	1, 2, 5	60.4
0.559	0.373 c	a	1, 2, 5	47.8
		b	3, 4	30.8

Mean correlation = 0.366
Rep = 0.91
Rep_I = 0.88
I = 0.24

Index score and cut-off point		% in population	No. of respondents in sample
Low	0	21.0	845
Medium	1	33.3	1,319
	2	31.2	1,271
High	3	14.4	564
		100	3,999

6   FREQUENCY OF TALKING WITH WORKMATES

			%
(a)	Do you have the opportunity to talk with other workers while you are doing your own job?	1 Very often	25.0
		2 Rather often	39.6
		3 Rather seldom	19.8
		4 Very seldom	14.9
		5 Don't know	0.7
(b)	Does it happen that you talk with other workers when you take a break, e.g. to smoke, go to the toilet or take a rest?	1 Very often	14.7
		2 Rather often	40.8
		3 Rather seldom	26.4
		4 Very seldom	16.6
		5 Don't know	1.5
(c)	Does it happen that you talk with other workers at lunch breaks?	1 Very seldom	5.9
		2 Rather seldom	8.0
		3 Rather often	32.0
		4 Very often	52.9
		5 Don't know	1.2

Correlations between items a		Item	Positive response alternatives	% positive
0.555	b	c	3, 4	84.9
0.268	0.513 c	a	1, 2	64.6
		b	1, 2	55.5

Mean correlation = 0.446
Rep = 0.93
Rep_I = 0.90
I = 0.30

Index score and cut-off point		% in population	No. of respondents in sample
Low	0	5.4	220
	1	23.6	879
Medium	2	31.4	1,292
High	3	39.5	1,608
		100	3,999

7   INTEGRATION INTO WORKGROUP

			%
(a)	Do you feel that you yourself belong to a	1 No, certainly not	26.3
		2 No, perhaps not	18.6

clique or gang in your department/shop?

3 Yes, perhaps   28.4
4 Yes, surely   19.5
5 Don't know   7.3

(b) Imagine that there is to be a large-scale reorganization here at this firm so that many workers must move to new places of work. Which ones would you most prefer as closest workmates?

1 Others than those
   I now work with   1.1
2 Doesn't matter   50.1
3 Those whom I now
   work with   41.6
4 Don't know   7.1

Item	Positive response alternatives	% positive
a	3, 4, 5	55.2
b	3	41.6

Correlation between items = 0.355

Index score and cut-off point	% in population	No. of respondents in sample
Low 0	30.6	1,283
Medium 1	42.1	1,673
High 2	27.3	1,043
	100	3,999

8 WORKGROUP COHESIVENESS

%

(a) Is it the usual thing that workers in your department/shop stick together so much that you could speak of cliques or gangs?

1 Not at all usual 17.4
2 Not especially
   usual   36.3
3 Yes, perhaps   25.7
4 Yes, certainly   11.6
5 Don't know   9.0

(b) Do you feel there is much or little feeling of unity among the workers in your department/shop?

1 Very little   5.2
2 Rather little   11.5
3 Neither little
   nor much   25.0
4 Rather much   40.3
5 Very much   16.1
6 Don't know   1.9

Item	Positive response alternatives	% positive
b	4, 5, 6	58.3
a	3, 4	37.3

Correlation between items = 0.539

Index score and cut-off point	% in population	No. of respondents in sample
Low 0	32.7	1,368
Medium 1	38.6	1,541
High 2	28.7	1,090
	100	3,999

9   STRENGTH OF THE WORKERS' COLLECTIVITY

%

(a) Suppose that a worker in your department/shop is trying to get in good with his superiors. Would you bet that the other workers can get together and see that he changes?

		%
1	Yes, certainly	15.2
2	Yes, perhaps	29.2
3	No, perhaps not	18.3
4	No, certainly not	16.2
5	Don't know	21.1

(b) Assume that a new man comes to your department/shop and works entirely too hard. Would you bet that the other workers can agree to seeing that he slows down?

1	No, certainly not	15.0
2	No, perhaps not	17.0
3	Yes, perhaps	36.9
4	Yes, certainly	18.2
5	Don't know	12.9

(c) Assume that management treats a worker in your department/shop in a manner which most think is unfair. Would you bet that the other workers can agree to seeing that he receives fair treatment?

1	Yes, certainly	31.4
2	Yes, perhaps	38.6
3	No, certainly not	9.2
4	No, perhaps not	9.3
5	Don't know	11.5

(d) Assume that there is a foreman or time-study man in your department/

1	No, certainly not	5.0
2	No, perhaps not	7.4

shop who is trying to do the workers a bad turn and lower their earnings. Would you guess that the workers can get together on doing something to put an end to it?

3	Yes, perhaps	40.0
4	Yes, certainly	39.8
5	Don't know	7.9

Correlations between items			Item	Positive response alternatives	% positive
a					
0.524	b		d	3, 4	79.8
0.613	0.465	c	c	1, 2	70.0
0.446	0.494	0.769	d	b	3, 4	55.1
				a	1, 2	44.4

Mean correlation = 0.552
Rep = 0.92
Rep_I = 0.88
I = 0.34

Index score and cut-off point		% in population	No. of respondents in sample
Low	0	8.3	301
	1	13.9	478
Medium	2	24.1	905
	3	27.7	1,137
High	4	26.0	1,178
		100	3,999

10   SELECTIVE POWER OF SUPERVISORS

				%
(a)	Do your immediate supervisors have any possibility of granting privileges to a worker whom they particularly like?	1	Very great possibility	17.3
		2	Rather great possibility	31.1
		3	Rather small possibility	21.1
		4	Very small possibility	14.2
		5	Don't know	16.3
(b)	Do your immediate supervisors have any means of doing a worker they dislike a bad turn?	1	Very small means	9.6
		2	Rather small means	19.0
		3	Rather great means	36.1

                                    4 Very great means   15.7
                                    5 Don't know   19.7

Item	Positive response alternatives	% positive
b	3, 4, 5	71.5
a	1, 2	47.4

Correlation between items = 0.439

Index score and cut-off point	% in population	No. of respondents in sample
Low 0	19.3	804
Medium 1	41.4	1,600
High 2	39.2	1,595
	100	3,999

11   MANAGEMENT CONSIDERATION WITHIN DEPARTMENT

                                                              %

(a) Do you think that it is   1 Very easy   6.5
     easy or difficult to get   2 Rather easy   27.5
     management to straighten   3 Rather difficult 41.0
     out a cause of dissatis-   4 Very difficult   14.0
     faction in your   5 Don't know   11.0
     department/shop?

(b) Do you think that   1 No, certainly not 13.4
     management tries to take   2 No, perhaps not   20.2
     into consideration what   3 Yes, perhaps   42.8
     the workers think about   4 Yes, certainly   13.4
     various conditions in   5 Don't know   10.2
     your department/shop?

(c) Do you think that the   1 Very well   8.1
     planning and preparation   2 Rather well   38.3
     of work functions well   3 Rather poorly   26.2
     or poorly in your   4 Very poorly   17.3
     department/shop?   5 Don't know   10.1

Correlations between items		Item	Positive response alternatives	% positive
a				
0.577 b		b	3, 4, 5	66.4
0.565 0.562 c		c	1, 2, 5	56.5
		a	1, 2	34.0

Mean correlation = 0.567
Rep = 0.93
Rep_I = 0.85
I = 0.55

Index score and cut-off point		% in population	No. of respondents in sample
Low	0	19.2	980
Medium	1	27.1	1,179
	2	31.3	1,082
High	3	22.4	758
		100	3,999

12   EVALUATION OF FIRM AS AN EMPLOYER

			%
(a)	Do you ever have the feeling that this company puts unpleasant pressure on the workers in order to get as much out of them as possible?	1 Very seldom	17.4
		2 Rather seldom	23.9
		3 Rather often	36.0
		4 Very often	13.8
		5 Don't know	8.8
(b)	Do you ever have the feeling that this company treats the workers like machines?	1 Very often	15.7
		2 Rather often	29.1
		3 Rather seldom	20.9
		4 Very seldom	23.9
		5 Don't know	10.4
(c)	Do you think that on the whole the workers here at this company regard it as a good place to work or a poor place to work?	1 Very good place to work	7.5
		2 Rather good place to work	63.1
		3 Rather poor place to work	16.6
		4 Very poor place to work	2.8
		5 Don't know	10.0

Correlations between items a		Item	Positive response alternative	% positive
0.769	b	c	1, 2, 5	80.6
0.646	0.598 c	a	1, 2, 5	50.1
		b	3, 4	44.8

Mean correlation = 0.670
Rep = 0.96
Rep_I = 0.89
I = 0.61

Index score and cut-off point		% in population	No. of respondents in sample
Low	0	13.2	595
	1	30.0	1,186
Medium	2	24.8	991
High	3	32.0	1,227
		100	3,999

13 OFF-THE-JOB CONTACTS WITH WORKERS FROM FIRM

				%
(a)	Does it happen that you visit other workers who work here at this company at their homes or that they visit you?	1	Almost never	31.3
		2	A few times a year	33.0
		3	A few times a month	21.0
		4	A couple of times a week or more	11.5
		5	No answer	3.2
(b)	With whom do you mostly associate on your time off: with people who work here at this company or with other acquaintances?	1	Mostly with people from the company	9.4
		2	Mostly with other acquaintances	56.3
		3	Equally much with both	31.0
		4	No answer	3.2

Item	Positive response alternatives	% positive
b	1, 3	40.4
a	3, 4	32.5

Correlation between items = 0.760

Index score and cut-off point		% in population	No. of respondents in sample
Low	0	50.3	2,122
Medium	1	26.5	1,091
High	2	23.2	786
		100	3,999

14 LABOUR MOVEMENT SUPPORT

				%
(a)	If you were to buy an evening paper and had to choose between 'Expressen' and 'Aftonbladet' which would you bet you would choose?	1	'Expressen'	22.4
		2	'Aftonbladet'	45.4
		3	Wouldn't matter	32.3
		4	No answer	0
(b)	If you had to choose between shopping at a co-operative store or another store next to it, which would you bet that you would choose?	1	The other store	15.1
		2	The co-operative	38.8
		3	Wouldn't matter	46.0
		4	No answer	0.1

Item	Positive response alternatives	% positive
a	2	45.3
b	2	38.8

Correlation between items = 0.600

Index score and cut-off point	% in population	No. of respondents in sample
Low 0	41.4	1,298
Medium 1	33.1	1,299
High 2	25.5	1,402
	100	3,999

15 PERCEIVED MEMBERSHIP INFLUENCE IN THE WORKS CLUB

				%
(a)	In your opinion does the works club committee take into enough consideration what the members think?	1	Yes, certainly	21.7
		2	Yes, perhaps	36.5
		3	No, perhaps not	18.9
		4	No, certainly not	7.8
		5	Don't know	15.1
(b)	In some clubs a single person makes most of the decisions. In other clubs there are many who participate in the decision-making. How	1	One decides most everything	3.0
		2	A few decide	28.0
		3	Quite a few participate in the decisions	24.7

do you think it is in this works club?	4 Many participate in the decisions	9.6
	5 Don't know	34.8

Item	Positive response alternatives	% positive
a	1, 2, 5	73.3
b	3, 4	34.3

Correlation between items = 0.490

Index score and cut-off point	% in population	No. of respondents in sample
Low 0	21.8	756
Medium 1	48.9	1,739
High 2	29.3	1,504
	100	3,999

16   INTERNAL CONFLICTS ON WORKS CLUB POLICY

			%
(a)	Would you say that the workers in your department/shop are in agreement or disagreement about what the works club should do?	1 Very much in disagreement	4.4
		2 Rather much in disagreement	23.3
		3 Rather much in agreement	44.6
		4 Very much in agreement	5.2
		5 Don't know	22.4
(b)	Does it ever happen that workers in your department/shop have quarrelled over what the works club should do?	1 Very often	2.3
		2 Rather often	13.3
		3 Rather seldom	31.4
		4 Very seldom	28.3
		5 Don't know	24.7

Item	Positive response alternatives	% positive
b	1, 2, 3	47.0
a	1, 2	27.7

Correlation between items = 0.510

Index score and cut-off point	% in population	No. of respondents in sample
Low 0	43.8	1,582
Medium 1	37.7	1,590
High 2	18.5	827
	100	3,999

17   PERCEIVED BARGAINING POWER OF WORKS CLUB

%

(a) Do you think that the works club board here can really put up a stiff front if piece-rate negotiations with the company get tough?

		%
1	Yes, certainly	23.4
2	Yes, perhaps	36.8
3	No, perhaps not	13.1
4	No, certainly not	14.0
5	Don't know	12.6

(b) Do you think that the works club board does anything to raise the earnings of the workers?

1	Nothing	5.4
2	Rather little	41.2
3	Rather much	27.5
4	Much	7.6
5	Don't know	18.3

(c) Do you think that the works club board has succeeded in getting through any increases in earnings during the past year?

1	Almost none	12.9
2	Rather small	44.6
3	Rather large	17.3
4	Very large	1.2
5	Don't know	24.1

(d) Assume that in piece-rate negotiations the works club asks quite a bit more than the company wants to agree to.   How much would you guess that the club gets?

1	Almost everything	0.6
2	Rather much	10.0
3	Rather little	52.2
4	Almost nothing	13.2
5	Don't know	24.0

(e) Have you ever had a feeling that the works club board lets in too easily to the views of the company?

1	Very often	12.5
2	Rather often	27.5
3	Rather seldom	22.5
4	Very seldom	7.4
5	Don't know	30.1

(f) Do you think that the works club negotiators are strong or weak if

1	Very strong	2.4
2	Rather strong	28.8
3	Rather weak	30.3

		4 Very weak	7.8
you compare with the		5 Don't know	30.6
company negotiators?			

Correlations
between items

a
0.783 b
0.708 0.556 c
0.894 0.744 0.649 d
0.677 0.798 0.985 0.771 e
0.777 0.613 0.725 0.673 0.680 f

Item	Positive response alternative	% positive
a	1, 2, 5	72.8
f	1, 2, 5	61.8
c	3, 4, 5	42.6
b	3, 4	35.1
e	3, 4	29.9
d	1, 2	10.6

Mean correlation = 0.736
Rep = 0.93
Rep_I = 0.88
I = 0.42

Index score and cut-off point		% in population	No. of respondents in sample
Low	0	16.2	635
	1	14.6	555
Medium	2	18.3	586
	3	22.0	746
High	4	14.1	565
	5	9.0	522
	6	5.7	390
		100	3,999

18 PERCEIVED MEMBERSHIP INFLUENCE IN UNION

				%
(a)	Do you think that the average members have enough influence in the Metal Workers' Union?	1	Yes, certainly	4.9
		2	Yes, perhaps	17.7
		3	No, perhaps not	30.0
		4	No, certainly not	26.2
		5	Don't know	21.2

(b) Do you think that the
national union leaders
know enough about how it
really is to be a worker
these days?

1   No, certainly not   25.0
2   No, perhaps not   27.4
3   Yes, perhaps   22.7
4   Yes, certainly   11.9
5   Don't know   12.9

(c) Do you think that the
national union leaders
have good or poor contact
with the workers?

1   Very good contact   3.2
2   Rather good
    contact   30.2
3   Rather poor
    contact   33.6
4   Very poor contact   12.4
5   Don't know   20.7

Correlations between items		Item	Positive response alternatives	% positive
a				
0.946	b	c	1, 2, 5	54.1
0.611	0.513 c	b	3, 4	34.6
		a	1, 2	22.6

Mean correlation = 0.690
Rep = 0.95
Rep_I = 0.90
I = 0.46

Index score and cut-off point		% in population	No. of respondents in sample
Low	0	34.5	1,477
Medium	1	31.3	1,172
High	2	22.7	820
	3	11.5	530
		100	3,999

19   CRITICISM OF UNION POLICY

(a) Do you ever have the
feeling that the leaders
of the national union
let in too easily to the
views of the employers?

%

1   Very often   13.4
2   Rather often 31.2
3   Rather seldom 19.0
4   Very seldom   6.4
5   Don't know   30.1

(b) Do you think that in
collective bargaining
the national union
leaders pay

1   Yes, certainly   23.1
2   Yes, perhaps   28.8
3   No, perhaps not   11.5
4   No, certainly not 4.7

<table>
<tr><td>too much attention to
what is thought in
government circles?</td><td>5 Don't know</td><td>31.9</td></tr>
</table>

Item	Positive response alternatives	% positive
a	3, 4, 5	25.4
b	3, 4	16.2

Correlation between items = 0.644

Index score and cut-off point	% in population	No. of respondents in sample
Low 0	40.1	1,707
Medium 1	48.2	1,735
High 2	11.7	557
	100	3,999

20   DENSITY OF UNION ACTIVISTS IN DEPARTMENT

				%
(a)	Is there any worker in your department/shop of whom the others can ask advice in regard to getting unsatisfactory working conditions corrected?	1 2 3 4	No, no one Yes, one Yes, two or more Don't know	12.2 39.3 37.8 10.7
(b)	Is there any worker in your department/shop of whom others can ask advice regarding matters which have been discussed at union meetings?	1 2 3 4	No, no one Yes, one Yes, two or more Don't know	11.5 38.9 35.6 14.0
(c)	Is there any worker in your department/shop of whom the other workers can ask advice regarding the labour contract?	1 2 3 4	No, no one Yes, one Yes, two or more Don't know	9.3 41.7 36.7 12.3

Correlations between items a	Item	Positive response alternatives	% positive
0.761 b	a	2, 3	77.1
0.646 0.861 c	b	3	35.6
	c	3	36.7

Mean correlation = 0.756
Rep = 0.96
Rep_I = 0.87
I = 0.71

Index score and cut-off point		% in population	No. of respondents in sample
Low	0	18.5	630
Medium	1	39.8	1,449
	2	15.2	700
High	3	26.4	1,220
		100	3,999

21   KNOWLEDGE OF NATIONAL UNION AFFAIRS

			%
(a)	What is the name of the president of the Metal Workers' Union? Write his name here if you remember it:...........	1 Wrong answer 2 Correct answer 3 Don't know	16.8 28.5 54.7
(b)	The Metal Workers' Union opened a new school during the autumn of 1965. Do you happen to remember where the school is located?	1 Runö 2 Skåvsjöholm 3 Brunnsvik 4 Gladtjärn 5 Bommersvik 6 Don't remember	5.9 17.9 5.8 2.5 3.4 64.4
(c)	About how many members do you think that the Metal Workers' Union has now?	1 130,000 2 330,000 3 530,000 4 730,000 5 930,000 6 Don't remember	2.1 18.4 8.9 15.8 8.1 46.7
(d)	Which do you think is the highest decision-making organ in the union according to the union statutes?	1 The executive board 2 The union council 3 Collective bargaining council	17.1 13.5 5.7

| | | | | 4 | The union congress | 25.4 |
| | | | | 5 | Don't remember | 38.3 |

Correlations between items			Item	Positive response alternatives	% positive
a					
0.789 b			a	2	28.5
0.714	0.611	c	d	4	25.4
0.515	0.616	0.478 d	c	2	18.4
			b	2	17.9

Mean correlation = 0.614
Rep = 0.91
Rep_I = 0.88
I = 0.25

Index score and cut-off point		% in population	No. of respondents in sample
Low	0	50.0	1,496
Medium	1	25.0	924
High	2	13.6	655
	3	7.3	500
	4	4.0	424
		100	3,999

22   INFORMAL ADVISERS ON UNION MATTERS

				%
(a)	Has it occurred during the past year that one of the workers has asked your advice about something that has to do with the labour contract?	1	No, never	43.6
		2	Yes, once	9.0
		3	Yes, two-three times	21.0
		4	Yes, four times or more	13.7
		5	Don't remember	12.7
(b)	Has it occurred during the past year that one of the workers has asked your advice in a matter discussed at a union meeting?	1	No, never	55.8
		2	Yes, once	8.7
		3	Yes, two-three times	14.1
		4	Yes, four times or more	7.2
		5	Don't remember	14.2
(c)	Has it occurred during the past year that one of the	1	No, never	45.3
		2	Yes, once	9.1

<table>
<tr><td>workers has asked you what he should do in order to bring about a change in an unsatisfactory working condition?</td><td>3</td><td>Yes, two-three times</td><td>17.7</td></tr>
<tr><td></td><td>4</td><td>Yes, four times or more</td><td>11.9</td></tr>
<tr><td></td><td>5</td><td>Don't remember</td><td>16.0</td></tr>
</table>

Correlations between items		Item	Positive response alternative	% positive
a				
0.887	b	a	2, 3, 4	43.7
0.767	0.749 c	c	2, 3, 4	38.7
		b	2, 3, 4	30.0

Mean correlation = 0.801
Rep = 0.93
Rep_I = 0.87
I = 0.51

Index score and cut-off point		% in population	No. of respondents in sample
Low	0	42.8	1,305
Medium	1	21.4	721
High	2	16.4	659
	3	19.4	1,314
		100	3,999

23   LEVEL OF POLITICAL INTEREST

			%
(a)	Are you interested or uninterested in politics?	1 Entirely uninterested	12.3
		2 Rather uninterested	30.9
		3 Rather interested	44.0
		4 Very interested	8.8
		5 Don't know	3.9
(b)	Do you usually read editorials and other articles on politics in the newspapers?	1 Almost never	22.3
		2 A few times a year	16.4
		3 A few times a month	16.0
		4 A few times a week	17.8
		5 Almost every day	24.2
		6 Don't know	3.3

(c) Did you attend any   1 No, none   79.2
     election meeting or   2 Yes, one   10.8
     political speech before   3 Yes, two or more   6.3
     the communal election   4 Don't remember   3.8
     this past fall?

Correlations between items a		Item	Positive response alternatives	% positive
0.813	b	a	3, 4	52.8
0.741	0.756 c	b	4, 5	42.0
		c	2, 3	17.1

Mean correlation = 0.770
Rep = 0.96
Rep_I = 0.90
I = 0.63

Index score and cut-off point		% in population	No. of respondents in sample
Low	0	38.3	1,172
Medium	1	23.8	881
High	2	25.7	1,096
	3	12.2	850
		100	3,999

24 INFORMAL POLITICAL ACTIVISM

(a) Does it happen that you   1 Almost never   65.3
     try to interest a fellow   2 A few times a
     worker in reading an   year   17.5
     editorial or political   3 A few times a
     article in a newspaper?   month   7.5
                                       4 A few times a
                                          week   4.5
                                       5 Don't know   5.2

(b) Does it happen that you   1 Almost never   42.1
     yourself raise a   2 A few times a
     political question for   year   29.0
     discussion with your   3 A few times a
     workmates   month   16.1
                                       4 A few times a
                                          week or more   9.1
                                       5 Don't know   3.7

(c) Did it happen that in connection with the communal election this autumn you tried to interest some workmates in listening to or watching an election programme on the radio or television?

1	Yes, a couple of times or more	20.7
2	Yes, once	6.2
3	No, never	60.6
4	Don't remember	12.6

(d) Did you try to interest any fellow workers in voting for the party that you yourself intended to vote for in the communal election this past autumn?

1	Yes	21.2
2	No	74.0
3	Don't remember	4.6

(e) Did it happen that in connection with the communal election this autumn some workers asked your advice about something that was being discussed in the election campaign?

1	Yes, two or more times	14.3
2	Yes, once	6.9
3	No, never	65.0
4	Don't remember	13.8

Correlations
between items
a
0.885 b
0.848 0.729 c
0.802 0.732 0.870 d
0.862 0.726 0.828 0.837 e

Item	Positive response alternatives	% positive
b	2, 3, 4	54.2
c	1, 2	26.9
d	1	21.2
e	1, 2	21.1
a	3, 4	12.0

Mean correlation = 0.812
Rep = 0.95
Rep_I = 0.90
I = 0.53

Index score and cut-off point		% in population	No. of respondents in sample
Low	0	38.0	1,165
Medium	1	27.5	949
	2	13.5	529
High	3	8.9	465
	4	6.3	409
	5	5.8	482
		100	3,999

25   ACCEPTANCE OF UNOFFICIAL STRIKES

		%

(a) Imagine that negotiations are going on in your department/shop about a piece rate that all the workers think is too low. The management refuses to raise the rate.   The negotiations lead nowhere. Do you think that the workers should resort to a sit-down strike or a similar strike in order to put pressure on management?

1   Yes, certainly   18.4
2   Yes, perhaps   27.0
3   No, perhaps not   15.4
4   No, certainly not   23.7
5   Don't know   15.5

(b) Imagine that a foreman or time-study man at your department/shop tries to do the workers a bad turn and lower their earnings. Management doesn't want to move him to another job. Do you think that the workers should resort to a sit-down strike or a similar strike in order to try to get rid of him?

1   No, certainly not   16.6
2   No, perhaps not   13.4
3   Yes, perhaps   30.4
4   Yes, certainly   23.2
5   Don't know   16.5

(c) Assume that the company here wants to hurt a man who is leaving by giving him a poor recommendation. It's not possible to change the recommendation

1   Yes, certainly   14.9
2   Yes, perhaps   23.3
3   No, perhaps not   16.7
4   No, certainly not   24.0
5   Don't know   21.1

through negotiation.
Do you think that the
other workers should
resort to a sit-down
strike or a similar
strike as a protest?

(d) Assume that the company
     wants to do a worker in
     your department/shop a
     bad turn and therefore
     moves him to a new job
     with poorer earnings.
     It's not possible to get
     him back through negotia-
     tions. Do you think the
     other workers should
     resort then to a sit-down
     strike or a similar
     strike to show what they
     think about it?

1 No, certainly not 15.5
2 No, perhaps not   18.1
3 Yes, perhaps   31.1
4 Yes, certainly   18.6
5 Don't know   16.8

(e) Assume that a man in your
     department/shop gets the
     sack and everybody thinks
     it is unfair.   It's not
     possible to get him back
     through negotiations.
     Do you think the other
     workers should resort to
     a sit-down strike or a
     similar strike as protest?

1 Yes, certainly   26.5
2 Yes, perhaps   30.8
3 No, perhaps not   13.0
4 No, certainly not 15.1
5 Don't know   14.6

Correlations
between items
a
0.800 b
0.663 0.665 c
0.563 0.584 0.738 d
0.580 0.567 0.753 0.860 e

Item	Positive response alternative	% positive
e	1, 2, 5	71.9
d	3, 4, 5	66.5
b	3, 4	53.6
a	1, 2	45.4
c	1, 2	38.2

Mean correlation =
0.677
Rep = 0.92
Rep_I = 0.85
I = 0.45

Index score and cut-off point		% in population	No. of respondents in sample
Low	0	15.1	725
	1	9.3	389
Medium	2	18.9	684
	3	18.4	685
High	4	18.6	730
	5	19.7	786
		100	3,999

26   INEQUITY OF WORKERS' SHARE OF FIRM PROFITS

<table>
<tr><td></td><td></td><td></td><td></td><td>%</td></tr>
<tr><td>(a)</td><td>Do you think that workers here at this firm can come up to a decent wage without having to drudge and toil in an unpleasant way?</td><td>1
2
3
4
5</td><td>No, certainly not
No, perhaps not
Yes, perhaps
Yes, certainly
Don't know</td><td>32.6
19.0
30.1
12.5
5.8</td></tr>
<tr><td>(b)</td><td>Do you think that workers here at this firm get a decent share of the money the firm takes in?</td><td>1
2
3
4
5</td><td>Yes, certainly
Yes, perhaps
No, perhaps not
No, certainly not
Don't know</td><td>4.7
17.4
24.7
33.4
19.7</td></tr>
</table>

Item	Positive response alternatives	% positive
b	3, 4	58.1
a	1, 2, 5	57.4

Correlation between items = 0.419

Index score and cut-off point		% in population	No. of respondents in sample
Low	0	23.1	812
Medium	1	38.2	1,566
High	2	38.7	1,621
		100	3,999

27   PERCEIVED CLASS DIFFERENCES IN SOCIETY

<table>
<tr><td></td><td></td><td></td><td></td><td>%</td></tr>
<tr><td>(a)</td><td>Do you think that in this country the son of a</td><td>1
2</td><td>Much less chance
Somewhat less chance</td><td>13.2

24.5</td></tr>
</table>

	worker has a greater or lesser chance to be a medical doctor or a lawyer than the son of someone with a lot of money?	3	Just as much a chance	50.3
		4	Somewhat greater chance	2.3
		5	Much greater chance	1.4
		6	Don't know	8.2

(b) Do you think that the police in this country are more apt to see through their fingers in a case of speeding if it involves a high-placed salaried employee or a big businessman than if it involves a worker?

1	No, certainly not	29.8
2	No, perhaps not	16.8
3	Yes, perhaps	26.3
4	Yes, certainly	16.2
5	Don't know	8.2

(c) Do you think there is a greater risk for a worker to be arrested for drunkenness than there is for a high civil servant if both have drunk just as much?

1	No, certainly not	28.7
2	No, perhaps not	15.1
3	Yes, perhaps	25.4
4	Yes, certainly	21.0
5	Don't know	9.8

Correlations between items		Item	Positive response alternatives	% positive
a				
0.343	b	b	3, 4, 5	53.4
0.576	0.295 c	c	3, 4	46.4
		a	1, 2, 6	45.9

Mean correlation = 0.405
Rep = 0.579
Rep_I = 0.463
I = 0.216

Index score and cut-off point		% in population	No. of respondents in sample
Low	0	22.5	812
Medium	1	27.7	1,107
	2	31.5	1,287
High	3	18.3	793
		100	3,999

28   EARLY ECONOMIC HARDSHIP

				%
(a)	Do you remember if your father/guardian was un- employed longer than three months at a time when you were growing up?	1	Yes	25.6
		2	No	41.5
		3	Don't remember	32.9
(b)	Would you say that your childhood home was poor or economically well-off during the greater part of your childhood?	1	Very poor	11.4
		2	Rather poor	41.9
		3	Rather well-off	36.2
		4	Very well-off	3.1
		5	Don't know	7.5

Item	Positive response alternatives	% positive
b	1, 2, 5	60.8
a	1	25.6

Correlation between items = 0.443

Index score and cut-off point	% in population	No. of respondents in sample
Low 0	33.2	1,194
Medium 1	47.2	1,914
High 2	19.2	891
	100	3,999

29   INDEX OF UNION PARTICIPATION

	Estimated % in pop- ulation	No. of respondents in sample
Local leaders (chairman of works club, branch or group organization, member of works club or branch board)	0.8	322
Marginal office-holders (other elected position and belongs to stratum 1 or 2)	1.6	498
Regular participants (others in stratum 2 or has elected position but belongs to stratum 3)	9.4	1,122

	Estimated % in population	No. of respondents in sample
Marginal participants (indicates having attended at least one union meeting during last twelve months but belongs to stratum 3)	35.9	847
Outsiders (has not attended a union meeting during last twelve months and belongs to stratum 3)	52.4	1,209

30 INDEX OF UNION ROLE

Full-time works club official (more than 35 hours of weekly working time in union work)	0.1	40
Part-time official (4-35 hours of weekly working time in union work)	0.5	172
Marginal officials (less than 4 hours of weekly working time in union work)	1.8	609
Regular participants	9.4	1,122
Marginal participants	35.9	847
Outsiders	52.4	1,209

31 INDEX OF PARTY PREFERENCE

Based on the questions: 'Which party do you now like best?' and 'Which party do you now like second best?'

Communist (first preference)	10.3	420
Left-wing Social Democrat (Communist Party second best)	21.4	1,031

	Estimated % in population	No. of respondents in sample
Centre Social Democrat (no second best party preference indicated)	21.4	882
Right-wing Social Democrats (bourgeois party second best)	13.8	649
Bourgeois (a bourgeois party as first preference)	10.2	330
No answer	22.7	687

32   TIME FOR RESPONSE TO QUESTIONNAIRE

At premises of firm	84.5	3,557
After first mailing	11.0	309
After second mailing	3.2	86
After third mailing	0.7	24
After fourth mailing	0.5	19
After fifth mailing	0.2	4

33   SIZE OF FIRM

	No. of workers	No. of firms in sample		
Small	1 40-63	5	0.5	210
	2 79-89	4	0.7	237
	3 106-70	5	1.2	363
Medium	4 252-92	4	2.3	314
	5 309-635	8	6.5	732
Large	6 869-1388	7	15.6	692
	7 1486-1982	5	16.3	469
	8 2198-2893	5	22.8	493
	9 3050-4281	5	34.0	489

	Estimated % in pop- ulation	No. of respondents in sample
34 TYPE OF COMMUNITY AND SIZE OF FIRM		
Big city - small firm	0.4	129
Big city - medium-sized firm	2.9	280
Big city - large firm	33.5	671
Communities dominated by single large firm (employing more than 45% of labour force)	41.6	966
Industrial community - small firm	0.7	210
Industrial community - medium-sized firm	3.7	436
Industrial community - large firm	10.7	400
Mixed community - medium-sized firms	5.4	502
Mixed community - small firms	1.1	405
35 TYPE OF PRODUCTION TECHNOLOGY AND SIZE OF FIRM		
Standardized production - small firm	1.6	514
Standardized production - medium-sized firm	6.7	732
Standardized production - large firm	20.5	485
Auto assembly - large firm	18.5	366
Steel work - large firm	14.0	399
Unit or small batch - small firm	0.8	296

	Estimated % in population	No. of respondents in sample
Unit or small batch - medium-sized firm	2.1	314
Unit or small batch - large firm	13.9	494
Shipyard - large firm	21.8	399

36   TURNOVER OF PERSONNEL IN FIRM

No. of workers quitting their jobs during the year as proportion of no. of workers employed at the beginning of the year. Average for the two years preceeding the survey.

Low (-20%)	31.4	1,283
Medium (21-34%)	32.8	1,392
High (35+%)	35.5	1,324

37   STRATA IN THE SECOND SAMPLING STAGE

Stratum 1. Members of works club boards	0.5	275
Stratum 2. Registered on attendance lists at union meetings	5.3	1,526
Stratum 3. Other workers	94.2	2,198

SELECTED QUESTIONS

1 About how long have you been employed at this company?

1	Less than six months	5.7	157
2	Six-twelve months	6.0	191
3	One-three years	21.5	679
4	Four-seven years	18.4	716
5	Eight-fifteen years	17.0	823

		Estimated % in population	No. of respondents in sample
6	More than fifteen years	31.0	1,420
7	No answer	0.3	13

2   Have you worked in agriculture or forestry after the age of 15?

1	No	61.4	2,482
2	Yes, less than one year	7.1	319
3	Yes, one-three years	12.1	469
4	Yes, four years or more	16.4	643
5	No answer	3.0	86

3   About how long have you worked in industry (both in the metal industry and in other branches of industry)?

1	Less than four years	17.8	458
2	Four-seven years	15.5	521
3	Eight-fifteen years	20.4	743
4	More than fifteen years	44.6	2,226
5	No answer	1.8	51

4   Do you think that you will leave this company on your own accord within the next five years?

1	Yes, certainly	9.3	382
2	Yes, perhaps	18.1	713
3	No, perhaps not	15.6	648
4	No, certainly not	19.8	815
5	Don't know	31.4	1,219
6	Retire within five years	5.5	208
7	No answer	0.3	13

5   Do you think that there is any risk for workers here at this company being temporarily or permanently laid off within the next five years because of changes in the production?

1	Very great risk	9.1	454
2	Rather great risk	14.2	684
3	Rather small risk	23.2	900
4	Very small risk	21.1	673
5	Don't know	32.5	1,288

	Estimated % in pop- ulation	No. of respondents in sample

6 How much have you earned per hour on the average during the past three months?

1	Less than 7 kronor	6.9	249
2	7.00-7.99	14.2	632
3	8.00-8.99	23.6	970
4	9.00-9.99	23.0	954
5	10.00-10.99	20.2	747
6	11.00-11.99	8.4	259
7	12 kronor or more	3.2	171
8	No answer	0.5	17

7 Are you on the whole satisfied or dissatisfied with your present hourly earnings?

1	Very satisfied	2.8	100
2	Rather satisfied	23.3	922
3	Neither satisfied nor dis- satisfied	37.1	1,498
4	Rather dissatisfied	21.6	864
5	Very dissatisfied	14.1	585
6	Don't know	1.0	30

8 Would you think that you could get a job at another company in this town which pays better than what you have now?

1	Yes, certainly	13.8	464
2	Yes, perhaps	25.2	1,905
3	No, perhaps not	24.7	997
4	No, certainly not	19.5	851
5	Don't know	16.9	682

9 Do you work mainly on piece-rate or do you have a fixed wage as hourly wage, weekly wage, or monthly wage?

1	Mainly piece-rate	64.9	2,596
2	Mainly hourly wage	28.8	1,174
3	Mainly weekly wage	3.1	113
4	Mainly monthly wage	0.9	29
5	Mixed forms	1.8	64
6	No answer	0.5	23

	Estimated % in population	No. of respondents in sample

10 Do you have mainly straight piece-rate or mixed piece-rate?

1	Mainly straight piece-rate	41.1	1,781
2	Mainly mixed piece-rate	28.9	976
3	Do not work on piece-rate	28.2	1,166
4	No answer	1.8	76

11 Do you have individual piece-rate or group piece-rate right now?

1	Individual piece-rate	35.7	1,774
2	Group piece-rate	32.6	943
3	Do not work on piece-rate	28.4	1,172
4	No answer	3.2	108

12 What type of piece-rate do you have right now?

1	Piece-rate based on work studies or other piece-rate base	33.5	1,510
2	MTM piece-rate	9.4	246
3	UMS piece-rate	1.5	48
4	Foreman's piece-rate	6.1	322
5	Averaged piece-rate for group or section	9.9	246
6	Piece-rate determined after the job is finished	5.4	197
7	Other type. What? ...	2.3	111
8	Do not work on piece-rate	26.8	1,141
9	No answer	5.1	178

13 Do you have large or small possibilities to decide yourself how your own work is to be done?

1	Very small possibilities	21.8	726
2	Rather small possibilities	23.5	897
3	Rather large possibilities	36.6	1,598
4	Very large possibilities	14.8	660
5	Don't know	3.4	118

14 Do you work on an assembly line?

1	No	83.4	3,501
2	Yes	14.4	420
3	No answer	2.2	78

	Estimated % in pop- ulation	No. of respondents in sample

15 Can you do your job and still think about other things most of the time?

1	Very often	12.4	502
2	Rather often	24.7	1,089
3	Rather seldom	29.4	1,131
4	Very seldom	30.6	1,177
5	Don't know	2.9	100

16 Which would you guess to be the worst in your section/ shop: to be on bad terms with management or to be on bad terms with the other workers?

1	Much worse with management	11.3	359
2	Somewhat worse with management	12.8	448
3	Somewhat worse with the workers	19.3	777
4	Much worse with the workers	38.0	1,755
5	Don't know	18.6	660

17 About how great a part of the workers in your section/ shop would you guess to be of foreign origin?

1	A very small part	34.3	1,886
2	A rather small part	18.6	824
3	A rather large part	26.3	749
4	A very large part	16.0	387
5	Don't know	4.7	153

18 Have you been to any union meeting (of your works club, branch or group organization) during the last twelve months?

1	No, not once	48.9	1,151
2	Yes, once	15.9	531
3	Yes, twice	10.5	480
4	Yes, three times	8.2	442
5	Yes, four times	3.5	312
6	Yes, five times or more	8.7	956
7	Don't remember	4.4	127

	Estimated % in pop- ulation	No. of respondents in sample

19 Does it happen that you read the 'Metal-Worker'?

1 Don't get the 'Metal-Worker'	6.7	170
2 No, almost never	4.5	128
3 Read it sometimes	19.9	666
4 Read it rather often	22.0	811
5 Read it every week	46.2	2,199
6 No answer	0.7	25

20 Have you participated in any study circle or course on union matters or social questions during the last five years?

1 No, none	77.1	2,538
2 Yes, one	12.7	584
3 Yes, two or more	7.8	800
4 Don't remember	2.3	74
5 No answer	0	3

21 People are members of the union for many different reasons. Which would you say is the most important reason for yourself being a member? (Encircle only one alternative.)

1 Am not a member of the union	3.5	84
2 I felt obliged to join	7.7	234
3 I wasn't very interested but joined none the less	8.6	238
4 I personally benefit from being in the union	36.9	1,547
5 I think that one should be solidaristic with the labour movement	40.8	1,810
6 Other reason. What? ...	0.5	33
7 No answer	1.9	53

22 Do you think that the national union leaders should have opposed the introduction of motion-time studies into the metal industry?

1 Yes, certainly	19.7	792
2 Yes, perhaps	22.5	887
3 No, perhaps not	22.8	943
4 No, certainly not	17.8	793
5 Don't know	17.2	584

	Estimated % in population	No. of respondents in sample

23 Which of these alternatives gives everything which is necessary if one is to receive a holiday wage?

1 Worked at the company at least one year	5.8	239
2 Worked the day just before the holiday	2.5	78
3 Worked the day just before and just after the holiday	19.4	628
4 Worked the day just before and just after the holiday and have worked enough to have earned at least four days of vacation	59.5	2,621
5 Don't remember	12.7	433

24 Does it happen that people discuss politics in your section/shop?

1 Almost every day	9.5	464
2 A few times a week	17.9	824
3 A few times a month	29.7	1,291
4 Almost never	35.0	1,186
5 Don't know	7.9	234

25 Would you say that those working in your section/shop have similar or dissimilar ideas on political questions?

1 Very dissimilar ideas	11.5	421
2 Rather dissimilar ideas	41.2	1,630
3 Rather similar ideas	23.9	1,198
4 Very similar ideas	2.0	120
5 Don't know	21.4	630

26 Are you a man or a woman?

1 Man	89.4	3,690
2 Woman	10.6	309

27 When were you born?

1 Before 1906	9.0	336
2 1906-15	17.5	823
3 1916-25	19.6	1,003
4 1926-35	19.0	781

		Estimated % in pop- ulation	No. of respondents in sample
5	1936-45	26.5	808
6	1945 or since	8.4	247
7	Not possible to code	0	1

28 In which country were you born?

1	Sweden	78.9	3,543
2	Finland	11.9	234
3	Denmark	1.8	53
4	Norway	1.1	30
5	Other country	6.3	137
6	No answer	1.4	44

29 Where did you live most of the time before you were 15 years old?

1	In Stockholm, Göteborg or Malmö	12.4	449
2	In another city or large town	18.4	840
3	In a small town	14.6	637
4	In the countryside	35.7	1,641
5	In a country other than Sweden	17.0	378
6	No answer	1.9	54

30 How long all together have you lived in the community where you live now?

1	Almost all my life	30.6	1,425
2	More than fifteen years	24.8	1,190
3	Seven-fifteen years	16.0	616
4	Three-six years	11.6	380
5	Less than three years	15.4	343
6	No answer	1.6	45

31 Are you married or not married?

1	Not married	31.5	1,014
2	Married	65.1	2,875
3	Widower (Widow)	1.9	71
4	No answer	1.4	38

	Estimated % in population	No. of respondents in sample

32 What kind of education did you have?

1 Elementary school	71.0	2,973
2 New elementary school, vocational course	2.6	74
3 New elementary school, general or college preparatory course	0.6	18
4 Vocational school	10.8	429
5 Industrial training school or apprenticeship	5.2	186
6 People's high school ('folkhögskola')	2.2	99
7 High school or other secondary school	5.5	154
8 Other education. What? ...	0	3
9 No answer	2.0	63

33 What occupation did your father/guardian have during most of your childhood? (Write in detail, for example, farmer with own farm, conductor with the State Railways, bank clerk, metal-worker, farm-worker, electrician with own business.)

1 Entrepreneurs (Social Groups I + II)	3.3	148
2 Salaried employees, etc. (Social Groups I + II)	6.9	230
3 Independent farmers (Social Groups I + II)	16.1	678
4 Lower salaried employees (Social Group III)	4.4	156
5 Workers in manufacturing (Social Group III)	21.9	898
6 Other workers in secondary and tertiary sectors (Social Group III)	23.9	990
7 Workers in farming, forestry, etc. (Social Group III)	10.6	464
8 Combination of worker and small-holder (Social Group III)	0.4	24

	Estimated % in population	No. of respondents in sample

34 Do you happen to remember if your father/guardian was active in any labour union when you were growing up?

1	Was not active	43.4	1,793
2	Was rather active	13.0	625
3	Was very active	8.5	380
4	Don't know	35.1	1,199

35 Do you happen to remember which party your father/guardian favoured most during your childhood?

1	People's party	4.7	159
2	Communist party	3.3	152
3	Conservative party	2.4	93
4	Social Democratic party	46.0	2,072
5	Centre Party (Farmers' party)	6.9	304
6	Other party. Which? ...	0.3	6
7	Don't know	36.4	1,211
8	No answer	0	2

36 Have you yourself been unemployed more than a month at a time since you were 18 years old?

1	Yes	33.8	1,323
2	No	63.5	2,606
3	No answer	2.7	70

37 Are you now a member of any sports club?

1	No	72.0	2,818
2	Yes	25.1	1,103
3	No answer	2.8	78

38 Does it happen that you go to church or religious meetings (apart from marriages, christenings or funerals)?

1	Almost never	68.0	2,681
2	Once a year	12.3	536
3	Two-five times a year	10.9	460
4	Six-twelve times a year	2.3	78
5	More than twelve times a year	3.4	145
6	No answer	3.2	99

	Estimated % in pop-ulation	No. of respondents in sample

39 Do you have any close relative who is a worker here at this company?

1	No, no one	56.2	2,390
2	Yes, one	21.0	838
3	Yes, two	9.6	341
4	Yes, three or more	9.1	321
5	Don't know	4.2	109

40 Have you any near relative who is a white-collar employee here at the company?

1	Yes	12.6	468
2	No	83.6	3,430
3	Don't know	3.8	107

41 Does it happen that you visit any white-collar employees or someone with his own business or that they visit you?

1	No, almost never	52.6	2,271
2	Yes, sometimes	25.5	1,108
3	Yes, rather often	7.0	346
4	Yes, often	3.9	113
5	Don't know	5.4	161

42 How are you living now?

1	In company housing	11.4	314
2	In a rented apartment	37.5	1,492
3	In a 'purchased' apartment	14.6	630
4	In my own home	18.3	970
5	With my parents	10.3	372
6	As a boarder	4.6	132
7	In some other way. What? ...	0.5	20
8	No answer	2.9	69

43 Do you now have any commissions of trust in the union?

0	Not applicable or no answer	81.2	2,568
1	Yes	8.4	972
2	No	10.3	459

	Estimated % in population	No. of respondents in sample

44 During how many years have you held commissions of trust in the union?

		Estimated % in population	No. of respondents in sample
0	Not applicable or no answer	84.9	2,683
1	Less than one year	1.0	75
2	One-two years	3.7	260
3	Three-five years	4.4	350
4	Six-ten years	3.1	294
5	Eleven-fifteen years	0.8	120
6	More than fifteen years	2.1	217

45 How much of your regular working time do you estimate that you have spent in union work on the average during the last 12 months?

0	Not applicable or no answer	83.1	2,641
1	Hardly any time	11.1	630
2	Less than one hour	1.7	205
3	1-3 hours	2.6	278
4	4-10 hours	0.9	126
5	11-20 hours	0.3	50
6	21-35 hours	0.1	25
7	More than 35 hours	0.4	44

46 Have you participated in any negotiations with the firm as a representative of the union during the last 12 months?

0	Not applicable or no answer	82.8	2,622
1	None	14.4	922
2	Yes, one	0.8	86
3	Yes, two	0.4	61
4	Yes, three-four	0.8	83
5	Yes, five or more	1.0	225

47 Total number of positions presently held in the union

0	None	91.7	3,035
1	One	5.5	425
2	Two	1.5	237
3	Three	0.7	140
4	Four	0.4	86
5	Five	0.1	45
6	Six	0.1	21
7	Seven	0	7
8	Eight	0	3

Appendix 3

Turnout in elections to the Riksdag by sex and socioeconomic status (social groups), mobilization of the electorate by the socialist and the bourgeois parties, distribution of the two-bloc vote and left-wing proportion of total socialist vote, 1911-76

Election year	Turnout Social group I Men %	Women %	Social group II Men %	Women %	Social group III Men %	Women %	Total %	Mobilization of electorate Enfranchized citizens voting for Socialist parties %	Bourgeois parties %	Distribution of voters Socialist % of two-bloc vote %	Left-wing % of socialist vote %
1911	68		61		52		57.0	16.2	40.5	28.5	
1914	79		68		62		66.2	23.9	41.4	36.4	
1917	74		68		62		65.8	25.6	39.8	39.2	20.6
1921	67	60	66	49	58	44	54.2	23.8	30.0	44.0	17.8
1924	75	70	62	49	57	43	53.0	24.4	28.5	46.2	11.0
1928	85	83	76	67	69	58	67.4	29.3	38.0	43.4	14.8
1932							67.6	33.7	33.2	50.0	16.6
1936	86	85	81	73	77	68	74.5	39.8	33.3	53.6	14.4
1940	85	85	75	71	70	65	70.3	40.1	29.4	58.0	6.2
1944	85	86	77	71	72	66	71.6	40.7	30.4	57.2	18.1
1948	93	92	88	84	82	78	83.0	43.2	39.1	52.4	12.0
1952	92	92	86	83	79	77	79.5	39.7	39.0	50.3	8.6
1956	95		88		83		79.8	39.4	40.0	49.6	10.0
1960	96		92		89		85.9	44.7	40.7	52.3	8.6
1964	91		88		87		83.9	43.7	38.1	53.4	9.9
1968	96		92		93		89.3	47.1	40.2	53.9	5.7
1970	97		93		91		88.3	44.2	42.0	51.2	10.3
1973	98		95		93		90.8	44.3	44.3	50.0	11.8
1976	99		96		94		91.8	43.4	46.4	48.4	10.6

Notes

CHAPTER 1   GRAVE-DIGGERS OR ANGELS IN MARBLE?

1 Quoted in McKenzie and Silver (1968, p. ii).
2 Sweden has, of course, frequently also served as a
   'bad' example in the political debate abroad (e.g.
   Huntford, 1971).   For discussions of different aspects of Swedish society see e.g. Childs, 1961;
   Scase, 1976, 1977; Stephens, 1976; Martin, 1975;
   Jones, 1976.
3 For a partly different usage of the term welfare
   capitalism see Marshall (1972).
4 The nature of the relationship between the material
   base and the 'superstructure' has been subject to
   considerable discussion (see e.g. Althusser, 1969;
   Parkin, 1975).
5 Dahrendorf thus appears to overlook the exercise of
   non-legitimate power for the formation of classes.
   This is an important omission.
6 Industrial societies with communist regimes, however,
   are assumed to be unstable since their political institutions are not functional for industrialism (see
   the discussion in Goldthorpe, 1971, pp. 270-4).   The
   present book, however, does not consider societies
   under Communist rule.
7 In France, unionization in these sectors has been increasing, while it appears to have stagnated among
   manual workers (Shorter and Tilly, 1974).
8 It can be noted that 'stratification' research often
   takes the dependent variables of class theories, e.g.
   income and prestige, as its independent variables.
9 The theories on coalition formation in small groups
   are strikingly, but probably inadvertently, Marxian
   in their stress on the distribution of power resources
   and in their disregard for status differences as a

base for coalition formation.   See Caplow (1968) and
Gamson (1961).

10 The structural-functional interpretation of stratification is presented and discussed in Bendix and Lipset
(1966, pp. 47-72).

11 Parkin (1974) has referred to similar processes as
strategies for social closure.

CHAPTER 2   SOCIAL CONFLICT AND STRUCTURAL CHANGE

1 For a discussion of the labour aristocracy and other
issues of relevance in this context, see Hobsbawm
(1964).

2 See the discussion in Hyman (1971, pp. 17-20).

3 This section is adapted from Korpi (1974a).

4 Another theoretical approach has been based on the
concept of 'strain';   see Smelser (1963).   For cri-
tiques of this approach see Currie and Skolnick (1970)
and Oberschall (1973, pp. 19-24).

5 For exceptions see Blalock (1967), Gamson (1968),
Grimshaw (1970, pp. 9-20), Rex (1961) and Schmid
(1968).

6 Some points of departure for a connection and comparison of these two traditions can be suggested.   The
basic idea in the cross-cutting cleavage theories is
that, if the possible lines of cleavage in a society
are not superimposed but rather cut across parties,
the probability of manifest conflict will decrease,
and society is 'sewn together' by its inner conflicts.
This theory thus apparently assumes that each party is
internally heterogeneous and has internally opposed
interests.   Mobilization of power resources therefore
incurs high costs, making coalition formation and conflict less likely.   In coalition theory on the other
hand, it is assumed that parties are homogeneous with
respect to interests.   Mobilization of power resources is therefore easy and does not incur high costs,
something that facilitates coalition formation and
conflict.

7 For an exception see Dahlström (1966).   Even in exchange analyses where inequalities in power resources
are recognized, the consequences of such inequalities
often are not assumed to be crucial for the result of
the exchange;   see Homans (1961, pp. 77-8) and Blau
(1964, pp. 157-8).   Westergaard and Resler (1975)
have an interesting discussion on the effects of
power for the processes of distribution.

8 We adhere here to the sociological convention of de-

fining relative deprivation in terms of the perceived discrepancy between, on the one hand, the actual position or state of the actor with respect to some good or value dimension, and on the other hand the level of aspiration (or the normative expectations) of the actor with respect to that dimension, i.e. what he believes he is justifiably entitled to.

9   This assumption is similar to the position by Lenski (1966, p. 44) that 'power will determine the distribution of nearly all of the surplus possessed by the society'.   On the international scene one example of the differential use of power resources was given by the United States during the oil crisis in the mid-1970s with a more or less unveiled threat of a military intervention if the oil-producing countries drive too hard a bargaining on oil prices based on supply and demand.

10   Hirschman (1970) discusses similar issues in terms of Exit, Voice and Loyalty.

11   The use of power resources by collectivities has also been termed 'collective action'; see Olson (1965) and Coleman (1971).

12   Such probabilistic relationships allowing for influences from variables not included in the model are also assumed among the other variables in the model.

13   Atkinson (1964, p. 242) assumes utility or the value of achieving the goal to be a multiplicative function of an actor's motivation (need) to achieve the goal, and of incentives (objective rewards or punishments associated with the goal).   The costs associated with reaching the goal should be deducted from its objective incentive value to find the 'net' value of reaching the goal.   Utility is thus here regarded as 'net' utility derived from different types of outcomes as, for example, costs of reaching the goal and improved exchange rates.

14   To the extent that power resources overlap with investments, this assumption is parallel to the 'rule of distributive justice' proposed by Homans (1961, ch. 12), but has different implications.

15   The prediction of some degree of decrease in the probability of manifest conflict around the point of parity in power resources derives from an assumption that changes in the difference in power resources have somewhat different effects on the probability of initiation or attack as compared with the probability of retaliation or defence in a conflict situation.   This aspect of the power difference model of conflict is developed in Korpi (1974b).

16 A very high utility can of course sometimes offset the
effects of decreasing expectancy of success. Utility, being a multiplicative function of motivation and
incentives (Atkinson, 1964, p. 242), can be very high
in situations that are of vital concern for the actor
and where incentives thus are exceedingly high. For
example, where extermination is threatened, mobilization can be expected in spite of very low prospects
for success.

17 For an interpretation of changes in the level of industrial conflict over time in terms of changes in
mobilization and organizational power resources, see
Shorter and Tilly (1974). The difference in power
resources may decrease also if for some reason the
power resources of the 'ruling class' decline.

18 Robinson (1966, pp. xvii-xviii) also assumes, with
some supporting evidence, that relative shares of workers of the results of production are affected by the
bargaining power of labour.

19 We are here referring to realistic rather than to
wish levels of aspiration.

20 The analysis here thus goes contrary to Giddens'
(1973, pp. 112-15) assumption that the development of
capitalism will only lead to 'conflict consciousness'
among the workers, i.e. to a recognition of opposition
of interest with another class, but not to 'revolutionary consciousness', involving the recognition of
the possibility of an alternative organization of the
economy which can be brought about through collective
action. Revolutionary consciousness, according to
Giddens (1973, pp. 116-17) does not originate in class
conflict but only in 'contradiction', with 'the clash
between a "backward", agrarian order, and the impact
of "advanced" technique' as the paradigm case.

21 The exceedingly wide definition of the state suggested
e.g. by Poulantzas (1973), which includes political
parties, trade unions, the mass media and also the
family, is unfruitful because it makes the state encompass the major part of society. It thus becomes
a concept reminding one of 'the social system'.

22 For recent discussions of the state from Marxian
points of view see e.g. Miliband (1969), Baran and
Sweezy (1966), Offe (1972) and Westergaard and Resler
(1975).

23 In a similar way, Poulantzas (1976, pp. 72-5) has
later come to the conclusion that
by State power one can only mean the power of certain classes to whose interest the State corres-
ponds ... [and that] the relative autonomy of the

capitalist State stems precisely from the contradictory relations of power between social classes
[and is] a 'resultant' of the relations of power
between classes, [why] the State should be seen ...
as a condensate of a relation of power between
struggling classes.

CHAPTER 3   THE SWEDISH LABOUR MOVEMENT AND CLASS CONFLICT

1 Sources on the modern social, economic and political
   history of Sweden include Jörberg (1961), Koblik
   (1975), Samuelsson (1968) and Hadenius et al. (1974).
   For a comparative analysis of industrialization and
   organized labour in Scandinavia, see Lafferty (1971).
2 The percentage of workers in firms with more than
   1000 workers thus only increased from 8 per cent in
   1923 to 19 per cent in 1970. The proportion in firms
   with less than 200 workers has been almost constant,
   while the proportion in medium-sized firms has decreased (SOS, Industri, annual publications).
3 Hard data on this development are scarce (see however
   LO, 1966). The major factor affecting skill level
   can be assumed to be the extent to which the quality
   of production is affected by, and dependent on, the
   individual judgment of workers. With the change from
   craft to mass-production industry, the quality as well
   as quantity of production has become more and more
   dependent on machinery.
4 At this time Sweden had a lower proportion of its population with voting rights than many other Western
   countries, including Britain and the United States.
5 An organization among typographers in Stockholm formed
   in 1846 is often regarded as the first union in
   Sweden, although it did not begin to function as a
   union until in the 1880s (Hansson, 1938, p. 15;
   Björklund, 1965).
6 Through majority vote the local union branches can
   affiliate their members to the local Social Democratic
   Party organizations collectively, but with individual
   rights of reservation. The proportion of LO members
   affiliated through collective membership was 45 per
   cent in 1912, 30 per cent in 1929, 32 per cent in
   1933, 33 per cent in 1954 and 32 per cent in 1967
   (Karlbom, 1969, p. 44). These union members have
   constituted about 60 per cent of the membership of the
   party (Elvander, 1969).
7 In estimating the organizational level, the number of
   workers is based on the censuses (Carlsson, 1966), in

which a division into workers and salaried employees
was made up to the census of 1965. The LO also has a
minority of members, primarily in the public sector,
who are classified as salaried employees in the censuses. Therefore the level of unionization is here
overestimated to some extent.

8 Generally known as the Akarp Law.

9 An employers' organization in the engineering industry
was formed the same year but stayed outside the SAF
until 1917.

10 The first industry-wide contract was signed in the
tobacco industry in 1896.

11 At this time, the unions were interested primarily in
limiting the rights of employers to hire and fire and
to find ways of protecting themselves against strike-
breakers.

12 Attempts to use strike-breakers were made primarily
by firms outside the SAF.

13 The largest group is the syndicalist union (SAC).

14 The level of unionization in agriculture and forestry
is difficult to estimate since a large proportion of
persons listed in the censuses as working in this
sector are relatives of the owners. The level of
unionization among the regular wage-workers in this
sector is now probably higher than the one given here.

15 De anställdas centralorganisation, DACO.

16 The difference in the level of unionization between
the sexes is perhaps of the magnitude of 15 per cent.

17 The figures are based on a random sample of the Swedish population (N = 6000) and are taken from the
1974 Level of Living Survey. A smaller white-collar
union, the SR, has recently amalgamated with the SACO.
Here their members are added together. Farmers' organizations are excluded.

18 The early history of the Swedish Social Democratic
Party is described in Lindgren (1927).

19 Moderata Samlingspartiet, Folkpartiet och Center-
partiet.

20 In the 1960s several reshuffles among parties to the
left of the Social Democrats have taken place. The
dominating group is however the Communist Left Party
(Vpk) which has support of about 4-5 per cent of the
electorate.

21 Sweden has thus not had any 'realigning' elections in
the American sense (see Campbell et al., 1960).

22 Increasing urbanization, improved communications, more
up-to-date voting registers and improved possibilities
to vote at the post offices prior to the election day
have of course also contributed to the increase in
voting participation.

23   See e.g. Milbrath (1965).

24   Lewin (1974) has made an attempt to use ecological
     data to estimate the social composition of supporters
     for the different parties during the present century.
     His results, however, appear to be unreliable
     (Quensel, 1973).

CHAPTER 4   THE POLITICAL IDEAS AND STRATEGIES OF THE
SWEDISH LABOUR MOVEMENT

1   Discussions and documentations of the ideological
    debate and the party programmes of the Social Demo-
    cratic Party can be found in Lindhagen (1972a and b),
    Gunnarsson (1971), Ahlsén et al. (1972) and Tingsten
    (1973).

2   See Ahlsén et al. (1972) and Lindhagen (1972a).

3   E.g. Branting (1929a, p. 130) wrote in 1896: 'For us
    the universal suffrage is thus not so much a goal in
    itself, but more one of the most powerful *means* to our
    final goal: a completely reshaped society.'

4   See Branting (1929b, pp. 302-3).

5   The first youth organization left the party in 1908
    and transformed itself into a party, the Young Soc-
    ialist Party, which was of only small significance.
    The second youth organization was founded in 1903 by
    groups more loyal to the party, but soon they too
    became a nucleus of opposition, leaving the party in
    the split in 1917.

6   See e.g. Lindeberg (1968).   For a description of the
    conditions of the unemployed in these years see e.g.
    Erlander (1972, pp. 163-6).   The bourgeois parties
    maintained that in the frequent industrial disputes,
    which often were lockouts to back demands for wage
    decreases, the neutrality of the state required the
    withdrawal of support to the unemployed in branches
    with disputes and also required that the unemployed
    accept work in firms involved in disputes, and thus
    act as strike-breakers.

7   Named after the British industrialist, Sir Albert
    Mond, who sponsored a conference to increase co-opera-
    tion between labour and employers after the General
    Strike in 1926, which was lost by the workers.   This
    idea was taken up in several European countries.   The
    Swedish conference resulted in the establishment of a
    committee for co-operation between the parties on the
    labour market, which however did not become of major
    importance, and was dissolved after the military in-
    tervention in the demonstrations in Ådalen in 1931.

8   These ideas were presented in the so-called 'Göteborg programme' worked out in 1919 primarily by Ernst Wigforss (1951, pp. 121ff.). Because of the attempts of the party leadership to revive the coalition with the Liberals, the relatively radical programme was shelved (Wigforss, 1967).

9   For discussions of the background to these policies see Steiger (1972, 1973), Landgren (1960, 1972), Wigforss (1967), Öhman (1970), Lewin (1967) and Unga (1976).

10 See Nyman (1944), Hellström (1976) and Söderpalm (1976) for discussions of this agreement.

11 These efforts included the appointment of special commissions to study the problems of various sectors of the economy and subsidies to industry through loans and export guarantees. Company taxation was changed from progressive to proportional taxation. Rules favouring re-investment of profits in the firm and discouraging high dividends to shareholders were also introduced.

12 The Main Agreement was also an attempt by the parties on the labour market to avoid the legislation in this area that had often been proposed in the Riksdag.

13 The work by Karleby (1926) appears to have played an important role in this process.

14 This idea was formulated by Östen Undén, professor of law and long-time member of the Social Democratic government.

15 A modern variety of this ideology was proposed by Adler-Karlsson (1967).

16 These persons included three of the most influential publicists within the party, Richard Lindström, Karl Fredriksson and K.J. Ohlsson, who were editors of the main newspapers of the party.

17 Hayek's 'The Road to Serfdom' gave the main arguments in this debate (see Lewin, 1967, ch. 4).

18 Ohlin (1949), Lundberg (1958) and Öhman (1973).

19 After its principal inventors, Gösta Rehn and Rudolf Meidner, this model is known as the Rehn-Meidner model.

20 Others have seen these developments as the final delivery of the party from the assumed Marxian fatalism and as a 'sobering-up' period.

21 The comparison is with the following nations: Belgium, Canada, Denmark, Finland, France, Germany, the Netherlands, Italy, Norway, Spain, the United Kingdom and the United States.

22 The decline in strike activity in Sweden from the first to the second half of the 1930s is rather

unique. In the United States, where an organizational drive among the industrial unions set in at the
latter period, the frequency of disputes increased.
This period is in some ways a parallel to the early
organizational period of the Swedish union movement.

23 For descriptions and analyses of Swedish labour market
legislation, see Schmidt (1962), Edlund (1967) and
Eklund (1973, 1974). The law concerning mediation in
industrial disputes originates from 1906. In 1915
the Supreme Court ruled that collective agreements
were legally binding and that strikes in breach of the
agreements were punishable by fines. Laws concerning
arbitration were enacted in 1920. See also Forsebäck
(1976).

24 Ingham (1974, ch. 3) regards the differences between
Britain and Sweden in the levels of industrial conflict as a reflection of differences in the extent of
institutionalization of industrial conflict, but considers the institutions as intervening variables reflecting differences in industrial substructure. He
argues that industrial substructures can differ with
respect to (i) industrial concentration, (ii) complexity of technical and organizational structure, and
(iii) product differentiation and specialization. In
comparison with Britain, Sweden has had a higher industrial concentration but lower complexity and product differentiation, something which underlies the
higher degree on institutionalization of industrial
relations and the lower degree of industrial conflict
in Sweden. Ingham's only empirical data on substruc-
tural differences between Sweden and Britain concern
industrial concentration. He refers to data indicating that the percentage of employment accounted for by
the twenty largest plants in selected industries is,
on the average, considerably higher in Sweden than in
Britain. This 'twenty-plant concentration index',
however, is misleading in this context. Since the
maximum size of a plant usually is about 5,000-10,000
workers, the proportion of the total employment
accounted for by the twenty largest plants can be expected to decrease with the size of the labour market.
The percentage distribution of employees among enterprises of different sizes in manufacturing industry in
Britain and Sweden indicates that, if anything, Britain has a higher proportion of employees in the
largest firms (Scase, 1977, p. 22). At any rate, no
major changes in the industrial substructure or in the
development of institutions of industrial relations
are found to precede changes in the level of industrial conflict in Sweden.

25 From 1911 to 1957 statistics on unemployment among
    union members were based on monthly reports from the
    unions regarding the proportion of members whose mem-
    bership dues were cancelled because of unemployment.
    This method yielded higher unemployment figures than
    the statistics introduced by the Labour Market Board
    in 1955, which were based on the registration of un-
    employment on one day each month (Skog, 1963, pp.
    134-8). Because of the great increase in the 1960s
    of the number of organized salaried employees having
    a lower level of unemployment, I have here given un-
    employment figures for workers in manufacturing.
26 For a discussion see Martin (1973).
27 For an analysis of factors affecting the rate of
    social assistance in the postwar period see Korpi
    (1975).
28 Data are from the Level of Living Survey in 1968,
    except for the youngest cohorts, who come from the
    survey in 1974. The fact that the responses from the
    youngest persons were given six years later introduces
    additional sources of error in the comparisons.
29 For an analysis of the economic effects of wartime
    measures on the households, see Abukhanfusa (1975).
30 Primarily because of increasing levels of employment,
    the income distribution among women has however become
    more equal. Since there are indications that the in-
    creasing female employment has taken place more in the
    middle- and upper-class households than in working-
    class families (e.g. Erikson, 1971, pp. 58, 60), it is
    doubtful if the distribution of household incomes has
    become more equal.
31 I wish to thank Lena Ekman and Jerzy Sarnecki for aid
    in the collection of this material.
32 Of the four leaders of the Social Democratic Party the
    first and the latest (Branting and Palme) have had
    distinctively upper-class backgrounds, the second
    (Hansson) came from the working class and the third
    (Erlander) from the lower middle class.
33 In comparison with Britain, for instance, it would
    appear that the egalitarian forces in Sweden have been
    considerably stronger. Thus, for example, no new
    peerages have been created in Sweden since 1917; the
    leaders of the Social Democratic Party and of the LO
    on principle have refused to accept honours and the
    system of royal honours was discontinued in 1975.
    The king has been devested of his remaining political
    power and retains only a limited ceremonial role.
    The use of occupational titles in the telephone direc-
    tory, often commented upon by social scientists from
    abroad, was discontinued in 1975.

34 The differences between cohorts can, of course, re-
    flect age differences as well as generational differ-
    ences.
35 Sweden would appear to be perhaps the most secular
    nation in the West.   The confessional party has
    attracted only about 2 per cent of the votes in the
    elections since the 1960s.   According to a Gallup
    poll from 1968, the following percentages of the pop-
    ulation in twelve countries stated that they believed
    in God ('New York Times', 26 December 1968; quoted in
    Stephens, 1976, pp. 482-3):

	%
United States	98
Greece	96
Uruguay (cities)	89
Austria	85
Switzerland	84
Finland	83
West Germany	81
Netherlands	79
Britain	77
France	73
Norway	73
Sweden	60.

CHAPTER 5   WORK AND WORK ORIENTATIONS

1 Since this chapter was written I have become acquainted with the work of Braverman (1974), which in some
   ways parallels the analysis carried out here.
2 The following figures are based on secondary analyses
   of data from the survey on the living conditions of
   the Swedish people carried out by the Central Bureau
   of Statistics.   The socioeconomic classification of
   occupations used here is described in note 2 to
   chapter 10.
3 Figures not given here indicate that monotonous jobs
   are considerably more common in mining and manufacturing than in building construction or in the primary
   and tertiary sectors.   Only small differences, however, are found with respect to good learning opportunities.   Jencks et al. (1972, ch. 3) refer to empirical data which he interprets to show that job satisfaction has little relationship to occupational
   status.   The occupational classification system used
   by Jencks - nine occupational groups including categories like 'Processing', 'Machine trades' and 'Bench
   work' - are however internally so heterogeneous that

the major part of the variation in job satisfaction
can be expected to be found within rather than between
these groups. His index of job satisfaction is also
conceptually very heterogeneous. When measuring experiences of intrinsic rewards from work, care must be
taken so that differences in levels of aspiration and
response sets do not confound the results (cf.
Blauner, 1960).

4 These studies include Walker and Guest (1952), Blauner
(1960, 1964), Vroom (1964, pp. 126-50), Friedman
(1961), Turner and Lawrence (1965), Sheppard and Herrick (1972), Kornhauser (1965), Goldthorpe et al.
(1968a, ch. 2), Wedderburn and Crompton (1972, ch. 2),
Dahlström et al. (1966), Gardell (1971, 1976), Herzberg, Mausner and Snyderman (1959).

5 Path coefficients below 0.10 are excluded from this
diagram, since their effects generally can be disre-
garded.

6 Gardell (1971, ch. 10) has also found that among industrial workers piece rates tend to decrease job
satisfaction.

7 A description of indices concerning union activity and
political interest is found in Appendix 2.

8 The relationship between level of intrinsic job satisfaction and off-the-job activities is however relatively weak. It thus appears that it is the work
characteristics rather than the level of job satisfaction that are of importance here.

9 Also, Goldthorpe et al. (1968a) stress the necessity
of tracing the social background of work orientations
to the typical life experiences of the individuals.

10 The workers included in the study were sampled from
three different firms, an auto assembly, a.ballbear-
ing company and a chemical process industry.   Only
high-paid, married workers 21-46 years of age were
included (N = 250).

11 Goldthorpe et al. (1969, p. 86, fn. 1) point out that
the concept of 'traditional worker' must be seen as a
sociological and not a historical concept.   Implicit
in the theory of increasingly instrumental work orientations, however, is the assumption that solidarist
work orientations were more common in the earlier
stages of industrialism.

12 Gardell (1971, pp. 174-5) mixes the normative expectations concerning intrinsic rewards from work implied
in the concept 'orientations to work' with the actual
experiences of intrinsic job satisfaction.

CHAPTER 6   SOCIAL RELATIONS IN WORK AND COMMUNITY

1   Since the index on the strength of the workers' col-
    lectivity is cumulative, the lowest scores on the
    index reflect the perceived probability of collective
    actions against management while the two highest
    scores reflect the probability of collective action
    against the workmates who break the norms of the col-
    lectivity.   It can be noted that the index reacts to
    variation in selective power of management and in
    management consideration only at its lower levels,
    while the perceived importance of sanctions from work-
    mates tends to increase over the whole range of the
    index.
2   This question refers to perceived attitudes towards
    the firm among other workers rather than to the res-
    pondent's own views.   The evaluations may be based on
    different aspects of the firm as a place of work, in-
    cluding the work environment, social relations with
    other workers, pay levels and relations to management.
3   Figures not given here indicate that this trend is
    broken in the auto assemblies and large batch firms,
    where workers in jobs with the lowest skill require-
    ments are less positive than those in jobs with medium
    skill requirements.

CHAPTER 7   THE UNION AT THE WORKPLACE

1   In 1964 the Swedish Foundry Workers' Union with about
    10,000 members was amalgamated with the Metal Workers'
    Union.
2   In one-plant communities, where a single firm totally
    dominates the labour market, the branch functions as
    the firm's works club.   In the small firms where
    works clubs are not found, one or two 'contact men'
    are usually appointed, to keep in touch with the
    local union branch.   In some of the larger communi-
    ties special 'occupational clubs' bring together the
    works clubs of those smaller firms with identical
    types of production, e.g. auto repair or forge shops.
3   The hiring of foreign workers, in practice, requires
    the consent of the works club.
4   Nationwide sample surveys show somewhat lower propor-
    tions of union membership.   Data from the 1968 Level
    of Living Survey indicate that, among male and female
    workers in the metal-working, manufacturing, wood,
    paper, building, textile, leather and foodstuff in-
    dustries, 85 per cent claim union membership (figures

based on data in von Otter, 1973, Table 1).   The
absence of the smallest firms in our study increases
the level of union membership.

5 Figures not given here indicate that labour movement
support is related to this set of independent variables in approximately the same way as union involvement.

6 The discrepancy between self-reported and registered
attendance at union meetings is probably partly related to the shorter time period covered by the attendance lists, the omission of branch meetings and some
meetings in the group organization as well as to some
degree of over-reporting of attendance in the survey.

7 According to a law from 1974, works club representatives are remunerated for this by the firm.   Previously various types of arrangements had been worked
out in different firms where, however, the firm usually contributed substantial amounts to cover the wage
of the union representatives.

8 In the preparatory stages of this survey an attempt
was made to use the familiar 'control graph' technique
to describe the distribution of power within the works
club (cf. Tannenbaum and Kahn, 1957).   Because of
difficulties of the respondents in responding in terms
of differences in power between the various levels of
the works club hierarchy this remained an attempt
only.

9 Also, other characteristics of the clubs have been related to the perceived membership influence in the
club, but only weak or inconsistent associations were
found.   There is a slight tendency that, in clubs
with a low turnover in persons on the board, perceived
membership influence is somewhat lower than in clubs
with higher turnover.   Participation rates at works
club meetings are unrelated to average membership influence.   Neither do the characteristics of the
workers' representatives participating in the latest
five negotiations relate consistently to the perceived membership influence within the clubs.

10 The classification of firms according to proportion of
Communist workers is done on the basis of estimates
from our survey data: 'Low' = below 10 per cent;
'Medium' = 10-15 per cent and 'High' = 16+ per cent.

11 Five of the large workplaces in our sample had Communist chairmen in the works club.   Of the 48 plants,
13 were classified as having had a high frequency of
contests in works club elections in recent years, 24
as having a medium level and 11 as having a low level.

12 This partly reflects the fact that wages are deter-

mined, in principle at least, through centrally negotiated contracts and not through workplace bargaining.
13 Union membership among workers in most Western European countries and in North America hovers in the
region of 25-75 per cent.

CHAPTER 8 UNION DEMOCRACY AND MEMBERSHIP INFLUENCE

1 These studies include Lazarsfeld, Berelson and Gaudet
(1944), Berelson, Lazarsfeld and McPhee (1954), Campbell et al. (1960) and Lipset (1960).
2 Some of the significant works are Sartori (1962),
Kornhauser (1960), Almond and Verba (1963), Dahl
(1961, 1956), Key (1961), Schattschneider (1960),
Bachrach and Baratz (1970) and Bachrach (1967). For
Swedish reviews and contributions in this debate see
Lewin (1970, 1977), Westerståhl (1971) and Johansson
(1971b).
3 Swedish union officials who resign before retirement
age usually go to other branches of the labour movement, or to public service.
4 It would appear that the International Typographers'
Union studied by Lipset is just about the only union
that has had a functioning party system.
5 See Elvander (1969, ch. 3) for a survey of internal
democracy within Swedish voluntary organizations.
6 Lind (1938b), who was editor of the LO journal and
perhaps the most important 'ideologe' within the LO
at that time, argued for this drive partly in out-
spokenly elitist terms.
7 The unusual character of these negotiations is illustrated by the fact that they were the first direct
negotiations between the LO and the SAF since the
general strike in 1909.
8 Prior referendums were held in 1907, 1908, 1915 and
1918.
9 When a contract proposal covered more than one sector,
only a majority of the total vote (not a majority in
each sector) was required. A major exception occurred in the big engineering strike of 1945, when the
executive board signed the contract proposal when
also the fourth referendum failed to give a majority
in support of the course favoured by the union executive (cf. chapter 9).
10 It is often suggested that employer concessions granted after negative outcomes in referendums only prove
that employers are more cautious, and do not yield as
much as they otherwise would when they know that the

contract proposal will be submitted to a referendum.
Since usually less than half of the contract proposals are turned down in the first referendum, and
amended proposals are also subject to a referendum,
this reasoning implies that labour will lose in a bargaining system where referendums are used. It
appears, however, that both employers and union representatives have an interest in presenting members
with a proposal that will be accepted in the first
referendum. Employers can therefore be expected to
concede as much as they regard as necessary and possible already before the first referendum.

11 Expulsion because of failure to pay membership dues
is, however, decided by the branch.

12 This rule is still valid. Since the 1950s, however,
the small branches are again over-represented to some
extent, since the executive board now adjusts representation to give the large branches the minimum possible representation required by the present rules.

13 This was at the congress in 1919, which had a strong
left-wing opposition.

14 These figures exclude officials in the construction
sector with very special functions in the measurement
of the volume of production on behalf of the members.

15 The regional district organization of the union, in
existence from 1916 to 1926, constituted a possible
base for an opposition as long as its executive board
was elected directly by the members concerned. When
the congress began to elect representatives to the
district boards, the possibility of these organizations to function as power bases for the opposition
was undercut. Some LO unions, however, have maintained regional organizations (Carlsson, 1969, pp.
103-5).

16 In recent years also the largest works clubs have been
authorized to introduce an elected assembly to replace
the membership meeting in the works club.

17 The study activities in the union have expanded
strongly in recent years. In 1975-6 about 5 per cent
of the members participated in study groups on union
organization, collective bargaining or work environment. Another 5 per cent participated in language
training courses for immigrants.

18 At least since the early 1940s a ten-minute time limit
for speeches by the elected delegates has been imposed
at the beginning of the congress, while no time limit
has been set for those presenting the views and proposals of the union council. The elected delegates
have made the majority of the speeches and proposals

throughout this period, but here also the same tendency towards decreasing activity from the elected delegates can be observed.

19 The association between perceived membership influence in the works club and in the union is presumably also a result of 'spurious' factors which affect both variables, and not merely differences in the functioning of the works club.

20 The income of some of the leaders of the LO and the unions are of course considerably higher because of increments coming from other positions and tasks that follow with union leadership.

21 The Nothin Commission had, in fact, argued that, by increasing centralization through giving the union executive decisive power in collective bargaining, and by abolishing referendums on contract proposals, important contributions could be made to industrial peace. The increase in centralization introduced with the new 'normal statutes' in 1941 were partly motivated by the argument that the LO was now also to become an organization for attack. The union commission behind this proposal did however recognise the limited relevance of this argument by stating that (LO, 1941, p. 197):

> when the right of organization has been recognized and the labour market has become stabilized through organization and cooperation between the organizations of workers and of employers, open conflicts no longer have the same importance as before.

22 The figures given here are also supported by other data. In a study among LO members carried out in 1974, Lewin (1977, p. 172) found that 73 per cent of the LO members agreed with the following statement: 'The board members of the national unions and the top officials in the LO can be justly criticized for too much domination in union affairs.'

CHAPTER 9 THE INTERNAL UNION OPPOSITION

1 The Liberal influence was most persistent in the Typographers' Union, where it lasted up to the end of the First World War (Björklund, 1965, pp. 161-204). From 1899 to 1910 a liberal, 'yellow' union organization existed outside the LO (Myrman, 1973).

2 Ideally, one would like to make some kind of a cluster analysis of voting patterns, and to define the opposition in terms of consistency of support for, or opposition to, the proposals of the union leadership.

This, however, can not be attempted here, partly because voting has only occasionally been done through roll calls. The method used here is admittedly more arbitrary.

3 Johan-Olov Johansson was treasurer of the LO up to 1936. He was also Social Democratic chairman of the city council of Stockholm, author of several books on the life of the common people in the iron industry and a popular radio reciter.

4 For male workers the index of real hourly wages (money wages in relation to a cost of living index, including taxes and social benefits) changed in the following way:

1939	100
1940	95
1941	90
1942	90
1943	93
1944	94

The decrease in real wages was somewhat less among men in the metal-working industry (SOS, 1952, pp. 79-80).

5 At the contract conference in May, Westerlund was thus convinced that the majority of the members would accept a contract proposal that was not as good as the original proposal of the executive board which was turned down in the second referendum in the middle of March, and considerably worse than the proposal that was to be turned down at the fourth referendum in the end of June.

6 Four different ways of describing branches and communities have been explored: size of branch; size of the community in which the branch is located; the proportion of metal-workers in the economically active population in the community (Ahlberg, 1953, pp. 289-91 and Tables XII and XV); and a combination of community size and size of firm. The last-named way yields the strongest and most consistent association with opposition strength and will therefore be used in the analysis that follows.

7 The classification of branches is based on data on size of firms in the 1919 membership registry of the SAF, and on data on industrial structure on the community level in SOS (1919).

8 Branches are classified on the basis of information in the 1944 contract inventory of the union on the number of workers in different firms in the branches.

9 Information is taken from the contract inventories of the union, the official statistics on general elections in the years 1918-20 and 1941-4, the membership

registry of the SAF for 1919, and from SOS: Industri (1920 and 1945).

10 Since 1916, the Eskilstuna branch appears to have sent only one oppositional delegate to any of the congresses of the Metal Workers' Union. This delegate was called in as a substitute at the 1919 congress, when the originally elected delegate was rejected by the left-wing congress majority on the grounds that, in an extra job in a newsstand, he had sold newspapers boycotted by the typographers because strike-breakers had been used by these papers.

11 For individual workers the damages have been maximized to 200 kronor. In 1976, however, the Labour Court was authorized to increase damages for individual workers. The firing of workers leading unofficial strikes was also legalized in the mid-1970s.

CHAPTER 10   WORKING-CLASS POLITICS AND THE UNION

1 These data are based on secondary analyses of panel surveys on party preferences in the Swedish population carried out by the Central Bureau of Statistics. Information on occupation and income are taken from the 1970 census and from the tax registers. I wish to thank Staffan Sollander and Bo Wärneryd of the Central Bureau of Statistics for aid in the data processing.

2 The occupational classification used here is based on a multi-dimensional system of socioeconomic classification of occupations proposed by Carlsson et al. (1974). A basic dimension in the system is the distinction between entrepreneurs and employees. Among the entrepreneurs a distinction is made between farmers and others. Employed persons are separated into two broad categories according to the traditional lines of differentiation between occupational groups organized by the LO or by the unions for salaried employees. This is a broad distinction between 'blue-collar' and 'white-collar' employees, but some categories of lower salaried employees are included in the LO unions. Among the employees a further distinction is made according to the number of years of formal training above compulsory schooling normally required for the job. This is taken as an indication of position of the job in the organizational hierarchy of the employing organization.

3 The survey of party preferences by the Central Bureau of Statistics is also used here.

4 These differences may partly reflect differences in

age, the Communists being on the average somewhat younger than the Social Democrats.

5   These data can be found in Petersson and Särlvik (1974).

6   These occupations include e.g. sales clerks, postmen, train conductors, firemen, policemen and hospital workers.

7   The occupational categories are: (i) manual workers; (ii) lower white collar; (iii) other white collar; (iv) self-employed entrepreneurs, and (v) farmers.

8   The limitation of these data to persons in the labour force imply that in the youngest age groups those involved in higher education, who are especially likely to support the bourgeois parties, are excluded. Other data bases, however, also indicate that in the younger non-manual groups socialist support is considerably higher than in the older age groups.

9   The slight increase in social mobility, which probably has taken place in Sweden in the postwar period (Erikson, 1971), may also have contributed to decrease differences in voting patterns between manual and non-manual occupations.

10 The proportion of married women in the labour force increased from 14 per cent in 1950 to 58 per cent in 1975.

11 The pattern of inter-generational political change among sons of Social Democratic fathers and the choice of a 'second-best' party among the Social Democratic metal-workers indicates that among them the Communist Party has been a closer alternative than the bourgeois parties.   This need not, however, always have been so.   A study by Dahlström (1954) indicates that, when the Social Democrats and the Agrarian Party were in a government coalition during the Cold War period, only a small minority of industrial workers preferred the Communist Party as the second-best party.   Among all Social Democratic voters in 1973 the bourgeois parties were preferred as 'second-best' parties over the Communist Party by approximately 2 to 1 (Petersson and Särlvik, 1974).   Among the Social Democratic workers the Communist Party is thus apparently more often the alternative party than among other party supporters.

12 Figures not given here indicate that the pattern of inter-generational political change among women and foreign-born workers is largely the same as the ones reported here for the Swedish-born men.

13 Because of the skewed distribution in the dependent variable (small proportions of Communists), certain 'ceiling effects' may appear in the analysis (cf. Andrews et al., 1973).

14   The Communist proportion is slightly lower in the
     small firms. In the very small firms with less than
     fifty workers, which were not represented in our
     sample, the Communist proportion might be even lower.
15   Processes of downward social mobility are partly in-
     volved here.   Of fathers indicated to have bourgeois
     party preferences, 75 per cent were farmers or in
     middle-class occupations as against 26 per cent of
     all fathers.
16   The decrease in bourgeois party preferences with in-
     creasing length of employment in industry is presum-
     ably to some extent also a result of selective upward
     social mobility.
17   The proportional reduction of error when predicting
     the party preference of the son with, rather than
     without, knowledge of the party preference of the
     father in firms with a low, medium and high level of
     political competition is 0, 6 and 8 per cent respec-
     tively.   The number of workers with Communist fathers
     in firms with low, medium and high levels of political
     competition was 36, 48 and 29, respectively.   Of all
     workers in our population 31 per cent were in firms
     with a low level of political competition, 48 per cent
     in firms with a medium level and 22 per cent in firms
     with a high level of political competition.
18   In a survey of a random sample of LO members in 1974,
     Lewin (1977, p. 144) found that 64 per cent of rank-
     and-file members, 56 per cent of members of branch
     boards and 33 per cent of elected officials at the
     national level agreed with the following statement:
     'Collective affiliation to the Social Democratic Party
     is a bad form for membership in a political party.'

CHAPTER 11   THE LABOUR MOVEMENT IN WELFARE CAPITALISM

1   These involve e.g. expenditures for education, health,
    housing, roads, public services, unemployment benefits
    and public work projects.
2   Several of the problems discussed here, especially
    those connected with pollution of the environment,
    finite resources and meaningful jobs are found also in
    industrialized Communist countries.
3   This is the case irrespective of whether the working
    class is defined in terms of the censuses or whether
    more refined categorizations of the census data are
    made in Marxist terms (Therborn, 1976).
4   The opportunities for career mobility, however, may
    have been retained, partly because adult education in
    Sweden has expanded very rapidly since the 1960s.

5   Immigrants from the common Nordic labour market have
    the same social rights as Swedish citizens.   After
    receiving residence permits, immigrants from other
    countries have right to employment which is not res-
    tricted in time nor to a particular employer, right to
    social services, right to language training during
    paid working time and, since 1976, the right to vote
    in communal and regional elections.

6   Data from retrospective questions in the Level of
    Living Survey indicate that among persons born before
    1930, somewhat above 30 per cent had lived in more
    than one community during their childhood.   This
    figure has increased to somewhat above 50 per cent
    among persons born in the late 1950s.

7   The general opinion in the public debate in Sweden is
    that social segregation in housing has increased in
    recent years.   This assumption thus can not be cor-
    roborated with empirical data.

8   Ingham (1974) has suggested that the high level of
    organization among Swedish employers reflects struc-
    tural features, primarily the great importance of
    export industries which did not have to compete with
    each other.   This may have facilitated organization
    but it must be remembered that the home market indus-
    tries appear to have dominated the Swedish Employers'
    Federation (SAF).

9   A follow-up study of persons, who moved from northern
    Sweden to the south with the support of the Labour
    Market Board because of difficulties to find employ-
    ment, indicates that relatively large proportion
    moved back to their community of origin and that of
    those who remained, a large proportion indicated that
    they would return to their original community if they
    could find equivalent employment there (Åberg, 1974).

10 The majority proposal of the parliamentary commission
    working on the issue of enlarging the influence of
    employees in the firms was that the influence of
    the wage earners should be channelled through new
    organs for co-determination on the firm level, with
    equal representations for employees and management.
    Representatives of the LO and TCO on the commission
    dissented, presenting an alternative proposal, where
    the unions would be given greater bargaining rights
    and improved bargaining power.   The Social Democratic
    government followed the LO/TCO proposal.

11 In 1975 tax credits to industry amounted to 27,000
    million Sw. Crowns, or 11 per cent of the total value
    of machinery, buildings and stocks of industry (LO,
    1976, p. 54).   From 1953-7 to 1965-8 effective tax

rates in industry lessened from 47 per cent to 34 per
cent, and partly compensated falling profits (Bergström, 1973, pp. 33-4).   The rules for taxation
favour especially the expanding, profitable firms.
In 1974, e.g. Sweden's largest and profitable export
firm, the Volvo, paid no taxes to the state.

12   The profits from the shares controlled by the wage-
earners' funds were to be administered by a special
organ and to be used for buying shares as well as for
programmes to improve the ability of the employees
to exercise their influence, directed especially to
the employees in the small firms.

13   This report, however, also recognized that the uneven
distribution of shareholding was an important obstacle
to general acceptance of high profits in private
firms.   In therefore discussed various ways of broadening ownership of shares, suggesting the creation of
funds administered by employees, to which the firms
would supply dues in relation to the sum of their
wages.   A large number of such funds should be created, acting independently of one another, without
attempting to achieve a dominant proportion of shares
in any one firm.

14   During this campaign, the ratings of the Social Democrats in response to the question: 'Which party do
you think is best today?' fell from 44 per cent in
February to 38.5 per cent in April according to the
SIFO poll.

15   These data come from the 'Party Preference Surveys'
carried out by the Central Bureau of Statistics and
comprising about 9000 respondents.   In the survey
from September 1976, the trend in the data is arrived
at through the following procedure.   The accumulated
number of interviews carried out up to a specific
date is taken as the basis for an estimation of party
choice in the electorate.   It is thus possible to
obtain estimates of voting intentions in the electorate for each day in the two-week period preceding
the election day, 19 September.   Since respondents
were not randomly distributed with respect to the date
for the interview, systematic errors are here possible.   Controls on data collected in the three other
party preference surveys carried out in 1976, two in
the first half of the year and the last one after the
election, does not, however, indicate similar trends
in the development of party preferences during the
two-week data collection period.

16   These data come from a mail survey carried out after
the election by the Swedish Radio and comprising 700

respondents.   In this survey, 9 per cent of the respondents indicated that the issue of nuclear energy
was *the* decisive issue for their party choice as
against 4 per cent for whom the 'wage-earners' funds'
had played a similar role.   I wish to thank Ronney
Henningsson for providing me with these figures.

17   In comparison with the 1973 election the Social Democrats lost 0.9 per cent of the vote.   According to
the SIFO poll, the proportion regarding the programme
of their own party as 'very good' increased among the
Social Democrats from 51 per cent in 1973 to 55 per
cent in 1976.   In 1973 only 37 per cent of the electorate preferred the Social Democratic leader, Palme,
as prime minister while 39 per cent preferred his
bourgeois opponent, Fälldin.   In 1976 Palme was preferred by 48 per cent of the respondents as against
29 per cent for Fälldin (SIFO, 1976).

18   According to Lenin's well-known assumption workers and
unions, by themselves, can develop only 'trade union
consciousness', i.e. demands limited to improvements
within the capitalistic system, while policies trans-
cending the capitalist system require participation by
intellectuals in vanguard political parties.   Similar
flattering assumptions are still common among intellectuals (Parkin, 1971, p. 91; Mann, 1973, p. 73).
The present analysis indicates that social consciousness and levels of aspiration depend on relative power
resources.   A weak working class is limited to 'economism'.   As the LO proposal on wage-earners' funds
indicates, powerful class-based union organizations
will come to question also the control structure in
industry and clearly transcend 'trade union consciousness'.

Bibliography

ABUKHANFUSA, K. (1975), 'Beredskapsfamiljernas Försörj-
ning' (The provision of soldiers' families), Stockholm:
Liber.
ADLER-KARLSSON, G. (1967), 'Functional Socialism', Stock-
holm: Prisma.
AHLBERG, G. (1953), 'Befolkningsutveckling och Urbanis-
ering i Sverige 1911-50' (Population Development and Ur-
banization in Sweden 1911-50), Stockholm: Stockholms
Kommunalförvaltning.
AHLSÉN, B. et al. (1972), 'Från Palm till Palme' (From
Palm to Palme), Stockholm: Rabén & Sjögren.
ALFORD, R.R. (1963), 'Party and Society', Chicago: Rand
McNally.
ALFORD, R.R. (1967), Class voting in the Anglo-American
political systems, in S.M. Lipset and S. Rokkan (eds),
'Party Systems and Voter Alignments', New York: Free
Press, pp. 67-94.
ALLARDT, E. (1964a), A theory on solidarity and legiti-
macy conflicts, in E. Allardt and Y. Littunen (eds),
'Cleavages, Ideologies and Party Systems', Helsinki:
Transactions of the Westermarck Society, X, pp. 78-96.
ALLARDT, E. (1964b), Patterns of class conflict and work-
ing class consciousness in Finnish politics, in E. Allardt
and Y. Littunen (eds), 'Cleavages, Ideologies and Party
Systems', Helsinki: Transactions of the Westermarck
Society, X, pp. 97-131.
ALLEN, V.L. (1954), 'Power in Trade Unions', London:
Longman.
ALMOND, G.A. and VERBA, S. (1963), 'The Civic Culture',
Princeton University Press.
ALTHUSSER, L. (1969), 'For Marx', Harmondsworth: Allen
Lane.
ANDRÉ, C.G. (1975), Proletära organisationsformer 1917:
militärdemonstrationerna och arbetarkommittén (Forms of

proletarian organization in 1917: anti-military demonstrations and the Workers Committee), 'Arkiv för Studier i Arbetarrörelsens Historia',(7-8), pp. 88-108.

ANDREWS, F.A. et al. (1973), 'Multiple Classification Analysis. A Report on a Computer Program for Multiple Regression Using Categorical Predictions', Ann Arbor, University of Michigan Press.

ARGYRIS, C. (1964), 'Integrating the Individual and the Organization', New York: Wiley.

ARON, R. (1967), '18 Lectures on Industrial Society', London: Weidenfeld & Nicholson.

ARVIDSSON, H. (1975), Sprängningen av Sveriges Kommunistiska Parti 1924 (The break in the Swedish Communist Party in 1924), in S.E. Olsson (ed.), 'Från SKP till VPK', Lund: Zenit/Cavefors, pp. 54-81.

ARVIDSSON, H. and BERNTSSON, L. (1975), Kommunistiska Internationalen (The Communist International), in S.E. Olsson (ed.), 'Från SKP till VPK', Lund: Zenit/Cavefors, pp. 9-32.

ASPELIN, G. (1969), 'Karl Marx: Samhällsforskare och Samhällskritiker' (Karl Marx: Social Scientist and Social Critic), Lund: Gleerup.

ASPELIN, G. (1972), 'Karl Marx som Sociolog' (Karl Marx as a Sociologist), Lund: Gleerup.

ATKINSON, J.W. (1964), 'An Introduction to Motivation', Princeton: Van Nostrand.

ATKINSON, A.B. (1975), 'The Economics of Inequality', Oxford: Clarendon Press.

AVINERI, S. (1968), 'The Social and Political Thought of Karl Marx', Cambridge University Press.

AXELROD, R. (1970), 'Conflict of Interest', Chicago: Markham.

BACHRACH, P. (1967), 'The Theory of Democratic Elitism', Boston: Little, Brown.

BACHRACH, P. and BARATZ, M.S. (1970), 'Power and Poverty', London: Oxford University Press.

BACK, P.E. (1963), 'Svenska Metallindustriarbetareförbundets Historia 1925-1940' (The History of the Swedish Metal Workers' Union 1925-1940), Stockholm: Tiden

BAGGE, G. et al. (1933), 'Wages in Sweden, 1860-1930', London: King & Son.

BALDWIN, A. (1972), The costs of power, 'Journal of Conflict Resolution', 15, pp. 145-55.

BARAN, A. and SWEEZY, P.M. (1966), 'Monopoly Capital', New York: Monthly Review Press.

BARRY, B.M. (1970), 'Sociologists, Economists and Democracy', London: Macmillan.

BELL, D. (1972), 'The Coming of the Post-Industrial Society', New York: Basic Books.

BENDIX, R. (1956), 'Work and Authority in Industry',
New York: Wiley.
BENDIX, R. (1974), Inequality and social structure: a
comparison of Marx and Weber, 'American Sociological
Review', 39 (2), pp. 149-61.
BENDIX, R. and LIPSET, S.M. (1966), 'Class, Status and
Power: Social Stratification in Comparative Perspective',
New York: Free Press.
BENGTSSON, S.E. (1971), 'Vi eller Dom: Om Facklig
Demokrati' (We or Them: On Union Democracy), Stockholm:
Tiden.
BENTZEL, R. (1952), 'Inkomstfördelningen i Sverige' (The
Income Distribution in Sweden), Stockholm: Industrins
Utredningsinstitut.
BERELSON, B., LAZARSFELD, P.F. and MCPHEE, W.N. (1954),
'Voting', Chicago University Press.
BERGLIND, S. (1974), An analysis of Leif Lewin's 'The
Swedish Electorate', 'Statsvetenskaplig Tidskrift', 77,
pp. 113-22.
BERGSTRÖM, L. (1970), What is a conflict of interest?,
'Journal of Peace Research', 7 (3), pp. 197-218.
BERGSTRÖM, V. (1965), Övergiven utjämningspolitik? (Is
equality policy deserted?), 'Tiden', 57 (7), pp. 401-7.
BERGSTRÖM, V. (1973), 'Kapitalbildning och Industriell
Demokrati' (Capital Formation and Industrial Democracy),
Stockholm: Tiden.
BJÖRKLUND, B. (1965), 'Svenska Typografförbundet' (The
Swedish Typographers' Union), Stockholm: Tiden.
BLAKE, D.J. (1960), Swedish trade unions and the Social
Democratic Party, 'The Scandinavian Economic History
Review', VIII (1), pp. 19-44.
BLALOCK, H.M. (1967), 'Toward a Theory of Minority Group
Relations', New York: Wiley.
BLAU, P.M. (1964), 'Power and Exchange in Social Life',
New York: Wiley.
BLAU, P.M. and DUNCAN, O.D. (1967), 'The American Occupa-
tional Structure', New York: Wiley.
BLAUNER, R. (1960), Work satisfaction and industrial
trends in modern society, in W. Galenson and S.M. Lipset
(eds), 'Labor and Trade Unionisms: An Inter-Disciplinary
Reader', New York: Wiley, pp. 339-60.
BLAUNER, R. (1964), 'Alienation and Freedom: the Factory
Worker and his Industry', Chicago University Press.
BOALT, G. (1954), 'Arbetsgruppen.   En Undersökning av
Formell och Informell Gruppbildning i Industrin' (The Work
Group.   A Study of Formal and Informal Group Formation in
Manufacturing), Stockholm: Tiden.
BOALT, G. (1968), Ståndscirkulationen i Stockholm och
invandringen (Social mobility and migration in Stockholm),

in C.-G. Janson (ed.), 'Det Differentierade Samhället' (The Differentiated Society), Stockholm: Prisma, pp. 217-24.

BONACICH, E. (1972), A theory of ethnic antagonism: the split labor market, 'American Sociological Review', 37 (October), pp. 547-59.

BONACHICH, E. (1975), Abolition, the extension of slavery, and the position of the free blacks: a study of split labor markets in the United States, 1830-1863, 'American Journal of Sociology', 81 (3), pp. 601-28.

BORKENAU, F.C. (1962), 'A History of the Communist International', Ann Arbor: University of Michigan Press.

BOTTOMORE, T.B. and RUBEL, M. (eds) (1967), 'Karl Marx: Selected Writings in Sociology and Social Philosophy', London: Pelican.

BRANTING, H. (1929a), 'Tal och skrifter I. Socialistisk samhällssyn' (Speeches and Writings I. Socialistic Views on Society), Stockholm: Tiden.

BRANTING, H. (1929b), 'Tal och skrifter III. Kampen för Demokratin' (Speeches and Writings III. The Fight for Democracy), Stockholm: Tiden.

BRAVERMAN, H. (1974), 'Labor and Monopoly Capital. The Degradation of Work in the Twentieth Century', New York: Monthly Review Press.

BURNHAM, W.D. (1970), 'Critical Elections and the Mainsprings of American Politics', New York: Norton.

BURNS, T. and STALKER, G.M. (1961), 'The Management of Innovations', London: Tavistock.

BUTLER, D. and STOKES, D. (1969), 'Political Change in Britain', Harmondsworth: Penguin.

BÄCKSTRÖM, K. (1971), 'Arbetarrörelsen i Sverige' (The Labour Movement in Sweden), Stockholm: Rabén & Sjögren.

CAMPBELL, A. et al. (1960), 'The American Voter', New York: Wiley.

CAPLOW, T. (1968), 'Two Against One: Coalitions in Triads', Englewood Cliffs, New Jersey: Prentice-Hall.

CARLSSON, B. (1969), 'Trade Unions in Sweden', Stockholm: Tiden.

CARLSSON, C., DAHLIN, E. and NILSSON, E.T. (1976), SKP och 30-talet (The Swedish Communist Party and the 1930s), in S.E. Olsson (ed.), 'Från SKP till VPK', Lund: Zenit/ Cavefors, pp. 151-73.

CARLSSON, G. (1958), 'Social Mobility and Class Structure', Lund: Gleerup.

CARLSSON, G. et al. (1974), Socio-ekonomiska grupperingar (Socioeconomic groupings), 'Statistisk Tidskrift', 12 (5), pp. 381-401.

CARLSSON, S. (1966), Den sociala omgrupperingen i Sverige efter 1866 (The social regrouping in Sweden after 1866),

in A. Thompson (ed.), 'Samhälle och riksdag', Stockholm:
Almqvist & Wiksell, pp. 1-374.

CASPARSSON, R. (1966), 'LO: Bakgrund, Utveckling och
Verksamhet', (The LO: Background, Development and Activities), Stockholm: Tiden.

CASPARSSON, R. (1974), 'LO under Fem Årtionden' (The LO
During Five Decades), Stockholm: Tiden.

CASTLES, S. and KOSACK, G. (1973), 'Immigrant Workers and
Class Structure in Western Europe', London: Oxford University Press.

CHILD, J. (1972), Organizational structure, environment
and performance: the role of strategic choice, 'Sociology', 6 (January), pp. 1-22.

CHILDS, M. (1961), 'Sweden: The Middle Way', New Haven:
Yale University Press.

COHEN, J., HAZZELRIGG, L.E. and POPE, W. (1975), De-
Parsonizing Weber: a critique of Parson's interpretation
of Weber's sociology, 'American Sociological Review', 40
(April), pp. 229-41.

COHEN, P.S. (1968), 'Modern Social Theory', London:
Heinemann.

COLEMAN, J.S. (1957), 'Community Conflict', Chicago:
Free Press.

COLEMAN, J.S. (1961), 'The Adolescent Society', Chicago:
Free Press.

COLEMAN, J.S. (1971), Foundations for a theory of collective decisions, in B. Lieberman (ed.), 'Social Choice',
New York: Gordon & Breach.

CONVERSE, E. (1968), The war of all against all: a
review of the 'Journal of Conflict Resolution', 1957-1968,
'Journal of Conflict Resolution', 12, pp. 471-532.

COSER, L. (1956), 'The Functions of Social Conflict',
London: Routledge & Kegan Paul.

COSER, L. (1967), 'Continuities in the Study of Social
Conflict', New York: Free Press.

CRAIG, J.G. and GROSS, E. (1970), The forum theory of
organizational democracy: structural guarantees as time-
related variables, 'American Sociological Review', 35
(February), pp. 19-33.

CROMPTON, R. (1976), Approaches to the study of white-
collar unionism, 'Sociology', 10 (3), pp. 407-26.

CRONER, F. (1963), 'Tjänstemännen' (The Salaried Em-
ployees), Stockholm: Rabén & Sjögren (also available in
German, 'Soziologie der Angestellten', Köln: Kiepenheuer
& Witsch).

CROZIER, M. (1964), 'The Bureaucratic Phenomenon', Chicago
University Press.

CURRIE, E. and SKOLNICK, J.H. (1970), A critical note on
conceptions of collective violence, 'The Annals of the

American Academy of Political and Social Science', 391, pp. 34-45.

DAHL, R.A. (1956), 'A Preface to Democratic Theory', Chicago University Press.

DAHL, R.A. (1961), 'Who Governs? Democracy and Power in an American City', New Haven: Yale University Press.

DAHLSTRÖM, E. (1954), 'Tjänstemännen, Näringslivet och Samhället' (The Salaried Employees, Industry and Society), Stockholm: SNS.

DAHLSTRÖM, E. (1966), Exchange, influence and power, 'Acta Sociologica', 9 (3-4), pp. 237-80.

DAHLSTRÖM, E. et al. (1966), 'Teknisk Förändring och Arbetsanpassning' (Technological Change and Work Adjustment), Stockholm: Prisma.

DAHRENDORF, R. (1959), 'Class and Class Conflict in Industrial Society', Stanford University Press.

DAVIES, J.C. (1962), Toward a theory of revolution, 'American Sociological Review', 27 (February), pp. 5-18.

DAVIS, L.E. and TAYLOR, J.C. (eds) (1972), 'Design of Jobs', Harmondsworth: Penguin.

DAVIS, L.E. and TAYLOR, J.C. (1975), Technology effects on job, work and organizational structure: a contingency view, in L.E. Davis and A.B. Cherns, 'The Quality of Working Life: Problems, Prospects and the State of the Art', New York: Free Press, pp. 220-41.

DIAMOND, L. (1975), 'Royal Commission on the Distribution of Income and Wealth', Report no. 1, London: HMSO.

DONOVAN, Lord (1968), 'The Royal Commission on Trade Unions and Employers' Associations 1965-1968: Report', London: HMSO.

DOWNS, A. (1957), 'An Economic Theory of Democracy', New York: Harper & Row.

DREYFUSS, C. (1952), Prestige gradings: a mechanism of control, in R.K. Merton et al. (eds), 'Reader in Bureaucracy', Chicago: Free Press, pp. 258-64.

DUBIN, R. (1958), 'The World of Work', Englewood Cliffs, New Jersey: Prentice-Hall.

EDELSTEIN, J.D. (1967), An organizational theory of union democracy, 'American Sociological Review', 32 (February), pp. 19-39.

EDELSTEIN, J.D. and WARNER, M. (1976), 'Comparative Union Democracy', New York: Halsted Press.

EDLUND, S. (1967), 'Tvisteförhandlingar på Arbetsmarknaden. En Rättslig Studie av Två Riksavtal i Tillämpning (Negotiation Procedures in Labour Disputes. A Legal Study of the Functioning of Two National Collective Agreements), Stockholm: Norstedt.

EDLUND, S. (1973), Perspektiv på arbetsdomstolen (Perspectives on the Labour Court), in LO, 'Tvärsnitt', Stockholm: Prisma, pp. 455-84.

EKLUND, P. (1973), Rätten i klasskampen - en studie i
rättens funktioner (The law in class conflict - a study in
the functions of law), in LO, 'Tvärsnitt', Stockholm:
Prisma, pp. 399-454.
EKLUND, P. (1974), 'Rätten i Klasskampen' (The Law in the
Class Struggle), Stockholm: Tiden.
ELVANDER, N. (1969), 'Intresseorganisationerna i Dagens
Sverige (The Interest Organizations in Sweden Today),
Lund: Gleerup.
EMERY, F.E. and TRIST, E.L. (1960), Socio-technical sys-
tems, in C.W. Churchman and M. Verhulst (eds), 'Management
Science: Models and Techniques', vol. 2, Oxford Univer-
sity Press.
ENGELS, F. (1969), 'The Condition of the Working Class in
England', London: Panther Books.
ERIKSON, R. (1971), 'Uppväxtforhållanden och Social
Rörlighet' (Conditions during Childhood and Social Mobil-
ity), Stockholm: Allmänna Förlaget.
ERIKSON, R. (1976), Patterns of social mobility, in
R. Scase (ed.), 'Readings in Swedish Class Structure',
London: Pergamon, pp. 171-204.
ERIKSSON, K. (1973), Facklig demokrati (Union democracy),
report no. 6, Department of Sociology, University of
Göteborg (mimeo).
ERLANDER, T. (1972), 'Tage Erlander 1909-1939', Stockholm:
Tiden.
ERLANDER, T. (1973), 'Tage Erlander 1940-1949', Stockholm:
Tiden.
ETZIONI, A. (1961), 'A Comparative Analysis of Complex
Organizations', New York: Free Press.
FAUNCE, W.A. and DUBIN, R. (1975), Individual investment
in working and living, in L.E. Davis and A.B. Cherns,
'The Quality of Working Life: Problems, Prospects and the
State of the Art', New York: Free Press, pp. 299-316.
FEIERABEND, I.K., FEIERABEND, R.I. and NESVOLD, B.A.
(1969), Social change and political violence: cross-
national patterns, in H.D. Graham and T.R. Gurr (eds),
'Violence in America: Historical and Comparative Perspectives', Washington: US Government Printing Office.
FINK, C.F. (1968), Some conceptual difficulties in the
theory of social conflict, 'Journal of Conflict Resolution', 12, pp. 412-60.
FORSEBÄCK, L. (1976), 'Industrial Relations and Employment
in Sweden', Stockholm: The Swedish Institute.
FOX, A. (1966), 'Industrial Sociology and Industrial Relations', London: HMSO.
FOX, A. (1973), Industrial relations: a social critique
of pluralist ideology, in J. Child (ed.), 'Man and Organization', London: Allen & Unwin, pp. 185-233.

FOX, A. (1974), 'Beyond Contract: Work, Power and Trust Relations', London: Faber & Faber.

FREDRIKSSON, G., STRAND, D. and SÖDERSTEN, B. (1970), 'Per-Albin-linjen'(The Per Albin line), Stockholm: Pan/ Norstedts.

FRIEDMAN, G. (1961), 'The Anatomy of Work, The Implications of Specialization', London: Heinemann.

FULCHER, J. (1973), Class conflict in Sweden, 'Sociology', 7, pp. 49-70.

GALBRAITH, J.K. (1967), 'The New Industrial State', New York: Signet Books.

GALTUNG, J. (1966), Rank and social integration, in J. Berger, M. Zelditch Jr and B. Anderson (eds), 'Sociological Theories in Progress', Boston: Houghton Mifflin.

GAMSON, W.A. (1961), A theory of coalition formation, 'American Sociological Review', 26 (4), pp. 373-82.

GAMSON, W.A. (1968), 'Power and Discontent', Homewood, Illinois: Dorsey Press.

GARDELL, B. (1971), 'Produktionsteknik och Arbetsglädje' (Production Technology and Joy in One's Work), Stockholm: PA-rådet.

GARDELL, B. (1976), 'Arbetsinnehåll och Livskvalitet' (Job Content and Quality of Life), Stockholm: LO/Prisma.

GIDDENS, A. (1973), 'The Class Structure of the Advanced Societies', London: Hutchinson.

GOLDSTEIN, J. (1952), 'The Government of British Trade Unions', London: Allen & Unwin.

GOLDTHORPE, J.H. (1966), Social stratification in industrial society, in R. Bendix and S.M. Lipset (eds), 'Class, Status and Power', New York: Free Press.

GOLDTHORPE, J.H. (1971), Theories of industrial society: reflections on the recrudescence of historicism and the future of futurology, 'European Journal of Sociology', XII, pp. 263-88.

GOLDTHORPE, J.H. et al. (1968a), 'The Affluent Worker: Industrial Attitudes and Behaviour', Cambridge University Press.

GOLDTHORPE, J.H. et al. (1968b), 'The Affluent Worker: Political Attitudes and Behaviour', Cambridge University Press.

GOLDTHORPE, J.H. et al. (1969), 'The Affluent Worker in the Class Structure', Cambridge University Press.

GORZ, A. (1964), 'Strategy for Labour', Boston: Beacon Press.

GREEN, B.F. (1954), Attitude measurement, in G. Lindzey (ed.), 'Handbook of Social Psychology' (vol. 1), Cambridge, Massachusetts: Addison-Wesley, pp. 335-69.

GRIMSHAW, A.D. (1970), Interpreting collective violence: an argument for the importance of social structure, 'The

Annals of the American Academy of Political and Social
Science', 391, pp. 9-20.
GUNNARSSON, G. (1971), 'Socialdemokratiskt Idéarv' (The
Ideological Heritage of Social Democracy), Stockholm:
Tiden.
GURR, T.R. (1970),''Why Men Rebel', Princeton University
Press.
GUSTAFSSON, B. (1965), Det religiösa livet (The religious
life), in E. Dahlström (ed.), 'Svensk Samhällsstruktur i
Sociologisk Belysning, Stockholm: Svenska Bokförlaget,
pp. 313-47.
GUSTAFSSON, B. (1969), The established church and the
decline of church attendence in Sweden, in N. Birnbaum and
G. Lenzer (eds), 'Sociology and Religion', Englewood
Cliffs, New Jersey: Prentice-Hall, pp. 360-6.
GUSTAFSSON, G. (1974), 'Partistyrka och Partistyrkeförsk-
jutningar (Party Strength and Changes in Party Strength),
Lund: Studentlitteratur.
GÄRDVALL, L. (1974), 'Revolutionärerna i fackföreningsrörelsen - Organiserad opposition i svensk fackföreningsrörelse 1917-1922' (The Revolutionaries in the Union Movement - Organized Opposition in the Swedish Union Movement,
1917-1922), University of Uppsala: Department of History
(mimeo).
GÄRDVALL, L. (1975), 'Enhetsfront med.socialdemokrater,
syndikalister och partilösa' (The United Front with
Social Democrats, Syndicalists and Independents), University of Uppsala: Department of History (mimeo).
HAAVIO-MANNILA, E. and JOHANSSON, S. (1974), 'Finska ut-
vandrares levnadsnivå i Sverige' (The Level of Living of
Finnish Emigrants in Sweden), Sosiologia (4), pp. 192-205.
HADENIUS, A. (1976), 'Facklig organisationsutveckling.
En studie av Landsorganisationen i Sverige' (The Develop-
ment of Union Organization. A Study of the Swedish LO),
Stockholm: Rabén & Sjögren.
HADENIUS, S. et al. (1974), 'Sverige efter 1900'(Sweden
after 1900), Stockholm: Aldus.
HAMILTON, R.F. (1967), 'Affluence and the French Worker in
the Fifth Republic', Princeton University Press.
HAMILTON, R.F. (1972), 'Class and Politics in the United
States', New York: Wiley.
HANSSON, P.A. (1929), 'Folk och klass' (People and Class),
Stockholm: Tiden, 21 (6), pp. 329-39.
HANSSON, S. (1938), 'Den Svenska Fackföreningsrörelsen'
(The Swedish Union Movement), Stockholm: Tiden.
HARSANYI, J.C. (1962), Measurement of social power, oppor-
tunity costs, and the theory of two-person bargaining
games, 'Behavioral Science', 7, pp. 68-80.
HAUSER, R.M. (1970), Context and consex: a cautionary

tale, 'American Journal of Sociology', 75 (4), pp. 645-64.
HAUSER, R.M. (1974), Contextual analysis revisited, 'Sociological Methods and Research', 2, pp. 365-75.
HAYEK, F.A. (1944), 'The Road to Serfdom', London: Routledge & Sons.
HELLSTRÖM, G. (1976), 'Jordbrukspolitik i industrisamhället' (Agricultural Policy in Industrial Society), Stockholm: LTs förlag.
HENTILÄ, S. (1974), Orsaker till reformismens genombrott i svensk socialdemokrati (Causes of the reformistic breakthrough in Swedish social democracy), 'Arkiv för Studier i Arbetarrörelsens Historia, (5), pp. 3-20.
HERMANSSON, C.H. (1959), 'Koncentration och Storföretag' (Concentration and Big Companies), Stockholm: Arbetarkultur.
HERZBERG, F. (1968), 'Work and the Nature of Man', London: Staples.
HERZBERG, F., MAUSNER, B. and SNYDERMAN, B.B. (1959), 'The Motivation to Work', New York: Wiley.
HIBBS, Jr, D.A. (1973), 'Industrial Conflict in Advanced Industrial Societies', Cambridge, Massachusetts: Massachusetts Institute of Technology Press.
HIMMELSTRAND, U. (1975), 'Structural Contradictions; Predicaments and Social Change in Sweden', paper presented to the British Sociological Association's Annual Conference at the University of Kent, Canterbury.
HIRDMAN, Y. (1974), 'SKP 1939-1945' (The Swedish Communist Party, 1939-1945), Stockholm: Liber.
HIRSCHMAN, A.O. (1970), 'Exit, Voice and Loyalty', Cambridge, Massachusetts: Harvard University Press.
HOBSBAWM, E.J. (1964), 'Labouring Men', London: Weidenfeld & Nicolson.
HOLMBERG, S. (1974), 'Riksdagen Representerar Svenska Folket' (The Riksdag Represents the Swedish People), Lund: Studentlitteratur.
HOMANS, G.C. (1961), 'Social Behaviour: Its Elementary Forms', New York: Harcourt, Brace & World.
HUNTFORD, R. (1971), 'The New Totalitarians', London: Allen Lane.
HYMAN, H.H. (1959), 'Political Socialization', Chicago: Free Press.
HYMAN, R. (1971), 'Marxism and the Sociology of Trade Unionism', London: Pluto.
HYMAN, R. (1972), 'Strikes', London: Fontana.
INGHAM, G.K. (1970), 'Size of Industrial Organization and Worker Behaviour', Cambridge University Press.
INGHAM, G.K. (1974), 'Strikes and Industrial Conflict: Britain and Scandinavia', London: Macmillan.
JACOBSSON, A. (1970), 'Om Flyttningar i Sverige' (On Mobility in Sweden), Stockholm: Statistiska Centralbyrån.

JACOBSSON, L. and LINDBECK, A. (1969), Labor market conditions and inflation - Swedish experiences 1955-67, 'Swedish Journal of Economics', 81 (2), pp. 64-103.

JANSON, C.G. (1961), 'Mandattilldelning och Regional Röstfördelning (Mandate Allocation and Regional Vote Distribution), Stockholm: Esselte.

JANSON, C.G. (1965), Urbanisering och flyttning (Urbanization and mobility), in E. Dahlström (ed.), 'Svensk Samhällsstruktur i Sociologisk Belysning (Sociological Perspectives on Swedish Social Structure), Stockholm: Svenska Bokforlaget, pp. 184-225.

JENCKS, C. et al. (1972), 'Inequality: A Reassessment of the Effect of Family and Schooling in America', New York: Harper & Row.

JEVONS, W.S. (1970), 'The Theory of Political Economy' (first published in 1871), Harmondsworth: Penguin.

JOHANNESSON, C. (1975), 'De Centrala Avtalsförhandlingarna och den Fackliga Demokratin (Centralized Collective Bargaining and Union Democracy), Lund Political Studies, Report no. 18, University of Lund.

JOHANSSON, S. (1971a), 'Om Levnadsnivåundersökningen' (On the Level of Living Survey), Stockholm: Allmänna Förlaget.

JOHANSSON, S. (1971b), 'Politiska Resurser' (Political Resources), Stockholm: Allmänna Förlaget.

JOHANSSON, S. (1974), 'När är Tiden Mogen?' (When is the Time Ripe?), Stockholm: Tiden.

JOHANSSON, S.-Å. (1967), 'Arbetsstudier: Begrepp och Metodik' (Work Studies: Concepts and Methods), Stockholm: Aldus.

JOHNSTON, T.L. (1962), 'Collective Bargaining in Sweden', London: Allen & Unwin.

JONES, H.G. (1976), 'Planning and Productivity in Sweden', London: Croom Helm.

JUNGENFELDT, K.G. (1966), 'Löneandelen och den Ekonomiska Utvecklingen' (The Share of Wages and the Economic Development), Stockholm: IUI.

JÄRNEK, M. (1971), 'Studier i Hushållens Inkomstförhållanden 1925-1964' (Studies in the Distribution of Income in Households, 1925-1964), Lund: Studentlitteratur.

JÖRBERG, L. (1961), 'Growth and Fluctuations of Swedish Industry 1869-1912', Lund: Gleerup.

JÖRBERG, L. (1966), Några tillväxtfaktorer i 1800-talets svenska industriella utveckling (Some growth factors in industrial development in Sweden in the nineteenth century), in R. Lundström (ed.), 'Kring Industrialismens Genombrott i Sverige', Stockholm: Wahlström & Widstrand.

JÖRBERG, L. (1970), 'The Industrial Revolution in Scandinavia', London: Fontana.

KARASEK, Jr, R.A. (1976), 'The Impact of the Work Environment on Life outside the Job', Swedish Institute for Social Research and Massachusetts Institute of Technology (mimeo.).
KARLBOM, T. (1955), 'Den Svenska Fackföreningsrörelsen' (The Swedish Union Movement), Stockholm: Tiden.
KARLBOM, T. (1969), 'Arbetarnas Fackföreningar' (The Unions of the Workers), Stockholm: Bok & Bild.
KARLEBY, N. (1926), 'Socialismen inför Verkligheten' (Socialism facing Reality), Stockholm: Tiden.
KASSALOW, E.M. (1969), 'Trade Unions and Industrial Relations', New York: Random House.
KENNERSTRÖM, B. (1974), 'Mellan Två Internationaler: Socialistiska Partiet 1929-1937' (Between Two Internationals: The Socialist Party 1927-1939), Lund: Arkiv Avhandlingsserie.
KENNERSTRÖM, B. (1976), Sprängningen av Sveriges Kommunistiska Parti 1929 (The break in the Swedish Communist Party in 1929), in S.E. Olsson (ed.), 'Från SKP till VPK', Lund: Zenit/Cavefors, pp. 82-105.
KERR, C. (1968), 'Marshall, Marx and Modern Times: The Multidimensional Society', Cambridge University Press.
KERR, C. and SIEGEL, A. (1954), The inter-industry propensity to strike, in A. Kornhauser, R. Dubin and A. Ross (eds), 'Industrial Conflict', New York: McGraw-Hill.
KERR, C. et al. (1960), 'Industrialism and Industrial Man', Cambridge, Massachusetts: Harvard University Press.
KERR, C. et al. (1973), 'Industrialism and Industrial Man' (second edn), Harmondsworth: Penguin.
KEY, Jr, V.O. (1961), 'Public Opinion and American Democracy', New York: Knopf.
KEY, Jr, V.O. (1966), 'The Responsible Electorate', Cambridge, Massachusetts: Harvard University Press.
KILBOM, K. (1953), 'Ur Mitt Livs Äventyr' (From the Adventure of my Life), Stockholm: Tiden.
KLOCKARE, S. (1967), 'Svenska Revolutionen 1917-1918' (The Swedish Revolution 1917-1918), Stockholm: Prisma.
KNOWLES, K.G.J.C. (1952), 'Strikes - A Study in Industrial Conflict', Oxford: Basil Blackwell.
KOBLIK, S. (1975), 'Sweden's Development from Poverty to Affluence 1750-1970', Minneapolis: University of Minnesota Press.
KORNHAUSER, A. (1965), 'Mental Health of the Industrial Worker', New York: Wiley.
KORNHAUSER, A. (1960), 'The Politics of Mass Society', London: Routledge & Kegan Paul.
KORPI, W. (1964), 'Social Pressures and Attitudes in Military Training', Stockholm: Almqvist & Wiksell.
KORPI, W. (1970), 'Varför Strejkar Arbetarna? En

Betraktelse över Konflikter, Makt och Rätt på Arbetsmarknaden (Why do Workers Strike?   An Essay on Conflicts, Power and Justice on the Labour Market), Stockholm: Tiden.
KORPI, W. (1971), Working class communism in western
Europe: rational or nonrational?, 'American Sociological
Review', 36 (December), pp. 971-84.
KORPI, W. (1972), Some problems in the measurement of
class voting, 'American Journal of Sociology', 78 (Novem-
ber), pp. 627-42.
KORPI, W. (1974a), Conflict, power and relative depriva-
tion, 'American Political Science Review', vol. LXVIII,
no. 4, December, pp. 1569-78.
KORPI, W. (1974b), Conflict and the balance of power,
'Acta Sociologica', 17 (2), pp. 99-114.
KORPI, W. (1975), Social policy and poverty in post-war
Sweden, 'Acta Sociologica', 18 (2-3), pp. 120-41.
KUHN, W. (1961), 'Bargaining in Grievance Settlement',
New York: Columbia University Press.
KUPFERBERG, F. (1972), Byggnadsarbetarstrejken 1933-34
(The strike among the construction workers 1933-34),
'Arkiv för Studier i Arbetarrörelsens Historia' (2),
pp. 36-60.
KUUSE, J. (1970), 'Inkomstutveckling och förmögenhetsför-
delning' (Changes in Income and Distribution of Property),
Report no. 23 from the Department of Economic History,
University of Göteborg.
KYLLÖNEN, T. (1951), Social characteristics of active
unionists, 'American Journal of Sociology', 55, pp. 528-
33.
LABOVITZ, S. (1967), Some observations on measurement and
statistics, 'Social Forces', 46 (December), pp. 151-60.
LABOVITZ, S. (1970), The assignment of numbers to rank
order categories, 'American Sociological Review', 35
(June), pp. 515-25.
LAFFERTY, W.M. (1971), 'Economic Development and the Res-
ponse of Labor in Scandinavia', Oslo: Universitetsfor-
laget.
LANDGREN, K.G. (1960), 'Den "Nya Ekonomin" i Sverige:
J.M. Keynes, E. Wigforss, B. Ohlin och Utvecklingen
1927-39' (The 'New Economics' in Sweden: J.M. Keynes,
E. Wigforss, B. Ohlin and the Development 1927-39),
Uppsala: Almqvist & Wiksell.
LANDGREN, K.G. (1972), Bakgrunden till 1930-talets kris-
politik (The background to the crises policy in the
1930s), 'Arkiv för Studier i Arbetarrörelsens Historia',
no. 2, pp. 96-107.
LAWRENCE, P.R. and LORSCH, J.W. (1967), 'Organization and
Environment', Boston: Harvard Business School.

423   Bibliography

LAZARSFELD, P.F., BERELSON, B. and GAUDET, H. (1944), 'The People's Choice', New York: Duell, Sloan & Pearce.
LAZARSFELD, P.F. and THIELENS, W. (1958), 'The Academic Mind', Chicago: Free Press.
LEGGETT, J.C. (1968), 'Class Race and Labor', New York: Oxford University Press.
LENSKI, G.E. (1966), 'Power and Privilege', New York: McGraw-Hill.
LERNER, D. (1958), 'The Passing of Traditional Society. Modernization in the Middle East', New York: Free Press.
LESTER, R.A. (1958), 'As Unions Mature: An Analysis of the Evolution of American Trade Unionism', Princeton University Press.
LEWIN, L. (1967), 'Planhushållningsdebatten' (The Debate on the Planned Economy), Stockholm: Almqvist & Wiksell.
LEWIN, L. (1970), 'Folket och Eliterna' (The People and the Elites), Stockholm: Almqvist & Wiksell.
LEWIN, L. (1974), 'The Swedish Electorate', Stockholm: Almqvist & Wiksell.
LEWIN, L. (1977), 'Hur styrs facket?   Om demokratin inom fackföreningsrörelsen' (How are the Unions Governed?   On Democracy in the Union Movement), Stockholm: Rabén & Sjögren.
LEWIN, L., JANSSON, B. and SÖRBOM, D. (1972), 'The Swedish Electorate 1887-1968', Stockholm: Almqvist & Wiksell.
LIKERT, R. (1961), 'New Patterns of Management', New York: McGraw-Hill.
LIND, A. (1938a), 'Facklig Demokrati' (Union Democracy), Stockholm: Tiden.
LIND, A. (1938b), 'Solidarisk Lönepolitik och Förhandsförhandlingar' (Solidaristic Wage Policy and Advance Negotiations), Stockholm: Tiden.
LINDBLAD, I. (1960), 'Svenska Kommunalarbetareförbundet 1910-1960' (The Swedish Municipal Workers' Union, 1910-1960), Stockholm: Tiden.
LINDBOM, T. (1938), 'Den Svenska Fackföreningsrörelsens Uppkomst' (The Origin of the Swedish Union Movement), Stockholm: Tiden.
LINDEBERG, S.O. (1968), 'Nödhjälpsarbete och Samhällsneutralitet: Svensk Arbetslöshetspolitik 1920-1923' (Relief Work and State Neutrality: Swedish Unemployment Policy 1920-1923), Lund: Gleerup.
LINDEROTH, S. (1972), 'Masslinjen' (The Mass Line), Stockholm: Arbetarkultur.
LINDGREN, J. (1927), 'Det Socialdemokratiska Partiets Uppkomst i Sverige, 1881-1889' (The Origin of the Social Democratic Party in Sweden, 1881-1889), Stockholm: Tiden.
LINDGREN, J. (1938), 'Svenska Metallindustriarbetareför-

bundets Historia 1888-1905' (The History of the Swedish
Metal Workers' Union), Stockholm: Tiden.
LINDGREN, J., TINGSTEN, H. and WESTERSTÅHL, J.
(1948),
'Svenska Metallindustriarbetareförbundets Historia,
1906-1925' (The History of the Swedish Metal Workers'
Union, 1906-1925), Stockholm: Tiden.
LINDHAGEN, J. (1972a), 'Socialdemokratins Program. I
Rörelsens tid 1890-1930' (The Social Democratic Programme.
In the time of the movement, 1890-1930), Stockholm:
Tiden.
LINDHAGEN, J. (1972b), 'Bolsjevikstriden' (The Fight with
the Bolsheviks), Stockholm: Tiden.
LINDSTRÖM, R. (1949), 'Föregångsmän' (Pioneers), Stock-
holm: Tiden, 41 (4), pp. 261-9.
LIPSET, S.M. (1960), 'Political Man', London: Mercury
Books.
LIPSET, S.M. (1964), The changing class structure of con-
temporary European politics, 'Daedalus', 63 (Winter), pp.
271-303.
LIPSET, S.M., TROW, M. and COLEMAN, J.S. (1956), 'Union
Democracy: The Internal Politics of the International
Typographic Union', Garden City, New York: Anchor Books.
LO (1941), 'Fackföreningsrörelsen och näringslivet' (The
Union Movement and Industry), Stockholm: Tiden.
LO (1951), 'Fackföreningsrörelsen och den Fulla
Sysselsättningen' (Trade Unions and Full Employment),
Stockholm: Tiden.   A modified version has been transla-
ted into English - see Turvey (1952).
LO (1961), 'Samordnad Näringspolitik', Stockholm: Tiden.
Translated into English (T.L. Johnson ed.) (1963), 'Eco-
nomic Expansion and Structural Change', London: Allen &
Unwin.
LO (1966), 'Fackföreningsrörelsen och den Tekniska
Utvecklingen', Stockholm: Prisma.   Translated into
English (1967), 'Trade Unions and Technological Change',
London: Allen & Unwin.
LO (1973), 'Tvärsnitt.   7 Forskningsrapporter Utgivna
till LO's 75-års-Jubileum' (Cross-Section.   Seven Re-
search Reports to the 75th Anniversary of the LO), Stock-
holm: Prisma.
LO (1974), 'LO-statistik' (Statistics on the LO), Stock-
holm: Tiden.
LO (1976), 'Kollektiv Kapitalbildning Genom Löntagarfon-
der' (Collective Capital Formation Through Wage-Earners'
Funds), Stockholm: Prisma.
LOCKWOOD, D. (1958), 'The Blackcoated Worker', London:
Allen & Unwin.
LUNDBERG, E. (1958), 'Konjunkturer och ekonomisk politik'
(Business Cycles and Economic Policy), Stockholm: SNS.

LYSGAARD, S. (1961), 'Arbeiderkollektivet' (The Workers' Collectivity), Oslo: Universitetsforlaget.

LYSGAARD, S. (1965), 'Arbeidernes Syn på Facklige og Politiske Spörsmål' (The Workers' Views on Union and Political Issues), Oslo: Universitetsforlaget.

MCCARTHY, W.E.J. (1967), 'The Role of Shop Stewards in British Industrial Relations', London: HMSO.

MCGREGOR, D. (1960), 'The Human Side of Enterprise', New York: McGraw-Hill.

MCGREGOR, D. (1966), 'Leadership and Motivation', Cambridge, Massachusetts: Massachusetts Institute of Technology Press.

MCKENZIE, R. (1964), 'British Political Parties', London: Mercury Books.

MCKENZIE, R. and SILVER, A. (1968), 'Angels in Marble: Working Class Conservatives in Urban England', London: Heinemann.

MALLET, S. (1963), 'La Nouvelle Classe Ouvrière', Paris: Éditions du Seuil.

MANN, M. (1970), The social cohesion of liberal democracy, 'American Sociological Review', 35 (3), pp. 423-39.

MANN, M. (1973), 'Consciousness and Action Among the Western Working Class', London: Macmillan.

MARCH, J.G. and SIMON, H.A. (1958), 'Organizations', New York: Wiley.

MARCUSE, H. (1964), 'One-Dimensional Man', Boston: Beacon Press.

MARSHALL, T.H. (1950), 'Citizenship and Social Class', Cambridge University Press.

MARSHALL, T.H. (1970), 'Social Policy in the Twentieth Century', London: Hutchinson.

MARSHALL, T.H. (1972), Value problems of welfare-capitalism, 'Journal of Social Policy', vol. 1, January, pp. 15-32.

MARTIN, A. (1973), 'The Politics of Economic Policy in the United States: A Tentative View from a Comparative Perspective', Beverly Hills, California: Sage.

MARTIN, R. (1968), Union democracy: an explanatory framework, 'Sociology', 2 (2), pp. 205-20.

MARX, K. (1967), 'The Capital', vols I-III, New York: International Publishers.

MARX, K. (1969), 'Theories of Surplus Value', London: Lawrence & Wishart.

MASLOW, A.H. (1954), 'Motivation and Personality', New York.

MAYER, L.S. (1972), Using monotonic regression to estimate a correlation coefficient, in H.L. Costner (ed.), 'Sociological Methodology 1972', San Francisco: Jossey-Bass, pp. 200-12.

MAYO, E. (1945), 'The Social Problems of an Industrial
Civilisation', Cambridge, Massachusetts: Harvard University Press.
MEIDNER, R. (1973), Samordning och solidarisk lönepolitik
under tre decennier, in LO, 'Tvärsnitt', Stockholm:
Prisma, pp. 7-73.   Also in English (1974), 'Co-ordination
and Solidarity: An Approach to Wage Policy', Stockholm:
LO.
MEIDNER, R. and ÖHMAN, B. (1972), 'Solidarisk Lönepolitik', Stockholm: Tiden.   Also in English (1972), 'Fifteen Years of Wage Policy', Stockholm: LO.
MEIDNER, R. HEDBORG, A. and FOND, G. (1975), 'Löntagar-
fonder', (Wage Earners' Funds), Stockholm: Tiden.   Re-
vised edition in English, 'Employee Investment Funds: An
Approach to Capital Formation', London: Allen & Unwin.
MEISSNER, M. (1971), The long arm of the job: a study of
work and leisure, 'Industrial Relations', 10 (3), pp.
239-60.
MICHELS, R. (1970), 'Soziologie des Parteiwesens', Stutt-
gart: Kröner.
MILBRATH, L. (1965), 'Political Participation', Chicago:
Rand McNally.
MILIBAND, R. (1969), 'The State in Capitalist Society',
London: Weidenfeld & Nicolson.
MILL, J.S. (1952), 'Representative Government', London:
Encyclopedia Britannica.
MILLS, C.W. (1963), 'The Marxists', Harmondsworth:
Penguin.
MYRDAL, G. (1945), Tidens industrikritik, 'Tiden', 37,
pp. 107-15.
MYRDAL, G. (1953), 'The Political Element in the Develop-
ment of Economic Theory', London: Routledge & Kegan Paul.
MYRMAN, Y. (1973), 'Maktkampen på Arbetsmarknaden 1905-
1907' (The Power Struggle on the Labour Market 1905-1907),
Department of Political Science, University of Stock-
holm.
NATIONAL CENTRAL BUREAU OF STATISTICS (1975), 'Living Con-
ditions: Yearbook 1975', Stockholm: Liber/Allmänna
Förlaget.
NICOLAUS, M. (1968), The unknown Marx, 'New Left Review',
48, pp. 41 ff.
NYMAN, O. (1944), 'Krisuppgörelsen mellan Socialdemokra-
terna och Bondeförbundet 1933' (The Crisis Deal between
the Social Democrats and the Agrarians in 1933), Stockholm: Almqvist & Wiksell.
OBERSCHALL, A. (1973), 'Social Conflict and Social Movements', Englewood Cliffs, New Jersey: Prentice-Hall.
O'BRIEN, F.S. (1965), Industrial conflict and business
fluctuations: a comment, 'Journal of Political Economy',
73, pp. 650-4.

OFFE, C. (1972), 'Strukturprobleme des Kapitalistischen Staats', Frankfurt: Suhrkampf.

OHLIN, B. (1949), 'The Problem of Employment Stabilization', New York.

OLOFSSON, G. (1976), Arbetarklass och underklass i Sverige 1870-1930 (Working Class and Under Class in Sweden 1870-1930), 'Zenit', no. 45, pp. 31-50.

OLSON, Jr, M. (1965), 'The Logic of Collective Action: Public Goods and Theory of Groups', Cambridge, Massachusetts: Harvard University Press.

OLSSON, T. (1976), SKP:s politiska utveckling 1943-1950 (The political development of the Swedish Communist Party 1943-1950), in S.E. Olsson, 'Från SKP till VPK', Lund: Zenit/Cavefors, pp. 174-224.

OLSSON, U. (1970), 'Lönepolitik och Lönestruktur: Göteborgs Verkstadsarbetare 1920-1949' (Wage Policy and Wage Structure: Engineering Workers in Göteborg, 1920-1949), Report no. 19, Department of Economic History, University of Göteborg.

VON OTTER, C. (1973), Arbetarnas fackliga organisationsgrad (The level of unionization among workers), 'Arkiv för Studier i Arbetarrörelsens Historia', no. 4, pp. 21-38.

VON OTTER, C. (1975), Sweden: labour reformism reshapes the system, in S. Barkin (ed.), 'Worker Militancy and Its Consequences, 1965-75', New York: Praeger, pp. 194-234.

PARKIN, F. (1971), 'Class Inequality and the Political Order', London: MacGibbon and Kee.

PARKIN, F. (1975), 'A Marxist Sociology of the Superstructure', paper presented to the British Sociological Association's Annual Conference at the University of Kent, Canterbury.

PARKIN, F. (ed.) (1974), 'The Social Analysis of Class Structure', London: Tavistock.

PARSONS, T. (1966), 'Societies: Evolutionary and Comparative Perspectives', Englewood Cliffs, New Jersey: Prentice-Hall.

PATCHEN, M. (1970), Models of cooperation and conflict: a critical review, 'The Journal of Conflict Resolution', 14 (September), pp. 389-408.

PAUL, W.J. and ROBERTSON, K.B. (1970), 'Job Enrichment and Employee Motivation', London: Gower Press.

PEARLIN, L.I. and RICHARDS, H.E. (1960), Equity: a study of union democracy, in W. Galenson and S.M. Lipset (eds), 'Labour and Trade Unionism', New York: Wiley, pp. 265-319.

PERROW, C. (1961), The analysis of goals in complex organisations, 'American Sociological Review', 26 (6), pp. 854-66.

PERROW, C. (1967), A framework for the comparative

analysis of organizations, 'American Sociological Review',
32 (2), pp. 194-208.
PERROW, C. (1970), 'Organizational Analysis: A Sociologi-
cal View', London: Tavistock.
PETERSON, O.A. (1954), Industrial conflict - Sweden, in
A. Kornhauser, R. Dubin and A.M. Ross (eds), 'Industrial
Conflict', New York: McGraw-Hill, pp. 487-98.
PETERSSON, O. and SÄRLVIK, B. (1974), Valet 1973 (The
1973 election), Stockholm: The Central Bureau of Statis-
tics (mimeo.).
PHILLIPS, A.W. (1958), The relation between unemployment
and the rate of change of money wage rates in the United
Kingdom, 1861-1957, 'Economica', 25, pp. 283-99.
POPE, W., COHEN, J. and HAZELRIGG, L.E. (1975), On the
divergence of Weber and Durkheim: a critique of Parson's
convergence thesis, 'American Sociological Review', 40
(August), pp. 417-27.
POULANTZAS, N. (1976), 'Pouvoir Politique et Classes
Sociales', Paris: Maspéro.
POULANTZAS, N. (1973), The problem of the capitalist
state, in J. Urry and J. Wakeford (eds), 'Power in Bri-
tain', London: Heinemann, pp. 291-305.
POULANTZAS, N. (1976), The capitalist state: a reply to
Miliband and Laclau, 'New Left Review', no. 95 (January-
February), pp. 63-83.
PRANDY, K. et al. (1974), Concepts and Measures: The Ex-
ample of Unionateness, 'Sociology', 8 (3), pp. 427-46.
QUENSEL, C.E. (1973), Leif Lewin et al., 'The Swedish
Electorate 1887-1968', 'Statsvetenskaplig Tidskrift', 76,
pp. 73-83.
REES, A. (1952), Industrial conflict and business fluctua-
tions, 'Journal of Political Economy', 60, pp. 371-82.
REEVES, T.K., TURNER, B.A. and WOODWARD, J. (1970), Tech-
nology and organizational behaviour, in J. Woodward (ed.),
'Industrial Organization: Behaviour and Control', London:
Oxford University Press, pp. 4-18.
REHN, G. (1945), 'Sant och Osant i Ekonomidebatten'
(Truths and Untruths in the Economic Debate), Stockholm:
LO.
REX, J. (1961), 'Key Problems of Sociological Theory',
London: Routledge & Kegan Paul.
RIKER, W.H. (1962), 'The Theory of Political Coalitions',
New Haven: Yale University Press.
ROBINSON, J. (1966), 'An Essay on Marxian Economics',
London: Macmillan.
ROSE, R. (ed.), 'Electoral Behaviour: A Comparative Hand-
book', New York: Free Press.
ROSE, R. (1976), 'Party Politics', Harmondsworth:
Penguin.

RUDEBECK, L. (1965), Det politiska systemet i Sverige (The political system in Sweden), in E. Dahlström (ed.), 'Svensk Samhällsstruktur i Sociologisk Belysning (Sociological Perspectives on Swedish Social Structure), Stockholm: Svenska Bokförlaget, pp. 421-67.

RUNCIMAN, G. (1967), 'Relative Deprivation and Social Justice', London: Routledge & Kegan Paul.

SAMUELSSON, K. (1968), 'From Great Power to Welfare State: 300 Years of Swedish Social Development', London: Allen & Unwin.

SARTORI, G. (1962), 'Democratic Theory', Detroit: Wayne State University Press.

SAYLES, L.R. (1958), 'Behaviour of Industrial Work Groups', New York: Wiley.

SCASE, R. (1974), Relative deprivation: a comparison of English and Swedish manual workers, in D. Wedderburn (ed.), 'Poverty Inequality and Class Structure', Cambridge University Press, pp. 197-216.

SCASE, R. (ed.),(1976), 'Readings in Swedish Class Structure', London: Pergamon Press.

SCASE, R. (1977), 'Social Democracy in Capitalist Society: Working Class Politics in Britain and Sweden', London: Croom Helm.

SCHATTSCHNEIDER, E.E. (1960), 'The Semisovereign People: A Realist's View of Democracy in America', New York: Holt, Rinehart & Winston.

SCHELLING, T.C. (1960), 'The Strategy of Conflict', London: Oxford University Press.

SCHILLER, B. (1967), 'Storstrejken 1909', (The General Strike of 1909), Göteborg: Akademiförlaget.

SCHMID, H. (1968), Peace research and politics, 'Journal of Peace Research', 5, no. 3, pp. 217-32.

SCHMIDT, F. (1962), 'The Law of Labour Relations in Sweden', Stockholm: Norstedt.

SCHUESSLER, K. (1971), 'Analyzing Social Data', Boston: Houghton Mifflin.

SCHUMPETER, J.A. (1947), 'Capitalism, Socialism and Democracy' (second edn), New York: Harper & Row.

SCOTT, W.H., et al. (1956), 'Technical Change and Industrial Relations', Liverpool University Press.

SEGERSTEDT, T.T. and LUNDQUIST, A. (1952), 'Människan i industrisamhället: Arbetslivet' (Man in Industrial Society: Working Life), Stockholm: Studieförbundet Näringsliv och Samhälle.

SEGERSTEDT, T.T. and LUNDQUIST, A. (1955), 'Människan i industrisamhället: Fritidsliv-Samhällsliv' (Man in Industrial Society: Leisure Time and Community Life), Stockholm: Studieförbundet Näringsliv och Samhälle.

SHEPPARD, H.L. and HERRICK, N.Q. (1972), 'Where Have All

the Robots Gone?   Worker Dissatisfaction in the '70s',
New York: Free Press.
SHORTER, E. and TILLY, C. (1974), 'Strikes in France,
1830-1968', Cambridge University Press.
SIFO (1975), 'Indikator', Stockholm: Svenska Institutet
för Opinionsundersökningar.
SIFO (1976), 'Indikator', Stockholm: Svenska Institutet
för Opinionsundersökningar.
SILENSTAM, P. (1970), 'Arbetskraftsutbudets Utveckling i
Sverige 1870-1965' (The Development of Labour Force Supply
in Sweden 1870-1965), Stockholm: Industrins
Utredningsinstitut.
SILVERMAN, D. (1970), 'The Theory of Organizations',
London: Heinemann.
SIMON, A. (1957), 'Models of Man', New York: Wiley.
SKOG, S. (1963), 'Arbetets Marknad' (The Market of Work),
Stockholm: Almqvist & Wiksell.
SKÖLD, L. and HALVARSSON, A. (1966), Riksdagens sociala
sammansättning under hundra år (The social composition of
the Riksdag during a hundred years), in A. Thompson (ed.),
'Samhälle och Riksdag', Stockholm: Almqvist & Wiksell,
pp. 375-493.
SMELSER, N.J. (1963), 'Theory of Collective Behaviour',
New York: Free Press.
SNYDER, D. and TILLY, C. (1972), Hardship and collective
violence in France, 1830 to 1960, 'American Sociological
Review', 37, pp. 520-32.
SORRENTINO, C. (1972), Unemployment in nine industria-
lized countries, 'Monthly Labour Review', 95 (June), pp.
29-33.
SOS (1921), 'Industri, 1919' (Manufacturing, 1919),
Stockholm: Kommerskollegium.
SOS (1942), 'Lönestatistisk årsbok för Sverige 1940'
(Annual Wage Statistics for Sweden 1940), Stockholm:
Socialstyrelsen.
SOS (1952), 'Lönestatistisk årsbok för Sverige 1950'
(Annual Wage Statistics for Sweden 1950), Stockholm:
Socialstyrelsen.
SOU (1935: 65-66), 'Betänkande om Folkförsörjning och
Arbetsfred' (Report on Provision of the People and Labour
Peace), Stockholm: Socialdepartementet.
SOU (1968: 7), 'Ägande och Inflytande i det Privata
Näringslivet' (Ownership and influence in the private in-
dustry), Stockholm: Finansdepartementet.
SOU (1971: 39), 'Den Svenska Köpkraftsfördelningen' (The
Distribution of Buying Power in Sweden), Stockholm:
Inrikedepartementet.
SOU (1975: 1), 'Demokrati på Arbetsplatsen' (Democracy at
the Place of Work), Stockholm: Arbetsmarknadsdepartemen-
tet.

SPINRAD, W. (1960), Correlates of trade union participation: a summary of the literature, 'American Sociological Review', 25 (2), pp. 237-44.

SPÅNT, R. (1975), 'Förmögenhetsfördelningen i Sverige' (The Distribution of Wealth in Sweden), Stockholm: Prisma.

SPÅNT, R. (1976), 'Den Svenska Inkomstfördelningens Utveckling' (The Development of the Swedish Income Distribution), Uppsala: Studia Œconomica Uppsaliensia, no. 4.

STAGNER, R. and ROSEN, H. (1965), 'The Psychology of Union-Management Relations', London: Tavistock.

STEIGER, O. (1972), Bakgrunden till 30-talets socialdemokratiska krispolitik (The background to the Social Democratic policy in the 1930s), 'Arkiv för Studier i Arbetarrörelsens Historia', (1), pp. 4-28.

STEIGER, O. (1973), Bakgrunden till 1930-talets socialdemokratiska krispolitik (The background to the Social Democratic crises policy in the 1930s), 'Arkiv för Studier i Arbetarrörelsens Historia, (4), pp. 67-83.

STEPHENS, J. (1976), 'The Consequences of Social and Structural Change for the Development of Socialism in Sweden', unpublished PhD dissertation, Yale University.

STINCHCOMBE, A.L. (1965), Social structure and organization, in J.G. March (ed.), 'Handbook of Organizations', Chicago: Rand McNally, pp. 142-93.

SUNESSON, S. (1974), 'Politik och Organisation' (Politics and Organization), Stockholm: Arkiv Avhandlingsserie.

SVENNING, O. (1972), 'Socialdemokratin och Näringslivet' (Social Democracy and the Industry), Stockholm: Tiden.

SVENSKA METALLINDUSTRIARBETAREFÖRBUNDET (1919), 'Årsberättelse 1919' (Annual Report, 1919), Stockholm: Tiden.

SVENSKA METALLINDUSTRIARBETAREFÖRBUNDET (1938), 'Kongressprotokoll 1938' (Minutes from the 1938 Congress), Stockholm: Tiden.

SVENSKA METALLINDUSTRIARBETAREFÖRBUNDET (1945), 'Protokoll från den fortsatta avtalskonferensen inom verkstadsindustrin, maj 1945' (Minutes from the Continued Contract Conference in the Engineering Industry, May 1945), Stockholm: Tiden.

SVENSKA METALLINDUSTRIARBETAREFÖRBUNDET (1950), 'Kongressprotokoll 1950' (Minutes from the 1950 Congress), Stockholm: Tiden.

SVENSKA METALLINDUSTRIARBETAREFÖRBUNDET (1969), 'Kongressprotokoll 1969' (Minutes from the 1969 Congress), Stockholm: Tiden.

SVENSKA METALLINDUSTRIARBETAREFÖRBUNDET (1973), 'Förslag till Handlingsprogram' (Proposal for an Action Programme), Stockholm: Tiden.

SVERIGES INDUSTRIFÖRBUND (1976), 'Företagsvinster,

Kapitalförsörjning, Löntagarfonder' (Company profits,
capital provision and wage earners' funds), Stockholm:
Svenska Arbetsgivareföreningen.
SVERIGES RIKSDAG (1932), 'Andra Kammarens Protokoll'
(Minutes from the Second Chamber), no. 55, Stockholm:
Sveriges Riksdag.
SÄRLVIK, B. (1974), The social bases of parties in a
developmental perspective, in R. Rose (ed.), 'Electoral
Behaviour: A Comparative Handbook', New York: Free
Press, pp. 371-436.
SÖDERPALM, S.A. (1969), 'Storföretagarna och det Demo-
kratiska Genombrottet' (The Big Managers and the Democra-
tic Breakthrough), Stockholm: Zenit/Rabén & Sjögren.
SÖDERPALM, S.A. (1976), 'Direktörsklubben - Storindustrin
i Svensk Politik under 1930- och 1940-talen' (The Mana-
gers' Club - Big Business in Swedish Politics in the
1930s and the 1940s), Stockholm: Zenit/Rabén & Sjögren.
SÖDERSTEN, J. (1971), Företagsbeskattning och resursför-
delning (Company taxation and the distribution of re-
sources), in E. Lundberg et al., 'Svensk Finanspolitik i
Teori och Praktik', Stockholm: Aldus, pp. 322-59.
TAFT, P. (1954), 'The Structure and Government of Labour
Unions', Cambridge, Massachusetts: Harvard University
Press.
TANNENBAUM, A.S. (1965), Unions, in J.S. March (ed.),
'Handbook of Organizations', Chicago: Rand McNally, pp.
710-63.
TANNENBAUM, A.S. (1966), 'Social Psychology of the Work
Organization', London: Tavistock.
TANNENBAUM, A.S. and KAHN, R. (1957), Organizational con-
trol structure: a general descriptive technique as
applied to four local unions, 'Human Relations', 10 (2),
pp. 127-40.
TAYLOR, F.W. (1913), 'The Principles of Scientific Manage-
ment', New York: Harper.
TCO (1976), 'Löntagarkapital' (Wage Earners' Capital),
Stockholm: Tjänstemännens Centralorganisation.
THERBORN, G. (1971), 'Klasser och Ekonomiska System'
(Classes and Economic Systems), Lund: Zenit/Cavefors.
THERBORN, G. (1975), 'Science, Class and Society: On the
Formation of Sociology and Historical Materialism',
London: New Left Books.
THERBORN, G. (1976), The Swedish class structure: a
Marxist analysis, in R. Scase (ed.), 'Readings in Swedish
Class Structure', London: Pergamon, pp. 151-68.
THIBAUT, J.W. and KELLEY, H.H. (1959), 'The Social Psycho-
logy of Groups', New York: Wiley.
TILLY, C. (1973), Does modernization breed revolution?,
'Comparative Politics', 5, pp. 425-47.

TIMASHEFF, N.S. (1965), 'War and Revolution', New York: Sheed & Ward.

TINGSTEN, H. (1937), 'Political Behaviour: Studies in Election Statistics', London: King & Son.

TINGSTEN, H. (1973), 'The Swedish Social Democrats: Their Ideological Development', Totowa: Bedminster Press.

TOMASSON, R.F. (1970), 'Sweden: Prototype of Modern Society', New York: Random House.

TORSVALL, L. (1974), Något om den solidariska lönepolitiken och dess effekter på lönerna inom verkstadsindustrin under de tre senaste decennierna (On the solidaristic wage policy and its effects on wages in the engineering industry during the last three decades), Stockholm University Department of Sociology (mimeo.).

TOURAINE, A. (1974), 'The Post-Industrial Society', London: Wildwood House.

TOURAINE, A. and RAGAZZI, O. (1961), 'Ouvriers d'Origin Agricole', Paris: Éditions du Seuil.

TRESLOW, K. (1972),'Verkstadskonflikten 1945: en studie av arbetsmarknadens förhandlingssystem vid konflikt' (The engineering strike in 1945: a study of the bargaining system on the labour market in a conflict), University of Stockholm, Department of Political Science (mimeo.).

TRIST, E. et al. (1963), 'Organizational Choice', London: Tavistock.

TURNER, A.N. and LAWRENCE, P. (1965), 'Industrial Jobs and the Worker', Cambridge, Massachusetts: Harvard University, Graduate School of Business Administration.

TURVEY, R. (ed.),(1952), 'Wages Policy under Full Employment', London.

ULLENHAG, J. (1971), 'Den Solidariska Lönepolitiken i Sverige' (Solidaristic Wage Policy in Sweden), Stockholm: Läromedelsförlagen.

UNGA, N. (1976), 'Socialdemokratin och arbetslöshetsfrågan 1912-34' (The Social Democratic Party and the Unemployment Issue, 1912-34), Stockholm: Arkiv avhandlingsserie.

UUSITALO, H. (1975a), 'Income and Welfare', Research Group for Comparative Sociology, University of Helsinki (Report no. 8).

UUSITALO, H. (1975b), 'Class Structure and Party Choice: A Scandinavian Comparison', Research Group for Comparative Sociology, University of Helsinki (Report no. 10).

VROOM, V.H. (1964), 'Work and Motivation', New York: Wiley.

WADENSJÖ, E. (1972), Immigration och Samhällsekonomi (Immigration and the national economy), University of Lund Department of Economics (mimeo.).

WALKER, C.R. and GUEST, R.H. (1952), 'The Man on the Assembly Line', Cambridge, Massachusetts: Harvard University Press.

WEBER, M. (1968), 'Economy and Society', New York: Bedminster Press.
WEDDERBURN, D. and CROMPTON, R. (1972), 'Workers' Attitudes and Technology', Cambridge University Press.
WESOŁOWSKI, W. (1972), Klassdominans och intressegruppers
makt (Class dominance and the power of interest groups),
in G. Sidebäck (ed.), 'Historiesyn och klassteori' (His-
torical Perspectives and Class Theory), Stockholm:
Wahlström & Widstrand.
WESTERGAARD, J.H. (1970), The rediscovery of the cash
nexus, in R. Miliband and J. Saville (eds), 'The Socialist
Register 1970', London: Merlin Press, pp. 111-39.
WESTERGAARD, J. and RESLER, H. (1975), 'Class in a Capi-
talist Society', London: Heinemann.
WESTERSTÅHL, J. (1945), 'Svensk Fackföreningsrörelse' (The
Swedish Union Movement), Stockholm: Tiden.
WESTERSTÅHL, J. (1971), 'Den Kommunala Självstyrelsen'
(The Communal Self-Government), Stockholm: Almqvist &
Wiksell.
WESTLANDER, G. (1976), 'Arbetets Villkor och Fritidens
Innehåll' (Conditions at Work and the Content of Leisure),
Stockholm: PA-rådet.
WIGFORSS, E. (1951), 'Minnen 1914-1932' (Memories 1914-
1932), Stockholm: Tiden.
WIGFORSS, E. (1954), 'Minnen 1932-1949' (Memories 1932-
1949), Stockholm: Tiden.
WIGFORSS, E. (1967), Ideologiska linjer i praktisk politik
(Ideological directions in practical policy), 'Tiden',
59, pp. 525-33.
WILENSKY, H. (1960), Work, careers and social integration,
'International Social Science Journal', 12 (Fall), pp.
543-60.
WOODWARD, J. (1958), 'Management and Technology', London:
HMSO.
WOODWARD, J. (1965), 'Industrial Organization: Theory
and Practice', London: Oxford University Press.
WOODWARD, J. (ed.) (1970), 'Industrial Organization:
Behaviour and Control', London: Oxford University Press.
ZALEZNIK, A. and MOMENT, D. (1964), 'The Dynamics of
Interpersonal Behaviour', New York: Wiley.
ÅBERG, R. (1974), Changes in work conditions as a result
of changes in economic structure', University of Umeå,
Department of Sociology (mimeo.).
ÖHMAN, B. (1970), 'Svensk Arbetsmarknadspolitik 1900-
1947' (Swedish Labour Market Policy 1900-1947), Stockholm:
Prisma.
ÖHMAN, B. (1973), LO och arbetsmarknadspolitiken efter
andra världskriget (LO and labour market policy since the
second world war), in LO, 'Tvärsnitt', Stockholm: Prisma,
pp. 73-150.

Name index

Subject index

Routledge Social Science Series

Routledge & Kegan Paul   London, Henley and Boston

39 Store Street, London WC1E 7DD
Broadway House, Newtown Road, Henley-on-Thames,
Oxon RG9 1EN
9 Park Street, Boston, Mass. 02108

Contents

*Authors wishing to submit manuscripts for any series in
this catalogue should send them to the Social Science Editor,
Routledge & Kegan Paul Ltd, 39 Store Street,
London WC1E 7DD*

● *Books so marked are available in paperback
All books are in Metric Demy 8vo format (216 × 138mm approx.)*

International Library of Sociology

General Editor John Rex

GENERAL SOCIOLOGY

Barnsley, J. H. The Social Reality of Ethics. *464 pp.*
Belshaw, Cyril. The Conditions of Social Performance. *An Exploratory Theory. 144 pp.*
Brown, Robert. Explanation in Social Science. *208 pp.*
● Rules and Laws in Sociology. *192 pp.*
Bruford, W. H. Chekhov and His Russia. *A Sociological Study. 244 pp.*
Cain, Maureen E. Society and the Policeman's Role. *326 pp.*
●**Fletcher, Colin.** Beneath the Surface. *An Account of Three Styles of Sociological Research. 221 pp.*
Gibson, Quentin. The Logic of Social Enquiry. *240 pp.*
Glucksmann, M. Structuralist Analysis in Contemporary Social Thought. *212 pp.*
Gurvitch, Georges. Sociology of Law. *Preface by Roscoe Pound. 264 pp.*
Hodge, H. A. Wilhelm Dilthey. *An Introduction. 184 pp.*
Homans, George C. Sentiments and Activities. *336 pp.*
Johnson, Harry M. Sociology: *a Systematic Introduction. Foreword by · Robert K. Merton. 710 pp.*
●**Keat, Russell, and Urry, John.** Social Theory as Science. *278 pp.*
Mannheim, Karl. Essays on Sociology and Social Psychology. *Edited by Paul Keckskemeti. With Editorial Note by Adolph Lowe. 344 pp.*
Systematic Sociology: *An Introduction to the Study of Society. Edited by J. S. Erös and Professor W. A. C. Stewart. 220 pp.*
Martindale, Don. The Nature and Types of Sociological Theory. *292 pp.*
●**Maus, Heinz.** A Short History of Sociology. *234 pp.*
Mey, Harald. Field-Theory. *A Study of its Application in the Social Sciences. 352 pp.*
Myrdal, Gunnar. Value in Social Theory: *A Collection of Essays on Methodology. Edited by Paul Streeten. 332 pp.*
Ogburn, William F., and Nimkoff, Meyer F. A Handbook of Sociology. *Preface by Karl Mannheim. 656 pp. 46 figures. 35 tables.*
Parsons, Talcott, and Smelser, Neil J. Economy and Society: *A Study in the Integration of Economic and Social Theory. 362 pp.*
Podgórecki, Adam. Practical Social Sciences. *About 200 pp.*
●**Rex, John.** Key Problems of Sociological Theory. *220 pp.*
Sociology and the Demystification of the Modern World. *282 pp.*
●**Rex, John** (Ed.) Approaches to Sociology. *Contributions by Peter Abell, Frank Bechhofer, Basil Bernstein, Ronald Fletcher, David Frisby, Miriam Glucksmann, Peter Lassman, Herminio Martins, John Rex, Roland Robertson, John Westergaard and Jock Young. 302 pp.*
Rigby, A. Alternative Realities. *352 pp.*
Roche, M. Phenomenology, Language and the Social Sciences. *374 pp.*

Sahay, A. Sociological Analysis. *220 pp.*

Simirenko, Alex (Ed.) Soviet Sociology. *Historical Antecedents and Current Appraisals. Introduction by Alex Simirenko. 376 pp.*

Strasser, Hermann. The Normative Structure of Sociology. *Conservative and Emancipatory Themes in Social Thought. About 340 pp.*

Urry, John. Reference Groups and the Theory of Revolution. *244 pp.*

Weinberg, E. Development of Sociology in the Soviet Union. *173 pp.*

FOREIGN CLASSICS OF SOCIOLOGY

●**Durkheim, Emile.** Suicide. *A Study in Sociology. Edited and with an Introduction by George Simpson. 404 pp.*

●**Gerth, H. H.,** and **Mills, C. Wright.** From Max Weber: *Essays in Sociology. 502 pp.*

●**Tönnies, Ferdinand.** Community and Association. (*Gemeinschaft und Gesellschaft.*) *Translated and Supplemented by Charles P. Loomis. Foreword by Pitirim A. Sorokin. 334 pp.*

SOCIAL STRUCTURE

Andreski, Stanislav. Military Organization and Society. *Foreword by Professor A. R. Radcliffe-Brown. 226 pp. 1 folder.*

Carlton, Eric. Ideology and Social Order. *Preface by Professor Philip Abrahams. About 320 pp.*

Coontz, Sydney H. Population Theories and the Economic Interpretation. *202 pp.*

Coser, Lewis. The Functions of Social Conflict. *204 pp.*

Dickie-Clark, H. F. Marginal Situation: *A Sociological Study of a Coloured Group. 240 pp. 11 tables.*

Glaser, Barney, and **Strauss, Anselm L.** Status Passage. *A Formal Theory. 208 pp.*

Glass, D. V. (Ed.) Social Mobility in Britain. *Contributions by J. Berent, T. Bottomore, R. C. Chambers, J. Floud, D. V. Glass, J. R. Hall, H. T. Himmelweit, R. K. Kelsall, F. M. Martin, C. A. Moser, R. Mukherjee, and W. Ziegel. 420 pp.*

Johnstone, Frederick A. Class, Race and Gold. *A Study of Class Relations and Racial Discrimination in South Africa. 312 pp.*

Jones, Garth N. Planned Organizational Change: *An Exploratory Study Using an Empirical Approach. 268 pp.*

Kelsall, R. K. Higher Civil Servants in Britain: *From 1870 to the Present Day. 268 pp. 31 tables.*

König, René. The Community. *232 pp. Illustrated.*

●**Lawton, Denis.** Social Class, Language and Education. *192 pp.*

McLeish, John. The Theory of Social Change: *Four Views Considered. 128 pp.*

Marsh, David C. The Changing Social Structure of England and Wales, *1871-1961. 288 pp.*

Menzies, Ken. Talcott Parsons and the Social Image of Man. *About 208 pp.*

●**Mouzelis, Nicos.** Organization and Bureaucracy. *An Analysis of Modern Theories. 240 pp.*

Mulkay, M. J. Functionalism, Exchange and Theoretical Strategy. *272 pp.*

Ossowski, Stanislaw. Class Structure in the Social Consciousness. *210 pp.*

●**Podgórecki, Adam.** Law and Society. *302 pp.*

Renner, Karl. Institutions of Private Law and Their Social Functions. *Edited, with an Introduction and Notes, by O. Kahn-Freud. Translated by Agnes Schwarzschild. 316 pp.*

SOCIOLOGY AND POLITICS

Acton, T. A. Gypsy Politics and Social Change. *316 pp.*

Clegg, Stuart. Power, Rule and Domination. *A Critical and Empirical Understanding of Power in Sociological Theory and Organisational Life. About 300 pp.*

Hechter, Michael. Internal Colonialism. *The Celtic Fringe in British National Development, 1536–1966. 361 pp.*

Hertz, Frederick. Nationality in History and Politics: *A Psychology and Sociology of National Sentiment and Nationalism. 432 pp.*

Kornhauser, William. The Politics of Mass Society. *272 pp. 20 tables.*

●**Kroes, R.** Soldiers and Students. *A Study of Right- and Left-wing Students. 174 pp.*

Laidler, Harry W. History of Socialism. *Social-Economic Movements: An Historical and Comparative Survey of Socialism, Communism, Co-operation, Utopianism; and other Systems of Reform and Reconstruction. 992 pp.*

Lasswell, H. D. Analysis of Political Behaviour. *324 pp.*

Martin, David A. Pacifism: *an Historical and Sociological Study. 262 pp.*

Martin, Roderick. Sociology of Power. *About 272 pp.*

Myrdal, Gunnar. The Political Element in the Development of Economic Theory. *Translated from the German by Paul Streeten. 282 pp.*

Wilson, H. T. The American Ideology. *Science, Technology and Organization of Modes of Rationality. About 280 pp.*

Wootton, Graham. Workers, Unions and the State. *188 pp.*

CRIMINOLOGY

Ancel, Marc. Social Defence: *A Modern Approach to Criminal Problems. Foreword by Leon Radzinowicz. 240 pp.*

Cain, Maureen E. Society and the Policeman's Role. *326 pp.*

Cloward, Richard A., and **Ohlin, Lloyd E.** Delinquency and Opportunity: *A Theory of Delinquent Gangs. 248 pp.*

Downes, David M. The Delinquent Solution. *A Study in Subcultural Theory. 296 pp.*

Dunlop, A. B., and **McCabe, S.** Young Men in Detention Centres. *192 pp.*

Friedlander, Kate. The Psycho-Analytical Approach to Juvenile Delinquency: *Theory, Case Studies, Treatment. 320 pp.*

Glueck, Sheldon, and **Eleanor.** Family Environment and Delinquency. *With the statistical assistance of Rose W. Kneznek. 340 pp.*

5

Lopez-Rey, Manuel. Crime. *An Analytical Appraisal. 288 pp.*

Mannheim, Hermann. Comparative Criminology: *a Text Book. Two volumes. 442 pp. and 380 pp.*

Morris, Terence. The Criminal Area: *A Study in Social Ecology. Foreword by Hermann Mannheim. 232 pp. 25 tables. 4 maps.*

Rock, Paul. Making People Pay. *338 pp.*

● **Taylor, Ian, Walton, Paul,** and **Young, Jock.** The New Criminology. *For a Social Theory of Deviance. 325 pp.*

● **Taylor, Ian, Walton, Paul,** and **Young, Jock** (Eds). Critical Criminology. *268 pp.*

SOCIAL PSYCHOLOGY

Bagley, Christopher. The Social Psychology of the Epileptic Child. *320 pp.*

Barbu, Zevedei. Problems of Historical Psychology. *248 pp.*

Blackburn, Julian. Psychology and the Social Pattern. *184 pp.*

● **Brittan, Arthur.** Meanings and Situations. *224 pp.*

Carroll, J. Break-Out from the Crystal Palace. *200 pp.*

● **Fleming, C. M.** Adolescence: Its Social Psychology. *With an Introduction to recent findings from the fields of Anthropology, Physiology, Medicine, Psychometrics and Sociometry. 288 pp.*

● The Social Psychology of Education: *An Introduction and Guide to Its Study. 136 pp.*

● **Homans, George C.** The Human Group. *Foreword by Bernard DeVoto. Introduction by Robert K. Merton. 526 pp.*

● Social Behaviour: *its Elementary Forms. 416 pp.*

● **Klein, Josephine.** The Study of Groups. *226 pp. 31 figures. 5 tables.*

Linton, Ralph. The Cultural Background of Personality. *132 pp.*

● **Mayo, Elton.** The Social Problems of an Industrial Civilization. *With an appendix on the Political Problem. 180 pp.*

Ottaway, A. K. C. Learning Through Group Experience. *176 pp.*

Plummer, Ken. Sexual Stigma. *An Interactionist Account. 254 pp.*

● **Rose, Arnold M.** (Ed.) Human Behaviour and Social Processes: *an Interactionist Approach. Contributions by Arnold M. Rose, Ralph H. Turner, Anselm Strauss, Everett C. Hughes, E. Franklin Frazier, Howard S. Becker, et al. 696 pp.*

Smelser, Neil J. Theory of Collective Behaviour. *448 pp.*

Stephenson, Geoffrey M. The Development of Conscience. *128 pp.*

Young, Kimball. Handbook of Social Psychology. *658 pp. 16 figures. 10 tables.*

SOCIOLOGY OF THE FAMILY

Banks, J. A. Prosperity and Parenthood: *A Study of Family Planning among The Victorian Middle Classes. 262 pp.*

Bell, Colin R. Middle Class Families: *Social and Geographical Mobility. 224 pp.*

Burton, Lindy. Vulnerable Children. *272 pp.*

Gavron, Hannah. The Captive Wife: *Conflicts of Household Mothers. 190 pp.*

George, Victor, and **Wilding, Paul.** Motherless Families. *248 pp.*

Klein, Josephine. Samples from English Cultures.
1. Three Preliminary Studies and Aspects of Adult Life in England. *447 pp.*
2. Child-Rearing Practices and Index. *247 pp.*

Klein, Viola. The Feminine Character. *History of an Ideology. 244 pp.*

McWhinnie, Alexina M. Adopted Children. *How They Grow Up. 304 pp.*

● **Morgan, D. H. J.** Social Theory and the Family. *About 320 pp.*

● **Myrdal, Alva,** and **Klein, Viola.** Women's Two Roles: *Home and Work. 238 pp. 27 tables.*

Parsons, Talcott, and **Bales, Robert F.** Family: Socialization and Interaction Process. *In collaboration with James Olds, Morris Zelditch and Philip E. Slater. 456 pp. 50 figures and tables.*

SOCIAL SERVICES

Bastide, Roger. The Sociology of Mental Disorder. *Translated from the French by Jean McNeil. 260 pp.*

Carlebach, Julius. Caring For Children in Trouble. *266 pp.*

George, Victor. Foster Care. *Theory and Practice. 234 pp.*

Social Security: *Beveridge and After. 258 pp.*

George, V., and **Wilding, P.** Motherless Families. *248 pp.*

● **Goetschius, George W.** Working with Community Groups. *256 pp.*

Goetschius, George W., and **Tash, Joan.** Working with Unattached Youth. *416 pp.*

Hall, M. P., and **Howes, I. V.** The Church in Social Work. *A Study of Moral Welfare Work undertaken by the Church of England. 320 pp.*

Heywood, Jean S. Children in Care: *the Development of the Service for the Deprived Child. 264 pp.*

Hoenig, J., and **Hamilton, Marian W.** The De-Segregation of the Mentally Ill. *284 pp.*

Jones, Kathleen. Mental Health and Social Policy, 1845-1959. *264 pp.*

King, Roy D., Raynes, Norma V., and **Tizard, Jack.** Patterns of Residential Care. *356 pp.*

Leigh, John. Young People and Leisure. *256 pp.*

● **Mays, John.** (Ed.) Penelope Hall's Social Services of England and Wales. *About 324 pp.*

Morris, Mary. Voluntary Work and the Welfare State. *300 pp.*

Nokes, P. L. The Professional Task in Welfare Practice. *152 pp.*

Timms, Noel. Psychiatric Social Work in Great Britain (1939-1962). *280 pp.*

● Social Casework: *Principles and Practice. 256 pp.*

Young, A. F. Social Services in British Industry. *272 pp.*

SOCIOLOGY OF EDUCATION

Banks, Olive. Parity and Prestige in English Secondary Education: a Study in Educational Sociology. *272 pp.*

Bentwich, Joseph. Education in Israel. *224 pp. 8 pp. plates.*

●**Blyth, W. A. L.** English Primary Education. *A Sociological Description.*
 1. Schools. *232 pp.*
 2. Background. *168 pp.*

Collier, K. G. The Social Purposes of Education: *Personal and Social Values in Education. 268 pp.*

Dale, R. R., and **Griffith, S.** Down Stream: *Failure in the Grammar School. 108 pp.*

Evans, K. M. Sociometry and Education. *158 pp.*

●**Ford, Julienne.** Social Class and the Comprehensive School. *192 pp.*

Foster, P. J. Education and Social Change in Ghana. *336 pp. 3 maps.*

Fraser, W. R. Education and Society in Modern France. *150 pp.*

Grace, Gerald R. Role Conflict and the Teacher. *150 pp.*

Hans, Nicholas. New Trends in Education in the Eighteenth Century. *278 pp. 19 tables.*

● Comparative Education: *A Study of Educational Factors and Traditions. 360 pp.*

●**Hargreaves, David.** Interpersonal Relations and Education. *432 pp.*

● Social Relations in a Secondary School. *240 pp.*

Holmes, Brian. Problems in Education. *A Comparative Approach. 336 pp.*

King, Ronald. Values and Involvement in a Grammar School. *164 pp.*
 School Organization and Pupil Involvement. *A Study of Secondary Schools.*

●**Mannheim, Karl,** and **Stewart, W. A. C.** An Introduction to the Sociology of Education. *206 pp.*

Morris, Raymond N. The Sixth Form and College Entrance. *231 pp.*

●**Musgrove, F.** Youth and the Social Order. *176 pp.*

●**Ottaway, A. K. C.** Education and Society: An Introduction to the Sociology of Education. *With an Introduction by W. O. Lester Smith. 212 pp.*

Peers, Robert. Adult Education: *A Comparative Study. 398 pp.*

Pritchard, D. G. Education and the Handicapped: *1760 to 1960. 258 pp.*

Stratta, Erica. The Education of Borstal Boys. *A Study of their Educational Experiences prior to, and during, Borstal Training. 256 pp.*

Taylor, P. H., Reid, W. A., and **Holley, B. J.** The English Sixth Form. *A Case Study in Curriculum Research. 200 pp.*

SOCIOLOGY OF CULTURE

Eppel, E. M., and **M.** Adolescents and Morality: *A Study of some Moral Values and Dilemmas of Working Adolescents in the Context of a changing Climate of Opinion. Foreword by W. J. H. Sprott. 268 pp. 39 tables.*

●**Fromm, Erich.** The Fear of Freedom. *286 pp.*

● The Sane Society. *400 pp.*

Mannheim, Karl. Essays on the Sociology of Culture. *Edited by Ernst Mannheim in co-operation with Paul Kecskemeti. Editorial Note by Adolph Lowe. 280 pp.*

Weber, Alfred. Farewell to European History: *or The Conquest of Nihilism. Translated from the German by R. F. C. Hull, 224 pp.*

SOCIOLOGY OF RELIGION

Argyle, Michael and **Beit-Hallahmi, Benjamin.** The Social Psychology of Religion. *About 256 pp.*

Glasner, Peter E. The Sociology of Secularisation. *A Critique of a Concept. About 180 pp.*

Nelson, G. K. Spiritualism and Society. *313 pp.*

Stark, Werner. The Sociology of Religion. *A Study of Christendom.*
Volume I. *Established Religion. 248 pp.*
Volume II. *Sectarian Religion. 368 pp.*
Volume III. *The Universal Church. 464 pp.*
Volume IV. *Types of Religious Man. 352 pp.*
Volume V. *Types of Religious Culture. 464 pp.*

Turner, B. S. Weber and Islam. *216 pp.*

Watt, W. Montgomery. Islam and the Integration of Society. *320 pp.*

SOCIOLOGY OF ART AND LITERATURE

Jarvie, Ian C. Towards a Sociology of the Cinema. *A Comparative Essay on the Structure and Functioning of a Major Entertainment Industry. 405 pp.*

Rust, Frances S. Dance in Society. *An Analysis of the Relationships between the Social Dance and Society in England from the Middle Ages to the Present Day. 256 pp. 8 pp. of plates.*

Schücking, L. L. The Sociology of Literary Taste. *112 pp.*

Wolff, Janet. Hermeneutic Philosophy and the Sociology of Art. *150 pp.*

SOCIOLOGY OF KNOWLEDGE

Diesing, P. Patterns of Discovery in the Social Sciences. *262 pp.*

● **Douglas, J. D.** (Ed.) Understanding Everyday Life. *370 pp.*

● **Hamilton, P.** Knowledge and Social Structure. *174 pp.*

Jarvie, I. C. Concepts and Society. *232 pp.*

Mannheim, Karl. Essays on the Sociology of Knowledge. *Edited by Paul Kecskemeti. Editorial Note by Adolph Lowe. 353 pp.*

Remmling, Gunter W. The Sociology cf Karl Mannheim. *With a Bibliographical Guide to the Sociology of Knowledge, Ideological Analysis, and Social Planning. 255 pp.*

9

Remmling, Gunter W. (Ed.) Towards the Sociology of Knowledge. *Origin and Development of a Sociological Thought Style. 463 pp.*

Stark, Werner. The Sociology of Knowledge: *An Essay in Aid of a Deeper Understanding of the History of Ideas. 384 pp.*

URBAN SOCIOLOGY

Ashworth, William. The Genesis of Modern British Town Planning: *A Study in Economic and Social History of the Nineteenth and Twentieth Centuries. 288 pp.*

Cullingworth, J. B. Housing Needs and Planning Policy: *A Restatement of the Problems of Housing Need and 'Overspill' in England and Wales. 232 pp. 44 tables. 8 maps.*

Dickinson, Robert E. City and Region: *A Geographical Interpretation 608 pp. 125 figures.*

The West European City: *A Geographical Interpretation. 600 pp. 129 maps. 29 plates.*

● The City Region in Western Europe. *320 pp. Maps.*

Humphreys, Alexander J. New Dubliners: *Urbanization and the Irish Family. Foreword by George C. Homans. 304 pp.*

Jackson, Brian. Working Class Community: *Some General Notions raised by a Series of Studies in Northern England. 192 pp.*

Jennings, Hilda. Societies in the Making: *a Study of Development and Re-development within a County Borough. Foreword by D. A. Clark. 286 pp.*

●**Mann, P. H.** An Approach to Urban Sociology. *240 pp.*

Morris, R. N., and **Mogey, J.** The Sociology of Housing. *Studies at Berinsfield. 232 pp. 4 pp. plates.*

Rosser, C., and **Harris, C.** The Family and Social Change. *A Study of Family and Kinship in a South Wales Town. 352 pp. 8 maps.*

●**Stacey, Margaret, Batsone, Eric, Bell, Colin,** and **Thurcott, Anne.** Power, Persistence and Change. *A Second Study of Banbury. 196 pp.*

RURAL SOCIOLOGY

Haswell, M. R. The Economics of Development in Village India. *120 pp.*

Littlejohn, James. Westrigg: *the Sociology of a Cheviot Parish. 172 pp. 5 figures.*

Mayer, Adrian C. Peasants in the Pacific. *A Study of Fiji Indian Rural Society. 248 pp. 20 plates.*

Williams, W. M. The Sociology of an English Village: *Gosforth. 272 pp. 12 figures. 13 tables.*

SOCIOLOGY OF INDUSTRY AND DISTRIBUTION

Anderson, Nels. Work and Leisure. *280 pp.*

●**Blau, Peter M.,** and **Scott, W. Richard.** Formal Organizations: *a Comparative approach. Introduction and Additional Bibliography by J. H. Smith. 326 pp.*

Dunkerley, David. The Foreman. *Aspects of Task and Structure. 192 pp.*

Eldridge, J. E. T. Industrial Disputes. *Essays in the Sociology of Industrial Relations. 288 pp.*

Hetzler, Stanley. Applied Measures for Promoting Technological Growth. *352 pp.*

Technological Growth and Social Change. *Achieving Modernization. 269 pp.*

Hollowell, Peter G. The Lorry Driver. *272 pp.*

●**Oxaal, I., Barnett, T.,** and **Booth, D.** (Eds). Beyond the Sociology of Development. *Economy and Society in Latin America and Africa. 295 pp.*

Smelser, Neil J. Social Change in the Industrial Revolution: *An Application of Theory to the Lancashire Cotton Industry, 1770–1840. 468 pp. 12 figures. 14 tables.*

ANTHROPOLOGY

Ammar, Hamed. Growing up in an Egyptian Village: *Silwa, Province of Aswan. 336 pp.*

Brandel-Syrier, Mia. Reeftown Elite. *A Study of Social Mobility in a Modern African Community on the Reef. 376 pp.*

Dickie-Clark, H. F. The Marginal Situation. *A Sociological Study of a Coloured Group. 236 pp.*

Dube, S. C. Indian Village. *Foreword by Morris Edward Opler. 276 pp. 4 plates.*

India's Changing Villages: *Human Factors in Community Development. 260 pp. 8 plates. 1 map.*

Firth, Raymond. Malay Fishermen. *Their Peasant Economy. 420 pp. 17 pp. plates.*

Gulliver, P. H. Social Control in an African Society: a Study of the Arusha, Agricultural Masai of Northern Tanganyika. *320 pp. 8 plates. 10 figures.*

Family Herds. *288 pp.*

Ishwaran, K. Tradition and Economy in Village India: *An Interactionist Approach.*
Foreword by Conrad Arensburg. 176 pp.

Jarvie, Ian C. The Revolution in Anthropology. *268 pp.*

Little, Kenneth L. Mende of Sierra Leone. *308 pp. and folder.*

Negroes in Britain. *With a New Introduction and Contemporary Study by Leonard Bloom. 320 pp.*

Lowie, Robert H. Social Organization. *494 pp.*

Mayer, A. C. Peasants in the Pacific. *A Study of Fiji Indian Rural Society. 248 pp.*

Meer, Fatima. Race and Suicide in South Africa. *325 pp.*

11

Smith, Raymond T. The Negro Family in British Guiana: *Family Structure and Social Status in the Villages. With a Foreword by Meyer Fortes. 314 pp. 8 plates. 1 figure. 4 maps.*

Smooha, Sammy. Israel: Pluralism and Conflict. *About 320 pp.*

SOCIOLOGY AND PHILOSOPHY

Barnsley, John H. The Social Reality of Ethics. *A Comparative Analysis of Moral Codes. 448 pp.*

Diesing, Paul. Patterns of Discovery in the Social Sciences. *362 pp.*

●**Douglas, Jack D.** (Ed.) Understanding Everyday Life. *Toward the Reconstruction of Sociological Knowledge. Contributions by Alan F. Blum. Aaron W. Cicourel, Norman K. Denzin, Jack D. Douglas, John Heeren, Peter McHugh, Peter K. Manning, Melvin Power, Matthew Speier, Roy Turner, D. Lawrence Wieder, Thomas P. Wilson and Don H. Zimmerman. 370 pp.*

Gorman, Robert A. The Dual Vision. *Alfred Schutz and the Myth of Phenomenological Social Science. About 300 pp.*

Jarvie, Ian C. Concepts and Society. *216 pp.*

●**Pelz, Werner.** The Scope of Understanding in Sociology. *Towards a more radical reorientation in the social humanistic sciences. 283 pp.*

Roche, Maurice. Phenomenology, Language and the Social Sciences. *371 pp.*

Sahay, Arun. Sociological Analysis. *212 pp.*

Sklair, Leslie. The Sociology of Progress. *320 pp.*

Slater, P. Origin and Significance of the Frankfurt School. *A Marxist Perspective. About 192 pp.*

Smart, Barry. Sociology, Phenomenology and Marxian Analysis. *A Critical Discussion of the Theory and Practice of a Science of Society. 220 pp.*

International Library of Anthropology

General Editor Adam Kuper

Ahmed, A. S. Millenium and Charisma Among Pathans. *A Critical Essay in Social Anthropology. 192 pp.*

Brown, Paula. The Chimbu. *A Study of Change in the New Guinea Highlands. 151 pp.*

Gudeman, Stephen. Relationships, Residence and the Individual. *A Rural Panamanian Community. 288 pp. 11 Plates, 5 Figures, 2 Maps, 10 Tables.*

Hamnett, Ian. Chieftainship and Legitimacy. *An Anthropological Study of Executive Law in Lesotho. 163 pp.*

Hanson, F. Allan. Meaning in Culture. *127 pp.*

Lloyd, P. C. Power and Independence. *Urban Africans' Perception of Social Inequality. 264 pp.*

Pettigrew, Joyce. Robber Noblemen. *A Study of the Political System of the Sikh Jats. 284 pp.*

Street, Brian V. The Savage in Literature. *Representations of 'Primitive' Society in English Fiction, 1858–1920. 207 pp.*

Van Den Berghe, Pierre L. Power and Privilege at an African University. *278 pp.*

International Library of Social Policy

General Editor Kathleen Jones

Bayley, M. Mental Handicap and Community Care. *426 pp.*

Bottoms, A. E., and **McClean, J. D.** Defendants in the Criminal Process. *284 pp.*

Butler, J. R. Family Doctors and Public Policy. *208 pp.*

Davies, Martin. Prisoners of Society. *Attitudes and Aftercare. 204 pp.*

Gittus, Elizabeth. Flats, Families and the Under-Fives. *285 pp.*

Holman, Robert. Trading in Children. *A Study of Private Fostering. 355 pp.*

Jones, Howard, and **Cornes, Paul.** Open Prisons. *About 248 pp.*

Jones, Kathleen. History of the Mental Health Service. *428 pp.*

Jones, Kathleen, with **Brown, John, Cunningham, W. J., Roberts, Julian,** and **Williams, Peter.** Opening the Door. *A Study of New Policies for the Mentally Handicapped. 278 pp.*

Karn, Valerie. Retiring to the Seaside. *About 280 pp. 2 maps. Numerous tables.*

Thomas, J. E. The English Prison Officer since 1850: *A Study in Conflict. 258 pp.*

Walton, R. G. Women in Social Work. *303 pp.*

Woodward, J. To Do the Sick No Harm. *A Study of the British Voluntary Hospital System to 1875. 221 pp.*

International Library of Welfare and Philosophy

General Editors Noel Timms and David Watson

● **Plant, Raymond.** Community and Ideology. *104 pp.*

● **McDermott, F. E.** (Ed.) Self-Determination in Social Work. *A Collection of Essays on Self-determination and Related Concepts by Philosophers and Social Work Theorists. Contributors: F. P. Biestek, S. Bernstein, A. Keith-Lucas, D. Sayer, H. H. Perelman, C. Whittington, R. F. Stalley, F. E. McDermott, I. Berlin, H. J. McCloskey, H. L. A. Hart, J. Wilson, A. I. Melden, S. I. Benn. 254 pp.*

Ragg, Nicholas M. People Not Cases. *A Philosophical Approach to Social Work. About 250 pp.*

13

● **Timms, Noel,** and **Watson, David** (Eds). Talking About Welfare. *Readings in Philosophy and Social Policy. Contributors: T. H. Marshall, R. B. Brandt, G. H. von Wright, K. Nielsen, M. Cranston, M. Titmuss, R. S. Downie, E. Telfer, D. Donnison, J. Benson, P. Leonard, A. Keith-Lucas, D. Walsh, I. T. Ramsey. 320 pp.*

Primary Socialization, Language and Education

General Editor Basil Bernstein

Adlam, Diana S., *with the assistance of Geoffrey Turner and Lesley Lineker.* Code in Context. *About 272 pp.*

Bernstein, Basil. Class, Codes and Control. *3 volumes.*
  1. *Theoretical Studies Towards a Sociology of Language. 254 pp.*
  2. *Applied Studies Towards a Sociology of Language. 377 pp.*
● 3. *Towards a Theory of Educatiomal Transmission. 167 pp.*
Brandis, W., and **Bernstein, B.** Selection and Control. *176 pp.*
Brandis, Walter, and **Henderson, Dorothy.** Social Class, Language and Communication. *288 pp.*

Cook-Gumperz, Jenny. Social Control and Socialization. *A Study of Class Differences in the Language of Maternal Control. 290 pp.*
● **Gahagan, D. M.,** and **G. A.** Talk Reform. *Exploration in Language for Infant School Children. 160 pp.*

Hawkins, P. R. Social Class, the Nominal Group and Verbal Strategies. *About 220 pp.*
Robinson, W. P., and **Rackstraw, Susan D. A.** A Question of Answers. *2 volumes. 192 pp. and 180 pp.*
Turner, Geoffrey J., and **Mohan, Bernard A.** A Linguistic Description and Computer Programme for Children's Speech. *208 pp.*

Reports of the Institute of Community Studies

● **Cartwright, Ann.** Parents and Family Planning Services. *306 pp.*
  Patients and their Doctors. *A Study of General Practice. 304 pp.*
Dench, Geoff. Maltese in London. *A Case-study in the Erosion of Ethnic Consciousness. 302 pp.*
● **Jackson, Brian.** Streaming: *an Education System in Miniature. 168 pp.*
Jackson, Brian, and **Marsden, Dennis.** Education and the Working Class: *Some General Themes raised by a Study of 88 Working-class Children in a Northern Industrial City. 268 pp. 2 folders.*
Marris, Peter. The Experience of Higher Education. *232 pp. 27 tables.*
  Loss and Change. *192 pp.*
Marris, Peter, and **Rein, Martin.** Dilemmas of Social Reform. *Poverty and Community Action in the United States. 256 pp.*

Marris, Peter, and Somerset, Anthony. African Businessmen. *A Study of Entrepreneurship and Development in Kenya. 256 pp.*

Mills, Richard. Young Outsiders: *a Study in Alternative Communities. 216 pp.*

Runciman, W. G. Relative Deprivation and Social Justice. *A Study of Attitudes to Social Inequality in Twentieth-Century England. 352 pp.*

Willmott, Peter. Adolescent Boys in East London. *230 pp.*

Willmott, Peter, and Young, Michael. Family and Class in a London Suburb. *202 pp. 47 tables.*

Young, Michael. Innovation and Research in Education. *192 pp.*

●Young, Michael, and McGeeney, Patrick. Learning Begins at Home. *A Study of a Junior School and its Parents. 128 pp.*

Young, Michael, and Willmott, Peter. Family and Kinship in East London. *Foreword by Richard M. Titmuss. 252 pp. 39 tables.*

The Symmetrical Family. *410 pp.*

Reports of the Institute for Social Studies in Medical Care

Cartwright, Ann, Hockey, Lisbeth, and Anderson, John L. Life Before Death. *310 pp.*

Dunnell, Karen, and Cartwright, Ann. Medicine Takers, Prescribers and Hoarders. *190 pp.*

Medicine, Illness and Society

General Editor W. M. Williams

Robinson, David. The Process of Becoming Ill. *142 pp.*

Stacey, Margaret, *et al.* Hospitals, Children and Their Families. *The Report of a Pilot Study. 202 pp.*

Stimson, G. V., and Webb, B. Going to See the Doctor. *The Consultation Process in General Practice. 155 pp.*

Monographs in Social Theory

General Editor Arthur Brittan

●Barnes, B. Scientific Knowledge and Sociological Theory. *192 pp.*

Bauman, Zygmunt. Culture as Praxis. *204 pp.*

●Dixon, Keith. Sociological Theory. *Pretence and Possibility. 142 pp.*

Meltzer, B. N., Petras, J. W., and Reynolds, L. T. Symbolic Interactionism. *Genesis, Varieties and Criticisms. 144 pp.*

●Smith, Anthony D. The Concept of Social Change. *A Critique of the Functionalist Theory of Social Change. 208 pp.*

Routledge Social Science Journals

The British Journal of Sociology. *Editor – Angus Stewart; Associate Editor – Leslie Sklair. Vol. 1, No. 1 – March 1950 and Quarterly. Roy. 8vo. All back issues available. An international journal publishing original papers in the field of sociology and related areas.*

Community Work. *Edited by David Jones and Marjorie Mayo. 1973. Published annually.*

Economy and Society. *Vol. 1, No. 1. February 1972 and Quarterly. Metric Roy. 8vo. A journal for all social scientists covering sociology, philosophy, anthropology, economics and history. All back numbers available.*

Religion. Journal of Religion and Religions. *Chairman of Editorial Board, Ninian Smart. Vol. 1, No. 1, Spring 1971. A journal with an interdisciplinary approach to the study of the phenomena of religion. All back numbers available.*

Year Book of Social Policy in Britain, The. *Edited by Kathleen Jones. 1971. Published annually.*

Social and Psychological Aspects of Medical Practice

Editor   Trevor Silverstone

Lader, Malcolm. Psychophysiology of Mental Illness. *280 pp.*

● **Silverstone, Trevor,** and **Turner, Paul.** Drug Treatment in Psychiatry. *232 pp.*

Printed in Great Britain by
Lowe & Brydone Printers Limited, Thetford, Norfolk